INNOVATION, SOCIAL RESPONSIBILITY AND SUSTAINABILITY

DEVELOPMENTS IN CORPORATE GOVERNANCE AND RESPONSIBILITY

Series Editor: David Crowther

Recent Volumes:

DEVELOPMENTS IN CORPORATE GOVERNANCE AND
RESPONSIBILITY   VOLUME 22

INNOVATION, SOCIAL RESPONSIBILITY AND SUSTAINABILITY

EDITED BY

DAVID CROWTHER

Social Responsibility Research Network, UK

AND

SHAHLA SEIFI

Social Responsibility Research Network, UK

United Kingdom – North America – Japan
India – Malaysia – China

Emerald Publishing Limited
Emerald Publishing, Floor 5, Northspring, 21-23 Wellington Street, Leeds LS1 4DL

First edition 2024

Reprints and permissions service
Contact: www.copyright.com

British Library Cataloguing in Publication Data
A catalogue record for this book is available from the British Library

ISBN: 978-1-83797-463-4 (Print)
ISBN: 978-1-83797-462-7 (Online)
ISBN: 978-1-83797-464-1 (Epub)

ISSN: 2043-0523 (Series)

Printed and bound by CPI Group (UK) Ltd, Croydon, CR0 4YY

INVESTOR IN PEOPLE

CONTENTS

LIST OF CONTRIBUTORS

Adetayo Olaniyi Adeniran	Federal University of Technology Akure, Nigeria
Francisco Javier Andrades Peña	University of Cadiz, Spain
Victor Ediagbonya	University of Brighton, UK
Srushti Govilkar	MICA – The School of Ideas, India
Anna Katharina Grill	Vienna University of Economics and Business, Austria
Joseph Olanrewaju Ilugbami	Rufus Giwa Polytechnic, Owo-Rector's Office, Nigeria
Nausheen Bibi Jaffur	University of Mauritius, Mauritius
Pratima Jeetah	University of Mauritius, Mauritius
Manuel Larrán Jorge	University of Cadiz, Spain
Florian Kragulj	Knowledge Management Group, Vienna University of Economics and Business, Austria
Gopalakrishnan Kumar	University of Stavanger, Norway
Domingo Martinez Martinez	University of Cadiz, Spain
Ikpechukwu Njoku	Federal University of Technology Akure, Nigeria
Arminda do Paço	NECE Research Center in Business Sciences, University of Beira Interior, Portugal
Taral Pathak	MICA – The School of Ideas, India
Hajaina Ravoaja	ISCAM Business School, Madagascar
Raysa Geaquinto Rocha	University of Essex, UK; NECE Research Center in Business Sciences, University of Beira Interior, Portugal
Mobolaji Stephen Stephens	Federal University of Technology Akure, Nigeria
Oluwadamisi Toluwalase Tayo-Ladega	University of Bangor, UK
Ruchi Tewari	MICA – The School of Ideas, India

PART 1

DEVELOPING SOCIAL RESPONSIBILITY

CHAPTER 1

TOWARDS A MANDATORY CORPORATE SOCIAL RESPONSIBILITY FOR BANKS IN CHALLENGING INSTITUTIONAL CONTEXTS: A CASE STUDY OF NIGERIA

Victor Ediagbonya

ABSTRACT

Many corporations engage in corporate social responsibility (CSR) activities voluntarily, but there is an ongoing debate about whether the government should intervene in CSR, particularly in countries with challenging institutional contexts. While some have argued that CSR should remain a discretionary exercise, as any attempt to make CSR mandatory through any form of state intervention will negate the meaning and objectives of CSR. However, drawing on the institutional theory, this chapter argues for the need to have some form of legislated CSR for banks operating in countries with challenging institutional contexts. The chapter further acknowledges that a universal CSR framework would be difficult to achieve due to differences in institutional contexts between countries; consequently, the nature, scope, and application of CSR legislation would vary significantly amongst countries as CSR is context dependent. Nonetheless, given the crucial role banks plays in society besides acting as the country's payment system, banks also transform illiquid liabilities into liquid assets, therefore making the banks the drivers of national economic developments globally. Governments in developing and emerging markets (DEMs) should ensure that banks' CSR initiatives are not only meaningful

Innovation, Social Responsibility and Sustainability
Developments in Corporate Governance and Responsibility, Volume 22, 3–24
Copyright © 2024 Victor Ediagbonya
Published under exclusive licence by Emerald Publishing Limited
ISSN: 2043-0523/doi:10.1108/S2043-052320230000022001

but also impactful by implementing a limited legislated CSR framework. This framework would require banks to establish a CSR committee of the board, make mandatory non-financial disclosures on their CSR activities in their Annual Reports, provide mandatory CSR continuous professional development (CPD) training for bankers, and mandate banks to contribute a certain percentage of their yearly profits before tax to agreed CSR initiatives, among other requirements.

Keywords: Corporate governance; corporate social responsibility; institutional theory; banking regulation; institutional voids; developing and emerging markets

1. INTRODUCTION

Globally, banks are pivotal to national economic development in the countries they operate, not because they act as the payment systems of countries, but due to their ability to transform illiquid assets into liquid assets. One way banks carry out their operations is through acceptance of deposits from depositors usually in the short term while lending most of such funds to its customers for a longer period. This mismatch in maturity no doubt creates a material risk by exposing banks to impending financial challenges if not adequately and effectively managed. Whilst this is the nature of the banking operations globally, banks in the developing and emerging markets (DEMs) are further constrained by challenges unique to their institutional environment, these challenges are still persistent despite adopting regulatory approaches from developed economies. It is argued that corporate social responsibility (CSR), although a Western concept is one way of resolving the problem facing the banks including the challenges highlighted above. The debates revolving around the use of CSR in resolving the problems of banks are no longer contentious; however, what is now contentious is whether the approach to CSR should be voluntary or mandatory. The United Kingdom operates a more voluntary/discretionary approach to CSR and that same approach has been adopted by banks in Nigeria despite the differences in the institutional arrangements of both countries. The effect of such transplantation of policies and regulations from developed economies such as the United Kingdom by countries in the DEMs such as Nigeria without any modification has resulted in nothing but a failure to achieve the desired result. The failure stems from the fact the institutional contexts in these countries, developed economies and the DEM are fundamentally different. The nature, extent and application of CSR should be context-dependent. Thus, this chapter advocates for a mandatory CSR framework for banks in the DEMs based on the peculiarity of these countries.

The rest of the chapter is structured as follows. The chapter begins by deconstructing CSR through the exploration of the various concept of CSR. It went further to analyse some of the definitions offered by various scholars. The chapter suggests that the major problem with these definitions is that they present CSR from a voluntary context. The second section of this chapter explores the theoretical framework that underpins this chapter: the stakeholders and the institutional theories. It argues that for CSR to help realise SDG, particularly goals 1 (No poverty), 5 (Gender Equality), and 9 (Reduced Inequality), CSR framework in the banking sector in challenging institutional contexts should be mandatory because CSR is context-dependent. The third section explores the justification for a legislated CSR. It examines various arguments for and against mandatory/legislated CSR.

The chapter argues that several corporations, particularly in the developed markets, now report on their purported CSR through annual reports and web-sites. This is not because of the regulatory framework for corporate social responsibility reporting in those climes but because of what they stand to benefit by showcasing themselves as a CSR-compliant corporation, such as giving such companies a competitive edge by attracting socially responsible investors and customers. The fourth section explores CSR in Nigeria, generally and in the banking sector in particular. It argues that while the country's institutional context is different, attempting to adopt a global approach to CSR has not yielded the desired result; it further argues that CSR is not a case of one size fits all, but rather CSR should be context-dependent. The fifth section proposes ways of having a legislated form of CSR as a way forward in the post-COVID-19 era, given that several people, particularly women and children, have been thrown into poverty, thereby widening the financial inclusion gap in most communities. The final section concludes the discussion in this chapter, drawing on lessons to be learnt by other countries, particularly developing and emerging markets with challenging institutional contexts and suggesting further research areas.

2. CONCEPT, NATURE, AND MEANINGS OF CORPORATE SOCIAL RESPONSIBILITY

CSR as a concept have been defined differently by various academics; this is not surprising at all, as CSR is both a multidisciplinary and interdisciplinary subject. It usually depends on the context necessitating the definitions and the particular discipline. However, these definitions have further created some misconceptions about the subject; therefore, to understand CSR fully, a definitional decon-struction of the subject is essential. As stated above, defining CSR is by no means easy because there are many connotations of what responsibilities corporations can be subjected to. Therefore, to lay a proper foundation for understanding the concept, each of the components of CSR will be individually explored, these are 'corporate', 'social' and 'responsibility'. While the concept of corporate/ corporation may seem relatively straightforward, it is necessary to explore the concept briefly as this will create a clear picture of the rationale behind its existence.

A company is also called a 'corporate' or 'corporation' which is derived from the Latin word 'corpus' meaning 'body' or 'organisation'. Merriam-Webster dictionary (1998) defines a corporation as 'any group of persons united or regarded as united in one body for a common purpose'. Bierce (1911) defines a corporation as an ingenious device for obtaining individual profit without individual responsibility. A corporation is a legally distinct entity with many rights attributed to individuals (*Solomon v. Solomon, 1897*). These rights include the ability to enter into contracts, borrow money, own assets, pay taxes, sue and be sued, amongst others. A corporation is formed when individuals or group of persons acquires shares in the corporation in pursuit of the corporate goal. Those who have exchanged money for shares in the corporation are known as shareholders. Therefore, due to their investment, they are entitled to profits. Generally, due to the doctrine of limited liability, the losses incurred by these shareholders are limited to the amount invested (*Solomon v. Solomon, 1897*). In *O'Neill v Phillips [1999]* Lord Hoffmann held that 'A corporation is an association of persons for an economic purpose, usually entered into with legal advice and some degree of formality'.

Corporations date back to mediaeval times (Davoudi, McKenna, & Olegario, 2018; Laski, 1917), and their goals have always been to maximise profit for the benefit of their shareholders. This doctrine is rooted in classical economic theory postulated by Adam Smith (1776/1982) in his work entitled 'The Wealth of Nations'. He argued that markets tend to work best when the government leaves them alone, as corporations would naturally find the most efficient way of producing their goods and services to maximise profits for the benefit of their owners. He further argues that government regulation is potentially detrimental to economic growth, inhabiting corporations' ability to maximise profits, given that a corporation that does not profit will eventually fold up. It is evident from the above that neoliberal economists such as Adam Smith argue that where corporations are unable to make profits they would not fulfil their other obligation, such as paying taxes and job creation. Despite how convincing the above argument may seem, given the fact that no country can grow without the payment of taxes and provision of employment from the corporation, that does not in any way obscure the general purpose of establishing corporations by the shareholders, which is to maximise profits for their benefits.

Having explored the concept of 'corporate', the next task in deconstructing the meaning of CSR is to briefly explore the concept of 'social'. What does the word 'social' connote? According to Collins (2008), social means relating to society or how society is organised. From this definition, the concepts' 'social' and 'society' are indistinguishably linked, given that Emile Durkheim's study of social facts underpins them (Durkheim, 1982). The term social identifies society at a very functional and practical level; Durkheim, while defining society, divides it into two categories: the internal society and the external society. The internal society establishes the beliefs and attitudes pertinent and inherent to society, whereas the external society compels and influences the individual to act accordingly (Durkheim, 1982). Hence, if people fail to conform to 'society', they could be compelled to do so through relevant laws. Law was central to Durkheim's study of sociology, he argued that law can be seen as an institutional social fact which provides an index to social solidarity (Durkheim, 1933).

Moreover, in applying the above meaning of social and society, it is evident that law can be manifested in the 'internal' as well as external society (Durkheim,

Lukes, & Scull, 1983). Therefore, from the above analysis, one would argue that the term 'social' does not translate to voluntariness and dilute the responsibility of corporations; in fact, the law is embedded within the social context. The last and final task in deconstructing CSR is to explore the concept of responsibility. The term 'responsibility' has been examined by various scholars in recent times and as stated above, there is a need to understand what it entails as it relates to CSR.

Abdulrachman (2006) argues that responsibility takes its root from the word 'response', which means to 'answer' or 'compliance'; thus, responsibility means 'being able to respond to the requirements of something or being responsible to something else'. So responsibility would mean accountability or answerability. Barry and Shaw (1979) defined responsibility as a sphere of duty or obligation assigned to a person by the nature of that person's position, function or work. From the above definition, one would argue that responsibility is a bundle of obligations assigned to a person according to persons based on the nature of their position or status. Responsibility can mean 'primary rules', which may be in the form of regulatory obligations, for example, disclosure or 'secondary rules', such as the consequences for breach of regulatory obligations (Nollkaemper, 2006). Therefore, one could argue that responsibility is not just calling on those in positions of authority or those who hold certain positions to answer questions. However, for responsibility to be effective, it requires setting out rules and legal sanctions, which could be preventive, punitive, or reparative sanctions (Cane, 2002). Given the above definitions of responsibility, it is safe to conclude that responsibility is a form of accountability, requiring persons who hold certain positions to give account in terms of their actions and if they fail to conform to the laid down rules, then there will be consequences in the form of any of the sanction identified above (Bottomley & Forsyth, 2007).

It is argued that though the concept of responsibility could easily be applied to individuals who hold certain positions and to the government to a large extent; however, it poses some difficulties when used in the context of corporations. This is because the concept of responsibility requires that corporations be accountable not just to only shareholders but also to society at large. Corporations must operate within the complexity of social and economic relationships and strike a balance between maximising profit for shareholders' benefit and promoting the interests of other stakeholder groups. Achieving this will require the need for proper accountability. Demanding such accountability from corporations has given rise to various contentious debates. For example, Friedman (1970) argues that the social responsibility of a business is to increase its profits for the benefit of its shareholders. A position that has previously gained judicial prominence through several decided cases. In the case of *Dodge v. Ford Motor Company* (1919), Michigan Supreme Court held that:

> There should be no confusion (of which there is evidence) of the duties which Mr. Ford conceives that he and the stockholders owe to the general public and the duties ... he and his codirectors owe to ... minority stockholders. A business corporation is organised and carried on primarily for the profit of the stockholders. The powers of the directors are to be employed for that end. The discretion of directors is to be exercised in the choice of means to

attain that end and does not extend to a change in the end itself, to the reduction of profits or to... devot[ing] them to other purposes.

It is evident from the above decision that directors are accountable to shareholders and not to anyone else, even though the law resonates with the various concepts that make up CSR, 'social and responsibility' as discussed above. These debates are not unconnected with how various scholars have attempted to define CSR, which has been informed by the multidisciplinary and interdisciplinary nature of the subject; given this dynamic nature, it is argued that CSR needs to be context-dependent. Adopting a universal or global notion of CSR based on philanthropism somehow erodes the meaning and impact CSR is meant to achieve, particularly in countries with challenging institutional contexts. Therefore, before exploring the theoretical framework which underpins this work, at this point, it will be helpful to examine some of the key definitions of CSR to establish the problem evident with these definitions and how to resolve this definitional defect.

According to the European Commission (2001), CSR is 'a concept whereby companies integrate social and environmental concerns in their business operations and in their interactions with their stakeholders on a voluntary basis'. However, the Commission in 2011 went further to define CSR as actions by companies over and above their legal obligations towards society and the environment. Certain regulatory measures create an environment more conducive to enterprises voluntarily meeting their social responsibility (European Commission, 2011). As evident from these definitions, the Commission portrays CSR purely from a voluntary perspective; even if the law must be involved, its purpose is to create an enabling environment where corporations can voluntarily deliver societal expectations. The Department for Business Innovation and Skills (2014) adopted with minimal modification the European Commission's definition stated above by suggesting that corporate responsibility is the voluntary action businesses take over and above legal requirements to manage and enhance economic, environmental and societal impacts. It is about being a responsible business and part of an integrated and strategic approach, creating shared value for business and society (Department for Business Innovation and Skills, 2014). The main difference between the two definitions is that the latter has dispensed with social in the concept, thus basing the definition on corporate responsibility. This does not change the meaning, as the obligation required of corporations in both instances remains the same; this is based on the fact that the phrasings of both definitions are the same. The other point that is of interest here is that the Department for Business Innovation and Skills aligns with the voluntariness of CSR.

Berliner and Prakash (2014) argue that CSR pertains simply to policies and activities aimed at creating public goods (or mitigating public bads) which firms pursue beyond their legal requirements. They described CSR as obligations that require corporations to produce public goods beyond the requirements of applicable government laws (Berliner & Prakash, 2014). They suggested that a bonafide CSR programme seeks to encourage businesses to embrace socially responsible principles as an integral part of their activities (Berliner & Prakash, 2014). The above definition also showcases CSR as voluntary gestures that corporations embark on; it tilts towards moral rather than legal obligations that corporations owe to society. The above is also in tandem with the definition postulated by Gjølberg (2010), who argues that the concept of corporate social responsibility is the notion that business has a responsibility to contribute to social and environmental goals on a voluntary basis.

According to Ollong (2014) CSR is the relationship between business and society, where the role of business is purported to go beyond the mere quest for profit to include have regards to the social and environmental impact of their activities. It is a mode corporations use to achieve commercial success in ways that honour ethical, legal, environmental, and other societal expectations. It considers a corporation not just a self-centred profit-making entity but also an integral part of the economy, society and environment in which corporations exist. In comparison, McWilliams and Siegel (2001) viewed CSR as 'actions that appear to further some social good, beyond the interests of the corporation and that which is required by law. CSR means going beyond obeying the law'.

Shamir (2010) defined CSR as a phenomenon whereby commercial entities deploy social and environmental policies that go beyond their formal legal duties and potentially beyond their goal of maximising profits for shareholders; like the others explored above, these definitions see CSR from a voluntary standpoint. Vogel (2005) opined that CSR is a 'business virtue' indicating 'practices that improve the workplace and benefit the society in ways that go above and beyond what companies are legally required to do'. Another definition worthy of consideration is that propounded by World Bank. It defined CSR as the commitment of business to contribute to sustainable economic development – working with employees, their families, the local community and society to improve the quality of life in ways that are both good for business and development (World Bank, 2006).

World Business Council for Sustainable Development (1999) argues that 'CSR is the continuing commitment by businesses to contribute to economic development while improving the quality of life of the workforce and their families as well as of the community and society at large'. CSR is also defined as a commitment to improve community well-being through discretionary business practices and contributions of corporate resources (Kotler & Lee, 2005). Given all the definitions explored above, it is evident that CSR has been construed purely from a voluntary or discretional angle. However, Carroll's postulated a four-part definition of CSR as he argued that CSR encompasses the economic, legal, ethical and discretionary (philanthropic) expectations that society has of organisations at a given point in time (Carroll, 1979, 1991, 1999). Carroll's CSR pyramid has greatly influenced CSR scholarships, particularly regarding its broad scope. Dahlsrud (2008) examined 37 definitions of CSR and suggested that almost all these definitions suggest that a philanthropic/voluntary nature underpins CSR.

Philanthropic/charitable gestures characterise Carroll's four-part definition of CSR by corporations. Corporation purporting to give back to society through philanthropic contribution has significantly hindered the scope for regulating CSR, thus giving corporations opportunities to exploit the system, particularly in countries with challenging institutional contexts. In light of the above definitional ambiguity evidenced by the lack of an exact and uncontroversial meaning of the concept, it is argued that such confusion has caused a mismatch between CSR initiatives with societal needs, particularly in countries with challenging institutional contexts such as Nigeria. Before exploring the nature of CSR in Nigeria, the following section explores two fundamental CSR theories, the Institutional and Stakeholder theory, which underpins this work.

3. CORPORATE SOCIAL RESPONSIBILITY THEORIES: INSTITUTIONAL AND STAKEHOLDER THEORIES

Given the rise in the debates on the terminology and the definitions of CSR that have emerged in recent times, especially since the second half of the twentieth century, so have the associated theories, this field has grown significantly and today contains a significant proliferation of theories. The increased scholarship has evidenced the expansion of these theories on corporate governance, and CSR since the 1950s, notably since Bowen (1953) wrote the seminal book entitled the *Social Responsibilities of the Businessman*. This chapter is not intended to explore all the associated theories within this field, as this is beyond its scope; therefore, the focus here will include the two core theories, the institutional and stakeholder theories.

3.1 Institutional Theory

The institutional theory is premised on the perception that economic behaviour, whether by individuals or by firms, is affected by the institutional setting in which actors find themselves (Ohnesorge, 2007). Institutional theory is also based on the notion of 'institutions' this means rules, norms and beliefs that describe reality for the organisation, explaining what is and is not, what can be acted upon and what cannot (Hoffman, 1999). Various scholars have further explored the notion of institutional theory. For example, Hodgson (2006) submitted that institutional theory is a systems of established and prevalent social rules that structure social interactions, which comprises formal and informal procedures, routines, norms and conventions embedded in the organisational structure of the polity or political economy (Hall & Taylor, 1996). Acemoglu (2009) suggested that institutional theory includes such things as the structure of property rights, the presence of markets, and the contractual opportunities available to individuals and companies. Therefore, it is argued that institutions (not only public/ governmental agencies) regulate societal behaviour. The institutional theory is based on the notion that institutions influence market participation; therefore, institutions supporting market development are crucial for economic growth and poverty reduction (Tebaldi & Mohan, 2010).

Given the above description of the institutional theory, the next step is to explore the challenging institutional frameworks in developing and emerging markets due to the institutional voids in those economies. Institutional voids or challenging institution contexts connotes weak and non-functioning institutions (Palepu & Khanna, 1997). Formal legal institutions create enabling environments by providing for and enforcing, among others, rights and obligations, providing incentives for social actors' behaviour; consequently, since institutional settings are heterogenous, CSR should be context-dependent. This is in agreement with the *OECD Principles of Corporate Governance*, which state that a sound legal, regulatory and institutional framework for corporate governance includes a mix of legislation, regulation, self-regulatory arrangements, voluntary commitments and business practices that are the result of a country's specific circumstances, history and tradition (OECD, 2015).

Institutional theory shows that CSR can be a form of regulation and a regulatory tool. This could be achieved by being regulated by law through several methods (Osuji, 2011, 2015; Osuji & Obibuaku, 2016). CSR can be utilised as substantive regulation; for example, one could adopt CSR through the use of self-regulation, co-regulation, third-party and state regulation; CSR could also be regulated by law as disclosure regulation. Therefore, it is argued that rather than seeing CSR purely as a realm of voluntary action, institutional theory suggests seeking to situate CSR explicitly into a broader field of economic governance characterised by different modes, including the market, state regulation and beyond (Brammer, Jackson, & Matten, 2012).

3.2 Stakeholder Theory

The stakeholder theory is one of the core theories in management science that rejects the shareholder theory idea of the corporation. While the shareholder theory postulates that directors only have one legal obligation: to protect shareholders' interests because shareholders have a privileged place in an organisation as they bear the residual risks in the organisation, the stakeholder theory tends to counter this assertion (Freeman & Reed, 1983). Edward Freeman, who served as the foundation for this stakeholder idea by popularising the stakeholder concept of CSR, argued that shareholders are not the only ones in the organisation that bear the residual risk (Freeman, 1984). Other stakeholders in the corporation also bear some form of residual risk if the corporation becomes insolvent; these include employees, unsecured creditors and customers. Therefore, while pursuing profits, corporations must promote the interests of other interest groups, including the employees, customers, suppliers and creditors, without going against the moral values on which the corporation is built (Freeman, 1984; Alfonso & Castrillón, 2021).

One core criticism of the stakeholder's theory is the uncertainty resulting from defining those that will fall within the stakeholder's group from which directors should be accountable. Sternberg (1997) argued that the fundamental problem with the stakeholder's theory is that the understanding can be stretched so that virtually everything, everywhere, can now be regarded as stakeholders. The above argument might seem convincing to a certain extent; however, stakeholders will generally include shareholders, taxpayers, local communities, government, employees, consumers, suppliers and creditors (Hill & Jones, 1992). Freeman's definition of stakeholders shows the important bi-directionality of stakeholders, he defined stakeholders as: 'Any group or individual who can affect or [be] affected by the achievement of an organisation's objectives' (Freeman, 1984). Stakeholders can affect or be affected by the organisation's objective; it is also possible for some stakeholders to be on both sides, thus affecting and being affected by the organisation's objective (Freeman, 1984). In the view of the stakeholder theory, corporations cannot maximise the shareholder's interest at the expense of the other stakeholders, as this is not morally or economically efficient. Within the evolving research, the stakeholder theory has been conceptualised in three ways: the descriptive, instrumental and normative stakeholder theory (Donaldson & Preston, 1995).

Although proponents of stakeholder theory argue that corporations consider the interest of all stakeholders, they do not stipulate how this should be addressed based on the varying interests of the stakeholder group. As a result, stakeholder theory has been criticised as unsuited with business operations and incapable of providing better corporate governance, business performance or business conduct (Donaldson & Preston, 1995). In this context, Michael Jensen (2001) suggests that stakeholder theory can add to this a specification that the objective function of a firm is to maximise the overall long-term firm value and that all satisfaction is achieved when the overall long-term firm value is maximised. In this way, corporate executives may be better able to assess trade-offs between competing interest groups within the organisation (Jensen, 2001).

4. JUSTIFICATIONS FOR CORPORATE SOCIAL RESPONSIBILITY

There have been several reasons scholars in the field have suggested to justify why corporations should engage in CSR, particularly relating to the benefit it gives to society. While this has been the case, most literature focuses on the benefits of CSR to the community and other stakeholders such as employees and customers, thereby ignoring how much benefits engaging in CSR brings to the corporations themselves. In light of the above, the focus of this section is to explore the business case arguments for CSR activities/practices by corporations. The fundamental question that needs to be answered is what do corporations get from engaging in CSR policies, initiatives and practices? The benefits to be derived by corporations for CSR policies, initiatives, and practices include reputation and legitimacy, cost and risk reduction, attracting socially responsible investors and customers, employee retention and gaining competitive advantage. Therefore, it is worth further exploring the above benefits in the subsection below.

4.1 Reputation and Legitimacy

Studies have shown that corporations that engage in CSR activities, policies, initiatives, and practices tend to enhance their reputation and give these corporations some form of legitimacy. According to Suchman (1995), legitimacy is a generalised perception or assumption that the actions of an entity are desirable, proper or appropriate within some socially constructed system of norms, values, beliefs and definitions. Feldman and Vasquez-Parraga (2013) argued that CSR is today interconnected with the social consequences of commerce, business and marketing and thus aims at mitigating and limiting the negative impacts while enhancing and augmenting the positive effects of trade, business and marketing. Corporate philanthropy is another CSR initiative which aims to strengthen corporate legitimacy and reputation. Chen, Patten, and Roberts (2008) suggest that corporate philanthropy may be a legitimisation tool. They argue that some corporations with negative social performance in environmental issues and product safety use charitable contributions to build their legitimacy (Chen et al., 2008). Therefore, it is argued that corporations not only use CSR activities, policies, initiatives and practices to enhance their corporate reputation but also a strategy to help protect businesses from reputation damage and accelerate their recovery after a crisis. Corporations may also use corporate philanthropy to strengthen their legitimacy by managing local dependency and creating trusts (Kamens, 1985).

4.2 Cost and Risk Reduction

The correlation between CSR activities, policies, initiatives and practices and cost and risk reduction have been explored by various authors in recent times (Attig, Ghoul, Guedhami, & Suh, 2013; Goss & Roberts, 2011; Weber, 2018; Ye & Zhang, 2011). Though there are divergent opinions on this relationship, some argue that there is a negative correlation between CSR performance and the cost of equity capital, which means that CSR is a crucial risk-pricing factor in the capital market (El Ghoul, Guedhami, Kwok, & Mishra, 2011). Albuquerque, Koskinen, and Zhang (2018) argued that corporations that engage in CSR face less price elastic demand and can charge higher prices at things being equal; consequently, these corporations' cash flows become less volatile over the business cycle, resulting in higher optimal leverage. Harjoto and Jo (2015) argue that CSR activities, policies, initiatives, and practices tend to reduce information asymmetry, market risk, transaction costs and, in turn, the cost of equity capital. Xu, Liu, and Huang (2015) suggested that CSR activities, policies, initiatives and practices indulged in by listed companies can reduce the cost of equity capital, especially during an economic downturn. Some scholars have argued that although CSR is vital to businesses as a whole as it helps in cost reduction and mitigates business risk, this is only possible in economies where lower levels of assertiveness and higher levels of humane orientation and institutional collectivism (Matthiesen & Salzmann, 2017).

4.3 Attracting Socially-Responsible Investors and Customers

Generally, investors are more likely to invest in corporations that engage in CSR initiatives, policies, activities and practices. CSR is an essential strategy for branding and retaining customers; this is somehow coupled with the CSR strategy of reputation and legitimacy discussed above. Thus, if a corporation purports to engage in CSR, it can help build a good reputation, which can lead to trust and loyalty among customers. Consumer patronage is essential for a business to remain a going concern because the company would not exist without them. Smith (2003) contends that CSR initiatives, policies, activities and practices enhance the ability of corporations to attract consumers and investors. He further states that consumers report that many claims to be influenced in their purchasing decisions by the CSR reputation of companies (Smith, 2003). The Global Sustainability Study 2021, conducted by Global Strategy and Pricing Consultancy Simon Kucher and Partners, reveals significant global paradigm shifts in how consumers view sustainability and the associated generational differences in willingness to pay for sustainable products and services. The study shows that globally, 85% of people have shifted their purchase behaviour towards being more sustainable in the past five years and are willing to pay more for a product or service if the companies prioritise sustainability (Kucher, 2021). This signifies that consumers will prefer to patronise companies that are not just profit-seeking but also ensures that they are CSR compliant.

4.4 Employee Retention

Recently, employee retention has been a topical issue, leading to several studies conducted to ascertain the nexus between CSR and employee retention. CSR has been proven to impact employees in terms of creative involvement, relationships and employee retention (Aguinis & Glavas, 2012; Bhattacharya, Sen, & Korschun, 2008; Glavas, 2016). Engaging in CSR initiatives, policies, activities and practices can lead to greater employee engagement and, subsequently, higher retention rates. It is argued that a strong commitment to effective CSR initiatives, policies, activities and practices increases employees' commitment, affinity and engagement (Burbano, 2014). This will enhance job performance, increase productivity, reduce turnover, lower absenteeism and even reduce the incidence of employee corruption. A 2015 study conducted by The Lewis Institute for Social Innovation at Babson College indicates that businesses with a commitment to CSR could see productivity increases by 13% and turnover reductions by up to 50% (Rochlin, Bliss, Jordan, & Kiser, 2015). The report stated that companies that engage in CSR are perceived as more attractive employers than those lower in CSR. Thus, prospective applicants' job pursuit, the probability of an interview and the likelihood of accepting a job offer are positively associated with a company's CSR initiatives, policies, activities and practices (Rochlin et al., 2015).

4.5 Gaining Competitive Advantage

Gaining competitive advantage justification is predicated upon the argument that corporations could use CSR initiatives, policies, activities and practices to build a competitive advantage. According to Smith (2003), corporations may improve their competitiveness by engaging in specific CSR initiatives, policies, activities and practices. Smith further argues that companies may build their competitive advantage through CSR strategies if their social responsibility strategy is genuinely and carefully conceived and should be unique (Smith, 2003). The uniqueness serves as a basis for setting the company apart from others, giving it a competitive advantage. Kurucz, Colbert, and Wheeler (2008) argue that corporations can turn stakeholder demands into an opportunity to be competitive. Corporations can achieve this by strategically managing their resources to meet stakeholders' needs and promoting their relationships with stakeholders.

5. CORPORATE SOCIAL RESPONSIBILITY IN THE NIGERIAN BANKING SECTOR

There have been few attempts to have some form of legislated CSR in Nigeria; however, these various attempts to have a legislated form of CSR have not been successful. The first attempt was when Mr Chukwumerije, a member of the Nigerian Senate in 2007, sponsored a Corporate Social Responsibility Bill requiring companies to set aside 3.5% of gross profits for CSR activities; however, the bill did not eventually pass the committee stage. Similarly, an attempt was made in 2015 by the House of Representatives to introduce a Corporate Social Responsibility Bill which mandates companies to spend at least three per cent of their average net profits on CSR activities. This bill, like its predecessor, did not go past the committee stage as many businesses vehemently opposed it. Technically there is no established legal framework for CSR in Nigeria. Therefore CSR is based on voluntariness and philanthropy, so banks purport to spend less than 1% of profit on numerous CSR initiatives (Ediagbonya, 2020). The majority of the Nigerian Bank CSR claimed that they engage in CSR to give back to society; however, businesses equally benefit from CSR (Amaeshi, Adi, Ogbechie, & Amao, 2006). One main problem of CSR in Nigerian banks is a lack of stakeholders' involvement in the banks' CSR initiative, which has resulted in the limited recognition of stakeholders and protection of their interests, such as employees and customers.

6. A CASE FOR A CHANGE IN THE CORPORATE SOCIAL RESPONSIBILITY PARADIGM IN COUNTRIES WITH CHALLENGING INSTITUTIONAL CONTEXTS

This has been an area of debate in this area in recent times. Is evidenced by the way several scholars attempted to define CSR as a voluntary concept (Carroll,

1979; Friedman, 1970). It has been argued that companies should be at liberty to determine if they want to include CSR activities in their core business or not (Clark, 2020). The argument is that corporations should be allowed to develop their CSR initiative and voluntarily enforce CSR. The reason for this is not farfetched, as previously discussed above; The traditional view of the corporation is that corporations are established solely for profit maximisation for the benefit of shareholders only (Sternberg, 1997). The above argument is also embedded in legislation; for example, under s.172 UK Companies Act 2006, it includes a new overriding duty broadly equivalent to the old common law duty to act in the company's best interest. This duty is set out in s.172 UK Companies Act 2006. It provides that 'a director must act in the way he considers, in good faith, would be most likely to promote the success of the company for the benefit of its members as a whole'. This is very similar to the existing common law duty to act in the company's best interests. However, s.172 UK Companies Act 2006 also sets out a list of non-exhaustive factors, including customers, suppliers, employees, and the environment, which directors must consider when 'promoting the success of the company'. It is therefore argued that notwithstanding s. 172 listing some other constituents, the overriding duty the director owes to the company is to promote the company's success, which is the corporate goal; thus, this corporate goal is confined to shareholder interest, and shareholder interest equals profit max-imisation for their benefit. The Companies and Allied Matter Act (CAMA) 2020, the principal legislation regulating companies in Nigeria, also requires directors to act in the company's best interest. In discharging their fiduciary duty to the company, directors are to act in the interests of shareholders s.305 CAMA 2020 is in *pari materia* with the provision of s.172 of the UK Companies Act 2006. As embedded in these legislations, the UK Companies Act 2020, CAMA 2020, directors' overriding duty is to promote the company's corporate purpose. This corporate purpose aligns with shareholders' interests, maximising profit for their benefit. It is argued that achieving this will be deemed the company's success.

In light of the above objective, there is a need to have some form of legislated CSR, although the free market theory argument suggests that free market forces should regulate CSR, not hard laws and mandatory rules. Corporations have become so powerful in their drive to succeed that they have been granted enor-mous rights and liberty. In *Louis K. Liggett Co v. Lee*, Justice Louis Brandeis considered corporations 'the Frankenstein monster which states have created by their corporation laws'. Mintzberg (1983) argued that large corporations have immense power to influence social issues profoundly, circumvent government regulations, and resist social pressures. Recent studies have shown that over half of the world's wealthiest entities are corporations (CIA World Factbook, 2021, Fortune Global 500, 2022) which has given corporations power to determine what people wear, the content they watch, what they read and the food they eat. These large companies have too much influence on the government, which is attuned to condone the excesses of this 'Frankenstein monster', a creation of corporate law.

Wilks (2013) argued that the rise of CSR can only be explained in the context of other significant changes in society, the economy and political ideology.

Among those changes is the increased criticism of the corporation; of course, CSR reflects much more profound changes. He argued that, indeed, the CSR phenomenon illustrates and provides evidence for corporate political power; thus, every mention of corporate social responsibility is simultaneously an affirmation of market power and hence a recognition that perfectly competitive markets are an illusion (Wilks, 2013).

In light of the above, one would argue that there is a need for mandatory CSR. This view might seem unpopular to several scholars who tend to suggest that having a mandatory/legislated form of CSR is a move that negates the meaning and objective of CSR. This position is not true as going through the various word that forms the concept of CSR, it is evident that law is intertwined with CSR in all forms. Besides, the argument that corporations will generally engage in CSR without the intervention of the law is preposterous, not to say the least. This assumption is premised on the fact that all companies are the same and institutional contexts are also the same.

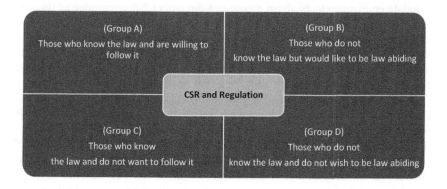

The diagram above illustrates the different behavioural patterns of companies. According to McInerney (2007), there are four types of companies with which regulators must deal. Those who know the law and are willing to follow it will fall under Group A; those who do not know the law but would like to be law-abiding, this category will fall into Group B; the next group will be those who know the law and do not want to follow it these will fall into category Group C and comes those who do not know the law and do not wish to be law-abiding this will fall into Group D. However, most CSR literature does not even reflect these difference in the behavioural patterns of companies let alone highlighting the difference in the institutional contexts of countries. From the above analysis, companies that fall within Group A are willing to comply on intrinsic grounds. Voluntary CSR proponents tend to assume that only Group A companies exist; however, companies may not be law-abiding in the face of weak enforcement mechanisms. Therefore, most companies in countries with challenging institutional contexts will fall into Group C and D due to the weak enforcement mechanisms. There is a need to have a mandatory/legislated framework for banks in developing and emerging markets to address the challenges these countries face, particularly regarding gender equality, infrastructure, poverty, healthcare and education. Mandatory/legislated CSR can be embedded into the Nigerian corporate governance framework for banks in several ways. Companies can mandate to contribute a certain percentage of their profits to help address the above problem like other countries, such as Mauritius, India and Nepal, have taken this step. For example, as part of the legislation on CSR, all Mauritius companies must contribute 2% of their net profit to a CSR fund to carry out intervention as per the 10th Schedule of the Income Tax Act 1995, which includes social welfare, sports, environment protection and various other areas. India also has a similar provision under its Company Act 2013, by virtue of s. 135 (1) requires companies to spend in every financial year a minimum of 2% of the average net profits made during the three immediately preceding financial years as per CSR initiatives. There is a need to have a CSR developmental plan where companies can key into one of the critical areas that require interventions. There is also the need to mandate companies to establish a board of directors CSR committee as this will foster all stakeholder interests. Thus, implementing such a mandatory governance structure requires the board of directors to be composed of representatives of various stakeholders through a CSR Committee. The CSR Committee will enact, implement and supervise the company's CSR initiatives, policies, activities and practices in conjunction with other relevant stakeholders such as employees, customers, host committees, and employees. Mandatory Continuous Professional Development is one way of continuously inculcating the tenets of effective CSR in the bank's staff besides introducing CSR as a core module in the banker's training programme. Mandatory or legislated CSR can also take the form of companies disclosing extensive information about several things, including environmental, social and governance aspects of their business. Last but not least, mandatory or legislated CSR requires companies to carry out compulsory due diligence; this regulatory approach requires companies to identify social and environmental risks associated with their business operation and establish and execute reasonable plans to prevent harm resulting from the identified risks. One of the first countries to adopt this approach is Indonesia. By of virtue of Article 74 of the Indonesia Company Act 2007, companies doing business in the field of and/or concerning natural resources must put into practice environmental and social responsibility; the environmental and social responsibilities constitute an obligation of the company which are budgeted and accounted for as an expense of the company that the implementation is done with regard to the appropriateness and fairness. France is another country that has adopted this mandatory due diligence approach to CSR. The French Corporate Duty of Vigilance Law passed in 2017 requires large companies with at least 5,000 employees in France or 10,000 worldwide, either directly or in their subsidiaries, to draw up, implement and publish a due vigilance plan. The plan must include 'due diligence measures such as to identify risks and forestall serious infringements of or harm to human rights and fundamental freedoms, personal health and safety and the environment'. Thus it covers the activities of the company, its direct or indirect subsidiaries, and subcontractors and suppliers with which it maintains an established business relationship insofar as those activities are linked to that relationship.

7. RECOMMENDATIONS

There are several criticisms against mandatory CSR that must be highlighted. One such criticism suggests that mandatory CSR limits the ability to respond to changes in a timely manner because of the bureaucracy involved in amending the law. While this is correct to an extent, particularly relating to the process involved in amending any key legislation, the core argument in this chapter is to have some form of mandatory CSR regulation, which the companies themselves are already doing. The focus is to have an organised or strategic form of CSR rather than an uncoordinated one. Following on from the above is also the argument that mandatory CSR tends to limit activities to what is legislated rather than what is needed; as a result, it inhibits the development of best practices. However, one would argue that in the context of countries in challenging institutional contexts, having a CSR developmental plan that companies can key into would address what is needed, as this will be reviewed regularly.

Some may argue that mandatory CSR, like all regulations, is to ensure compliance rather than to develop good practices; as a result, get a minimalist approach, whereas all the evidence shows that CSR develops through the best practice of those companies with a developed social conscience. While the above argument may seem plausible, mandatory CSR does not limit the ability of companies to develop best practices, what the law suggests that they must engage in some core practices; however, they are not constrained from doing more. Companies will generally do more, notably the large ones, due to their reputation and competitive advantage. There's also the possibility of companies copying each other, mostly the small and medium companies, mimicking the large ones as formal and informal institutions regulate behaviours.

Furthermore, more recently, there has been a move by corporations to ensure their survival rather than to maximise profits in the short term for the benefit of shareholders because ensuring the survival of the company leads to long-term profit maximisation. Several companies have adopted this approach; for example, in 2019, around 200 US Chief Executive Officers, including Apple, Pepsi, Walmart and JPMorgan Chase, issued a new statement of purpose declaring that they were now fundamentally committed to serving all their stakeholders (Gelles & Yaffe-Bellany, 2019). These stakeholders include employees, suppliers, customers and communities and not only the shareholders to whom they had long catered for. In the United Kingdom, there is also clamour for the triple bottom line to ensure the survival of the companies. The triple-bottom-line CSR framework advocates for profit, people, and the planet while ensuring the company's survival (Księżak & Fischbach, 2018). Given the above, CSR can be considered an instrument of profit maximisation.

8. CONCLUSION

The chapter has explored the various definitions and meanings of the concept of CSR; it is agreed that there is no universally accepted definition of the subject; the majority of these definitions are confusing and misleading. This has come to light from deconstructing and analysing the individual concept that constitutes CSR. Defining CSR as a voluntary or philanthropic gesture has given businesses room to perpetuate all forms of corporate irresponsibilities to the detriment of other stakeholders. The chapter also highlights the business case for CSR, exploring some of the key benefits businesses derive from engaging in CSR activities, policies, initiatives, and practices. This does not in any way undermine the benefit to be derived by other stakeholders if CSR activities, policies, initiatives and practices are properly implemented, particularly in countries with challenging institutional contexts. The pandemic has broadened the financial exclusion gap in most Developing and Emerging Markets. CSR in developing and emerging markets must address poverty in line with the UN Sustainable Development Goals 1 eradication of poverty (UN SDG, 2015), particularly in the post-pandemic era. According to the UNDP, income losses are expected to exceed $220 billion in developing countries, and an estimated 55% of the global population have no access to social protection (UNDP, 2020). In the most severe cases, the losses have affected education, human rights, basic food security and nutrition. Therefore, a mandatory CSR framework is required in developing and emerging markets countries to achieve a fairer society.

BIBLIOGRAPHY

Abdulrachman, S. M. (2006). *Public ethics and responsibility: Western and Islamic perspectives.* Marawi: University Book Center, Mindanao State University.

Acemoglu, D. (2009). *Introduction to modern economic growth.* Princeton, NJ: Princeton University Press.

Aguinis, H., & Glavas, A. (2012). What we know and don't know about corporate social responsibility. *Journal of Management, 38*(4), 932–968.

Albuquerque, R., Koskinen, Y., & Zhang, C. (2018, October). Corporate social responsibility and firm risk: Theory and empirical evidence. *Management Science, 65*(10), 4451–4469.

Alfonso, M., & Castrillón, G. (2021). *The concept of corporate governance* (Vol. 173). Visión de Futuro. Universidad Nacional de Misiones, Argentina.

Amaeshi, K. M., Adi, B. C., Ogbechie, C., & Amao, O. O. (2006). Corporate social responsibility in Nigeria: Western mimicry or indigenous influences? *The Journal of Corporate Citizenship, 24*, 83–99.

Attig, N., Ghoul, S. E., Guedhami, O., & Suh, J. (2013). Corporate social responsibility and credit ratings. *Journal of Business Ethics, 117*(4), 679–694.

Barry, V., & Shaw, W. H. (1979). *Moral issues in business.* Belmont: Wadsworth.

Berliner, D., & Prakash, A. (2014). The United Nations global compact: An institutionalist perspective. *Journal of Business Ethics, 122*(2), 217–223. http://www.jstor.org/stable/42921430

Bhattacharya, C. B., Sen, S., & Korschun, D. (2008). Using corporate social responsibility to win the war for talent. *MIT Sloan Management Review, 49*(2), 37–44.

Bierce, A. (1911). *The devil's dictionary.* New York, NY: Neale Publishers.

Bottomley, S., & Forsyth, A. (2007). The new corporate law: Corporate social responsibility and employees' interests. In D. McBarnet, A. Voiculescu, & T. Campbell (Eds.), *The new corporate accountability: Corporate social responsibility and the law* (Ist ed., pp. 307–335). Cambridge: Cambridge University Press.

Bowen, H. R. (1953). *Social responsibilities of the businessman.* New York, NY: Harper & Row.

Brammer, S., Jackson, G., & Matten, D. (2012). Corporate social responsibility and institutional theory: New perspectives on private governance. *Socio-Economic Review, 10*(1), 3–28. doi:10. 1093/ser/mwr030

Burbano, V. C. (2014). Can firms pay less and get more... by doing good? *Field experimental evidence of the effect of corporate social responsibility on employee salary requirements and performance (Working Paper).* Los Angeles, CA: UCLA Anderson School of Management. Retrieved from https://corporate-sustainability.org/wp-content/uploads/arcs-2014-Burbano.pdf

Cane, P. (2002). *Responsibility in law and morality.* London: Bloomsbury Publishing.

Carroll, A. B. (1979). A three-dimensional conceptual model of corporate performance. *Academy of Management Review, 4*(4), 497–505.

Carroll, A. B. (1991). The pyramid of corporate social responsibility: Toward the moral management of organisational stakeholders. *Business Horizons, 34*(4), 39–48.

Carroll, A. B. (1999). Corporate social responsibility: Evolution of a definitional construct. *Business & Society, 38*(3), 268–295.

Chen, J. C., Patten, D. M., & Roberts, R. (2008). Corporate charitable contributions: A corporate social performance or legitimacy strategy? *Journal of Business Ethics, 82,* 131–144.

CIA World Factbook. (2021). Retrieved from https://www.cia.gov/the-world-factbook/countries/

Clark, S. (2020). *What corporate social responsibility looks like in 2020.* Leadership June 8. Retrieved from https://www.reworked.co/leadership/what-corporate-social-responsibility-looks-like-in-2020/

Collins. (2008). *Collins english dictionary home edition.* London: HarperCollins UK Publishers Ltd.

Companies and Allied Matter Act 2020.

Dahlsrud, A. (2008). How corporate social responsibility is defined: An analysis of 37 definitions. *Corporate Social Responsibility and Environmental Management, 15,* 1–13. doi:10.1002/csr.132

Davoudi, L., McKenna, C., & Olegario, R. (2018, December). The historical role of the corporation in society. *Journal of the British Academy, 6*(s1), 17–47. doi:10.5871/jba/006s1.017

Department for Business Innovation and Skills. (2014). *Corporate responsibility: Good for business & society.* Government Response to Call for Views on Corporate Responsibility. Retrieved from https://assets.publishing.service.gov.uk/government/uploads/system/uploads/attachment_data/file/300265/bis-14-651-good-for-business-and-society-government-response-to-call-for-views-on-corporate-responsibility.pdf

Dodge v. Ford Motor Company, 204 Mich. 459, 170 N.W. 668 (Mich. 1919).

Donaldson, T., & Preston, L. (1995). The stakeholder theory of the corporation: Concepts, evidence, and implications. *Academy of Management Review, 20,* 65–91.

Durkheim, E. (1933/1964). *The division of labour in society* (Trans. G. Simpson) (p. c1933). New York, NY; London: Free Press, Collier Macmillan.

Durkheim, E. (1982). In S. Lukes (Ed.), *The rules of sociological method and selected texts on sociology and its method* (translated. W. D. Halls). New York, NY: The Free Press.

Durkheim, É., Lukes, S., & Scull, A. T. (1983). In S. Lukes & A. T. Scull (Eds.), *Durkheim and the law.* Oxford: Martin Robertson Oxford.

Ediagbonya, V. (2020). Incorporating CSR in corporate governance of banking institutions in a challenging institutional context: A case study of Nigeria. In D. Crowther & S. Seifi (Eds.), *Governance and sustainability. Approaches to global sustainability, markets, and governance* (pp. 21–41). Singapore: Springer.

El Ghoul, S., Guedhami, O., Kwok, C. C., & Mishra, D. R. (2011). Does corporate social responsibility affect the cost of capital? *Journal of Banking & Finance, 35*(9), 2388–2406.

European Commission. (2001). Promoting a European framework for corporate social responsibility. Retrieved from https://ec.europa.eu/commission/presscorner/detail/en/DOC_01_9

European Commission. (2011). A renewed E.U. strategy for corporate social responsibility. Retrieved from https://eur-lex.europa.eu/LexUriServ/LexUriServ.do?uri=COM:2011:0681:FIN:EN:PDF

Feldman, P. M., & Vasquez-Parraga, A. Z. (2013). Consumer social responses to CSR initiatives versus corporate abilities. *Journal of Consumer Marketing, 30,* 100–111.

Fortune Global 500. (2022). Retrieved from http://fortune.com/global500/list

Freeman, E. (1984). *Strategic management: A stakeholder approach*. Boston: Pitman.

Freeman, E., & Reed, D. (1983). Stockholders and stakeholders: A new perspective on corporate governance' 25 California. *Management Review, 88*, 90.

French corporate Duty of Vigilance Law 2017.

Friedman, M. (1970, September 13). A Friedman doctrine–The social responsibility of business is to increase its profits. *New York Times Magazine, 13*(32–33), 122–126.

Gelles, D., & Yaffe-Bellany, D. (2019, August 19). Shareholder value is no longer everything, top C.E.O.'s say. *New York Times*. Retrieved from https://www.nytimes.com/2019/08/19/business/business-roundtable-ceos-corporations.html

Gjølberg, M. (2010, June). Varieties of corporate social responsibility (CSR): CSR meets the 'Nordic model'. *Regulation and Governance, 4*(2), 203–229.

Glavas, A. (2016). Corporate social responsibility and employee engagement: Enabling employees to employ more of their whole selves at work. *Frontiers in Psychology, 7*(796), 1–10.

Goss, A., & Roberts, G. S. (2011). The impact of corporate social responsibility on the cost of bank loans. *Journal of Banking & Finance, 35*(7), 1794–1810.

Hall, P. A., & Taylor, R. C. R. (1996). Political science and the three new institutionalism. *Political Studies, 44*, 936–957. doi:10.1111/j.1467-9248.1996.tb00343.x

Harjoto, M. A., & Jo, H. (2015). Legal vs. Normative CSR: Differential impact on analyst dispersion, stock return volatility, cost of capital, and firm value. *Journal of Business Ethics, 128*, 1–20. doi:10.1007/s10551-014-2082-2

Hill, C., & Jones, T. (1992). Stakeholder-agency theory. *Journal of Management Studies, 29*, 131. doi:10.1016/S0959-6526(03)00075-1

Hodgson, G. M. (2006). What are institutions? *Journal of Economic Issues, 40*(1), 1–25. http://www.jstor.org/stable/4228221

Hoffman, A. J. (1999). Institutional evolution and change: Environmentalism and the U.S. Chemical industry. *Academy of Management Journal, 42*(4), 351–371.

Indian Companies Act 2013. Retrieved from chrome-extension://efaidnbmnnnibpcajpcglclefindmkaj/https://www.mca.gov.in/Ministry/pdf/CompaniesAct2013.pdf

Indonesia Company Act 2007. Retrieved from chrome-extension://efaidnbmnnnibpcajpcglclefindmkaj/https://cdn.indonesia-investments.com/documents/Company-Law-Indonesia-Law-No.-40-of-2007-on-Limited-Liability-Companies-Indonesia-Investments.pdf

Jensen, M. (2001). Value maximisation, stakeholder theory, and the corporate objective function. 7 *European Financial Management, 7*, 297–300.

Kamens, D. H. (1985). A theory of corporate civic giving. *Sociological Perspectives, 28*, 29–49.

Kotler, P., & Lee, N. (2005). *Corporate social responsibility: Doing the most good for company and your cause*. Hoboken, NJ: John Wiley & Sons, Inc.

Księżak, P., & Fischbach, B. (2018). Triple bottom line: The pillars of CSR. *Journal of Corporate Responsibility and Leadership, 4*(3), 95–110.

Kucher, S. (2021). *Global sustainability study 2021*. Retrieved from https://www.simon-kucher.com/sites/default/files/studies/Simon-Kucher_Global_Sustainability_Study_2021.pdf

Kurucz, E., Colbert, B., & Wheeler, D. (2008). The business case for corporate social responsibility. In A. Crane, A. McWilliams, D. Matten, J. Moon, & D. Siegel (Eds.), *The Oxford handbook of corporate social responsibility* (pp. 83–112). Oxford: Oxford University Press.

Laski, H. J. (1917, April). The early history of the corporation in England. *Harvard Law Review, 30*(6), 561–588.

Louis K. Liggett Co. v. Lee. (1933). 288 U.S. 517, 53 S. Ct. 481.

Matthiesen, M. L., & Salzmann, A. J. (2017). Corporate social responsibility and firms' cost of equity: How does culture matter? *Cross Cultural & Strategic Management, 24*(1), 105–124.

Mauritius income and Tax Act 1995. Retrieved from chrome-extension://efaidnbmnnnibpcajpcglclefindmkaj/https://www.mra.mu/download/ITAConsolidated.pdf

McInerney, T. (2007). Putting regulation before responsibility: Towards binding norms of corporate social responsibility. *Cornell International Law Journal, 40*(1), 171–199.

McWilliams, A., & Siegel, D. (2001). Corporate social responsibility: A theory of the firm perspective. *Academy of Management Review, 26*(1), 117–127. doi:10.2307/259398

Mintzberg, H. (1983). The case for corporate social responsibility. *Journal of Business Strategy*, 3.

Nollkaemper, A. (2006). Responsibility of transnational corporations in international environmental law: Three perspectives. In G. Winter (Ed.), *Multilevel governance of global environmental change: Perspectives from science, sociology and the law*. Cambridge: Cambridge University Press.

O'Neill v Phillips [1999] 1 WLR 1092.

OECD. (2015). *G20/OECD principles of corporate governance*. Paris: OECD Publishing. doi:10.1787/9789264236882-en

Ohnesorge, J. K. (2007). Developing development theory: Law and development orthodoxies and the Northeast Asian experience. *University of Pennsylvania Journal of International Economic Law*, *28*, 219–308.

Ollong, K. A. (2014). The role of multinational corporations in community development initiatives in Cameroon. In E. Ariwa (Ed.), *Green technology applications for enterprise and academic innovation* (pp. 87–101). Hershey, PA: IGI Global. doi:10.4018/978-1-4666-5166-1.ch006

Osuji, O. K. (2011). Fluidity of regulation CSR nexus: The multinational corporate corruption example. *Journal of Business Ethics*, *103*(1), 31–57.

Osuji, O. K. (2015). Corporate social responsibility, juridification and globalisation: 'Inventive interventionism' for a 'paradox. *International Journal of Law in Context*, *11*(3), 265–298.

Osuji, O. K., & Obibuaku, U. L. (2016). Rights and corporate social responsibility: Competing or complementary approaches to poverty reduction and socioeconomic rights? *Journal of Business Ethics*, *136*(2), 329–347.

Palepu, K. G., & Khanna, T. (1997). Institutional voids and policy challenges in emerging markets. *The Brown Journal of World Affairs*, *5*(1), 71–78. Retrieved from http://www.jstor.org/stable/24589954

Rochlin, S., Bliss, R., Jordan, S., & Kiser, C. Y. (2015). Defining the competitive and financial advantages of corporate responsibility and sustainability, IO sustainability. Retrieved from https://www.babson.edu/media/babson/site-assets/content-assets/academics/centers-and-institutes/the-lewis-institute/project-roi/Project-ROI-Report.pdf

Salomon v. Salomon Ltd. (1897). AC 22.

Shamir, R. (2010). Capitalism, governance, and authority: The case of corporate social responsibility. *Annual Review of Law and Social Science*, *6*(1), 531–553.

Smith, A. (1776/1982). In A. Skinner (Ed.), *The Wealth of Nations books I – III* (Penguin classic reprinted edition). London: Penguin Group, Penguin book Limited.

Smith, N. C. (2003). Corporate social responsibility: Whether or how? *California Management Review*, *45*, 52–76.

Sternberg, E. (1997). The defects of stakeholder theory. *Corporate Governance: An International Review*, *5*(1), 3–10.

Suchman, M. C. (1995). Managing legitimacy: Strategic and institutional approaches. *Academy of Management Journal*, *20*, 571–610.

Tebaldi, E., & Mohan, R. (2010). Institutions and poverty. *Journal of Development Studies*, *46*(6), 1047–1066. Taylor and Francis Journals.

U.K. Companies Act 2006.

UNDP. (2020). COVID-19: Looming crisis in developing countries threatens to devastate economies and ramp up inequality. Retrieved from https://www.undp.org/press-releases/covid-19-looming-crisis-developing-countries-threatens-devastate-economies-and-ramp-inequality

U.N. Sustainable Development Goals. (2015). Retrieved from https://sdgs.un.org/goals

Vogel, D. (2005). *The market for virtue: The potential and limits of corporate social responsibility*. Brookings Institution Press. Retrieved from http://www.jstor.org/stable/10.7864/j.ctt1287b7x

Weber, J. L. (2018). Corporate social responsibility disclosure level, external assurance and cost of equity capital. *Journal of Financial Reporting & Accounting*, *16*(4), 694–724.

Wilks, S. (2013). *The political power of the business corporation*. Cheltenham: Edward Elgar Publishing.

World Bank. (2006). *Beyond corporate social responsibility: The scope for corporate investment in community driven development*. Washington, DC: World Bank.

World Business Council for Sustainable Development. (1999). CSR definition. Retrieved from http://www.wbcsd.org/workprogram/business-role/previous-work/corporate-social-responsibility.aspx

Xu, S., Liu, D., & Huang, J. (2015). Corporate social responsibility, the cost of equity capital and ownership structure: An analysis of Chinese listed firms. *Australian Journal of Management, 40*(2), 245–276.

Ye, K., & Zhang, R. (2011). Do lenders value corporate social responsibility? Evidence from China, *Journal of Business Ethics, 104*(2), 197.

CHAPTER 2

FACTORS INFLUENCING WILLINGNESS-TO-REPURCHASE AIRLINE SERVICES IN NIGERIA

Adetayo Olaniyi Adeniran, Ikpechukwu Njoku and Mobolaji Stephen Stephens

ABSTRACT

This study examined the factors influencing willingness-to-repurchase for each class of airline service, and integrate the constructs of service quality, satisfaction and willingness-to-repurchase which were rooted on Engel-Kollat-Blackwell (EKB) model. The study focuses on the domestic and international arrival of passengers at Murtala Muhammed International Airport in Lagos and Nnamdi Azikwe International Airport in Abuja. Information was gathered from domestic and foreign passengers who had post-purchase experience and had used the airline's services more than once. The survey data were obtained concurrently from arrival passengers at two major international airports using an electronic questionnaire through random and purposive sampling techniques. The data was analysed using the ordinal logit model and structural equation model. From the 606 respondents, 524 responses were received but 489 responses were valid for data analysis and reporting and were obtained mostly from economy and business class passengers. The study found that the quality of seat pitch, allowance of 30 kg luggage permission, availability of online check-in 24 hours before the departing flight, quality of space for legroom between seats, and the quality of seats that can be converted into a fully flatbed are the major service factors influencing willingness-to-repurchase economy and business class tickets. Also, it was found that passengers' willingness to repurchase is influenced majorly by service quality, but not necessarily influenced by satisfaction. These results reflect the passengers'

Innovation, Social Responsibility and Sustainability
Developments in Corporate Governance and Responsibility, Volume 22, 25–64
ISSN: 2043-0523/doi:10.1108/S2043-052320230000022002

consciousness of COVID-19 because the study was conducted during the heat of COVID-19 pandemic. Recommendations were suggested for airline management based on each class.

Keywords: Service attributes; willingness-to-repurchase; service quality; satisfaction; ordinal logit model; airline classes

LIST OF ABBREVIATIONS

A—Agree
Ac—Airline Culture
Ap—Airline Promotions and Offers
BASAs—Bilateral Air Service Agreements
C—Convenience
D—Disagree
Df—Date of Flight
EKB—Engel-Kollat-Blackwell
Fd—Flight Duration
I—Income
ICAO—International Civil Aviation Organization
Js—Journey Stage
MMIA—Murtala Muhammed International Airport
NAD—Neither Agree nor Disagree
NAIA—Nnamdi Azikwe International Airport
Oa—Origin Airport
OLR—Ordinal Logistic Regression
Pc—Price of Competitors
Pct—Penalty for Changes in Ticket
POM—Proportional Odds Model
Pr—Price
Pw—Punctuality Warranties or Reliability
Qs—Quality of Service
SA—Strongly Agree
SD—Strongly Disagree
T—Taste
Tp—Trip Purpose
Tv—Time Value
WTR—Willingness-to-Repurchase

1. BACKGROUND

The construct of service quality has become a major focus of interest in academics and the service industry; meanwhile, there are disagreements regarding the measurement and evaluation of services from the customer's point of view (Olorunniwo, Hsu, & Udo, 2017). Apart from these disagreements, assessing the level of service quality is broadly carried out using customers' satisfaction (Lee & Hwan, 2017), which does not necessarily imply that customers may reuse or repurchase the particular service from the same service provider (Tsoukatos & Rand, 2017).

It is pertinent to note that the 21st century is driven by technology and globalisation that is shaping the service sectors of many countries most especially in the area of air transportation and has made the service sector contribute significantly to nations' development. The service sector in the United States contributes about 74% to the GDP and employment generation from 2000 to 2020 (Patricia & Rumki, 2020; Statista, 2021). Similarly, the service sector contributes to GDP in parts of North America, Asia, Europe, and Australia. For example, 70.2% in Canada, 62% in Hong Kong, 70% in The Netherlands, and 78.6% in Australia respectively. In Nigeria, Plecher (2020) revealed that the service sector contributed about 51% to the Nation's GDP from 2000 to 2020.

The transportation industry is among the service sector that is recently influenced by technology, politics, and economic changes. As a result of these changes, service quality has been a key issue for both passengers and airlines. Aviation contributes significantly to global economic growth by carrying people and things across borders, so encouraging economic activity, job creation, tourism, and commerce. The total number of scheduled passengers transported by the worldwide aviation sector in 2021 was 2.19 billion (IATA, 2022b), a 21% increase over the 1.81 billion recorded in 2020. The rise of the global airline business has been aided by the expansion of the tourism sector, which has seen an increase in the number of international visitors travelling by air, as well as trade and service liberalisation (ACI, 2022). Meanwhile, the tremendous expansion in passenger transportation is being disrupted by two worldwide crises: the COVID-19 epidemic and the European conflict.

The COVID-19 epidemic has been termed the most disastrous danger to the aviation sector in history, ranking among previous global shocks such as the 1979 oil price crisis, the Gulf War, 9/11, and the 2008 Global Financial Crisis (IATA, 2021). In perspective, the COVID-19 epidemic reversed over two decades of passenger traffic growth. The global economic impact of the pandemic on the aviation sector is projected to be $3.5 trillion, or nearly 4.1% of global GDP (IATA, 2022b).

According to the International Air Transport Association (IATA), by 2040, passenger volume will still be 6% lower than predicted before the outbreak, highlighting the pandemic's long-term impact. The aircraft sector, on the other hand, was still recuperating from the epidemic when the several competitors of Ukraine-Russia attacked it, causing a spiral impact on multiple fronts.

First, as of 2021, the shutdown of Ukrainian airspace halts around 3.3% of all air passenger travel in Europe and 0.8% of total traffic globally (IATA, 2022). Furthermore, around 40 nations have closed their airspace to Russian airlines, with Russia retaliating by prohibiting most of those countries from visiting or flying over Russia. The Ukraine conflict has a significant influence on air travel between Europe and Asia, as well as between Asia and North America (ACI, 2022). Air travel between Russia and the rest of the world is expected to account for 5.2% of global international traffic in 2021, with Russian domestic Revenue Passenger-Kilometers (RPKs) accounting for 4.5% of worldwide RPKs (IATA, 2022).

The COVID-19 epidemic, in line with the global trend, had a detrimental influence on Nigeria's aviation sector. Due to the March 2020 air travel limitation, the local aviation industry saw negative growth of 36.98% in 2020, compared to a GDP increase of 13.22% in 2019. Nonetheless, the aviation industry rose by 19.7%, returning to pre-pandemic levels if the travel ban is entirely lifted in 2021 (IATA, 2022b). According to the National Bureau of Statistics (NBS), around 13 million passengers passed through Nigerian airports in 2021, marking a 43.41% increase from 9 million in 2020. Meanwhile, growth is being hampered by persistent pressure points, which is consistent with global patterns (Phillipsconsulting, 2022).

Since the introduction of airline deregulation in the late 1970s, considerable changes have been recorded in the air travel industry. Among the changes are the increasing number of flight operations, construction of more functional airports, affordability of airline tickets, and increasing air traffic. Apart from these, intense competition among the airlines is a direct result of deregulation (Alivand, Hochmair, & Srinivasan, 2015; Hangjun, Qiong, & Qiang, 2018). Due to intense competition, airlines aimed at maintaining quality services so that they can retain passengers. For a customer to be retained and willing to repurchase, this implies that such a customer must have positive intentions about the services offered, value the services as quality, receive value for their money and be satisfied.

The air transport industry is evolving because of the changing dynamics of urbanisation, globalisation, digitalisation and socio-economic shift among other factors. As a result of these changes, the global economy was predicted to be dominated by Asia, America and Europe in the year 2030 (Anta, Pérez-López, Martínez-Pardo, Novales, & Orro, 2016; Gill, 2020; Hamish, 2018). Therefore, service organisations like airlines must be rightly positioned where the business is, and be able to fulfil the customers' wants. With the constraint of Bilateral Air Service Agreements (BASAs), airlines are forming strategic alliances by sharing code to expand global network coverage, dominate new routes, and offer quality service at reduced costs (James & Paul, 2018).

In the airline industry, the evaluation of airline services is germane to determine its performance. Airline traffic is the amount of airline output that is sold or consumed. The form of traffic can either be passenger traffic, cargo traffic or both, which can include air freight, mail and passenger baggage. Airlines are generally categorised based on the nature of traffic; cargo airlines primarily transport air freight, while passenger airlines primarily transport the combination of passengers, passenger baggage, mail and air freight (Bhat, Astroza, & Bhat, 2016; Bieger & Laesser, 2016; Peter, Amedeo, & Cynthia, 2009).

Traditionally, airlines have three travel classes in which a passenger may buy the ticket; in terms of hierarchy, they are first class, business class, and economy class of airlines based on the level of service offerings. The services offered in each of the classes are usually influenced by the changing dynamics earlier identified (technology, taste, income); therefore, airline requires huge effort to deliver services with good levels of quality. Airline services are essential services that a passenger cannot do away with to gain air travel experience; therefore, evaluating the levels of airline services delivered is pertinent to understand the needs of the customers and areas for service improvement.

Passengers' evaluation of airline services is necessitated as price and quality service offerings are the major determinants that enhance airline competitive advantage (Jou, Michael, Henser, Chen, & Kuo, 2017; Li, Yu, Pei, Zao, & Tian, 2017). For airlines to survive, they must be able to deliver a total travel programme (such as non-stop flights, leisure programmes, hotels, and financial services, among all) through a central information system (Cavallaro, Ciari, Nocera, Prettenthaler, & Scuttari, 2017). Air passengers are more conscious of the value of their money and at the same time search for more cheap tickets (Al Rafaie, Bata, & Issam, 2019; Anastasia, 2019; Ozlem, Mahmut, & Sahap, 2019; Roy, Luke, & Beukering, 2017; Thomas, 2019).

The expectations of passengers regarding the quality service they receive, and expected value are increasing, and airlines are conscious of meeting these expectations. This implies that airline management must have an in-depth understanding of the dynamics in which passengers value service quality. Currently, with the increasing demand for air travel in Nigeria, airlines are confronted with the need to have a better understanding of passengers' travel behaviour (Adeola & Adebiyi, 2019), which will enable them to offer exact services that are appealing to the passengers when consumed. This is a means of achieving willingness-to-repurchase, justifying and improving the satisfaction of passengers. Since service quality and customers satisfaction are essential to achieve a willingness to repurchase (Azman, Iiyani, Rabaah, & Norazryana, 2017; Mittal & Gera, 2020; Muhammad, 2015), the examination of factors that could influence willingness to repurchase will be more robust without exploring service constructs but solely dependent on service attributes.

Despite the significant pace achieved in recent years, the exact service attributes influencing willingness-to-repurchase different classes of airline service may not have been well researched. From the foregoing, this study seeks to examine the factors influencing willingness-to-repurchase for each class of airline service, using domestic and international airlines that are operating in Nigeria. This study is a post-consumption assessment of airline services; therefore, it focuses on the revealed preference of passengers. The airline evaluation was carried out using airline service attributes for first, business and economy classes because they will provide a robust quality assessment for determining the behaviour of customers based on the repurchase of the ticket.

Moreover, this study was limited to airline services which are the primary aviation services for different classes of airline service (first class, business class and economy class) which a passenger must consume before having a post-consumption travel experience. Information was elicited from domestic and international passengers that have post-consumption experience and must have consumed the airline services more than once. The category of domestic passengers must also have international air travel experience. The air passengers were chosen because they are primary users of airline services. The study areas for this research were Murtala

Muhammed International Airport in Lagos and Nnamdi Azikwe International Airport in Abuja, Nigeria. The two airports were chosen for this study because they are located within the South and North zones respectively, and they facilitate high patronage in terms of passenger throughputs.

2. LITERATURE REVIEW

In recent times, consumer behaviour as a term is gaining traction in different fields, particularly in marketing, social sciences, engineering and technology literature (Anderl, Schumann, & Kunz, 2016). Consumer behaviour, as described by Becker and Jaakkola (2020), is the process through which people or groups select, acquire, utilise or dispose of objects, services, ideas or experiences to meet needs and desires (Schmidt & Spreng, 1996). It is a general evaluation process that is continuous and applicable to more than a moment (one-time consumption) (Hulland, Baumgartner, & Smith, 2018).

The traditional consumer decision-making process explains that the search for information is carried out internally to some extent, focusing on recalling stored information (Hanson, Jiang, & Dahl, 2019). Rosario, de Valck, and Sotgiu (2020) express how behaviours shaped towards different alternatives are crucial in whether that alternative was considered during the process of buying. Consumers' behaviour is key in marketing strategies because its changes influence the pattern of buying (Kranzbühler, Kleijnen, & Verlegh, 2019).

Baxendale, Macdonald, and Wilson (2015) further underline the need for investigating the entire consuming process, rather than simply the moment of exchange, because it is necessary to screen the customer before, during, and after a purchase (Kuehnl, Jozic, & Homburg, 2019). Because of the actual demand in the airline industry, and the changing attitude of customers (Hamilton & Price, 2019), there is a need to examine how they make decisions (Santini et al., 2020). As a result, Schamp, Heitmann, and Katzenstein (2019) observed that this examination is needed for effective marketing tactics, especially for airlines to retain more customers.

2.1 Willingness-to-Repurchase

Willingness-to-repurchase is a form of customers' repurchases intention; it is germane in the defensive marketing techniques and success of any business in general because they prevent customers from patronising other service providers (Vasudevan, Gaur, & Shinde, 2017), and post-consumption-feedback-from the users of service. An individual tends to repurchase a particular service after a one-time purchase (Chen & Chang, 2005; Schmidt & Bijmolt, 2020).

Eliasaph, Farida, and Balarabe (2016) identified two forms of repurchase, which are:

i. the intention to re-buy (repurchase); and
ii. the intention to engage in positive word-of-mouth and recommendation (referral).

While repurchase is the actual action, willingness-to-repurchase is defined as the customer's decision to engage in future intention to re-buy from a retailer or supplier (Akaka & Schau, 2019). According to Pizzutti, Gonçalves, and Ferreira (2022) and Kotler and Armstrong (2019), it is a form of consumer behaviour, and a dynamic nexus between the interaction of cognition, emotion and behaviour including feelings and thoughts that are experienced by consumers and their behaviour during the process of buying which is mostly influenced by the post-consumption experience (Pizzutti et al., 2022). Also, it encompasses the environment which affects consumers' cognition, emotion and behaviour, such as information concerning product price, comments emanating from other consumers, advertisements and product packaging, among others. In the study of Engel, Blackwell, and Miniard (1995), Norazryana and Khalil (2020), it was revealed that willingness-to-repurchase is highly connected to the post-consumption experience.

A great number of studies have found the nexus between service quality, customers satisfaction, customer value and willingness to repurchase (Cronin, Brady, & Hult, 2000; Chumpitaz & Paparoidamis, 2016; Vasudevan et al., 2017). Yananda and Duangkamol (2019) found a strong relationship between customer satisfaction and repurchase intention and as a result, satisfaction with services is crucial in enhancing willingness to repurchase. Premium price would be happily paid by customers to the same service provider because of the good post-consumption experiences and for the avoidance of risk (uncertainty). Rowley (2016) noted that customers' willingness to repurchase is a sign that customers have decided to be loyal to the service provider.

2.2 Factors Influencing Willingness-to-Repurchase Airline Services

The factors influencing willingness-to-repurchase airline services have been widely investigated, among are Lee and Luengo-Prado (2016) conducted a study on passengers' willingness to pay more for additional legroom in the US. In the study, panel data from 1998 to 2002 and primary data were analysed with regression and found that short-haul trip influences passengers' willingness to pay for an economy-class of airline. Also, passengers' willingness to pay more for additional legroom is influenced by the availability and quality of in-flight food services. Dixon (2017) employed SEM to analyse an alternative perspective on the relationships between loyalty and future store choices and found that repurchase intention is influenced by the quality of service received during past purchasing.

Feng and Jeng (2017) analysed airline service improvement strategy through importance and performance analysis in the Taiwan air market. The study employed primary data from 599 respondents (domestic passengers) and found that reliability of flight, trip purposes, gender, baggage delivery and flight safety are the key factors that lead to satisfaction, and such will influence willingness-to-repurchase airline service. Laws (2017) conducted a study on the management of passengers' satisfaction with airline meal service during journeys by air using the consumerist gap concept for analysis from the passenger's and airline staff's points of view and found that passengers demand a greater level of meals variety and safety on long-haul flights. The study also found that passengers are dissatisfied with the quality of meals, and there is an ineffective response from airline staff to the customers' complaints.

Fourie and Lubbe (2017) examined the determinants of the selection of full-service airlines and low-cost carriers on a business trip in South Africa using passengers that were mainly from South Africa, the UK, and Brazil. The study found that fast, accurate, friendly check-in services and low-price offerings are factors influencing willingness-to-repurchase for low-cost (economy class) carriers. Willingness to repurchase for full-service (first class and business class) carriers is largely influenced by the level of comfort in-flight and on-ground (lounges), flexible connectivity between flights and, most importantly, punctuality. Waterhouse, Kao, Edwards, Atkinson, and Reilly (2017) conducted a study on factors associated with food intake in passengers on long-haul flights using 361 passengers' eating habits across eight time zones. The study found that most of the passengers under study consumed their offered meals due to boredom on long flights, and their level of meal acceptance is mainly influenced by the circumstances and the time of meal service. The study further revealed that long-haul flight influences willingness-to-repurchase for meals on business class flights.

Chen and Chen (2010) examined the experience quality, perceived value, satisfaction and behavioural intention of heritage tourists using 447 respondents at the four main heritage sites in Tainan, Taiwan. SEM was employed for data analysis, and it revealed that the availability of price discounts and promotions are the factors influencing customers' repurchases. It also found the relationships between quality and satisfaction, perceived value and satisfaction, quality, perceived value, and satisfaction, and quality, perceived value, satisfaction and behavioural intentions. Moufakkir (2019) examined the pay-for-in-flight food and drinks policy and its impact on travellers' experience. Using 217 passengers that were randomly selected and regression analysis, the study found that passengers give less attention to food noted that when choosing a carrier, but still consider it important when repurchasing for medium and long-haul trips.

Zahari, Salleh, Kamaruddin, and Kutut (2019) investigated passengers' perceptions and acceptance of in-flight meals and the latter relationship with flight satisfaction and re-booking intention using a case study of a Mongolian airline. The cross-sectional survey was conducted on international flights from Ulaanbaatar to Tokyo, Seoul, Beijing, Bangkok, Moscow, and Berlin using convenience sampling and a sample of 303 respondents. Regression analysis revealed that in-flight meals do not only contribute to the prediction of satisfaction but slightly influence re-booking intentions. Also, in-flight service quality and flight safety influenced passengers' satisfaction and loyalty.

Juliet (2020) examined the influence of airline service quality on passengers' satisfaction and loyalty in the Uganda airline industry using 263 respondents (passengers) that were randomly sampled. Their responses were analysed with

Chi-square and found that the popularity of service providers, exposure to opportunities, ease of transaction, positive word-of-mouth from satisfied customers; customers' experience during the first-time patronage are the factors influencing customers' willingness-to-repurchase. Namukasa (2020) examined the influence of airline service quality on passenger satisfaction and loyalty in the Uganda airline industry using 303 respondents (passengers) that were randomly sampled. Their responses were analysed with Chi-square and found that the quality of pre-flight, in-flight and post-flight have a significant impact on satisfaction and loyalty which are indications of willingness-to-repurchase airline services.

Laming and Mason (2014) evaluated airline performance based on customer experience. The study employed IATA data collected over 12 months from a sample size of 18,567 passengers in Europe, the Middle East and Asia, and analysed with regression. The study found that class of flight were not related to satisfaction, loyalty and advocacy, but related to the length of the journey, the purpose of the trip and the in-flight meal. Mauricio (2019) employed an analytical model to assess airline expansion strategies using 904,736 customers. The analytical model of points and weights revealed that the income of the passenger is the main factor influencing the business class choice of an airline, and it has a huge effect on the willingness of a passenger to repurchase for such class of an airline. The study further revealed that price, price of competitors, the penalty for changes in the ticket, trip purpose, date of flight, airline promotions and offers, origin airport, taste, income, time value, flight duration (Short haul or Long haul), journey stage (completed, stop-over), airline culture, punctuality warranties or reliability, convenience, and quality of service pre-flight, in-flight and post-flight services are the factors influencing willingness-to-repurchase airline services, and each of the airline services is categorised based on the economy class, business class and first class or low-cost and full-service carriers.

From the foregoing, the study of Mauricio (2019) was quite similar, but it was not conducted in Nigeria. Also, the examination of factors that could influence willingness-to-repurchase will be more robust without exploring service constructs but solely dependent on service attributes; hence, this study seeks to examine the factors influencing willingness-to-repurchase for each class of airline service, using domestic and international airlines that are operating in Nigeria, and based on the post-consumption experience of passengers.

3. MODEL FRAMEWORK

3.1 Engel-Kollat-Blackwell (EKB) Model of Consumer Behaviour

Engel-Kollat-Blackwell (EKB) model (1968) is the most widely utilised model in marketing that explained five customers' decision-making processes (Darley, Blankson, & Luethge, 2010). This was adopted in this study because it encompasses several customer processes including post-purchase evaluation.These processes are sequential and are as follows:

(1) Identification of problem;
(2) Searching for information;
(3) Evaluation of alternatives;
(4) Purchase decision; and
(5) Post-purchase evaluation.

According to Wolny and Charoensuksai (2014), this model is mostly applicable to high-involvement products and services due to its schematic representation of consumer cognitive processes. Since air travel services and products represent high-involvement products, this model is preferred when studying travel consumer behaviour (Chua, Servillo, Marcheggiani, & Moere, 2016; Papathanassis & Knolle, 2011). Additionally, it is of high importance to study instances of changing consumer behaviours in response to satisfaction and monetary issues (Gerike & Schulz, 2018), hence, basic when developing marketing strategies.

However, there are conditions when the consumer does not pass through these entire processes and heuristics decisions are made (Gross & Grimm, 2018; Gühnemann, Kurzweil, & Mailer, 2021; Nuraeni, Arru, & Novani, 2015). Different studies revealed that the process of decision-making regarding travel is a more complex one even than the one illustrated in EKB-model (Gardiner, King, & Grace, 2013; Hardy et al., 2017; Hardy & Aryal, 2020; Nuraeni et al., 2015).

Elucidating on this theory helps to:

i. Appreciate the most significant variables that influence passengers to embark on purchasing a class of ticket of a particular airline, both deliberately and undeliberately;
ii. Reveal the preferences of airline customers vis-à-vis the airline marketing dynamics.

Buaphiban and Truong (2017), Borhan, Ibrahim, Miskeen, Rahmat, and Alhodairi (2017), Kim and Han (2010), Sirakayaa and Woodside (2017) stated that the decision-making process is affected by internal, external, psychological variables, and non-psychological variables that should be determined especially within the airline travel market to understand the pattern of consumer behaviour.

Buaphiban and Truong (2017) explain that there are some motivational factors covered in intentions that may influence behaviour. They further state that intention is the extent to which people are willing to engage in a particular behaviour. It can be noted that the stronger the intention, the more likely an individual will be willing to execute a particular behaviour. For instance, the stronger the passenger's intention to patronise a particular airline over time, the more committed that passenger is to actively search for information regarding that airline (cost, comfort, penalties attached to change in ticket, reliability, frequency, etc.).

Consequently, the success of behavioural predictions does not only depend on the intention, but also on non-motivational factors such as the available resources and opportunities (such as technological exposure, time, money, etc.) which enhance the transformation of someone's intention into action over the behaviours. Factors influencing customers' behavioural intentions are usually of great significance as they may determine customers' propensity to remain with a particular air service provider or leave. This is dependent on how favourable or unfavourable the factors are. Zeithaml, Berry, and Parasuraman (1996) grouped behavioural intentions into two categories: favourable and unfavourable behavioural intentions.

In the case of favourable behavioural intentions, the following are noticeable: customers often show a preference for one company over another; oftentimes, customers engage in positive word-of-mouth communication/observations; customers recommend a service provider to others; they increase their rate of spending on the company's products/services, and they are always willing to pay premium prices. These characteristics are signs that customers have a strong connection with the company. It can also be maintained that customer experiences may also influence behavioural intentions (Burton, Sheather, & Roberts, 2016; Hewer, Scott, & Gough, 2017; Hoogendoorn-Lanser, Schaap, & OldeKalter, 2015). In a situation where the experience is positive, Olorunniwo, Hsu, and Udo (2018) revealed that customers would tend to reuse the service repeatedly.

In the case of unfavourable behavioural intentions, the following are noticeable: customers perceived the performance of the service as inferior; they complain about the company's products/services; they are likely to ignore the company, and they make shifts or spend less with the company. Complaining is usually the result of dissatisfaction which may result in a negative response. Practitioners found that customer complaint is a useful dimension to understanding the dynamics of marketplace dissatisfaction (Janzen, Vanhoof, Smoreda, & Axhausen, 2018; Juschten & Hössinger, 2021). Customer complaint studies and their consequences have been found critical in explaining and predicting consumers' loyalty and repurchase intentions (Borhan et al., 2017; Buaphiban & Truong, 2017; Li, Yang, Shen, & Wu, 2019). Willingness to repurchase is a form of behaviour which is positively or negatively influenced as a result of previous encounters about the service or product offerings.

The adoption of the EKB model in understanding passengers' evaluation of airline services is not common, especially in predicting passengers' purchase or repurchase behaviour. It can be used in the context where airline tickets are grouped into classes. This is an area yet to be investigated as a context for the behavioural model using willingness-to-repurchase. Several studies have found the nexus between service quality, customer satisfaction, customer value and behavioural intentions (Cronin et al., 2000; Chumpitaz & Paparoidamis, 2016; Dean, Raats, & Shepherd, 2012; Lin, Kerstetter, Nawijn, & Mitas, 2018; Liu, Susilo, & Karlström, 2015).

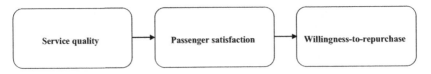

Fig. 2.1.   Conceptual Framework.

As a result, service quality, and passenger satisfaction are introduced as external factors, and two hypotheses were developed based on the theoretical foundation. Fig. 2.1 represents the proposed research model.

H1. Service quality negatively influences passenger satisfaction.

H2. Passenger satisfaction negatively influences willingness-to-repurchase.

4. METHODS

4.1 Method of Data Collection

The survey data were collected in the arrival halls of international and domestic terminals in the two major Nigerian international airports – Murtala Muhammed International Airport and Nnamdi Azikwe International Airport, in Lagos and Abuja respectively from 1st to 31st August 2021. The respondents included in this study were those that have more than 1-year air travel experience and patronised the airline more than once.

Items on the questionnaire were designed based on the related literature discussed above. The questionnaire was pre-tested by 60 people and revised properly to ensure content validity. The questions were refined based on interviewers' feedback and opinions regarding the questionnaire. Using the 60 samples, Cronbach's alpha values were obtained and ranged from 0.753 to 0.889, exceeding the recommended value of 0.7. The final version of the questionnaire was composed of 9 questions for demographic and travel-related characteristics, 7 questions for quality of airline inhibitors in economy class, 14 questions for quality of airline inhibitors in business class, 13 questions for quality of airline inhibitors in first class, and 28 questions for the four constructs. All questionnaire items for the three constructs were measured using a 5-point-Likert scale, ranging from 1 (strongly disagree) to 5 (strongly agree).

4.2 Ordinal Logistic Regression

The logistic regression model is the most dominant for analysing ordinal response variables (Wang et al., 2020), particularly the proportional odds model (POM) (Bender & Grouven, 1998; Fullerton & Xu, 2020). When the response variable is ordinal, the OLR model has been utilised often in past investigations (Adejumo & Adetunji, 2020; Fuks & Salazar, 2017; Gameroff, 2017). Ordinal models provide more generalising visualisations that compare the effects of independent variables at the class level (Citko, Milewska, Wasilewska, & Kaczmarski, 2020; Das & Rahman, 2019; Fasano & Durante, 2020).

OLR is used to predict group membership in models with continuous, discrete, dichotomous, or mixed variables (Field, 2009). This differs from linear regression because the dependent variable is in a binary or dichotomous form (Hosmer, Stanley, & Rodney, 2020; Maria, Laura, Carmen, & Gabriella, 2018) and the predictors do not need to meet the normality assumption, and no linear relationship is required between the dependent and independent variables. The identification of factors influencing willingness-to-repurchase airline tickets at Lagos and Abuja international and domestic airport terminals using the OLR model with ordered categories of strongly agree; agree; neither agree nor disagree; disagree and strongly disagree.

The equation of logistic regression models for this study as shown in Eq. (2.1) is as follows:

$$P_{WTR} = \frac{1}{1+e^{-\left(b_0+b_1 Pr+b_2 Pc+b_3 Pct+b_4 Tp+b_5 Df+b_6 Ap+b_7 Oa+b_8 T+b_9 I+b_{10} Tv+b_{11} Fd+b_{12} Js+b_{13} Ac+b_{14} Pw+b_{15} C+b_{16} Qs_{(1-n)}\right)}} \quad ......(Eq.\ 2.1)$$

where e represents the base of natural logarithms, b_0 is constant, and the factors influencing willingness-to-repurchase airline services were Price (Pr), Price of competitors (Pc), Penalty for ticket changes (Pct), Trip purpose (Tp), Date of flight (Df), Airline promotions and offers (Ap), Origin airport (Oa), Taste (T), Income (I), Time value (Tv), Flight duration (Short haul or Long haul) (Fd), Journey stage (Completed, Stop-over) (Js), Airline culture (Ac), Punctuality warranties or reliability (Pw), Convenience (C), and Quality of Service (inhibitors) (Qs $_{(1-n)}$) for each class of ticket are the independent or predictor variables). $P_{(WTR)}$ represents the probability for willingness-to-repurchase to occur for each class ticket. The probability of the occurrence of an event is divided by the probability of not occurring, and this is referred to as the odds ratio (Hair, Black, Babin, & Anderson, 2009).

4.3 Reliability Test

A confirmatory factor analysis (CFA) was performed to test the reliability and validity of the measurement model and assess the three constructs. The CFA found that the paths reaching from latent variables of perceived service quality factors based on economy and business class categories (PSQ), passenger satisfaction (PS), and willingness-to-repurchase (WtR) to the measurement variables were all significant ($p < 0.01$). Before conducting the CFA, the normality for the Likert scales was checked using skewness and kurtosis criteria, and the normality assumption was satisfied (Kline, 2011).

Convergent validity is evaluated by using standardised factor loading and the average variance extracted (AVE). To ensure convergent validity, all factor loadings should be greater than 0.70 and the AVE should be greater than 0.50 (Fornell & Larcker, 1981). The factor loadings of the items in the conceptual framework varied from 0.775 to 0.919, and all AVEs exceeded the recommended threshold, ranging between 0.820 and 0.921. The outcomes satisfied the proper

Table 2.1. Construct Reliability and Convergent Validity.

Construct	Item	Factor Loading	AVE	Composite Reliability	Cronbach's Alpha
Service quality	Quality of service for economy class ticket	0.813	0.865	0.904	0.894
	Quality of service for business class ticket	0.919			
Passenger satisfaction	Satisfaction with cabin services	0.849	0.820	0.847	0.821
	Satisfaction with onboard services	0.791			
	Satisfaction with ground services	0.775			
	Satisfaction with adherence to Covid-19 safety rules	0.781			
Willingness-to-repurchase	I Will repurchase for economy class ticket	0.834	0.921	0.830	0.837
	I Will repurchase for business class ticket	0.801			

degree of convergent validity. The model reliability was evaluated via composite reliability and Cronbach's alpha. It is recommended that the composite reliability should exceed 0.7 and the proper value for Cronbach's alpha should also exceed 0.7.

As shown in Table 2.1, all composite reliability values range between 0.830 and 0.904. The Cronbach's alpha values ranged from 0.821 to 0.894, exceeding the recommended value. The results satisfied the proper degree of reliability. Discriminant validity was assessed by comparing AVEs to the square of inter-construct correlations. All squared values of inter-construct correlation should be lower than the AVE values (Fornell & Larcker, 1981).

As shown in Table 2.2, all AVE values exceeded the square values of inter-construct correlation, and this ensured discriminant validity. Square inter-construct correlations and average variance extracted (AVEs) are shown in Table 2.2. AVEs are highlighted in the top diagonal of the matrix, and the square inter-construct correlations are presented diagonally under the AVEs. All inter-construct correlations are significant at the 0.05 significance level.

Table 2.2. Square Inter-construct Correlations and Average Variance Extracted.

	1 PSQ	2 PS	3 WtR
1 PSQ	0.756		
2 PS	0.617	**0.752**	
3 WtR	0.285	0.521	**0.821**

4.4 Structural Equation Model

For this study, a preliminary structural equation encompassing all of the survey items was created, and the early model's goodness of fit was assessed using confirmatory factor analysis. Then, based on the precondition criteria, we removed questions to increase the goodness of fit and built the final model. A structural equation model, also known as covariance structural modelling, searches for the relation between factors, which consists of a measurement model, confirmatory factor analysis, and structural model via multiple regression analysis/path analysis as following Eq. (2.1) (Hong, 2000; Kelloway, 1998; Ullman & Bentler, 2006).

$$V_1 = J_{11} + J_{12} + J_{13} + \cdots + J_{1p}$$

$$V_2 = J_{21} + J_{22} + J_{23} + \cdots + J_{1q}$$

$$V_3 = J_{31} + J_{32} + J_{33} + \cdots + J_{1p}$$

$$V_p = J_{p1} + J_{p2} + J_{p3} + \cdots + J_{pq}$$

where V: quantitative variable, J: quantitative or qualitative variable, p q: number of variables. GFI (goodness of fit index), NFI (normed fit index) (Bentler, 1990; Bentler & Bonett, 1980; McKercher, Hardy, & Aryal, 2019; Nawijn, Mitas, Lin, & Kerstetter, 2013; Schlemmer, Blank, Bursa, Mailer, & Schnitzer, 2019; Tucker & Lewis, 1973) and CFI (comparative fit index) (Bentler, 1990) were employed in this study. Root mean square of error approximation (RMSEA) supplementing the limitation of Chi statistics is recommended to be between 0.05 and 0.08 (Browne & Cudeck, 1992; Zhao, Lu, Liu, Lin, & An, 2018). CFI, GFI, NFI, and RMSEA as goodness of fit indexes were used concurrently with Chi statistics in this study since Chi statistics are sensitive to sample sizes, and in situations of above 400 sample size, it is usually assumed that it is statistically acceptable (Satorra & Bentler, 1988; Shoval & Ahas, 2016; van Nostrand, Sivaraman, & Pinjari, 2013; Vu, Li, Law, & Zhang, 2018).

5. RESULTS

Based on the survey conducted and valid information retrieved from 489 arrival passengers for this study between 1st August and 31st August 2021, there were 26 airlines (eight domestic airlines, 15 international airlines, and three domestic and international airlines) that arrived at the MMIA, Lagos, and NAIA, Abuja, domestic and international terminals as shown in Table 2.3. According to Chapter 5, Article 29 of the International Civil Aviation Organization (ICAO), the nature of flights are domestic and international depending on the points of

Table 2.3. Airlines Patronised by Passengers.

Airlines	Frequency	%	Airlines	Frequency	%
Aero Contractors	47	9.6	Ibom Air	47	9.6
Air France	7	1.4	Kenya Airways	11	2.2
Air Peace	22	4.5	KLM	15	3.1
Arik Air	32	6.5	Lufthansa	6	1.2
Azman Air	27	5.5	Max Air	20	4.1
British Airways	14	2.9	Overland Airways	48	9.8
Cally Air	46	9.4	Qatar Airways	9	1.8
Dana Air	28	5.7	Royal Air	11	2.2
Delta Airlines	7	1.4	Rwanda Air	7	1.4
Egypt Air	7	1.4	Swiss	14	2.9
Emirate	7	1.4	Turkish Airlines	7	1.4
Ethiopian Airline	13	2.7	United Air	18	3.7
Green Africa	13	2.7	Virgin Atlantic	6	1.2

origin and destination. For this survey, there were 335 domestic passengers, representing 68.5% while 154 international passengers, representing 31.5%.

The mean age of the respondents was 42.35 ± 10.39 years, with a minimum age of 12 and a maximum age of 71 years. This implies that the majority of the respondents were not older than 53 years, and were between the age of 32 and 53 years, which is referred to as the economic stimulating age (Oseni, Corral, Goldstein, & Winters, 2015). Most of the respondents (52.8%) were married and 200 respondents (40.9%) were self-employed while 192 respondents (40.1%) were privately employed as shown in Table 2.2. This implies that the majority of the people that can afford to travel by air are those in the self-employed or privately employed category.

The respondents for this survey were citizens from 19 countries. Meanwhile, more than half of the respondents (75.9%) were Nigerians. The majority of the respondents (95.3%) have international air travel experience, and the respondents (59.8%) have travel experience for more than two years as shown in Table 2.4. Also, 376 respondents (76.9%) have been travelling with that particular airline more than once, which implies that they were familiar with the specific airline's services. The majority of the respondents (72.4%) were economy-class passengers.

Regarding the reasonability of the airfare of the airline patronised, more than half of the respondents (80.8%) perceived that the airfares of the airline they patronised were reasonable. Meanwhile, 50.7% of respondents perceived that the airfares of competitors were more reasonable, and at the same time, the majority of the respondents (63.8%) perceived that the airlines offer promotional programs and offers. This is an implication that despite the oligopolistic market structure of the airline business, the nature of business is quite competitive as is evidenced by changes in industry practices, technological advancements, low-fare carriers, and frequent interaction with passengers, among others. Regarding the percentage of

Table 2.4. Demographic and Travel-Related Information ($n = 489$).

Variables	Indicators	N	%	Variables	Indicators	N	%
Nature of arrival flights	Domestic	335	68.5	International travel	No	23	4.7
	International	154	31.5		Yes	466	95.3
Age	Mean	42.35		Travel experience	>2 Years	291	59.8
	Std. Dev.	10.39	489		2 Years	198	40.8
Marital status	Divorced	75	15.3	First travel with the airline	No	376	76.9
	Married	258	52.8		Yes	112	22.9
	Single	97	19.8		Others	1	0.2
	Widowed	59	12.1				
Nature of employment	Government employed	92	18.8	Class of ticket	Business	134	27.4
	Privately employed	196	40.1		Economy	354	72.4
	Self-employed	200	40.9		Others	1	0.2
	Others	1	0.2	Reasonability of airfare	No	94	19.2
Nationality	America	9	1.8		Yes	395	80.8
	Benin	2	0.4	Reasonability of competitor's airfare	No	241	49.3
	China	8	1.6		Yes	248	50.7
	Dubai	4	0.8	Percentage of fare increase on the penalty for changes in ticket	10.0%	80	16.4
	France	2	0.4		20.0%	106	21.7
	Ghana	10	2.0		Others	303	62.0
	India	12	2.5				
	Italy	3	0.6	Airline promotions and offers	No	176	36.0
	Ivory Coast	1	0.2		Yes	312	63.8
	Jordan	2	0.4				
	Netherlands	1	0.2	Taste preference for airline service	Do not have a taste	24	4.9

(Continued)

Table 2.4. (*Continued*)

Variables	Indicators	N	%	Variables	Indicators	N	%
	Niger	1	0.2		Limited taste	138	28.2
	Nigeria	371	75.9		Very high taste	327	66.9
	Norway	1	0.2	Estimate monthly income		2	0.4
	South Africa	36	7.4		₦100,000 – ₦499,999	156	31.9
	Sweden	15	3.1		₦500,000 – ₦1,000,000	258	52.8
	UAE	1	0.2		Above ₦1,000,000	49	10.0
	UK	3	0.6		Below ₦100,000	24	4.9
	USA	7	1.4	Duration of flight	Long haul (more than 1 hour)	172	35.2
Travel with this Airline because of the time value	No	109	22.4		Short haul (less than 1 hour)	317	68.4
	Yes	380	77.7				
Stage of journey	Completed	447	91.4	Airlines' special form of culture	No	320	65.4
	Stop-over	42	8.6		Yes	169	34.6
Warranties on airline punctuality or reliability	Availability of free tickets for the same trip	22	4.5	Condition of space for legroom		2	0.4
	No compensation for flight delay	241	49.3		Small space for legroom within the seats	347	71.0
	Reimbursement of the cost of the ticket	226	46.2		Wide space for legroom within the seats	140	28.6

fare increase on the penalty for changes in the ticket, the majority of the respondents (62%) perceived that the fare increase is more than 20%, while 21% of respondents perceived that the increase is 20%.

Regarding the taste preference of passengers for airline service, 327 respondents representing 66.9% perceived that they have a very high taste for airline services, and the majority of them (77.7%) received that they travel with the airline because of the time value. This implies that taste and time are important factors that drive air passengers to patronise a particular airline. Hence, airlines should improve the quality of taste they dish out to passengers and at the same time be reliable in terms of swift operations and service frequency. Regarding the estimate of passengers' monthly income, it was revealed that the majority of passengers representing 84.7% earned between ₦100,000 and ₦1,000,000.

Flight duration is referred to as the total trip time which is measured from the 'true' origin (airport of origin) to the 'true' destination (airport of destination). Concerning the duration of the flight, as shown in Table 2.4, it was revealed the majority of the respondents (64.8%) perceived that they travelled on a short haul which is less than 1 hour. These are mostly passengers on domestic trips, while 35.2% of respondents were on the long haul trip whose duration is more than 1 hour; these are mostly the passengers on the international routes or those on the domestic route but a longer distance. The majority of the respondents (passengers) representing 91.4% have completed their journey, which implies that they reached their final airport destination upon arrival at the airport.

Regarding the specialised form of airline culture, more than half of the respondents (65.4%) perceived that the airlines they patronised do not have any special form of culture. This implies that many airlines especially domestic airlines do not sell culture to passengers in their operations. Concerning the warranties on airline punctuality or reliability, 49.3% of respondents perceived that there is no compensation for flight delay, while 46.2% of respondents perceived that there is reimbursement of the cost of a ticket. Finally is the condition of space for legroom, the majority of the respondents (71%) perceived that there was small space for legroom within the seats. It is pertinent to note that the condition of space for legroom is dependent on the class of ticket or cabin service; for instance, the space for an economy class flight will be quite different from the space for a business class.

The airline services were categorised into three classes (Economy class, Business class and First class). Each class determines the package of services that will be offered by the airline to the passengers when onboard; it is also among the criteria that determine the airfare. From the analysis shown in Fig. 2.2, it was revealed that the majority of the respondents (72.4%) purchased economy-class tickets, and there were no first-class passengers among the respondents.

The regression results, which were established to examine the factors influencing willingness-to-repurchase airline services, were presented in Tables 2.5 and 2.6 below. As earlier revealed in the descriptive analysis, there is no information on first-class services; hence, this section examines the factors influencing willingness-to-repurchase for economy and business classes of airline services.

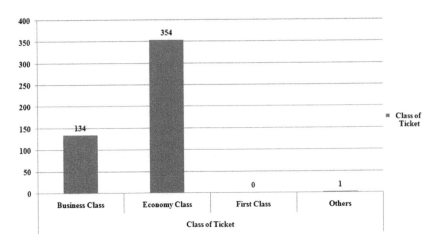

Fig. 2.2. Class of Ticket.

5.1 Factors Influencing Willingness-to-Repurchase for Economy-Class of Airline Services

In the model fitting shown in Table 2.5a, -2 Log likelihood ($-2LL$) reveals that the predicted model was compatible with the data (155.886). In other words, independent variables added to Model 0 provided a statistically significant contribution to logit estimation. In addition, the logistic model was found to be statistically significant in classifying the passengers responses (χ^2 ($N = 489$) = 501.146, $p < 0.05$). When considering the goodness-of-fit test as shown in Table 2.5b, it was revealed that deviance statistics with (p-value = 1.000) is large. This implies that the model fits the data well. Also, when considering the pseudo R^2 in Table 2.5c, it was revealed that the model explained 81.7% of the variance (Cox and Snell's R^2), 91.6% of the variance (Nagelkerke's R^2) and 76.3% of the variance in (McFadden's R^2) willingness-to-repurchase economic class of ticket.

Table 2.5a. Model Fitting Information.

Model	-2 Log Likelihood	Chi-Square	df	Sig.
Intercept only	657.033			
Final	155.886	501.146	81	0.000

Note: Link function: Logit.

Table 2.5b. Goodness-of-Fit.

	Chi-Square	Df	Sig.
Pearson	14884.241	587	0.000
Deviance	155.886	587	1.000

Note: Link function: Logit.

Table 2.5c. Pseudo R-Square.

Cox and Snell	0.817
Nagelkerke	0.916
McFadden	0.763

Note: Link function: Logit.

The thresholds shown in Table 2.5d represent the response variables in the Ordinal Logistic Regression. The threshold estimate for [WtR for economy class = 1) is the cutoff value between 'strongly disagree' and 'disagree', the threshold estimate for [WtR for economy class = 2) is the cutoff value between 'disagree' and 'neither agree nor disagree', the threshold estimate for [WtR for economy class = 3) is the cutoff value between 'neither agree nor disagree' and 'agree', and the threshold estimate for [WtR for economy class = 4) is the cutoff value between 'agree' and 'strongly agree'.

For WtR for economy class, this is the estimated cut point on the latent variable used to differentiate strongly disagree on WtR for economy class from disagreeing on WtR for economy class, neither agree nor disagree on WtR for economy class, agree on WtR for economy class and strongly agree on WtR for economy class when values of the predictors are evaluated at zero.

Quality of services; Warranties on airline punctuality or reliability; Trip purpose; Airline promotions and offers; Designation of airport origin; Taste preference; Estimate of monthly income; Time value; Duration of flight; Stage of the journey; Airline special form of culture; Warranties on airline punctuality or reliability; Condition of leg space for the economy class that had a value of − 18.789 or less on the underlying latent variables that gave rise to the 'WtR for economy class' variable would be classified under the strongly disagree.

Quality of services; Warranties on airline punctuality or reliability; Trip purpose; Airline promotions and offers; Designation of airport origin; Taste preference; Estimate of monthly income; Time value; Duration of flight; Stage of the journey; Airline special form of culture; Warranties on airline punctuality or reliability; Condition of leg space for the economy class that had a value of − 12.051 or less but not less than −18.789 on the underlying latent variables that gave rise to the 'WtR for economy class' variable would be classified under the disagree.

Quality of services; Warranties on airline punctuality or reliability; Trip purpose; Airline promotions and offers; Designation of airport origin; Taste preference; Estimate of monthly income; Time value; Duration of flight; Stage of the journey; Airline special form of culture; Warranties on airline punctuality or reliability; Condition of leg space for the economy class that had a value of − 6.137 or less but not less than −12.051 on the underlying latent variables that gave rise to the 'WtR for economy class' variable would be classified under the neither agree nor disagree.

Quality of services; Warranties on airline punctuality or reliability; Trip purpose; Airline promotions and offers; Designation of airport origin; Taste preference; Estimate of monthly income; Time value; Duration of flight; Stage of

Table 2.5d. Parameter Estimates.

		Estimate	Decision	Std. Error	Wald	df	Sig.	95% Confidence Interval	
								Lower Bound	Upper Bound
Threshold	WtR for economy class = 1	−18.789		71.280	0.069	1	0.792	−158.495	120.918
	WtR for economy class = 2	−12.051		71.275	0.029	1	0.866	−151.748	127.646
	WtR for economy class = 3	−6.137		71.263	0.007	1	0.931	−145.810	133.537
	WtR for economy class = 4	12.285		71.306	0.030	1	0.863	−127.472	152.042
Location	QSEC inches seat pitch = 2	15.315	SA	7.027	4.750	1	**0.029**	1.543	29.086
	QSEC inches seat pitch = 4	14.143	SA	6.610	4.578	1	**0.032**	1.187	27.099
	QSEC TV inches = 4	13.903	SA	5.434	6.547	1	**0.011**	3.254	24.553
	QSEC provision of airlines complimentary = 1	15.101	SA	3.851	15.379	1	**0.000**	7.554	22.648
	QSEC Availability of hot towels = 1	−19.019	SD	3.973	22.917	1	**0.000**	−26.805	−11.232
	QSEC luggage permission = 2	−14.390	D	3.465	17.250	1	**0.000**	−21.181	−7.599
	QSEC luggage permission = 4	−7.175	NAD	2.884	6.190	1	**0.013**	−12.827	−1.522
	QSEC the use of online checkin = 2	12.587	SA	4.750	7.021	1	**0.008**	3.277	21.898
	QSEC the use of online checkin = 3	12.228	A	4.994	5.994	1	**0.014**	2.439	22.016
	QSEC the use of online checkin = 4	16.530	SA	5.201	10.100	1	**0.001**	6.336	26.725
	Penalty for changes in Ticket = 2	2.658	A	1.293	4.224	1	**0.040**	0.123	5.193
	Trip Purpose = 5	−5.246	A	2.309	5.160	1	**0.023**	−9.772	−0.720
	Airline promotions and offers = 0	−4.409	A	1.645	7.184	1	**0.007**	−7.633	−1.185
	Taste preference for Airline = 1	4.559	A	1.461	9.731	1	**0.002**	1.694	7.423
	Estimate of monthly Income = 2	4.494	A	2.183	4.240	1	**0.039**	0.217	8.772
	Stage of Journey = 1	−5.056	A	2.228	5.151	1	**0.023**	−9.422	−0.690
	Warranties on punctuality = 2	5.406	A	2.739	3.895	1	**0.048**	0.037	10.775

Link function: Logit.
Note: The parameters set to zero were removed because they are redundant.
Strongly agree (SA); Agree (A); Neither agree nor disagree (NAD); Disagree (D); Strongly disagree (SD).

the journey; Airline special form of culture; Warranties on airline punctuality or reliability; Condition of leg space for the economy class that had a value of 12.285 or less but not less than −6.137 on the underlying latent variables that gave rise to the 'WtR for economy class' variable would be classified under the 'agree' section.

Quality of services; Warranties on airline punctuality or reliability; Trip purpose; Airline promotions and offers; Designation of airport origin; Taste preference; Estimate of monthly income; Time value; Duration of flight; Stage of the journey; Airline special form of culture; Warranties on airline punctuality or reliability; Condition of leg space for the economy class that had a value of that is above 12.285 on the underlying latent variables that gave rise to the 'WtR for economy class' variable would be classified under the strongly agree.

For the factors influencing willingness-to-repurchase for economy class of airline services, it was revealed in Table 2.5d that poor state of 30–32 inches seat pitch, good condition of 30–32 inches seat pitch, presence of 10.6 inch digital TV with more than 100 TV channels, non availability of free drinks and complimentary meals, non availability of hot towels after boarding and prior to landing, poor provision for 30 kg luggage permission, provision for 30 kg luggage permission, poor usage of online check-in 24 hours prior to the departing flight, fair usage of online check-in 24 hours prior to the departing flight, good usage of online check-in 24 hours prior to the departing flight, 20% increase on penalty for passenger changes in ticket, medical purpose of trip, lack of airline promotions and offers, limited taste preference of passengers for airline service, monthly income between 100,000 and 499,999, journey completed, and the availability of free ticket on same trip were the independent variables influencing willingness-to-repurchase for economy class of airline.

According to Wald test statistics for the predictors (Çokluk, 2019), few predictors of the economy class in the models were statistically significant ($p < 0.05$). Therefore, according to the Table 2.5d, logistic regression equation is as follows: Logit (odds in favor of being agree) = $-6.137 + 15.315 X_1 + 14.143 X_2 + 13.903 X_3 + 15.101 X_4 + (-19.019) X_5 + (-14.390) X_6 + (-7.175) X_7 + 12.587 X_8 + 12.228 X_9 + 16.530 X_{10} + 2.658 X_{11} + (-5.246) X_{12} + (-4.409) X_{13} + 4.559 X_{14} + 4.494 X_{15} + (-5.056) X_{16} + 5.406 X_{17}$.

Where the X variables for economy class tickets denote, poor quality of 30–32 inches seat pitch, fair quality of 30–32 inches seat pitch, good presence of 10.6 inches digital TV with more than 100 TV channels, non-availability of airlines' complimentary in-flight-magazine, duty-free magazines, and a selection of international newspapers, non-availability of hot towels after boarding and before landing, poor allowance for 30 kg luggage permission, good allowance for 30 kg luggage permission, poor usage of online check-in 24 hours before the departing flight, fair usage of online check-in 24 hours before the departing flight, good usage of online check-in 24 hours before the departing flight, 20% increase n penalty for ticket changes, the medical purpose of the trip, there is no airline promotions and offers, limited taste for the airline, ₦100,000 – ₦499,999 monthly income, stop-over journey stage, and availability of free ticket for the same trip respectively.

5.2 Factors Influencing Willingness-to-Repurchase for Business Class Airline Services

In the model fitting shown in Table 2.6a, -2 Log likelihood ($-2LL$) reveals that the predicted model was compatible with the data (6.637). In other words, independent variables added to Model 0 provided a statistically significant contribution to logit estimation. In addition, the logistic model was found to be statistically significant in classifying the passengers responses (χ^2 ($N = 489$) = 85.090, $p < 0.05$). When considering the pseudo R^2 in Table 2.6b, it was revealed that the model explained 48.6% of the variance (Cox and Snell's R^2), 94.9% of the variance (Nagelkerke's R^2) and 92.8% of the variance in (McFadden's R^2) willingness-to-repurchase business class of ticket.

The thresholds shown in Table 2.6c represent the response variables in the Ordinal Logistic Regression. The threshold estimate for [WtR for business class = 2) is the cutoff value between 'disagree' and 'neither agree nor disagree', the threshold estimate for [WtR for business class = 3) is the cutoff value between 'neither agree nor disagree' and 'agree', and the threshold estimate for [WtR for business class = 4) is the cutoff value between 'agree' and 'strongly agree'.

For WtR for business class, this is the estimated cut point on the latent variable used to differentiate disagree on WtR for business class from neither agree nor disagree on WtR for business class, agree on WtR for business class and strongly agree on WtR for business class when values of the predictors are evaluated at zero.

Quality of services; Warranties on airline punctuality or reliability; Trip purpose; Airline promotions and offers; Designation of airport origin; Taste preference; Estimate of monthly income; Time value; Duration of flight; Stage of the journey; Airline special form of culture; Warranties on airline punctuality or reliability; Condition of leg space for the business class that had a value of -993.383 or less on the underlying latent variables that gave rise to the 'WtR for business class' variable would be classified under the disagree.

Table 2.6a. Model Fitting Information.

Model	-2 Log Likelihood	Chi-Square	df	Sig.
Intercept only	91.727			
Final	6.637	85.090	54	0.004

Link function: Logit.

Table 2.6b. Pseudo R-Square.

Cox and Snell	0.486
Nagelkerke	0.949
McFadden	0.928

Note: Link function: Logit.

Table 2.6c. Parameter Estimates.

| | | Estimate | Decision | Std. Error | Wald | df | Sig. | 95% Confidence Interval | |
								Lower Bound	Upper Bound
Threshold	WtR for business class = 2	-993.383		706.113	1.979	1	0.159	-2377.339	390.572
	WtR for business class = 3	-991.850		706.112	1.973	1	0.160	-2375.803	392.103
	WtR for business class = 4	-983.338		706.116	1.939	1	0.164	-2367.300	400.624
Location	Penalty for changes in Ticket = 1	828.419	SA	174.016	22.663	1	0.000	487.353	1169.485
	Trip Purpose = 5	1498.016	SA	548.780	7.451	1	0.006	422.426	2573.605
	Airport Origin = Akure	-2918.865	D	726.593	16.138	1	0.000	-4342.961	-1494.769
	Airport Origin = Kano	2673.441	SA	964.883	7.677	1	0.006	782.305	4564.576
	Estimate of monthly Income = 2	-1338.851	D	634.222	4.456	1	0.035	-2581.904	-95.799
	Estimate of monthly Income = 3	-3236.852	D	434.773	55.427	1	0.000	-4088.991	-2384.712
	Duration of Flight = 1	-708.009	SA	221.842	10.186	1	0.001	-1142.812	-273.206
	Warranties on punctuality = 1	708.009	SA	221.883	10.182	1	0.001	273.125	1142.892
	Warranties on punctuality y = 2	2100.067	SA	161.012	170.117	1	0.000	1784.488	2415.645
	Space for Legroom = 2	-857.324	SA	344.185	6.205	1	0.013	-1531.914	-182.735
	QSBC Availability of seats to bed = 4	1045.166	SA	368.548	8.042	1	0.005	322.825	1767.506
	QSBC inches seat pitch = 2	-2047.202	SA	415.579	24.267	1	0.000	-2861.721	-1232.683
	QSBC inches seat pitch = 3	-2047.202	SA	415.585	24.266	1	0.000	-2861.733	-1232.671

Link function: Logit.
Note: The parameters set to zero were removed because they are redundant.

Quality of services; Warranties on airline punctuality or reliability; Trip purpose; Airline promotions and offers; Designation of airport origin; Taste preference; Estimate of monthly income; Time value; Duration of flight; Stage of the journey; Airline special form of culture; Warranties on airline punctuality or reliability; Condition of leg space for the business class that had a value of -991.850 or less but not less than -993.383 on the underlying latent variables that gave rise to the 'WtR for business class' variable would be classified under the neither agree nor disagree.

Quality of services; Warranties on airline punctuality or reliability; Trip purpose; Airline promotions and offers; Designation of airport origin; Taste preference; Estimate of monthly income; Time value; Duration of flight; Stage of the journey; Airline special form of culture; Warranties on airline punctuality or reliability; Condition of leg space for a business class that had a value of -983.338 or less but not less than -991.850 on the underlying latent variables that gave rise to the 'WtR for business class' variable would be classified under the agreement.

Quality of services; Warranties on airline punctuality or reliability; Trip purpose; Airline promotions and offers; Designation of airport origin; Taste preference; Estimate of monthly income; Time value; Duration of flight; Stage of the journey; Airline special form of culture; Warranties on airline punctuality or reliability; Condition of leg space for a business class that had a value of that is above -983.338 on the underlying latent variables that gave rise to the 'WtR for business class' variable would be classified under the strongly agree.

For the factors influencing willingness-to-repurchase business class ticket, it was revealed in Table 2.6c that 10% increase in the penalty for passenger changes in the ticket, the medical purpose of the trip, passengers whose designation of airport origin are Akure and Kano, monthly income between ₦100,000 and ₦499,999, between ₦500,000 and ₦1,000,000, completion of the journey, no compensation for flight delay, the availability of free ticket on the same trip, wide space for legroom between seats, availability of seats that can be converted into a fully flat bed, fair and poor condition of 79–87 inches seat pitch were the independent variables influencing willingness-to-repurchase for business class of airline ticket.

According to Wald test statistics for the predictors (Çokluk, 2019), few predictors of the business class ticket in the models were statistically significant ($p < 0.05$). Therefore, according to the Table 2.6c, logistic regression equation is as follows: Logit (odds in favor of being agree) $= -991.850 + 828.4195\ X_1 + 1498.016\ X_2 + (-2918.865)\ X_3 + 2763.441\ X_4 + (-1338.851)\ X_5 + (-708.009)\ X_6 + 708.009\ X_7 + 2100.067\ X_8 + (-857.324)\ X_9 + 1045.166\ X_{10} + (-2047.202)\ X_{11} + (-2047.202)\ X_{12}$

Where the X variables for business class tickets denote a 10% increase in the penalty for passenger changes in the ticket, the medical purpose of the trip, passengers whose designation of airport origin is Akure, designation of airport origin is Kano, monthly income between ₦100,000 and ₦499,999, monthly income between ₦500,000 and ₦1,000,000, completion of the journey, no compensation for flight delay, the availability of free ticket on the same trip, wide space for legroom between seats, availability of seats that can be converted into a fully flat bed, fair condition of 79–87 inches seat pitch, and poor condition of 79–87 inches seat pitch respectively.

5.3 Effect of Service Evaluation Constructs on Willingness-to-Repurchase

Checking the model fit and evaluating the hypotheses comprise the structural model analysis. The findings demonstrate that nearly all of the goodness of fit metrics are within their acceptable ranges: $\chi^2 = 495.240$ (df = 171, $p = 0.000$); GFI = 0.907; CFI = 0.953; NFI = 0.930; $\chi^2/df = 2.896$; RMSEA = 0.071 (see Table 2.7), because they meet the overall fitness level recommendation: GFI > 0.90); CFI > 0.95; NFI > 0.90; $\chi^2/df < 3$; RMSEA < 0.08 (Bentler, 1990; Bentler & Bonett, 1980; Tucker & Lewis, 1973).

The findings revealed that the research model fits well. The results of the hypotheses tests are summarised in Table 2.8. *H1* and *H2* were all rejected. That is, the perceived service quality and passenger satisfaction are statistically significant, and they positively influence passenger satisfaction; standardised coefficient of perceived service quality = 0.611 ($p < 0.05$). Among the variables affecting willingness-to-repurchase, passenger satisfaction has the most significant influence standardised coefficient is 0.471 ($p < 0.05$). The findings revealed that positive service quality increase passenger satisfaction; hence, passengers in the economy or business class that believed that the service is quality will be willing to repurchase.

The following were revealed from the test of mediations that were carried out:

i. There is a significant effect between service quality and passenger satisfaction; and
ii. The effect of service quality on willingness-to-repurchase was mediated by passenger satisfaction.

Table 2.7. Model's Goodness of Fit Index.

All	Model's Goodness of Fit Index					
	χ^2	RMSEA	GFI	CFI	NFI	χ^2/df
	495.240	0.071	0.907	0.953	0.930	2.896

Table 2.8. Hypotheses Test.

Hypotheses	Structural Coefficient	t-Value	p Value	Result
H01: PSQ → PS	0.611	11.676	0.000	Rejected
H02: PS → WtR	0.471	12.728	0.000	Rejected

Note: $p < 0.05$.

6. DISCUSSION

From the study, it was revealed that willingness-to-repurchase economy class tickets were influenced by the following in-flight service quality attributes such as quality of 30–32 inches seat pitch, presence of 10.6 inches digital TV with more than 100 TV channels, non-availability of airlines' complimentary in-flight-magazine, duty-free magazines, and a selection of international newspapers, non-availability of hot towels after boarding and before landing, allowance for 30 kg luggage permission, usage of online check-in 24 hours before the departing flight. Apart from the in-flight services, willingness-to-repurchase economy class tickets were influenced by the 20% increase that the airline levied on penalties for passenger changes in the ticket, the medical purpose of the trip, non-availability of airline promotions and offers, the limited taste of passengers for the airline, passengers that earn between ₦100,000 and ₦499,999 as income on monthly basis, and availability of free ticket for the same trip.

Furthermore, the study also revealed that willingness-to-repurchase business class tickets were influenced by the following in-flight service quality attributes such as wide space for legroom between seats; availability of seats that can be converted into a fully flat bed; and condition of 79–87 inches seat pitch. Apart from the in-flight services, willingness-to-repurchase business class tickets were influenced by a 10% increase in the penalty for passenger changes in ticket; the medical purpose of the trip; nature of airport origin (Akure and Kano); monthly income between ₦100,000 and ₦499,999; monthly income between ₦500,000 and ₦1,000,000; completion of the journey; no compensation for flight delay; availability of free ticket on the same trip.

It is pertinent to note that all passengers whether economy or business class tickets want to be comfortable when seating in the aircraft (Li, Yu, Chuan, & Baozhem, 2017), although the level of seating arrangement differs in each class. The economy passenger has access to the digital TV, enjoy the allowance of 30 kg luggage permission (Chou, Li-Jen, Sue-Fen, Jeng-Ming, & Tzeu-Chen, 2019), and uses online check-in 24 hours before the departing flight. The comfort of economy passengers with seat pitches, accessibility to digital TV during flight, allowance of 30 kg luggage permission, and availability of online check-in 24 hours before the departing flight will determine if they will patronise the airline again and that particular class of ticket. Regarding the provision of a warranty on airline punctuality and reliability, the willingness-to-repurchase economy class will not be enhanced if there is no compensation for flight delay. The study however found that economy passengers are not concerned with the availability of airlines' complimentary in-flight-magazine, duty-free magazines, and a selection of international newspapers and are not concerned with the availability of hot towels after boarding and before landing.

It is pertinent to note that business class passengers will be willing to repurchase if the space for legroom between seats is wide (79–87 inches seat pitch) and the seats can be converted into a fully flat bed. Most importantly, the comfort obtained in seating is what the business class passenger enjoys (Smith, 2020). The study also found that willingness-to-repurchase business class tickets were influenced by a 10% increase in the penalty for passenger changes in the ticket. Because of the high fare charged by airlines on business class passengers, and the fact that business class passengers are persons that usually belong to a particular class in society (as they earn monthly income between ₦500,000 and ₦1,000,000), they usually make quick decisions hence, they will always change ticket. The airlines must be considerate about any form of penalty for business class passengers. Regarding the provision of a warranty on airline punctuality and reliability, willingness-to-repurchase business class will be enhanced if there is the availability of a free ticket on the same trip. However, it will not be enhanced if there is no compensation for flight delays.

These findings support earlier studies of Šebjan, Polona, and Karin (2017), Chou et al. (2019), Li et al. (2017), and Smith (2020). Warnock-Smith, John, and Mahnaz (2017) determined the benefits of new opportunities and ancillary revenues for airlines. They found that seat comfort is more considered in business class and long-distance flights and that the passengers were more willing to pay for it.

In this study, service quality have a positive impact on passenger satisfaction, and passenger satisfaction is the most influential factor in predicting a passenger's willingness to repurchase. The results agree with the findings of previous studies which revealed that passenger satisfaction is an antecedent in understanding behavioural intention (Cronin, Brady, & Hult, 2019; Chen, 2008; Chang & Wildt, 1994; Zeithaml, 1988) and that passenger satisfaction is influenced by service quality (Liu & Lee, 2016; Rajaguru, 2016; Zeithaml, 1988). The results show that the experience of economy and business class passengers influences service quality, and their willingness to repurchase will increase when they have a positive perception about the airline service.

Service quality is important on the satisfaction level of economy and business passengers. This finding indicates that economy and business passengers would consider service quality first when evaluating the overall value of economy and business services. The findings agree with previous studies which emphasised the effect of service quality on passenger satisfaction (Chen & Chen, 2010; Chen, 2008). Percieved service quality also demonstrates a positive effect on passenger satisfaction of economy and business passengers. From the findings, it was suggested that if a passenger perceived that the service offering for the economy and business class is quality, the passenger will be satisfied with the level of service offered.

Based on the findings of this study, the seat pitch and baggage allowance for passengers were the major factors influencing willingness-to-repurchase airline (economy and business) services in Nigeria. Airplane seat pitch (the space between a seat and the one in front) has been shrinking as the airlines have attempted to pack in more passengers onto planes (Milne, Delcea, Cotfas, & Salari, 2019; Wittmann, 2019), and baggage spaces are being filled up which is a means of contacting infectious diseases such as COVID-19. Ashok (2020), Delcea, Cotfas, Craciun, and Molanescu (2018), and Laura (2022) found in their studies that seat pitches of airplanes are not convenient for all passengers. Cotfas, Delcea, Milne, and Salari (2020) found in their study that most of the present seat pitches for economy and business class airlines are not usually convenient for passengers who are 6 feet tall.

The World Health Organization (WHO, 2019) noted that social distancing must be at least one metre (three feet) distance between two persons who is coughing or sneezing. Social distancing of one meter, if applied to all airlines, the transmission of infectious diseases can be avoided in future. Social distancing in aircraft can be implemented on seat pitch and baggage storage. If the seat pitch and baggage storage are spacious, the risk of contacting infectious diseases in the aircraft will be minimised.

Since this study was conducted during the heat of COVID-19, passengers were more conscious of social distancing which necessitates for wider seat pitches and more space for baggage regardless of the airline class. In this study, majority of the respondents were economy class passengers, which implies that if an airline will come up with a sound policy, such airline must factor in the choice of economy class passengers. If an airline can increase the seat pitch and baggage space, passengers will be willing to repurchase the airline ticket in future.

7. CONCLUSIONS

The increasing demand for more comfortable travel options has prompted air-lines to strive to offer higher service quality at lower and reasonable prices and thereby enhance competition. The provision of economy and business class tickets represents one of these efforts to balance the quality of service offerings. Although air carriers have successfully implemented the economy and business classes, the willingness-to-repurchase economy and business class tickets have not been investigated repeatedly in the works of literature. The study identified the factors influencing willingness-to-repurchase for economy and business class tickets. It was concluded that seat comfort and baggage handling are most crucial in bth economy and business class tickets.

The results showed that service quality can enhance passenger satisfaction, and high passenger satisfaction can strongly influence willingness-to-repurchase. The proposed model was tested by using surveyed data retrieved through an electronic form of questionnaire from 489 arrival passengers in the international and domestic terminals of Murtala Muhammed International Airport, Lagos and Nnamdi Azikwe International Airport, Abuja. These were passengers who had international air travel experience and have air travel experience for more than one year. Because valid data were collected from 154 international and 335 domestic airline passengers who were citizens from 19 countries, the analysis excluded the effect of cultural and social characteristics of passengers from spe-cific regions. Also, the data covers passengers from 26 international and domestic airlines that arrived in the selected study airports.

According to Hugon-Duprat and O'Connell (2015), the economy class has been growing steadily while the business class has been static. Kuo and Jou (2017) stated that to realise the competitive benefits of economy class, airlines must first understand the elements that influence a traveller's decision regarding the selection of each class of the ticket (economy and business). To maintain long-term manageability and profitability, it is essential to evaluate passenger views and identify the factors that may impact repurchase decision-making. The outcomes of this study can assist airline practitioners in better understanding the correlates of factors that enhance passengers' willingness-to-repurchase. Also, the findings can provide insights for airlines to increase customer loyalty programs and sustainably develop each class of tickets. In addition, the proposed research model was well structured to sufficiently explain the passenger's willingness-to-repurchase while producing suitable values for model validity, reliability and goodness of fit.

A major finding from this study arises from the fact that increasing the passengers' seat pitch and creating more space for baggage or reducing baggage allowance for achieving more baggage space will help to reducing the risk of contacting infectious diseases in the aircraft. With increased social distancing, the passengers transmit fewer COVID-19 droplets onto the seated passengers they pass or seat next to, and will have little or no contact with baggage. This finding can be generalised to many international airlines. On a final note the airlines should understand that life is more important than profit.

8. RECOMMENDATIONS

Despite successful deployments, there is a dearth of study in the air transport literature on economic and business class tickets. Prior research has mostly focused on the rationale of economy class implementation and customer willingness to pay (Hugon-Duprat & O'Connell, 2015; Kuo & Jou, 2017). On the contrary, few studies were carried out on passengers' behavioural intentions over time. By presenting an improved EKB model, this study explored the perspectives of economic and business passengers on the factors influencing willingness-to-repurchase. As demand for economy and business class increases, a correct design and ongoing improved updates to the service is vital to improving the manageability and profitability of airlines in the long term. Indeed, constant improvement should be implemented as a need to drive the business into the unforeseeable future. Passenger satisfaction has the most significant impact on the willingness-to-repurchase economy and business tickets while being concurrently affected by service quality. Thus, airlines should improve on service offerings that generate significant attention.

8.1 Recommendation of Essential Services That Could Be Provided for Economy Class Ticket

Based on the findings, the management of airlines particularly for economy class should prioritise the quality of 30–32 inches seat pitch; accessibility to digital TV during flight; allowance of 30 kg luggage permission; and availability of online check-in 24 hours before the departing flight.

Based on the findings, the management of airlines particularly for economy class can remove airlines' complimentary in-flight-magazine, duty-free magazines and international newspapers; and hot towels after boarding and before landing.

Based on the findings, the management of airlines particularly for economy class should not increase the penalty for passenger changes in ticket above 20% to retain customers; they should increase their advert and promotions on medical trips and design their fares in a way that customers that earn between ₦100,000 and ₦499,999 can patronise. Regarding the provision of a warranty on airline punctuality and reliability, the airline should make free tickets available to economy passengers on that same trip.

8.2 Recommendation of Essential Services That Could Be provided for Business Class Ticket

Based on the findings, the management of airlines particularly for business class should prioritise the quality of space for legroom between seats wide (79–87 inches seat pitch) and the quality of seats that can be converted into a fully flat bed.

Because of the high fare charged by airlines on business class passengers, the penalty for passenger changes in a ticket should not be more than 10% increase to retain customers; they should increase their advert and promotions on medical trips and design their fares in a way that customers that earn above ₦500,000 can patronise.

Regarding the provision of a warranty on airline punctuality and reliability, the airline should make a free ticket available to business passengers on that same trip.

Recommendations for all airlines to curb the tranmission of infectious diseases.

In the future, there is need to plan for increasing the passengers' seat pitch and creating more space for baggage or reducing baggage allowance for achieving more baggage space will help to reducing the risk of contacting infectious diseases in the aircraft.

DECLARATIONS

Ethics Approval and Consent to Participate

N/A

Consent for Publication

N/A

Availability of Data and Materials

The datasets generated and/or analysed during the current study are available from the corresponding author on reasonable request, but cannot be made publicly available in order not to go against the declaration of confidentiality made to the participants.

Competing Interests

The author declares that there is no competing interest.

Funding

N/A

Authors' Contribution

AOA designed the manuscript; IN supervised and proofread the manuscript; MS: supervised and proofread the manuscript.
All authors have read and approved the manuscript.

ACKNOWLEDGEMENTS

We thank the Editor and Reviewers for their insightful contributions to the improvement of this article.

REFERENCES

ACI. (2022). *The impact of Covid-19 on the airport business and the path to recovery*. Retrieved from https://aci.aero/2022/02/24/the-impact-of-covid-19-on-the-airport-business-and-the-path-to recovery-4/

Adejumo, A. O., & Adetunji, A. A. (2020). Application of Ordinal Logistic Regression in the study of students' performance. *Mathematical Theory and Modeling, 3*, 10–19.

Adeola, M. M., & Adebiyi, S. O. (2019). Service quality perceived value and customers' satisfaction as determinants of airline choice in Nigeria. *International Letters of Social and Humanistic Sciences, 20*, 66–80.

Akaka, M. A., & Schau, H. J. (2019). Value creation in consumption journeys: Recursive reflexivity and practice continuity. *Journal of the Academy of Marketing Science, 47*, 499–515.

Al Rafaie, A., Bata, N. E., & Issam, J. (2019). Examining factors that affect passengers' overall satisfaction and loyalty: Evidence from Jordan Airport. *Jordan Journal of Mechanical and Industrial Engineering, 8*(2), 94–101.

Alivand, M., Hochmair, H., & Srinivasan, S. (2015). Analyzing how travelers choose scenic routes using route choice models. *Computers, Environment and Urban Systems, 50*, 41–52.

Anastasia, C. (2019). *Passengers' satisfaction with facility services in Terminal 2 of Tampere Airport* (pp. 1–61). Undergraduate Thesis at Tampere University of Applied SciencesPublished.

Anderl, E., Schumann, J. H., & Kunz, W. (2016). Helping firms reduce complexity in multichannel online data: A new taxonomy-based approach for customer journeys. *Journal of Retailing, 92*(2), 185–203.

Anta, J., Pérez-López, J. B., Martínez-Pardo, A., Novales, M., & Orro, A. (2016). Infuence of the weather on mode choice in corridors with time-varying congestion: A mixed data study. *Transportation, 43*, 337–355.

Ashok, K. R. (2020). Airlines seat pitch and social distancing – Impact of Novel Corona Virus. Retrieved from https://qz.com/quartzy/1324754/airline-seats-are-getting-narrower-and-passengers-dont-like-it/

Azman, I., Iiyani, R. R., Rabaah, T., & Norazryana, M. D. (2017). Relationship between service quality and behavioural intentions: The mediating effect of customers' satisfaction. *Etikonomi, 16*(2), 125–144.

Baxendale, S., Macdonald, E. K., & Wilson, H. N. (2015). The impact of different touch-points on brand consideration. *Journal of Retailing, 91*(2), 235–253.

Becker, L., & Jaakkola, E. (2020). Customer experience: Fundamental premises and implications for research. *Journal of the Academy of Marketing Science, 48*(4), 630–648.

Bender, R., & Grouven, U. (1998). Using binary logistic regression models for ordinal data with non-proportional odds. *Journal of Clinical Epidemiology, 51*(10), 809–816.

Bentler, P. M. (1990). Comparative fit indexes in structural models. *Psychology Bulletin, 107*, 238–246.

Bentler, P. M., & Bonett, D. G. (1980). Significance tests and goodness of fit in the analysis of covariance structures. *Psychological Bulletin, 88*, 588–606.

Bhat, C. R., Astroza, S., & Bhat, A. C. (2016). On allowing a general form for unobserved heterogeneity in the multiple discrete-continuous probit model: Formulation and application to tourism travel. *Transportation Research Part B: Methodological, 86*, 223–249.

Bieger, T., & Laesser, C. (2016). Information sources for travel decisions: Toward a source process model. *Journal of Travel Research, 42*, 357–371.

Borhan, M. N., Ibrahim, A. N. H., Miskeen, M. A. A., Rahmat, R. A. O. K., & Alhodairi, A. M. (2017). Predicting car drivers' intention to use low cost airlines for intercity travel in Libya. *Journal of Air Transport Management, 65*, 88–98.

Browne, M. W., & Cudeck, R. (1992). Alternative ways of assessing model fit. *Sociology Methods Research, 21*, 230–258.

Buaphiban, T., & Truong, D. (2017). Evaluation of passengers' buying behaviours toward low cost carriers in Southeast Asia. *Journal of Air Transport Management, 59*, 124–133.

Burton, S., Sheather, S., & Roberts, J. (2016). The effect of actual and perceived performance on satisfaction and behavioural intentions. *Journal of Service Research, 5*(4), 292–302.

Cavallaro, F., Ciari, F., Nocera, S., Prettenthaler, F., & Scuttari, A. (2017). The impacts of climate change on tourist mobility in mountain areas. *Journal of Sustainable Tourism, 25*, 1063–1083.

Chang, T. Z., & Wildt, A. R. (1994). Price, product information, and purchase intention: An empirical study. *Journal of the Academy of Marketing Science, 22*, 16–27.

Chen, C. F. (2008). Investigating structural relationships between service quality, perceived value, satisfaction, and behavioural intentions for air passengers: Evidence from Taiwan. *Transportation Research Part A: Policy Practice, 42*, 709–717.

Chen, F., & Chang, Y. (2005). Examining airline service quality from a process perspective. *Journal of Air Transport Management, 11*, 79–87.

Chen, C. F., & Chen, F. S. (2010). Experience quality, perceived value, satisfaction and behavioural intentions for heritage tourists. *Tourism Management, 31*, 29–35.

Chen, C., Ma, J., Susilo, Y., Liu, Y., & Wang, M. (2016). The promises of big data and small data for travel behavior (aka human mobility) analysis. *Transportation Research Part C: Emerging Technologies, 68*, 285–299.

Chou, C., Li-Jen, L., Sue-Fen, H., Jeng-Ming, Y., & Tzeu-Chen, H. (2019). An evaluation of airline service quality using the fuzzy weighted SERVQUAL method. *Applied Soft Computing, 11*, 2117–2128.

Chua, A., Servillo, L., Marcheggiani, E., & Moere, A. V. (2016). Mapping Cilento: Using geotagged social media data to characterize tourist fows in southern Italy. *Tourism Management, 57*, 295–310.

Chumpitaz, R., & Paparoidamis, N. G. (2016). Service quality and marketing performance in business-to-business markets: Exploring the mediating role of Client satisfaction. *Managing Service Quality, 14*(2/3), 235–248.

Citko, D., Milewska, A. J., Wasilewska, J., & Kaczmarski, M. (2020). Ordinal Logistic Regression for the analysis of skin test reactivity to common aeroallergens. *Studies Logic in Grammar Rhetoric, 29*, 87–98.

Çokluk, Ö. (2019). Logistic regression analysis: Kavram ve uygulama. *Kuram ve Uygulamada Eğitim Bilimleri, 10*, 1357–1407.

Cotfas, L. A., Delcea, C., Milne, R. J., & Salari, M. (2020). Evaluating Classical airplane boarding methods considering COVID-19 flying restrictions. *Symmetry*, *12*, 1087. doi:10.3390/sym12071087

Cronin, J. J., Brady, M. K., & Hult, G. T. M. (2000). Assessing the effects of quality, value and customers' satisfaction on consumer behavioural intentions in service environments. *Journal of Retailing*, *76*(2), 193–218.

Cronin, J. J., Brady, M. K., & Hult, G. T. M. (2019). Assessing the effects of quality, value and customers' satisfaction on consumer behavioural intentions in service environments. *Journal of Retailing*, *76*(2), 193–218.

Darley, W. K., Blankson, C., & Luethge, D. J. (2010). Toward an integrated framework for online consumer behavior and decision making process: A review. *Psychology and Marketing*, *27*(2), 94–116. doi:10.1002/mar.20322

Das, S., & Rahman, R. M. (2019). Application of Ordinal Logistic Regression analysis in determining risk factors of child malnutrition in Bangladesh. *Nutrition Journal*, *10*, 124.

Dean, M., Raats, M. M., & Shepherd, R. (2012). The role of self-identity, past behaviour, and their interaction in predicting intention to purchase fresh and processed organic food. *Journal of Applied Social Psychology*, *42*(3), 669–688.

Delcea, C., Cotfas, L. A., Craciun, L., & Molanescu, A. G. (2018). Are seat and aisle interferences affecting the overall airplane boarding time? An agent-based approach. *Sustainability*, *10*, 4217.

Dixon, J. (2017). An alternative perspective on relationships, loyalty and future store choice. *International Review of Retail Distribution & Consumer Research*, *15*(4), 351–374.

Eliasaph, I., Farida, B., & Balarabe, J. (2016). Consumer satisfaction and repurchase intentions. *Developing Country Studies*, *6*(2), 96–100.

Engel, J. F., Blackwell, R. D., & Miniard, P. W. (1995). *Consumer behaviour* (8th ed.). Fort Worth: Dryden Press.

Fasano, A., & Durante, D. (2020). *A class of conjugate priors for multinomial probit models which includes the multivariate normal one.* Retrieved from https://arxiv.org/abs/2007.06944

Feng, C. M., & Jeng, K. Y. (2017). Analyzing airline service improvement strategy through importance and performance analysis. *Journal of the Eastern Asia Society for Transportation Studies*, *6*(1), 782–797.

Field, A. (2009). *Discovering statistics using SPSS*. London: SAGE Publications Ltd.

Fornell, C., & Larcker, D. F. (1981). Evaluating structural equation models with unobservable variables and measurement error. *Journal of Marketing Research*, *18*, 39–50.

Fourie, C., & Lubbe, B. (2017). Determinants of selection of full-service airlines and low-cost carriers – A note on business travellers in South Africa. *Journal of Air Transport Management*, *12*(2), 98.

Fuks, M., & Salazar, E. (2017). Applying models for Ordinal Logistic Regression to the analysis of household electricity consumption classes in Rio de Janeiro, Brazil. *Energy Economics*, *30*(4), 1672–1692.

Fullerton, A. S., & Xu, J. (2020). The proportional odds with partial proportionality constraints model for ordinal response variables. *Social Science Research*, *41*(1), 182–198.

Gameroff, M. J. (2017). *Using the proportional odds model for health-related outcomes: Why, when, and how with various SAS procedures* (pp. 205–230). SUGI.

Gardiner, S., King, C., & Grace, D. (2013). Travel decision making: An empirical examination of generational values, attitudes, and intentions. *Journal of Travel Research*, *52*(3), 310–324. doi: 10.1177/0047287512467699

Gerike, R., & Schulz, A. (2018). Workshop synthesis: Surveys on long-distance travel and other rare events. *Transportation Research Procedia*, *32*, 535–541.

Gill, H. (2020). *Whoever leads in Artificial Intelligence in 2030 will rule the world until 2100.* The Brookings Institution. Retrieved from www.brookings.edu/blog/future-development/2020/01/17/whoever-leads-in-artificial- intelligence-in-2030-will-rule-the-world-until-2100/amp/

Gross, S., & Grimm, B. (2018). Sustainable mode of transport choices at the destination – Public transport at German destinations. *Tourism Review*, *73*, 401–420.

Gühnemann, A., Kurzweil, A., & Mailer, M. (2021). Tourism mobility and climate change – A review of the situation in Austria. *Journal Outdoor Recreation and Tourism*, *34*, 100382.

Hair, J., Black, W., Babin, B., & Anderson, R. (2009). *Multivariate data analysis* (7th ed.). New York, NY: Prentice-Hall.

Hamilton, R., & Price, L. L. (2019). Consumer journeys: Developing consumer-based strategy. *Journal of the Academy of Marketing Science, 47,* 187–191.

Hamish, M. (2018). *By 2030, economies like China and India will hold dominance over the west and influence our decisions.* Retrieved from www.independent.co.uk/voices/hsbc-economies-china-India-emerging-west-east-technology-a8556346.html%3famp

Hangjun, Y., Qiong, Z., & Qiang, W. (2018). Airline deregulation, market competition, and impact of high-speed rail on airlines in China. *Advances in Airline Economics, 7,* 79–101. doi:10.1108/S2212-160920180000007006

Hanson, S., Jiang, L., & Dahl, D. (2019). Enhancing consumer engagement in an online brand community via user reputation signals: A multi-method analysis. *Journal of the Academy of Marketing Science, 47*(2), 349–367.

Hardy, A., & Aryal, J. (2020). Using innovations to understand tourist mobility in national parks. *Journal of Sustainable Tourism, 28,* 263–283.

Hardy, A., Hyslop, S., Booth, K., Robards, B., Aryal, J., Gretzel, U., & Eccleston, R. (2017). Tracking tourists' travel with smartphone-based GPS technology: A methodological discussion. *Information Technology & Tourism, 17,* 255–274.

Hewer, M. J., Scott, D. J., & Gough, W. A. (2017). Diferences in the importance of weather and weather-based decisions among campers in Ontario parks (Canada). *International Journal of Biometeorology, 61,* 1805–1818.

Hong, S. H. (2000). The criteria for selecting appropriate fit indices in structural equation modeling and their rationales. *Korean Journal of Clinical Psychology, 19,* 161–177.

Hoogendoorn-Lanser, S., Schaap, N. T., & OldeKalter, M. J. (2015). The Netherlands mobility panel: An innovative design approach for web-based longitudinal travel data collection. *Transportation Research Procedia, 11,* 311–329.

Hosmer, D. W., Stanley, L., & Rodney, X. S. (2020). *Applied logistic regression.* Hoboken, NJ: John Wiley & Sons.

Hugon-Duprat, C., & O'Connell, J. F. (2015). The rationale for implementing a premium economy class in the long haul markets: Evidence from the transatlantic market. *Journal of Air Transport Management, 47,* 11–19.

Hulland, J., Baumgartner, H., & Smith, K. M. (2018). Marketing survey research best practices: Evidence and recommendations from a review of JAMS articles. *Journal of the Academy of Marketing Science, 46*(1), 92–108.

IATA. (2021). *IATA Press release.* Retrieved from https://www.iata.org/en/pressroom/2021-releases/2021-10-04-01/

IATA. (2022). *The impact of the conflict between Russia and Ukraine on aviation.* Retrieved from https://www.iata.org/en/iata-repository/publications/economic-reports/the-impact-of-the-conflict-between-russia-and-ukraine-on-aviation/

IATA. (2022b). *Fact sheet benefits aviation statistics.* Retrieved from https://www.iata.org/en/iata-repository/pressroom/fact-sheets/fact-sheet-benefits-aviation statistics/

James, R., & Paul, F. (2018). Strategic alliances as a competitive strategy. *International Journal of Commerce and Management, 19*(2), 93–114. doi:10.1108/10569210910967860

Janzen, M., Vanhoof, M., Smoreda, Z., & Axhausen, K. W. (2018). Closer to the total? Long-distance travel of French mobile phone users. *Travel Behaviour and Society, 11,* 31–42.

Jou, R., Michael, S. H., Henser, D. A., Chen, C., & Kuo, C. (2017). The effect of service quality and price on international airline competition. *Transportation Research Part E Logistics and Transportation Review, 44*(4), 580–592. doi:10.1016/j.tre.2007.05.004

Juliet, N. (2020). The influence of airline service quality on passengers' satisfaction and loyalty: The case of Uganda airline industry. *The TQM Journal, 25*(5), 520–532.

Juschten, M., & Hössinger, R. (2021). Out of the city – But how and where? A mode-destination choice model for urban-rural tourism trips in Austria. *Current Issues in Tourism, 24,* 1465–1481.

Kelloway, E. K. (1998). *Using LISREL for structural equation modeling: A researcher's guide* (1st ed.). Thousand Oaks, CA: SAGE Publications.

Kim, Y., & Han, H. (2010). Intention to pay conventional-hotel prices at a green hotel – A modification of the theory of planned behaviour. *Journal of Sustainable Tourism*, *18*, 997–1014.

Kline, R. (2011). *Structural equation modeling* (3rd ed.). New York, NY: Guilford.

Kotler, P., & Armstrong, G. (2019). *Principles of marketing*. London: Pearson.

Kranzbühler, A. M., Kleijnen, M. H. P., & Verlegh, P. W. J. (2019). Outsourcing the pain, keeping the pleasure: Effects of outsourced touchpoints in the customer journey. *Journal of the Academy of Marketing Science*, *47*(2), 308–327.

Kuehnl, C., Jozic, D., & Homburg, C. (2019). Effective customer journey design: Consumers' conception, measurement, and consequences. *Journal of the Academy of Marketing Science*, *47*(3), 1–18.

Kuo, C. W., & Jou, R. C. (2017). Willingness-to-pay for airlines' premium economy class: The perspective of passengers. *Journal of Air Transport Management*, *59*, 134–142.

Laming, C., & Mason, K. (2014). Customer experience - An analysis of the concept and its performance in airline brands. *Research in Transportation Business and Management*, *10*(1), 15–25.

Laura, B. B. (2022). Airplane seats are shrinking: Can the government fix it? FORBES. Retrieved from https://www.forbes.com/sites/laurabegleybloom/10/24/airplane-seats-are-shrinking-can-the-government-fix-it/?sh=24a17c9d39b1

Laws, E. (2017). Managing passenger satisfaction: Some quality issues in airline meal service. *Journal of Quality Assurance in Hospitality & Tourism*, *6*(1–2), 89–113.

Lee, M. C., & Hwan, I. S. (2017). Relationships among service quality, customers' satisfaction and profitability in the Taiwanese banking industry. *International Journal of Management*, *22*(4), 635–648.

Lee, D., & Luengo-Prado, M. J. (2016). Are passengers willing to pay more for additional legroom? *Journal of Air Transport Management*, *10*(6), 377–383.

Lin, Y., Kerstetter, D., Nawijn, J., & Mitas, O. (2018). Changes in emotions and their interactions with personality in a vacation context. *Tourism Management*, *40*, 416–424.

Liu, C. H. S., & Lee, T. (2016). Service quality and price perception of service: Influence on word-of-mouth and revisit intention. *Journal of Air Transport Management*, *52*, 42–54.

Liu, C., Susilo, Y. O., & Karlström, A. (2015). Investigating the impacts of weather variability on individual's daily activity-travel patterns: A comparison between commuters and non-commuters in Sweden. *Transportation Research Part A: Policy Practice*, *82*, 47–64.

Li, Y., Yang, L., Shen, H., & Wu, Z. (2019). Modeling intra-destination travel behavior of tourists through spatiotemporal analysis. *Journal of Destination Marketing & Management*, *11*, 260–269.

Li, W. S., Yu, H. P., Chuan, Z., & Baozhem, T. (2017). A hybrid approach based on fuzzy AHP and 2-tuple fuzzy linguistic method for evaluation in-flight service quality. *Journal of Air Transport Management*, *60*, 49–64.

Maria, G. B., Laura, E., Carmen, F., & Gabriella, M. (2018). Air transport passengers' satisfaction: An ordered logit model. *Transportation Research Procedia*, *33*, 147–154.

Mauricio, E. M. (2019). An analytical model for the assessment of airline expansion strategies. *Journal of Airline and Airport Management*, *4*(1), 48–77.

McKercher, B., Hardy, A., & Aryal, J. (2019). Using tracking technology to improve marketing: Insights from a historic town in tasmania, Australia. *Journal of Travel & Tourism Marketing*, *36*, 823–834.

Milne, R. J., Delcea, C., Cotfas, L. A., & Salari, M. (2019). New methods for two-door airplane boarding using apron buses. *Journal of Air Transport Management*, *80*, 101705.

Mittal, S., & Gera, R. (2020). Relationship between service quality dimensions and behavioural intentions: An SEM study of public sector retail banking customers in India. *Journal of Service Research*, *12*(2), 15–31.

Moufakkir, O. (2019). The pay for in-flight food and drinks policy and its impact on travelers' experience. *Tourism Analysis*, *15*(1), 99–110.

Muhammad, U. B. (2015). Impact of service value on service satisfaction and behavioural intentions: Mediating role of switching barrier. *IOSR Journal of Business and Management*, *17*(4), 47–51. doi:10.9790/487X-17414751

Namukasa, J. (2020). The influence of airline service quality on passengers' satisfaction and loyalty: The case of Uganda airline industry. *The TQM Journal, 25*(5), 520–532.

Nawijn, J., Mitas, O., Lin, Y., & Kerstetter, D. (2013). How do we feel on vacation? A closer look at how emotions change over the course of a trip. *Journal of Travel Research, 52,* 265–274.

Norazryana, A. J., & Khalil, M. N. (2020). A conceptual model of customer behavioural intentions: Moderating effects of switching barriers and social ties. *Jurnal Teknologi Social Sciences, 64*(3), 29–33.

Nuraeni, S., Arru, A., & Novani, S. (2015). Understanding consumer decision-making in tourism sector: Conjoint analysis. *Procedia, Social and Behavioral Sciences, 169,* 312–317. doi:10.1016/j.sbspro.2015.01.315

Olorunniwo, F., Hsu, M. K., & Udo, G. F. (2017). Service quality, customers' satisfaction and behavioural intentions in the service factory. *Journal of Services Marketing, 20*(1), 59–72.

Olorunniwo, F., Hsu, M. K., & Udo, G. F. (2018). Service quality, customers' satisfaction and behavioural intentions in the service factory. *Journal of Services Marketing, 20*(1), 59–72.

Oseni, G., Corral, P., Goldstein, M., & Winters, P. (2015). Explaining gender differentials in agricultural production in Nigeria. *Agricultural Economics, 46,* 285–310.

Ozlem, A., Mahmut, B., & Sahap, A. (2019). The role of in-flight service quality on value for money in business class: A logit model on the airline. *Industry Journal of Administrative Science, 9*(26), 1–15.

Papathanassis, A., & Knolle, F. (2011). Exploring the adoption and processing of online holiday reviews: A grounded theory approach. *Tourism Management, 32*(2), 215–224. doi:10.1016/j.tourman.2009.12.005

Patricia, B., & Rumki, M. (2020). The services powerhouse: Increasingly vital to world economic growth. Deloitte Insight. Retrieved from https://www2.deloitte.com/us/en/insights/economy/issues-by-the-numbers/trade-in-services-economy-growth.html

Peter, B., Amedeo, O., & Cynthia, B. (2009). *The global airline industry.* Hoboken, NJ: John Wiley & Sons Ltd.

Phillipsconsulting. (2022). *Nigeria's aviation industry: Customer satisfaction survey report 2022.*

Pizzutti, C., Gonçalves, R., & Ferreira, M. (2022). Information search behavior at the post-purchase stage of the customer journey. *Journal of the Academy of Marketing Science, 50,* 981–1010. doi: 10.1007/s11747-022-00864-9

Plecher, H. (2020). *Distribution of Gross Domestic Product (GDP) across economic sectors, Nigeria.* Retrieved from https://www.statista.com/statistics/382311/nigeria-gdp-distribution-across-economic-sectors/

Rajaguru, R. (2016). Role of value for money and service quality on behavioural intention: A study of full service and low-cost airlines. *Journal of Air Transport Management, 53,* 114–122.

Rosario, A. B., de Valck, K., & Sotgiu, F. (2020). Conceptualizing the electronic word-of-mouth process: What we know and need to know about e-WOM creation, exposure, and evaluation. *Journal of the Academy of Marketing Science, 48*(3), 422–448.

Rowley, J. (2016). Retention: Rhetoric or realistic agendas for the future of higher education. *International Journal of Educational Management, 17*(6), 248–253.

Roy, B., Luke, B., & Beukering, V. (2017). "A convenient truth": Air travel passengers' willingness to offset their Co2 emissions. *Climatic Change, 90*(3), 299–313. doi:10.1007/s10584-008-9414-0

Santini, F., Ladeira, W. J., Pinto, D. C., Herter, M. M., Sampaio, C. H., & Babin, B. J. (2020). Customer engagement in social media: A framework and meta-analysis. *Journal of the Academy of Marketing Science, 48,* 1211–1228.

Satorra, A., and Bentler, P. M. (1988). Scaling corrections for chi-square statistics in covariance structure analysis. In *ASA 1988 Proceedings of the Business and Economic Statistics* (pp. 308–313). Alexandria, VA: American Statistical Association.

Schamp, C., Heitmann, M., & Katzenstein, R. (2019). Consideration of ethical attributes along the consumer decision-making journey. *Journal of the Academy of Marketing Science, 47*(2), 328–348.

Schlemmer, P., Blank, C., Bursa, B., Mailer, M., & Schnitzer, M. (2019). Does health-oriented tourism contribute to sustainable mobility? *Sustainability, 11,* 2633.

Schmidt, J., & Bijmolt, T. H. A. (2020). Accurately measuring willingness-to-pay for consumer goods: A meta-analysis of the hypothetical bias. *Journal of the Academy of Marketing Science*, *48*(3), 499–518. doi:10.1007/s11747-019-00666-6

Schmidt, J. B., & Spreng, R. A. (1996). A proposed model of external consumer information search. *Journal of the Academy of Marketing Science*, *24*(3), 246–256.

Šebjan, U., Polona, T., & Karin, S. (2017). Multiple conceptual modelling of perceived quality of in-flight airline services. *Promet – Traffic & Transportation*, *29*, 311–319.

Shoval, N., & Ahas, R. (2016). The use of tracking technologies in tourism research: The frst decade. *Tourism Geographies*, *18*, 587–606.

Sirakayaa, E., & Woodside, A. G. (2017). Building and testing theories of decision making by travellers. *Tourism Management*, *26*(6), 815–832. doi:10.1016/j.tourman

Smith, G. (2020). Economy passengers 'increasingly research seat comfort'. Retrieved from https://www.businesstraveller.com/news/2020/11/18/economy-passengers-increasingly-research-seat-comfort/

Statista Research Department. (2021). *Distribution of Gross domestic Product (GDP) across economic sectors in the U.S.* Retrieved from https://www.statista.com/statistics/270001/distribution-of-gross-domestic-product-gdp-across-economic-sectors-in-the-us/

Thomas, K. O. (2019). Users' perceptions of service quality in Murtala Muhammed International Airport (MMA1), Lagos, Nigeria. *Journal of Marketing and Consumer Research – An Open Access International Journal*, *3*, 48–53.

Tsoukatos, E., & Rand, G. K. (2017). Path analysis of perceived service quality, satisfaction and loyalty in Greek insurance. *Managing Service Quality*, *16*(5), 501–519.

Tucker, L. R., & Lewis, C. (1973). A reliability coefficient for maximum likelihood factor analysis. *Psychometrika*, *38*, 1–10.

Ullman, J. B., & Bentler, P. M. (2006). *Structural equation modeling* (2nd ed.). Thousand Oaks, CA: SAGE Publications.

van Nostrand, C., Sivaraman, V., & Pinjari, A. R. (2013). Analysis of long-distance vacation travel demand in the United States: A multiple discrete-continuous choice framework. *Transportation*, *40*, 151–171.

Vasudevan, H., Gaur, S. S., & Shinde, R. K. (2017). Relational switching costs, satisfaction and Commitment. A study in the Indian manufacturing context. *Asia Pacific Journal of Marketing and Logistics*, *18*(4), 342–353.

Vu, H. Q., Li, G., Law, R., & Zhang, Y. (2018). Tourist activity analysis by leveraging mobile social media data. *Journal of Travel Research*, *57*, 883–898.

Wang, Y., Sha, Z., Tan, X., Lan, H., Liu, X., & Rao, J. (2020). Modelling urban growth by coupling localized Spatio-temporal association analysis and binary logistic regression. *Computers, Environment and Urban Systems*, *81*.

Warnock-Smith, D., John, F. O., & Mahnaz, M. (2017). An analysis of ongoing trends in airline ancillary revenues. *Journal of Air Transport Management*, *64*, 42–54.

Waterhouse, J., Kao, S., Edwards, B., Atkinson, G., & Reilly, T. (2017). Factors associated with food intake in passengers on long-haul flights. *Chronobiology International*, *23*(5), 985–1007.

WHO. (2019). Retrieved from https://www.who.int/emergencies/diseases/novel-coronavirus-2019/advice-for-public

Wittmann, J. (2019). Customer-oriented optimization of the airplane boarding process. *Journal of Air Transport Management*, *76*, 31–39.

Wolny, J., & Charoensuksai, N. (2014). Mapping customer journeys in multichannel decision-making. *Journal of Direct, Data and Digital Marketing Practice*, *15*(4), 317–326. doi10.1057/dddmp. 2014

Yananda, S., & Duangkamol, T. (2019). *Factors affecting customer repurchase intention of the low-cost airlines in Thailand*. In *The 2019 International Academic Research Conference in Vienna 180–185*.

Zahari, M., Salleh, N. K., Kamaruddin, M. S., & Kutut, M. Z. (2019). In-flight meals, passengers' level of satisfaction and re-flying intention. *World Academy of Science, Engineering and Technology, International Journal of Social, Behavioural, Educational, Economic, Business and Industrial Engineering*, *5*(12), 1982–1989.

Zeithaml, V. A. (1988). Consumer perceptions of price, quality, and value: A means-end model and synthesis of evidence. *Journal of Marketing, 52*, 2–22.

Zeithaml, V. A., Berry, L. L., & Parasuraman, A. (1996). The behavioural consequences of service quality. *Journal of Marketing, 60*(2), 31–46.

Zhao, X., Lu, X., Liu, Y., Lin, J., & An, J. (2018). Tourist movement patterns understanding from the perspective of travel party size using mobile tracking data: A case study of Xi'an, China. *Tourism Management, 69*, 368–383.

CHAPTER 3

PROFESSIONAL INTEGRATION OF DISPLACED PERSONS

Hajaina Ravoaja

ABSTRACT

This article reconstructs the conditions under which displaced persons are integrated into their workplaces with their hosts. It identifies the characteristics of this pathway and provides guidance on the support that should be provided to these people. This support is part of social responsibility. Theories on professional integration/labour market integration (LMI) have been categorised and then arranged in a logical order to determine the stages of this integration. Theories on professional integration support for refugees were also reviewed and examined in relation to this categorisation. Six stages characterise professional integration: getting a job, its sustainability and its wage adequacy, its security and sustainability, career continuity and employability, the fact of being a full and equal participant and being an integrated part of the workforce and the meaningfulness of that job. The level of professional integration marks the quality of this integration. Each level encompasses the previous levels. Displaced persons should be supported throughout their careers to go beyond technical and behavioural skills and take a more holistic view of their tasks to find meaning in their work. While most research focuses on getting a job as a characteristic of occupational integration, this study found five other characteristics that were ordered. It also links vocational integration with social responsibility and provides guidance on how to help displaced people reach the final stage of this integration.

Keywords: Professional integration; labour market integration; career; levels; displaced persons; social responsibility; CSR

Innovation, Social Responsibility and Sustainability
Developments in Corporate Governance and Responsibility, Volume 22, 65–81
Copyright © 2024 Hajaina Ravoaja
Published under exclusive licence by Emerald Publishing Limited
ISSN: 2043-0523/doi:10.1108/S2043-052320230000022003

1. THE NOTION OF SOCIAL INTEGRATION

In the US, the different migration periods allowed comparisons (Alba & Nee, 2003; Foner, 2001). Social differences between groups have decreased over time. In Europe, the formation of a minority among migrants has led to ethnic stratification. In countries such as the Netherlands, Great Britain and Germany, multiculturalist thinking has been supportive of assimilation policies. It was noted that for an immigrant to be incorporated on an equal footing and to be able to work in the basic institutions of society, it was necessary to acquire cultural skills (Heckmann, 2003).

In sociology, integration within social environments resulted from a progression towards a more coherent form. This coherence was the consequence of the increased functionality of the parts for the whole, which implied a growing differentiation of the roles played by the actors or by the groups of actors. All the parties incorporated the more or less independent social systems (Ritzer, 2000). In this functionalist perspective, integration was marked by stable and cooperative relationships. The process of integration was characterised not only by the attachment of additional actors or groups to an existing social system and its fundamental institutions, but also by the strengthening of relations within that social system (Heckmann, 2003).

Four dimensions of social integration have been identified: culturation, placement, interaction and identification (Esser, 2001). Esser defined social integration as the inclusion of individual actors in already existing social systems. This describes the cohesion of a larger entity. These four dimensions can be defined in a relational way. Three levels of analysis was considered: micro, median and macro. The micro level deals with the attitudes between individuals. The median level corresponds to institutional relations between groups or subgroups, between newcomers and hosts. Finally, at the macro level, local and national policy measures and legislation, including labour market development, can lead to population movements and demographic transformations (Heckmann, 2003).

Culturation refers to the acquisition, enlargement and transfer of competences, as well as the extent and distribution of these competences in the social environment in question. This is why institutional developments, events, relationships and identifications are important. That said, the terms system integration and systemic integration come from these interactions in a certain social environment. Culturation designates, on the one hand, practices that are beneficial to society and, on the other hand, behaviours that are antisocial, unhealthy and detrimental to social ascent. These latter behaviours are reworked to conform to traditional models.

The placement refers to the process that leads to different positions in society. It concerns the acquisition, maintenance or loss of resources related to individual or collective positions, especially in the fundamental areas of education, income, housing, mobility and health.

Several characteristics of the interactions were found: intensity, single or multiple, individual or collective, positive or negative emotive content, institutional, formal or informal communication, intra-group or inter-group, intra-generations or inter-generations and gender composition. Social groups or ethnic groups are in concurrence to access resources and to find social and economic opportunities. But a monopoly or impediment to this competition may occur. Some groups could defend their niches. Individuals and groups have and develop interdependent relationships over time and the distribution of power may vary between individuals and groups.

Identification includes self-ascription and other-ascription. Selfascription is the fact of conceiving of oneself as subject and other-ascription is the conceiving of other subjects. This involves representations, mutual stereotypes, feelings and manifestations of cing. Identification also covers symbolic manifestations of individual and collective interactions like figures of speech. The other-ascription between minorities and dominant groups and collective self-scription count to understand the power game.

For each of these dimensions, process levels matter. The following elements are to be considered: purposive behaviour of individuals, collective behaviour within and between formal and informal groups in favour of institutions. The entanglements of the dimensions of social positions, skills in carrying out the tasks and the results, the identification of individuals and groups and their representations on each other shape the integration of newcomers.

Displaced persons are those who were expelled or force to flee from their home or homeland. The United Nations High Commissioner for Refugees (UNHCR) notes that among the 89.3 million people worldwide forcibly displaced, 53.2 millions are internally displaced, remained within their country's borders. 36.1 millions try to find refuge outside their country (UNHCR, 2021). Refugees are 'individuals, regardless of their legal status, who have fled their home country to seek protection and security in another country, and cannot safely return due to a wellfounded fear of the prevailing circumstances in their country of origin' (Lee, Szkudlarek, Nguyen, & Nardon, 2020). Refugees are considered integrated when they are an integrated part of their host societies (Verwiebe et al., 2019; Wikström & Sténs, 2019).

2. THE CONCEPT OF PROFESSIONAL INTEGRATION

It is based on adaptation to society through work that can lead to social success and is marked by common values that could be unique to organizations. Regarding the four dimensions of assimilation in the concept of social integration: the cultural dimension is relative, for example, to language and norms, the structural dimension is related, among other things, to education and the labour market, the social dimension corresponds to friendships between natives and immigrants, and the identification dimension is linked to the feeling of belonging (Esser, 2001).

Currently, studies on LMI focus on refugees and asylum seekers. For host countries, dealing with these new arrivals is a significant resettlement challenge. For refugees and asylum seekers, integration is an important challenge that is highly dependent on local host country policies (Simadi & Nahar, 2009). But on arrival in their host countries, they face precarious financial circumstances, the lack of a network and support and traumatic experiences in social and professional integration (Hynie, 2018). Integration can be viewed as inclusion and participation in society through mainstream institutions and without any threat to people's physical and personal integrity, as well as the development of their individual and shared identities. Inclusion also involves equitable access to opportunities and resources (Ager & Strang, 2008; Hynie, 2018). Work is one of the most crucial areas of integration (Ager & Strang, 2008). Integration through employment is a key issue. Having a job will allow a refugee to provide for the immediate needs of her or his family and to regain a livelihood (Colic-Peisker & Tilbury, 2006). Policy makers, humanitarian organizations, and NGOs have moved from humanitarian work to meet people's basic needs to labour market measures to promote employment integration (Lenner & Turner, 2019), knowing that refugee employment reduces welfare dependency and improves the educational and health outcomes of children in their families (Pernice & Brook, 1996). Indeed, employment also leads to personal fulfilment and social inclusion (Fleay, Hartley, & Kenny, 2013).

The term refugee settlement refers to the process of basic adaptation to life, often in the early stages of transfer to the new country. This includes securing access to housing, education, health care, documentation and legal rights. Refugee integration can be seen as a long-term dynamic process in which a newcomer becomes a full and equal participant in the host society (Valtonen, 2016). Refugee integration focuses on social, cultural and structural dimensions. This process encompasses acquiring legal rights, mastering language and culture, seeking security and stability, developing social ties, and establishing components of integration, such as employment, housing and health (Puma, Lichtenstein, & Stein, 2018; Strang & Ager, 2010). Also, integration in the world of employment no longer stops at sociology, but extends to management.

3. LMI IS CONDITIONED PRIMARILY BY SUITABLE AND SECURE EMPLOYMENT AND REMUNERATION

Education and employment are two of the key pillars of integration (Ager & Strang, 2008), promoting the development of networks and increased participation in the local community (Harris, 2014; Harvey & Mallman, 2019). Through a qualitative study of Syrian refugees in Germany who have already had permanent or temporary jobs, a model of labour market integration has described the links between social capital and four stages of labour market integration. These stages are early integration support, labour market preparation support, labour market entry support and work support. It was found that four types of social capital can support and be accessed by refugees. Social capital can thus be related to bonding, corresponding to bridging, vertical and horizontal (Gericke, Burmeister, Löwe, Deller, & Pundt, 2018). Not only does bonding social capital emanate from the matching of backgrounds and characteristics of people who are part of close networks, but it also comes from the convergence of personal norms and values of these people. Bridging social capital arises from the fact that weakly connected people come into contact with people from other social groups and share information and resources with them. Furthermore, taking into account the social situation, vertical social capital refers to interactions between people of different social backgrounds, and horizontal social capital refers to relationships between people who, having common backgrounds, share the same knowledge and resources (Granovetter, 1973).

Ultimately, vertical bridging social capital is the most influential resource for obtaining suitable employment. In contrast, horizontal bridging social capital and independent job search methods tend to result in refugees obtaining low-skilled employment, or becoming underemployed. This suggests that refugees need to be supported, particularly in the development of vertical bridging social networks. Therefore, integration is seen as access to the labour market and job retention (Gericke et al., 2018). For blue-collar workers, optimising their recruitment helps to attract and retain them (Lin-Hi, Rothenhöfer, & Blumberg, 2019). Refugees with skills and qualifications have difficulty in asserting their credentials, and often work in jobs that do not allow them to use their skills (Risberg & Romani, 2021). For refugees, successful skill utilisation requires the redesign of employment, which improves motivation levels (Ortlieb & Weiss, 2020). Through interviews with Syrian refugees, employers and experts from governmental and non-governmental organizations in Turkey, it was deduced that suitable jobs and remuneration, as well as development opportunities mark the integration of refugees into the labour market. It has been reported that refugee women were more disadvantaged in employment and when origin and host countries kept the same traditional gender roles, their exclusion from work was reinforced and they were even considered as objects and sexually exploited and become more dependent and desperate (Knappert, Kornau, & Figengül, 2018). On the immigrant side, they find that work is an imperative to be integrated into their host societies and to feel accepted and respected by their local communities. This increases their self-esteem and their ability to adopt cultural habits and customs. It also allows them to build relationships (Välipakka, Zeng, Lahti, & Croucher, 2016). Career paths and transitions influence priorities and expectations at work (Fournier et al., 2019). Refugees career plans are prioritised to meet their needs, their life plans, such as starting a family (Fedrigo et al., 2021). One study examined social initiatives that can facilitate the employment of Sudanese refugee women in Australia. It was concluded that initiatives that focus on using existing skills can create new opportunities for refugees in the labour market, while initiatives that taught new skills were more likely to connect refugees to existing labour market opportunities (Gaillard & Hughes, 2014; Warriner, 2004). A high level of labour force integration is associated with obtaining stable, usually permanent and full-time employment, and adequately paid work that enormously matches the refugees skill level, thus providing adequate economic security (Schmitt, 2012).

A meaningful job is one that matches a person's skills, training and experience, is paid accordingly and gives employees a sense of purpose (Lysova, Allan, Dik,

Duffy, & Steger, 2019). Refugees find it difficult to obtain decent and meaningful jobs. Decent work is productive, respects employees' rights and provides social protection and social dialogue (International Labour Organization (ILO), 2013). The number of years spent as a refugee has an impact on the probability of finding meaningful employment (Codell, Hill, Woltz, & Gore, 2011). Meaningful work is an important factor for labour market integration (Codell et al., 2011). A sense of meaning leads to positive work behaviours, engagement, job satisfaction, empowerment, career development, personal fulfilment, well-being and a sense of dignity (Codell et al., 2011; Rosso, Dekas, & Wrzesniewski, 2010; Steger, Dik, & Duffy, 2012).

4. NO LMI WITHOUT A CAREER

Integration does not stop at accessing the desired job, it extends to doing it. It is in the latter sense that professional or career capital has been studied in relation to refugees seeking employment. This professional or career capital includes cultural, social and economic capital in labour market integration (Eggenhofer-Rehart et al., 2018). This is the case of a study that was conducted in Austria, a country that received a large number of asylum seekers during the height of the global refugee crisis in 2015 and 2016. It was noted that refugees often encounter hostile and unfamiliar processes in the country. This limits their successful integration into employment. From a series of semi-structured interviews with Afghan and Syrian refugee jobseekers, the relocation, acquisition and transformation of their career capital during their entry into an unfamiliar labour market was examined. It was found that when refugees attempted to integrate into the labour market of their host country, all forms of their career capital were undervalued or devalued. Refugees who tried to use their cultural capital were confronted with unknown rules, threats to their professional identity and loss of status. Thus, in order to acquire new career capital or to shape forms of career capital that are more valued by their host country, refugees need to be proactive through self-directed, forward-looking and change-oriented behaviour. In fact, the work allows to learn the culture of the host country, to create networks and to increase one's social capital (Eggenhofer-Rehart et al., 2018).

During the reconstruction of the newcomers' life stories (Macías Gómez-Estern, 2013) and identities (Vough, Bataille, Noh, & Lee, 2015), work role transitions require identity work. They have to develop a set of behaviours perceived as appropriate to a professional community (Smith, 2010). Forming, repairing, maintaining, strengthening or revising one's identity, also called work identity is a critical element in increasing employability (Smith, 2010). It consists on revising constructions of who they are in ways that bring a sense of coherence and distinctiveness (Brown, 2015). A qualitative study in Germany has shown that psychological barriers to the resettlement process have negative consequences for refugees' integration into society and the labour market. These barriers can undermine refugees' basic identity needs for self-worth, distinction, continuity and control. In the face of these challenges and threats, refugees have been able to develop proactive coping responses by protecting their previous identities and restructuring their identities to fit their new situation (Wehrle et al., 2018). This proactivity leads to positive psychological growth despite the adversity encountered in the resettlement and integration process. But this is conditional on holding sufficient psychosocial resources and proactive coping strategies. It is also important to be aware that employment-related stressors and refugees' coping strategies in the labour market integration process are related (Baranik, Hurst, & Eby, 2018). Drawing on the transactional theory of stress and coping (Lazarus & Folkman, 1984), a content analysis of open-ended survey responses collected from refugees was conducted in the US. The transactional model is a cognitive view of stress in which the appraisal phase is paramount and determines subsequent adjustment efforts. Appraisal is the way the persons perceives the situation, based on their values, expectations and history. It was found that the most frequently reported stressor, mentioned by 31% of the responses, was access and opportunities, which showed that refugees felt that their previous work experience was not valued when looking for work, high-lighting their difficulties in finding work and the exploitation they suffered as a result of low wages. Another stress factor revealed by 22% of respondents was acculturation, including learning the language of the host country. 13% of respondents mentioned discrimination and 11% mentioned interpersonal stressors. Coping strategies included reflection and relaxation (25%), problem-solving actions (24%), social resources (18%) and shelter-specific adaptation (17%). The latter coping strategy included improving language skills, participating in assimilation and multicultural activities, and seeking social support from other refugees. At the institutional level, solutions have included programmes to hire more refugees, expand diversity and inclusion initiatives, and provide them with practical advice on stress management (Baranik et al., 2018). This idea of adaptation is similar to that of job retention.

Besides, the study of the labour market integration of refugees can be extended over several years using longitudinal data. This is the case of the examination of the labour market integration of blue-collar workers in Sweden, which showed that the age of refugees is positively related to the time spent unemployed, while the time spent in the host country is negatively related to it. As well, refugees from culturally distant countries such as Iran and Iraq spent more time unemployed than refugees from less culturally distant countries such as Eastern Europe (Lundborg, 2013). Internally displaced persons (IDPs) flee conflict, violence or persecution, but remain in their own country. For them, having a job is a primary indicator of labour market integration. It is crucial to recover lost property, rebuild human capital, trust and dignity, overcome psychological trauma and restore social networks (World Bank, 2015).

In summary, studies on job search and labour market integration of refugees have announced that psychological characteristics related to personal agency, such as psychological capital which includes self-efficacy and resilience, career adaptability, can play an important role in the successful integration of refugees into the labour market of their host country. The conditions that were favourable for this personal agency were low personal, social and structural barriers.

This should have a positive impact on refugees' self-efficacy, job search success and entrepreneurial intentions. In addition, refugees' vertical bridging social capital and the broader concept of career capital can contribute to obtaining suitable and secure jobs. Nevertheless, it is important that policy-makers provide special support to particularly vulnerable sub-groups of refugees, such as women and those with low levels of education. Adaptable career building leads to professional integration. It is even more essential in the circumstances of displacement, stress, acculturation and oppression that impact on refugees' career development (Yakushko, Backhaus, Watson, Ngaruiya, & Gonzalez, 2008). However, being integrated into the labour market means having a career. In other words, a career is a sign of professional integration.

Generally, in their host countries, refugees' occupational status decreases. Often they were left with only undesirable jobs. In Australia, it was noted that the niche jobs for newly arrived refugees included cleaning services, aged care, meat processing, taxi driving, security and construction. These are low-value, low-paying jobs that locals avoid, except for the construction sector. This is due to the non-recognition of their previous qualifications, racial and cultural discrimination by employers, the lack of traditional social networks and government initiatives to allocate low-skilled jobs to migrants (Colic-Peisker & Tilbury, 2006). And employment agencies have placed refugees in easily accessible, low-skilled and low-paid jobs (Shutes, 2011).

A study of refugees in the US drew on social cognitive career theory and psychological contract theory. By the way, social cognitive career theory (Bandura, 1999; Lent, 2008; Lent, Brown, & Hackett, 1994) is based on reciprocal causality between the subject, his or her behaviours and the environment. Taking into account the concept of agentivity, the subject wants to implement proactive, goal-oriented behaviours, which she or he regulates according to constraints, external and internal resources and the results obtained. The latter are evaluated according to self-perception or representations of the self, the environment and the interaction between the two. These representations, constructed through recurrent feedback from the outcome of actions and the social environment, constitute cognitions that in turn determine the direction of actions or their goals, the choice of specific actions implemented and the intensity with which they are carried out. Four types of cognitions play a role in the self-regulation of behaviour: sense of self-efficacy, outcome expectations, perceived obstacles and goals (Lent, Brown, & Hackett, 2000; Lent & Brown, 2006). The psychological contract is defined as an individual's subjective understanding of the reciprocal promise-based exchanges between her or himself and the organization (Eckerd, Hill, Boyer, Donohue, & Ward, 2013; Rousseau, 1996). The psychological contract is related to the deep feelings and perceptions that both parties have about a working relationship (Alcover, Rico, Turnley, & Bolino, 2016). It is the perception by organizations and their employees of their mutual obligations (Erkutlu & Chafra, 2013). This contract is associated with employees' assumptions of employers' obligations and vice versa in employment relationships (Rayton & Yalabik, 2014). It involves an agreement of exchange (Alcover, Rico, Turnley, & Bolino, 2017) due to obligations and promises

(Latorre, Guest, Ramos, & Gracia, 2016; Montes, Rousseau, & Tomprou, 2015) made and believed to be already made between employees and their employers (Alcover et al., 2017). It includes perceptions at the economic level that are qualified as transactional contract, perceptions on social needs or relational contract and the balanced psychological contract that combines these first two types (Dabos & Rousseau, 2013; Jamil, Raja, & Darr, 2013; Mayes, Finney, Johnson, Shen, & Yi, 2017). Through this research on refugees in the US, it was reported that their occupational integration was conditioned by resilience, ability to cope with change, realism, support, self-evaluations, concession and self-sufficiency relative to fulfilment and dependency. Their occupational integration thus relates to getting jobs that match their qualifications and continuity of the psychological contract (Baran, Valcea, Porter, & Coleman Gallagher, 2018).

5. LMI DEPENDS ON SATISFACTION, WELL-BEING AND COMMITMENT

Refugees life satisfaction is largely dependent on their job and financial satisfaction (Colic-Peisker, 2009). Their LMI results from job satisfaction, life satisfaction and the desire to stay in their host countries (Baran et al., 2018). In a longitudinal study, based on the theory of cumulative disadvantage (O'Rand, 1996) where the effects of risk factors accumulate over time, the labour market outcomes of IDPs were examined. These outcomes included employment status, informal work and job satisfaction. These people fled persecution and conflict but remained in their own post-socialist countries in Eastern Europe and Central Asia such as Armenia, Croatia and Russia. Among a sample of over 10,000 people who participated in the Life in Transition II study conducted by the European Bank for Reconstruction and Development and the World Bank in 2010, 10% were displaced, 85% were unaffected by the conflict and 5% were non-migrants affected by the conflict. It has been reported that the likelihood of being short or long-term unemployed and of having lost one's job is higher for those displaced by the conflict more than ten years ago. Moreover, displaced women were more disadvantaged than men in terms of long-term employment, and young IDPs were more interested in education and training than young people not affected by the conflict. IDPs were more likely to work in the informal sector to support their families. Yet job satisfaction among IDPs was equal to that of non-displaced people. As a result, the need to provide special support to female IDPs and further training to young IDPs was stated (Ivlevs & Veliziotis, 2018). This was echoed by a qualitative study that demonstrated the vulnerability of refugee women in the displacement and resettlement process. Semi-structured interviews with young African women provided detailed accounts of their gendered experiences of oppression and abuse during the displacement and resettlement process. The interviews revealed that women's personal agency, importance and voice were stifled in the transition from poor conditions in their home country to

Australia. But targeted professional interventions with them can remedy this stifling (Abkhezr, McMahon, Glasheen, & Campbell, 2018).

Finally, the characteristics of the work and organizational climate influence refugees' work experiences. The perceived diversity climate has impacts on refugee employees' work attitudes. At a six-month interval, on 135 refugees in Australia from Iranian, Iraqi, Afghan/Hazara and Pakistani ethnic backgrounds, it was shown that perceived diversity climate is positively associated with psychological capital which is positively related to refugee employees' affective organizational commitment. Psychological capital includes hope, optimism, resilience and self-efficacy (Luthans et al., 2007). It should be noted that work is one of the most important ways to integrate quickly into a host society and participation in the local economy contributes significantly to sustainable integration in the host society. The links between perceived diversity climate, affective organizational commitment and turnover intentions through psychological capital have been found to be stronger when employees identify more with their ethnic group (Newman, Bimrose, Nielsen, & Zacher, 2018). Research on 75 male refugees in Italy revealed that their goals were more about well-being, security, starting families, meeting people, obtaining housing and financial resources than about self-realisation and development at work or free time, and they were not aware of their rights to decent work (Kosny et al., 2020). Social support from both work and non-work domains affects the well-being of refugee employees through their psychological capital. An examination of 190 refugee employees living in Australia illustrated that perceived organizational and family supports, not perceived supervisor support, are positively related to refugee employees' well-being. Psychological capital is a full mediator of the relationship between perceived organizational support and well-being, and a partial mediator of the relationship between perceived family support and well-being. This advocates for a supportive environment and psychological capital for refugee employees. Ultimately, on the one hand, individual factors such as qualifications and prior expectations, and on the other hand contextual factors such as employment practices, diversity climate and support significantly promote refugees' occupational adjustment and well-being (Newman et al., 2018).

A study of Syrian refugees found that increasing their psychological capital through their confidence in finding work was necessary to ameliorate their career adaptability (Pajic, Ulceluse, Kismihók, Mol, & den Hartog, 2018). Psychological capital develops positive work attitudes (Newman et al., 2018) and psychological well-being of refugee workers (Newman et al., 2018). Once they became employed, the psychological capital and perseverance of refugees fortified their engagement to work, their commitment to their organizations and their entrepreneurial behaviour (Fong, Busch, Armour, Heffron, & Chanmugam, 2007; Newman et al., 2018; Obschonka & Hahn, 2018).

6. LEVELS OF OCCUPATIONAL INTEGRATION

Initially, the analysis of integration was concerned with immigrants as they sought their place in their host countries. Four dimensions of assimilation were identified: cultural, structural, social and identification-related (Esser, 2001). It has been noted that occupational integration, which is included in structural integration, is the most important and determining component of this integration (Ager & Strang, 2008). The most extensive studies on LMI have focused on immigrants, refugees and IDPs because they are the most vulnerable in the struggle for integration since the skills they initially developed are often not recognised in their host countries or societies (Risberg & Romani, 2021).

Thus, getting a job is the first level of this integration into the labour force. Then, the suitability of that job (Gericke et al., 2018) and its wage adequacy (Schmitt, 2012) enter the next level of occupational integration. After that come the security and sustainability of that job and its remuneration (Gericke et al., 2018), stability, permanent status, full-time employment, skills (Schmitt, 2012) and long-term employment (Ivlevs & Veliziotis, 2018). Then, career adaptability (Eggenhofer-Rehart et al., 2018; Yakushko et al., 2008) and employability (Smith, 2010) constitute the next step of occupational integration. This implies personal agency, significance, voice (Abkhezr et al., 2018), continuity of the psychological contract, job satisfaction and a desire for IDPs to stay in their host countries (Baran et al., 2018), affective organizational commitment related to identification (Newman et al., 2018), and engagement to work and commitment to the organization (Fong et al., 2007; Newman et al., 2018; Obschonka & Hahn, 2018). Furthermore, diversity climate and support strongly influence work adjustments and well-being (Newman et al., 2018). On a higher scale is the fact of being an integrated part of the workforce or the labour market (Verwiebe et al., 2019; Wikström & Sténs, 2019). Afterwards, meaningful employment that provides a sense of purpose promotes this LMI (Lysova et al., 2019). In addition,

Finding meaning at work

Being an integrated part of the workforce or the labour market

Career adaptability and employability

Security, sustainability, stability, permanent status, full-time employment, long-term employment

The suitability of that job and its wage adequacy

Getting a job

Fig. 3.1.   Stages in the Professional Integration of Displaced Persons.

there is the opportunity to learn new skills (Gaillard & Hughes, 2014; Warriner, 2004). This leads us to the following classification.

The path of professional integration of displaced persons thus runs from bottom to top in this Fig. 3.1. These people are IDPs and refugees and the quality of their professional integration depends on the level in which they are in this classification, knowing that there are six consecutive stages: (1) getting a job (2) the suitability of that job and its wage adequacy (3) security, sustainability, stability, permanent status, full-time employment, long-term employment (4) career adaptability and employability (5) being an integrated part of the work-force or the labour market and (6) finding meaning at work.

After a job is obtained, whether it is the first or not, it must be suitable and the wage must be suitable, which includes the decency of the job. This corresponds to placement (Esser, 2001). Secondly, the security of the job, its durability, per-manent status, full time and long-term scope are the logical consequence. Sub-sequently, this leads to career adaptability and employability. After these personal characteristics, the elements concerning interactions with colleagues are the next step. Indeed, these interactions, similar to those mentioned by Esser, should lead to becoming an integral part of the workplace. Finally, all these steps lead to the finding of the meaning of work. Finally, each level encompasses the previous levels.

7. SOCIAL RESPONSIBILITY TO DISPLACED PERSONS

Creating employment opportunities which correspond to refugees' experience, qualifications, and aspirations is a high priority corporate social responsibility (CSR) goal (Lee et al., 2020). Therefore, human resource management (HRM) and CSR are, among others, linked by the integration of refugees into the workforce. Displaced people are often traumatised and come from a very different culture. Therefore, support for cultural adaptation is important. Refu-gees economic integration is a manifestation of CSR (Wang & Chaudhri, 2019). By providing language training, job-search aid, computer literacy, cross-cultural education, job referrals (Groutsis, van den Broek, & Harvey, 2015; Garkisch, Heidingsfelder, & Beckmann, 2017), information, social networks (Griffiths, Sigona, & Zetter, 2005; Nardon, Zhang, Szkudlarek, & Gulanowski, 2020), social support and knowledge of local labour market conditions (Steimel, 2017; Tom-linson & Egan, 2002), educational support, local language courses and vocational skills training (Clarke, 2014; Matikainen, 2003), non-profit organizations (NPOs) help refugees to find sustainable and meaningful employment (Groutsis et al., 2015; Garkisch et al., 2017). NPOs work closely with various stakeholders including governmental, educational, for-profit organizations (Kosny et al., 2020; Szkudlarek, 2019; Trinidad, Soneoulay-Gillespie, Birkel, & Brennan, 2018) and employers who may provide internships, recruit refugee candidates, and supply corporate volunteers as career coaches for refugee jobseekers (Lee et al., 2020). The integrative approach to HRM–CSR show that the convergence of stake-holders interests towards shared social impact creates a win–win situation, such as helping refugees find sustainable employment (Voegtlin & Greenwood, 2016). Job-readiness training is about developing technical skills and advancing task-centric knowledge necessary for on-the-job performance (Balcar, 2016; Wanberg, Zhang, & Diehn, 2010). This applies to displaced persons: IDPs and refugees. But aid agencies must bear in mind that displaced people have been on the move due to circumstances in their home areas and ideally want to return there when the situation improves. This means that they do not think about long-term integration at least initially in their host regions, which is a challenge for them to reach the sixth stage of integration. Thus, it would be interesting to know the proportion of displaced people who reach each of these six stages of professional integration.

8. CONCLUSION

While researchers have often focused on access to employment, this six-stage classification highlights the challenges of integrating displaced persons into the labour market. While these concepts have been scattered, they are now grouped and arranged in this model. By assisting these displaced persons through these six stages, employers and aid organisations at the micro, meso and macro levels fulfil their social responsibility. This will enhance diversity and inclusion. Of course, their recruitment must first be encouraged. Thus, refugees should be supported throughout their careers to go beyond technical and behavioural skills and take a more holistic view of their tasks to find meaning in their work. As a result, researchers and practitioners from several disciplines such as sociology, human resource management, psychology and economics, among others, will be able to better organise their efforts to study and manage the problem of professional integration, and these six elements can generate indicators for understanding this previously under-defined concept. Finally, this notion of professional integration can be extended not only to young people but also to any public seeking a place in the professional world.

REFERENCES

Abkhezr, P., McMahon, M., Glasheen, K., & Campbell, M. (2018). Finding voice through narrative storytelling: An exploration of the career development of young African females with refugee backgrounds. *Journal of Vocational Behavior*. doi:10.1016/j.jvb.2017.09.007

Ager, A., & Strang, A. (2008). Understanding integration: A conceptual framework. *Journal of Refugee Studies*. doi:10.1093/jrs/fen016

Alba, R., & Nee, V. (2003). *Remaking the American mainstream. Assimilation and contemporary immigration*. Cambridge, MA: Harvard University Press.

Alcover, C.-M., Rico, R., Turnley, W. H., & Bolino, M. C. (2016). Multi-dependence in the formation and development of the distributed psychological contract. *European Journal of Work & Organizational Psychology*. doi:10.1080/1359432X.2016.1197205

Alcover, C.-M., Rico, R., Turnley, W. H., & Bolino, M. C. (2017). Understanding the changing nature of psychological contracts in 21st century organizations. *Organizational Psychology Review*. doi:10.1177/2041386616628333

Balcar, J. (2016). Is it better to invest in hard or soft skills. *Economic and Labour Relations Review*, *27*(4), 453–470.

Bandura, A. (1999). Social cognitive theory: An agentic perspective. *Asian Journal of Social Psychology*. doi:10.1111/1467-839X.00024

Baranik, L. E., Hurst, C. S., & Eby, L. T. (2018). The stigma of being a refugee: A mixed-method study of refugees' experiences of vocational stress. *Journal of Vocational Behavior*. doi:10.1016/j.jvb.2017.09.006

Baran, B. E., Valcea, S., Porter, T. H., & Coleman Gallagher, V. (2018). Survival, expectations, and employment: An inquiry of refugees and immigrants to the United States. *Journal of Vocational Behavior*. doi:10.1016/j.jvb.2017.10.011

Brown, A. D. (2015). Identities and identity work in organizations. *International Journal of Management Reviews*. doi:10.1111/ijmr.12035

Clarke, J. (2014). Beyond social capital: A capability approach to understanding refugee community organisations and other providers for 'hard to reach' groups. *International Journal of Migration, Health and Social Care, 10*(2), 61–72.

Codell, J. D., Hill, R. D., Woltz, D. J., & Gore, P. A. (2011). Predicting meaningful employment for refugees: The influence of personal characteristics and developmental factors on employment status and hourly wages. *International Journal for the Advancement of Counselling*. doi:10.1007/s10447-011-9125-5

Colic-Peisker, V. (2009). Visibility, settlement success and life satisfaction in three refugee communities in Australia. *Ethnicities*. doi:10.1177/1468796809103459

Colic-Peisker, V., & Tilbury, F. (2006). Employment niches for recent refugees: Segmented labour market in twenty-first century Australia. *Journal of Refugee Studies*. doi:10.1093/jrs/fej016

Dabos, G. E., & Rousseau, D. M. (2013). Psychological contracts and informal networks in organizations: The effects of social status and local ties. *Human Resource Management*. doi:10.1002/hrm.21540

Eckerd, S., Hill, J., Boyer, K. K., Donohue, K., & Ward, P. T. (2013). The relative impact of attribute, severity, and timing of psychological contract breach on behavioral and attitudinal outcomes. *Journal of Operations Management*. doi:10.1016/j.jom.2013.06.003

Eggenhofer-Rehart, P. M., Latzke, M., Pernkopf, K., Zellhofer, D., Mayrhofer, W., & Steyrer, J. (2018). Refugees' career capital welcome? Afghan and Syrian refugee job seekers in Austria. *Journal of Vocational Behavior*. doi:10.1016/j.jvb.2018.01.004

Erkutlu, H., & Chafra, J. (2013). Effects of trust and psychological contract violation on authentic leadership and organizational deviance. *Management Research Review*. doi:10.1108/MRR-06-2012-0136

Esser, H. (2001). Integration und ethnische Schichtung. *Mannheimer Zentrum für Europäische Sozialforschung, 40*, 82.

Fedrigo, L., Udayar, S., Toscanelli, C., Clot-Siegrist, E., Durante, F., & Masdonati, J. (2021). Young refugees' and asylum seekers' career choices: A qualitative investigation. *International Journal for Educational and Vocational Guidance*. doi:10.1007/s10775-021-09460-9

Fleay, C., Hartley, L., & Kenny, M. A. (2013). Refugees and asylum seekers living in the Australian community: The importance of work rights and employment support. *Australian Journal of Social Issues*. doi:10.1002/j.1839-4655.2013.tb00294.x

Foner, N. (2001). *From Ellis Island to JFK. New York's two great waves of immigration*. New Haven, CT: Yale University Press.

Fong, R., Busch, N. B., Armour, M., Heffron, L. C., & Chanmugam, A. (2007). Pathways to self-sufficiency: Successful entrepreneurship for refugees. *Journal of Ethnic & Cultural Diversity in Social Work*. doi:10.1300/J051v16n01_05

Fournier, G., Lachance, L., Viviers, S., Lahrizi, I. Z., Goyer, L., & Masdonati, J. (2019). Development and initial validation of a multidimensional questionnaire on the relationship to work (RWQ). *International Journal for Educational and Vocational Guidance*. doi:10.1007/s10775-019-09397-0

Gaillard, D., & Hughes, K. (2014). Key considerations for facilitating employment of female Sudanese refugees in Australia. *Journal of Management and Organization*. doi:10.1017/jmo.2014.49

Garkisch, M., Heidingsfelder, J., & Beckmann, M. (2017). Third sector organizations and migration: A systematic literature review on the contribution of third sector organizations in view of flight, migration and refugee crises. *VOLUNTAS: International Journal of Voluntary and Nonprofit Organizations, 28*(5), 1839–1880.

Gericke, D., Burmeister, A., Löwe, J., Deller, J., & Pundt, L. (2018). How do refugees use their social capital for successful labor market integration? An exploratory analysis in Germany. *Journal of Vocational Behavior*. doi:10.1016/j.jvb.2017.12.002

Granovetter, M. S. (1973). The strength of weak ties. *American Journal of Sociology*. doi:10.1086/225469

Griffiths, D., Sigona, N., & Zetter, R. (2005). *Refugee community organisations and dispersal: Networks, resources and social capital*. Bristol: Policy Press.

Groutsis, D., van den Broek, D., & Harvey, W. S. (2015). Transformations in network governance: The case of migration intermediaries. *Journal of Ethnic and Migration Studies*, *41*(10), 1558–1576.

Harris, A. (2014). Conviviality, conflict and distanciation in young people's local multicultures. *Journal of Intercultural Studies*. doi:10.1080/07256868.2014.963528

Harvey, A., & Mallman, M. (2019). Beyond cultural capital: Understanding the strengths of new migrants within higher education. *Policy Futures in Education*. doi:10.1177/1478210318822180

Heckmann, F. (2003), From ethnic nation to universalistic immigrant integration. In Heckmann, F. & Schnapper, D. (Eds), *The integration of immigrants in European societies. National differences and trends of convergence*. De Gruyter Oldenbourg. doi:10.1515/9783110507324-004

Hynie, M. (2018). Refugee integration: Research and policy. Peace and Conflict. *Journal of Peace Psychology*. doi:10.1037/pac0000326

International Labour Organization (ILO). (2013). *Decent work indicators: Guidelines for procedures and users of statistical and legal framework indicators* (2nd ed.). International Labor Office. https://www.ilo.org/wcmsp5/groups/public/—dgreports/—integration/documents/publication/wcms_229374.pdf

Ivlevs, A., & Veliziotis, M. (2018). Beyond conflict: Long-term labour market integration of internally displaced persons in post-socialist countries. *Journal of Vocational Behavior*. doi:10.1016/j.jvb.2017.12.003

Jamil, A., Raja, U., & Darr, W. (2013). Psychological contract types as moderator in the breach-violation and violation-burnout relationships. *The Journal of Psychology: Interdisciplinary and Applied*. doi:10.1080/00223980.2012.717552

Knappert, L., Kornau, A., & Figengül, M. (2018). Refugees' exclusion at work and the intersection with gender: Insights from the Turkish-Syrian border. *Journal of Vocational Behavior*. doi:10.1016/j.jvb.2017.11.002

Kosny, A., Yanar, B., Begum, M., Al-khooly, D., Premji, S., Lay, M. A., & Smith, P. M. (2020). Safe employment integration of recent immigrants and refugees. *Journal of International Migration and Integration*. doi:10.1007/s12134-019-00685-w

Latorre, F., Guest, D., Ramos, J., & Gracia, F. J. (2016). High commitment HR practices, the employment relationship and job performance: A test of a mediation model. *European Management Journal*. doi:10.1016/j.emj.2016.05.005

Lazarus, R. S., & Folkman, S. (1984). *Stress, appraisal, and coping*. New York, NY: Springer.

Lee, E. S., Szkudlarek, B. A., Nguyen, D. C., & Nardon, L. (2020). Unveiling the canvas ceiling: A multidisciplinary literature review of refugee employment and workforce integration. *International Journal of Management Reviews*, *22*(2), 93–216.

Lenner, K., & Turner, L. (2019). Making refugees work? The politics of integrating Syrian refugees into the labor market in Jordan. doi:10.1080/19436149.2018.1462601

Lent, R. W. (2008). Une conception sociale cognitive de l'orientation scolaire et professionnelle: Considérations théoriques et pratiques. *L'orientation scolaire et professionnelle*. doi:10.4000/osp.159.

Lent, R. W., & Brown, S. D. (2006). On conceptualizing and assessing social cognitive constructs in career research: A measurement guide. *Journal of Career Assessment*. doi:10.1177/1069072705281364

Lent, R. W., Brown, S. D., & Hackett, G. (1994). *Toward a unifying social cognitive theory of career and academic interest, choice and performance*. doi:10.1006/jvbe.1994.1027

Lent, R. W., Brown, S. D., & Hackett, G. (2000). Contextual supports and barriers to career choice: A social cognitive analysis. *Journal of Counseling Psychology*. doi:10.1037/0022-0167.47.1.36

Lin-Hi, N., Rothenhöfer, L., & Blumberg, I. (2019). The relevance of socially responsible blue-collar human resource management. *Employee Relations.* doi:10.1108/ER-03-2018-0081

Lundborg, P. (2013). Refugees' employment integration in Sweden: Cultural distance and labor market performance. *Review of International Economics.* doi:10.1111/roie.12032

Luthans, F., Avolio, B. J., Avey, J. B., & Norman, S. M. (2007). Positive psychological capital: Measurement and relationship with performance and satisfaction. *Personnel Psychology.* doi: 10.1111/j.1744-6570.2007.00083.x

Lysova, E. I., Allan, B. A., Dik, B. J., Duffy, R. D., & Steger, M. F. (2019). Fostering meaningful work in organizations: A multi-level review and integration. *Journal of Vocational Behavior.* doi:10.1016/j.jvb.2018.07.004

Macías Gómez-Estern, B. (2013). 'And now I am here . . ., but then we were there': Space and social positioning in Andalusian migrants' narratives. *Journal of Multicultural Discourses.* doi:10. 1080/17447143.2013.820308

Matikainen, J. (2003). The Finnish Red Cross in refugee settlement: Developing the integration timeline as a tool for integration in the Kotopolku project. *Journal of International Migration and Integration, 4*(2), 273–295.

Mayes, B. T., Finney, T. G., Johnson, T. W., Shen, J., & Yi, L. (2017). The effect of human resource practices on perceived organizational support in the People's Republic of China. *International Journal of Human Resource Management.* doi:10.1080/09585192.2015.1114768

Montes, S. D., Rousseau, D. M., & Tomprou, M. (2015). *Psychological contract theory.* Wiley Encyclopedia of Management. doi:10.1002/9781118785317.weom110075

Nardon, L., Zhang, H., Szkudlarek, B., & Gulanowski, D. (2020). Identity work in refugee workforce integration: The role of newcomer support organizations. *Human Relations.* doi:10.1177/ 0018726720949630

Newman, A., Bimrose, J., Nielsen, I., & Zacher, H. (2018). Vocational behavior of refugees: How do refugees seek employment, overcome work-related challenges, and navigate their careers. *Journal of Vocational Behavior.* doi:10.1016/j.jvb.2018.01.007

Newman, A., Nielsen, I., Smyth, R., & Hirst, G. (2018). Mediating role of psychological capital in the relationship between social support and wellbeing of refugees. *International Migration.* doi:10. 1111/imig.12415

Newman, A., Nielsen, I., Smyth, R., Hirst, G., & Kennedy, S. (2018). The effects of diversity climate on the work attitudes of refugee employees: The mediating role of psychological capital and moderating role of ethnic identity. *Journal of Vocational Behavior.* doi:10.1016/j.jvb.2017.09.005

O'Rand, A. (1996). The precious and the precocious: Understanding cumulative disadvantage and cumulative advantage over the life course. *The Gerontologist.* doi:10.1093/geront/36.2.230

Obschonka, M., & Hahn, E. (2018). Personal agency in newly arrived refugees: The role of personality, entrepreneurial cognitions and intentions, and career adaptability. *Journal of Vocational Behavior.* doi:10.1016/j.jvb.2018.01.003

Ortlieb, R., & Weiss, S. (2020). Job quality of refugees in Austria: Trade-offs between multiple workplace characteristics. *German Journal of Human Resource Management.* doi:10.1177/ 2397002220914224

Pajic, S., Ulceluse, M., Kismihók, G., Mol, S. T., & den Hartog, D. N. (2018). Antecedents of job search self-efficacy of Syrian refugees in Greece and the Netherlands. *Journal of Vocational Behavior.* doi:10.1016/j.jvb.2017.11.001

Pernice, R., & Brook, J. (1996). Refugees' and immigrants' mental health: Association of demographic and post-immigration factors. *The Journal of Social Psychology.* doi:10.1080/00224545.1996. 9714033

Puma, J. E., Lichtenstein, G., & Stein, P. (2018). The RISE survey: Developing and implementing a valid and reliable quantitative measure of refugee integration in the United States. *Journal of Refugee Studies.* doi:10.1093/jrs/fex047

Rayton, B. A., & Yalabik, Z. Y. (2014). Work engagement, psychological contract breach and job satisfaction. *International Journal of Human Resource Management.* doi:10.1080/09585192. 2013.876440

Risberg, A., & Romani, L. (2021). Underemploying highly skilled migrants: An organizational logic protecting corporate 'normality'. *Human Relations.* doi:10.1177/0018726721992854

Ritzer, G. (2000). *Classical sociological theory*. New York, NY: McGraw Hill.

Rosso, B. D., Dekas, K. H., & Wrzesniewski, A. (2010). On the meaning of work: A theoretical integration and review. *Research in Organizational Behavior*. doi:10.1016/j.riob.2010.09.001

Rousseau, D. M. (1996). Changing the deal while keeping the people. *Academy of Management Executive, 10*(1), 50–59.

Schmitt, C. (2012). Labour market integration, occupational uncertainty, and fertility choices in Germany and the UK. *Demographic Research*. doi:10.4054/DemRes.2012.26.12

Shutes, I. (2011). Welfare-to-work and the responsiveness of employment providers to the needs of refugees. *Journal of Social Policy*. doi:10.1017/S0047279410000711

Simadi, F. A., & Nahar, G. S. (2009). Refugees in Jordan: Sociological perspective. *Social Responsibility Journal, 5*(2), 257–264. doi:10.1108/17471110910964522

Smith, V. (2010). Enhancing employability: Human, cultural and social capital in an era of turbulent unpredictability. *Human Relations*. doi:10.1177/0018726709353639

Steger, M. F., Dik, B. J., & Duffy, R. D. (2012). Measuring meaningful work: The work and meaning inventory (WAMI). *Journal of Career Assessment*. doi:10.1177/10690727114336160

Steimel, S. (2017). Negotiating refugee empowerment(s) in resettlement organizations. *Journal of Immigrant and Refugee Studies, 15*, 90–107.

Strang, A., & Ager, A. (2010). Refugee integration: Emerging trends and remaining agendas. *Journal of Refugee Studies*. doi:10.1093/jrs/feq046

Szkudlarek, B. (2019). *Engaging business in refugee employment: The employer's perspective*. Sydney: University of Sydney.

Tomlinson, F., & Egan, S. (2002). From marginalization to (dis)empowerment: Organizing training and employment services for refugees. *Human Relations, 55*, 1019–1043.

Trinidad, A. M. O., Soneoulay-Gillespie, T., Birkel, R. C., & Brennan, E. M. (2018). Parish collaboration and partnership in welcoming refugees: A case study. *Social Work and Christianity, 45*(3), 73–92.

UNHCR. (2021). *Figures at a glance*. https://www.unhcr.org/figures-at-a-glance.html

Välipakka, H., Zeng, C., Lahti, M., & Croucher, S. (2016). Experiencing cultural contact at work: An exploration of immigrants' perceptions of work in Finland. In S. Shenoy-Packer & E. Gabor (Eds), *Immigrant workers and meanings of work: Communicating life and career transitions* (pp. 21–32). Bern: Peter Lang.

Valtonen, K. (2016). *Social work and migration: Immigrant and refugee settlement and integration*. London: Routledge.

Verwiebe, R., Kittel, B., Dellinger, F., Liebhart, C., Schiestl, D., Haindorfer, R., & Liedl, B. (2019). Finding your way into employment against all odds? Successful job search of refugees in Austria. *Journal of Ethnic and Migration Studies*. doi:10.1080/1369183X.2018.1552826

Voegtlin, C., & Greenwood, M. (2016). Corporate social responsibility and human resource management: A systematic review and conceptual analysis. *Human Resource Management Review, 26*(3), 181–197.

Vough, H. C., Bataille, C. D., Noh, S. C., & Lee, M. D. (2015). Going off script: How managers make sense of the ending of their careers. *Journal of Management Studies*. doi:10.1111/joms.12126

Wanberg, C. R., Zhang, Z., & Diehn, E. W. (2010). Development of the 'Getting ready for your next job' inventory for unemployed individuals. *Personnel Psychology, 63*(2), 439–478.

Wang, Y., & Chaudhri, V. (2019). Business support for refugee integration in Europe: Conceptualizing the link with organizational identification 2019. *Media and Communication, 7*(2), 289–299.

Warriner, D. (2004). The days now is very hard for my family: The negotiation and construction of gendered work identities among newly arrived women refugees. *Journal of Language, Identity and Education*. doi:10.1207/s15327701jlie0304_4

Wehrle, K., Klehe, U.-C., Kira, M., & Zikic, J. (2018). Can I come as I am? Refugees' vocational identity threats, coping, and growth. *Journal of Vocational Behavior*. doi:10.1016/j.jvb.2017.10.010

Wikström, E., & Sténs, A. (2019). Problematising refugee migrants in the Swedish forestry sector. *Transfer: European Review of Labour and Research*. doi:10.1177/1024258919827133

World Bank. (2015). *Examining recovery and peacebuilding needs in Eastern Ukraine*. The World Bank.

Yakushko, O., Backhaus, A., Watson, M., Ngaruiya, K., & Gonzalez, J. (2008). Career development concerns of recent immigrants and refugees. *Journal of Career Development*. doi:10.1177/0894845308316292

CHAPTER 4

PRACTICE OF FEMALE GENITAL MUTILATION IN WEST AFRICA

Joseph Olanrewaju Ilugbami
and Oluwadamisi Toluwalase Tayo-Ladega

ABSTRACT

This study delves into the factors that influence the practice of female genital mutilation in West Africa, as well as the health implications. An online cross-sectional study was conducted with the use of electronic questionnaire. The study was targeted at adult females who were between the age of 18 and 50 years old. The Uniform Resource Locator (URL) of the electronic questionnaire was administered on social media platforms (Facebook and WhatsApp) only through convenience and snowball sampling techniques. A sample size of 3,119 adult females participated in the study. Spearman rank correlation (r) was employed to test the hypotheses. Responses were gathered from adult females whom originates from nine West African countries which are Nigeria, Ghana, Mali, Liberia, Benin, Cameroon, Chad, Gambia and Guinea. The study found a strong and positive relationship between culture and the practice of female genital mutilation in West Africa, and there was a weak and positive relationship between religion and education, and the practice of female genital mutilation in West Africa. Despite the health risks, it was revealed that female genital mutilation remained uninterrupted in West Africa. The findings of this study imply that the culture of the people, religious belief system and education are critical factors in efforts to be considered when discouraging the practice of female genital mutilation. Therefore, for healthy living, the practice of female genital mutilation should be discouraged in the study area. Based on the study outcome, recommendations were suggested.

Keywords: Female; genital mutilation; gender violence; health implications; practice; West Africa

Innovation, Social Responsibility and Sustainability
Developments in Corporate Governance and Responsibility, Volume 22, 83–97
Copyright © 2024 Joseph Olanrewaju Ilugbami and Oluwadamisi Toluwalase Tayo-Ladega
Published under exclusive licence by Emerald Publishing Limited
ISSN: 2043-0523/doi:10.1108/S2043-052320230000022004

LIST OF ABBREVIATIONS

COVID-19—Corona-Virus Disease 2019
FGC—Female Genital Cutting
FGM/C—Female Genital Mutilation/Cutting
FGM—Female Genital Mutilation
NDHS—Nigeria Demographic and Health Survey
UNICEF—United Nations International Children Emergency Fund
WHO—World Health Organization

1. BACKGROUND

Female genital mutilation (FGM), also known as female genital cutting (FGC) or female circumcision (FC), is still a major cause of illness and mortality among African women (Bogale, Markos, & Kaso, 2018). Despite persistent efforts to stop it, many ethnic groups, particularly in Africa, continue to practice it because it is based on socio-cultural beliefs (Zayed & Ali, 2021). FGM is defined by Alo and Gbadebo (2017); Bogale, Markos, and Kaso (2019); Dye, Reeder, and Terry (2020); World Health Organization (WHO, 2016a, 2016b); and Yirga, Kassa, Gebremichael, and Aro (2021) as 'all procedures that involve partial or total removal of the external female genitalia and/or injury to the female genital organs, whether for cultural or non-therapeutic reasons'.

Although generally condemned as a abuse and defiance of human rights, FGM is said to be an old practice developed by tribes seeking to control female sexual activity and maintain women's virginity by lowering sexual desire (Adeniran et al., 2015; Berg & Denison, 2020; Rafferty, 2020; WHO, 2017). The treatment is also performed by a significant number of healthcare practitioners in countries such as Egypt, Kenya, and Sudan. This is referred to as 'Medicalisation of FGM', and it refers to circumstances in which any type of healthcare practitioner performs FGM, whether in a private or public institution (Fahmy, El-Mouelhy, & Ragab, 2016; Fund & Gupta, 2020; Sipsma et al., 2021).

It also involves the technique of re-infibulation, which refers to the act of re-suturing the scar tissue caused by infibulation at any time in a woman's life (Berer, 2018; Kaplan, Hechavarría, Martín, & Bonhoure, 2017). In recent times, about 200 million females in the world have experienced some form of FGM in 30 nations including those in Africa, with another 30 million girls at danger in the next one decade (WHO, 2017). According to Ali (2021), eight African nations account for 80% of FGM, with the highest record (98%) in Somalia. The following countries such as Guinea, Djibouti, and Egypt account for 90%; other countries such as Eritrea, Mali, Sierra Leone and Sudan accounts for 80% or more (Arseneault, 2017; Galukande et al., 2018; Jacobson et al., 2018; Kandala & Komba, 2018).

There is increasing record of FGM among Nigerian girls aged 0–14 (United Nations International Children Emergency Fund [UNICEF], 2022). This level climbed from 16.9% in 2015 to 19.2% in 2018 (UNICEF, 2022). Nigeria and has the third largest number of women and children who have experienced this issue in the world, with an estimated 19.9 million survivors. The predominance of FGM among female aged 15–49 in Nigeria fell from 25% in 2016 to 20% in 2018, the predominance among girls aged 0–14 grew from 16.9% to 19.2% during the same time (Nigeria Demographic and Health Survey [NDHS], 2019).

Furthermore, 86% of girls had their hair cut before the age of 5, with the remaining 8% having their hair trimmed between the ages of 5 and 14. It is anticipated that 68 million girls worldwide would be at danger of FGM in 2030 (Dye et al., 2020; UNICEF, 2022). As COVID-19 destroys schools and disrupts activities that assist protect girls from this deadly operation, an additional 2 million cases of FGM may occur over the following decade (UNICEF, 2022). Almost 1 in every 4 Nigerian women aged 15–49 has been circumcised, with 'traditionalists' women having the highest proportion with 35% (NDHS, 2019).

In developing nations, some factors such as religion, culture, and other fundamental attitudes and faulty viewpoints, can keep women in danger, suppressed, and vulnerable. In light of this, FGM has serious immediate and long-term negative health implications, and lifelong psychological trauma to females. FGM is a deeply rooted practice in the majority of Sub-Saharan African countries (Baldry, Farrington, & Sorrentino, 2017; Barlett & Coyne, 2014; Barzilay et al., 2017; Bauerband & Galupo, 2014; Kaplan, Hechavarría, Martín, & Bonhoure, 2017).

Bhana and Mayeza (2016), Bockting, Miner, Swinburne Romine, Hamilton, and Coleman (2013), Contreras, Elacqua, Martinez, and Miranda (2016) and Diop and Askew (2015) stated that FGM continue to exist for mundane reasons such as culture, custom, religion and so on, that dehumanise, violate their female rights, endanger their health, and confuse them throughout their lives (Bradford, Reisner, Honnold, & Xavier, 2013; Dovlo, 2007; Kaplan et al., 2020). As a result, the argument for continuing experience of female genital mutilation in West Africa and Nigeria in particular is complex (Dey, 2019; Klomek, Sourander, & Elonheimo, 2015; Ladan, 2019).

It is essential to note that several studies have been carried out on female genital mutilation in West Africa, and the influence of religion, culture, and education on the practice of female genital mutilation, however, they may not be recent as many of the West African countries are presently facing different phases of social issues such as the rising state of insecurity, amongst all; hence, this study examine the practice of female genital mutilation in West Africa, with a view to reveal its influence by religion, culture and education, and it affects the health of victims.

2. LITERATURE REVIEW

According to Adam et al. (2016), executing female genital mutilation for non-medical reasons incurs obstetric expenses, leaving victims with vaginal difficulties such as discharge, itching, bacterial vaginosis and other infections, all of which harm their health in various ways. Furthermore, according to UNICEF (2018), female genital mutilation is both locally and globally recognised as a form of discrimination, subjection, and violation of female human rights and dignity (children, youth, and old). According to Epundu et al. (2018) and Koster and Price (2008), female genital mutilation is a life-threatening surgery with the potential for serious health repercussions, including emotional anguish that can last a victim's lifetime and occasionally lead to the victim's death.

According to Kaplan, Hechavarría, Martín, & Bonhoure (2017) and Mboho and Raphael (2018), the non-clinical causes underpinning female genital mutilation may be accountable for this demeaning practice practised by traditional circumcisers. Furthermore, the practice is prone to unprofessional and unhygienic behaviour, which may predispose FGM patients to health concerns (Mshelia, 2021; Mwatsiya & Rasool, 2021; Myhill, 2017). The WHO believes that the cutting and removal of female genital tissue linked with FGM is incorrectly carried out to prevent adultery and to maintain specific cultural or traditional behaviours (Babatunde et al., 2021; Mahmoud, 2016). This will eventually harm the female body's well-being and natural functioning, as well as reproductive processes (Nadama, 2019; WHO, 2020).

Due to the high hazards, WHO (2020) strongly warns against conducting FGM, even if it may be essential in rare and extreme medical situations to preserve the lives of medicalised patients. FGM, on the other hand, is classified into three types: I, II, and III, each of which has substantial short- and long-term health consequences (UNICEF, 2018). The WHO (2020) explicitly cited excruciating pain, copious bleeding (haemorrhage), swelling of the genital tissue, fever, infections such as tetanus, urinary issues (such as discharge, itching, bacterial vaginosis and other infections), wound healing problems, damage to the surrounding genital tissue, shock, and death as urgent health effects occurring from FGM (Odu, 2008; Rasool, 2022). Long-term adverse effects include bladder issues such as painful urination and urinary tract infections, but vaginal problems are also a worry.

Later treatments, such as vaginal sealing or narrowing (Type 3), may cause uncomfortable menstrual cycles, difficulty passing menstrual blood, and sexual difficulties such as pain during intercourse, decreased satisfaction, and so on (Rasheed, Abd-Ellah, & Yousef, 2017). A high tendency of complications during child-birth, such as difficult deliveries, excessive bleeding, caesarean sections, the need to resuscitate the child, and so on, as well as newborn deaths, might result in painful menstrual periods and difficulty shedding menstrual blood (depression, anxiety, posttraumatic stress disorder, low self-esteem, etc.) (Plo, Asse, Sei, & Yenan, 2019). FGM often result to death, it violates a person's right to health, safety, and physical integrity, as well as their right to life. It also breaches the right to be free of cruel, violent, or degrading treatment (Rosen & Nofziger, 2019; UNICEF, 2018).

Education would be an effective strategy for reducing the prevalence of female genital mutilation in Africa, especially in the West region (Garba, Muhammed, Abubakar, & Yukasai, 2021), the North Central region (Adeniran et al., 2018), and the East region (Ezenyeaku, Okeke, Chigbu, & Ikeako, 2017; Obi, 2019). Various traits, according to research, can predict or influence the practice of female genital mutilation. Culture (Smokowski, Evans, & Cotter, 2014; Yoder, Noureddine, & Arlinda, 2004), traditional demand, and promiscuity, for example, are decreasing (Geoffrey et al., 2018; Rufa, 2017), education level and religion are increasing (Ahinkorah, 2021; Vahida, 2022). However, the focus of this study is on the link between the determining elements of female genital cutting practice and the health repercussions sustained unknowingly by FGM victims.

According to Ezenyeaku et al. (2017), women in South-Eastern Nigeria have a similar perspective and fixation that female genital mutilation is a procedure that causes significant physical and mental difficulties that can last the victims' whole lives. This technique is not only hazardous in terms of health repercussions, but it may even result in death. Female genital mutilation has painful effects and outcomes, leaving the victim with nostalgia, psychological trauma, emotional bewilderment, regret and anger throughout a woman's lifetime, especially when the individual recalls any experience of painful penetration and unpleasant sexual encounters, including difficult deliveries (Adeniran et al., 2018; Rodriguez, Seuc, Say, & Hindin, 2016).

These obstacles may be the same as the happenings in West Africa. Because victims of genital mutilation may undergo psychological anguish, acute pains, infections, and even death, this surgery may have some obvious health consequences. Several studies have been carried out on female genital mutilation in West Africa, and the influence of religion, culture, and education on the practice of female genital mutilation, however, they may not be recent as many of the West African countries are presently facing different phases of social issues such as the rising state of insecurity, amongst all; hence, this study examine the practice of female genital mutilation in West Africa, with a view to reveal its influence by religion, culture, and education, and it affects the health of victims.

3. METHODS

An online cross-sectional study was used for the investigation. Co-relational research establishes a link between two or more variables to discover the relationship between variables (Nwankwo, 2020). In this scenario, the independent variables were education, culture and religious practice, while the dependent variable was health implications. For data gathering, the study used an electronic questionnaire. The electronic questionnaire's Uniform Resource Locator (URL) was solely sent via social media platforms (Facebook and WhatsApp).

The population of this study were adult females in West Africa who are between the age of 18 and 50 years of age. It is pertinent to note that the exact population that will be captured for the study is unknown, hence, the combination of convenience and snowball sampling techniques were employed. Convenience sampling was adopted because the online participants were reached based on convenience. Also, snowball sampling was adopted such that the URL of the electronic questionnaire can be shared by the participants to other online and social media users. The responses were gathered between June and November 2022. A sample size of 3,119 adult females participated in the study.

The questionnaire instrument was self-developed and validated by two research experts from the Department of Public Health at the National Open University of Nigeria. Corrections from the experts were integrated into the final draft of the instrument and used for the study. Pilot test was employed and results obtained were subjected to test the reliability of internal consistency using Cronbach's Alpha coefficient which yielded a coefficient of 0.736. Adeniran (2019) recommended an acceptable value of 0.7 for a good reliability coefficient. Since the reliability coefficient obtained is above this value, the instrument was considered suitable for the study.

The data were analysed using Spearman Rank Correlation (r) to achieve the objectives and test the hypotheses at a 95% confidence level. All analysis was carried out using the Statistical Package for Social Sciences (SPSS) version 23.0.

4. RESULTS

4.1 Characteristics of Participants

The valid participants (adult females) originates from nine West African countries which are Nigeria, Ghana, Mali, Liberia, Benin, Cameroon, Chad, Gambia and Guinea as shown in Table 4.1. Only responses that were received from adult females in West Africa were employed for the analysis. This implies that responses received from participants in other African countries aside West Africa were excluded. Responses received from male, and girl-children were also excluded from the analysis. For this study, adult females are individuals between the age of 15 and above. The age category is in-line with the African Charter as stated by Babalola and Fasiku (2015).

Regarding the marital and education status of participants, it was revealed that majority of the participants were married (69.19%) and holders of Higher National Diploma (ND) (29.91%), Bachelor of Arts (B.A), Bachelor of Science (B.Sc), Bachelor of Technology (B.Tech) (30.49%), which implies that majority of

Table 4.1. Nationality of Participants.

Countries	Frequency	Percentage
Nigeria	617	19.78
Ghana	402	12.89
Mali	142	4.55
Liberia	371	11.90
Benin	333	10.68
Cameroon	128	4.10
Chad	392	12.57
Gambia	423	13.56
Guinea	311	9.97
Total	*3,119*	*100*

Source: Authors' work (2022).

Table 4.2. Characteristics of Participants ($n = 3{,}119$).

Variables	Indicators	N	%
Marital status	Divorced	105	3.37
	Married	2,158	69.19
	Single	459	14.72
	Widowed	397	12.73
Education status	Senior Secondary Certificate Examination (SSCE), National Certificate Examination (NCE)	296	9.49
	Higher National Diploma	933	29.91
	Bachelor of Arts, Bachelor of Science, Bachelor of Technology	951	30.49
	Master of Arts, Master of Science, Master of Technology	151	4.84
	Doctor of Philosophy	26	0.83
	Others	762	24.58
Nature of employment	Government employed	491	15.74
	Privately employed	1,151	36.90
	Self-employed	1,176	37.70
	Others	301	9.65
Religion	Christianity	1,265	40.56
	Islamic	1,587	50.88
	Others	267	8.56

Source: IBM SPSS, Version 20 (2022).

the participants were educated (60.4%) and will be able to understand the issue of female genital mutilation. Hence, any information extracted from the participant will be reliable. Regarding the nature of employment and religion, it was revealed from the study that majority of the participants were privately employed (37.70%) and self employed (36.90%), and were Muslim (50.88%) as shown in Table 4.2. This implies that the majority of the participants have financial control.

4.2 Influence of Education on the Practice of Female Genital Mutilation

This study revealed a correlation value of 0.362 which implies a positive and weak association between education among females and the practice of female genital mutilation in West Africa, as shown in Table 4.3. This correlation value implies that the degree of education among females in West Africa accounts for 36.2% of the practice of female genital mutilation. Hence, the level of education among female may not necessarily predict the practice of female genital mutilation in West Africa. Similarly, there is significant difference ($0.041 < 0.05$) between education among female and the practice of female genital mutilation in West Africa. This indicates that as females get more enlightened and educated, they will have more information, and this will reduce the practice of female genital mutilation in West Africa.

Table 4.3. Correlation of the Relationship Between Education, Culture, Religious Belief, Health Conditions, and Practice of Female Genital Mutilation in West Africa.

Predictors	The Practice of Female Genital Mutilation	Significance	Decision at 5% Significance
Education	0.362 (Weak relationship)	0.041	Reject H_0
Culture	0.754 (Strong relationship)	0.023	Reject H_0
Religious belief	0.398 (Weak relationship)	0.038	Reject H_0
Health of victims	0.723 (Strong relationship)	0.001	Reject H_0
$N = 3,119$			

Source: SPSS output (2022).

4.3 Influence of Culture on the Practice of Female Genital Mutilation

This study revealed a correlation value of 0.754 which implies a positive and strong association between culture of females and the practice of female genital mutilation in West Africa as shown in Table 4.3. This correlation value implies that the degree of cultural practices in West Africa accounts for 75.4% of the practice of female genital mutilation. Hence, it can be inferred that culture was a substantial factor that influences the practice of female genital mutilation in West Africa. Similarly, there is a significant difference ($0.023 < 0.05$) between culture and the practice of female genital mutilation in West Africa. This implies that the increasing level of culture that supports female genital mutilation, so does the practice of female genital mutilation increases in West Africa.

4.4 Influence of Religious Belief on the Practice of Female Genital Mutilation

This study revealed a correlation value of 0.398 reveals a positive and weak association between religious belief and the practice of female genital mutilation in West Africa. This implies that the level of religious belief in West Africa accounts for 39.8% of the practice of female genital mutilation. Similarly, there is a significant difference ($0.038 < 0.05$) between religious belief and the practice of female genital mutilation in West Africa. Hence, as females are more deepened in religious activities, so does the practice of female genital mutilation in West Africa being impacted (See Table 4.3). The practice of female genital mutilation in West Africa can be reduced if head of religious organisations preaches against such act.

4.5 Health Implication of the Practice of Female Genital Mutilation

The correlating coefficient of 0.723 demonstrates a good and substantial association between victims' health and the practice of female genital mutilation in West Africa. This is an indication that the health of female victims in West Africa accounts for 72.3% of the practice of female genital mutilation. At $0.001 < 0.05$, this data shows that there is significant difference between the practice of female genital mutilation and the health problems of the victims in West Africa, which implies that if the practice of female genital mutilation increases, the health condition of female will become worsened (see Table 4.3).

5. DISCUSSION

The association between education level and the practice of female genital mutilation was 0.362, according to the findings. This suggests a favourable low association between education and female genital mutilation practice. This suggests that education has little influence on the practice of female genital mutilation in West Africa. This discovery was not surprising given that an individual's ethnic culture or custom may occasionally take precedence over their educational level. This finding agrees with the Integrated Regional Information Networks (IRIN) position, which states that despite being aware of the complications associated with FGC, educated Maasai men and women continue to practice it and that an uncircumcised girl is seen as one who cannot find a husband and thus faces rejection and isolation from the community, regardless of how highly educated or well-positioned a Maasai woman may be social.

This research contradicted the findings of Ahinkorah (2021), who discovered that highly educated women and their spouses in Chad have a preference for female genital mutilation. This contradicts Sherif, Ahmed, and Mostafa's (2018) claim that education improves knowledge and prognosis of female genital mutilation in Nigeria. Findings on the association between female genital mutilation culture and practice reveal a correlation value of 0.754, indicating a positive and strong relationship between the culture and practice of female genital mutilation in West Africa. This suggests that the culture of the people has a substantial effect on female genital mutilation. This finding is not surprising given that the people's culture acts as the Norm of that society and so affects their attitude and behaviour. This agrees with Ofor's (2018) contention that culture has a role in the humiliating effects on the dignity of girls exposed to female genital mutilation (including infants, adolescents and adults).

The association between religion and female genital mutilation is 0.398, indicating a positive and low relationship between religion and female genital mutilation practice. This means that as people are more rooted in religious belief, so does the practice of female genital mutilation in West Africa. This finding was unsurprising given that religion is a collection of beliefs and doctrines designed to mould individual's mentality and attitude toward doing what is proper and acceptable in the eyes of the one they worship. There is no text in the Holy Bible promotes female genital mutilation in the Christian religion. This result agrees with the findings of Ahmed et al. (2018), who demonstrated that there is no link between Islam and FGM. Also, there is not a single scripture in the Holy Quran that supports FGM; in fact, the Holy Quran has many passages that condemn any behaviour that endangers mankind. This study contradicts the findings of Ali (2021) and Ashimi, Aliyu, Shittu, and Mole (2019), which revealed that religion is a substantial predictor of female genital mutilation among Chadian women and girls.

The dominating factor that influences the practice of female genital mutilation is culture, which can also influence religion. Regarding culture, women will be made to belief that FGM is essential and parents will impose the practice of FGM on children that seems to percieve FGM as a wrong practice. It is pertinent to note that culture can influence the religious beliefs we hold because the place of our birth and our cultural environment heavily influence our behaviour; hence, if the practice of FGM is largely embraced by culture, it will be felt in religious belief as some beliefs will not completely preach against it.

Findings of female genital mutilation practices and effects on the health of victims show a correlation value of 0.723, indicating a positive and high relationship between the practice of female genital mutilation and the health consequences of victims. This demonstrates the extent of the issues involved with female genital mutilation. This outcome was predictable given that female genital mutilation is carried out or done by an unskilled practitioner using unsterile devices in an unsterile setting. It is sometimes performed without anaesthetic or painkillers.

According to WHO (2020), the immediate health consequences of female genital mutilation include tetanus, injury to surrounding genital tissue, genital tissue swelling, severe pain, death, excessive bleeding (haemorrhage), urinary problems and shock. Furthermore, the study corroborates with the results of Alsibiani and Rouzi's (2016); WHO (2016a, 2016b) which found that women who had genital mutilation experienced sexual dysfunction, including obstetric difficulties. Furthermore, the study supports reports of UNICEF (2018); Wolke and Lereya (2015) which found that sexual psychological difficulties (depression, anxiety, post-traumatic stress disorder, poor self-esteem, and so on), lower sexual satisfaction and an increased chance of birthing complications like haemorrhage.

6. CONCLUSIONS

This study examined religion, culture, and education as factors influencing the practice of female genital mutilation in West Africa, and how the practice of female genital mutilation affects the health of victims in West Africa. Information was gathered through convenience and snowball sampling techniques from 3,119 respondents who were adult females in West Africa.

The study found that there is a significant difference between education and the practice of female genital mutilation, culture and the practice of female genital mutilation, and religious beliefs and the practice of female genital mutilation, among females in West Africa. Culture is the major factor that influences the practice of female genital mutilation; this can also influence religion. The practice of religion is inseparably tied to our cultural habit; hence, if the practice of FGM is embraced by culture, it will be felt in religious belief. It was also established in this study that increasing practices of female genital mutilation, the more associated health issues.

These findings imply that the culture of the people, religious belief and education are critical factors to be considered when discouraging the practice of female genital mutilation. Based on the findings, the following recommendations were suggested:

- Governmental, educational, and religious groups or institutions should embark on public education campaigns concerning the health consequences of female genital mutilation.
- The public should be persuaded to oppose the culture that encourages female genital mutilation, which has both short- and long-term detrimental consequences.
- The general public should be persuaded to abandon the anti-modernity attitude that drives them to continue practising female genital cutting despite the health risks.
- Religious groups (Christianity and Islam) should take the lead in deterring their followers from partaking in female genital mutilation.
- Governments (regional, federal, state, and municipal) are urged to tighten and formulate implementable policies that are aimed at safeguarding the vulnerable population.

REFERENCES

Achia, T. N. (2019). Spatial modeling and mapping of female genital mutilation in Kenya. *BMC Public Health, 14*, 276. doi:10.1186/1471-2458-14-276

Adam, T., Bathija, H., Bishai, D., Bonnenfant, Y. T., Darwish, M., Huntington, D., & Johansen, E. (2016). Estimating the obstetric costs of female genital mutilation in six African countries. *Bulletin of the World Health Organization, 88*, 281–288.

Adeniran, A. O. (2019). Application of Likert scale's type and Cronbach's Alpha analysis in an airport perception study. *Scholar Journal of Applied Science Research, 2*(4), 1–5.

Adeniran, A., Fawole, A., Balogun, O., Ijaiya, M., Adesina, K., & Adeniran, P. (2015). Female genital mutilation: Knowledge, practice and experiences of secondary schoolteachers in North Central Nigeria. *South African Journal of Obstetrics and Gynaecology, 21*(2), 39–43.

Adeniran, A. S., Fawole, A. A., Balogun, O. R., Ijaiya, M. A., Adesina, K. T., & Adeniran, I. P. (2018). *Female genital mutilation/cutting: Knowledge, practice and experiences of secondary school teachers in North Central.*

Ahinkorah, B. O. (2021). Factors associated with female genital mutilation among women of reproductive age and girls aged 0–14 in Chad: A mixed-effects multilevel analysis of the 2019–2018 Chad demographic and health survey data. *BMC Public Health.* doi:10.1186/s12889-021-10293-y

Ahmed, H. M., Kareem, M. S., Shabila, N. P., & Morzi, B. Q. (2018). Knowledge and perspectives of female genital cutting among the local religious leaders in Erbil governorate, Iraqi Kurdistan region. *Journal of Reproductive Health, 15*, 44. doi:10.1186/s12978-018-0459-x

Akinsanya, A., & Babatunde, G. (2017). Intergenerational attitude change regarding female genital cutting in Yoruba speaking ethnic group of southwest Nigeria: A qualitative and quantitative enquiry. *Electronic Journal of Human Sexuality, 14.*

Ali, A. A. (2021). Knowledge and attitudes of female genital mutilation among midwives in Eastern Sudan. *Reproductive Health, 9*, 23.

Alo, O. A., & Gbadebo, B. (2017). Intergenerational attitude changes regarding female genital cutting in Nigeria. *Journal of Women's Health, 20*(11), 1655–1661.

Alsibiani, S. A., & Rouzi, A. A. (2016). Sexual function in women with female genital mutilation. *Fertility and Sterility, 93*(3), 722–724.

Arseneault, L. (2017). The long-term impact of bullying victimization on mental health. *World Psychiatry, 16*(1), 27–28.

Ashimi, A., Aliyu, L., Shittu, M., & Mole, T. (2019). A multicentre study on knowledge and attitude of nurses in West Africa concerning female genital mutilation. *European Journal of Contraceptive and Reproductive Healthcare, 19*, 134–140.

Babalola, O. E., & Fasiku, A. M. (2015). Youth empowerment: A panacea to sustainable democracy in Nigeria. *IOSR Journal of Humanities and Social Science, 20*(12), 33–39.

Babatunde, M. G., Adetokunbo, T. S., Rotimi, F. A., Mobolaji, M. S., Adeniyi, F. F., & Ayo, S. A. (2021). Cohort analysis of the state of female genital cutting in Nigeria: Prevalence, daughter circumcision and attitude towards its discontinuation. *BMC Women's Health, 21*, 182. doi:10.1186/s12905-021-01324-2

Baiocco, R., Santamaria, F., Lonigro, A., & Laghi, F. (2014). Beyond similarities: Cross-gender and cross-orientation best friends in a sample of sexual minority and heterosexual young adults. *Sex Roles, 70*(3–4), 110–121. doi:10.1007/s11199-014-0343-2

Baldry, A. C., Farrington, D. P., & Sorrentino, A. (2017). School bullying and cyberbullying among boys and girls: Roles and overlap. *Journal of Aggression, Maltreatment & Trauma, 26*(9), 937–951.

Barlett, C., & Coyne, S. M. (2014). A meta-analysis of sex differences in cyber-bullying behavior: The moderating role of age. *Aggressive Behavior, 40*(5), 474–488.

Barzilay, S., Klomek, A. B., Apter, A., Carli, V., Wasserman, C., & Hadlaczky, G. (2017). Bullying victimization and suicide ideation and behavior among adolescents in europe: A 10-country study. *Journal of Adolescent Health, 61*(2), 179–186.

Bauerband, L. A., & Galupo, M. P. (2014). The gender identity reflection and rumination scale: Development and psychometric evaluation. *Journal of Counseling and Development, 92*(2), 219–231. doi:10.1002/j.1556-6676.2014.00151.x

Behrendt, A., & Moritz, S. (2005). Posttraumatic Stress disorder and memory problems after female genital mutilation. *American Journal of Psychiatry, 162*, 1000–1002.

Berer, M. (2018). The history and role of the criminal law in anti-FGM campaigns: Is the criminal law what is needed, at least in countries like Great Britain?. *Reproductive Health Matters, 23*, 145–157.

Berg, R. C., & Denison, E. (2020). A tradition in transition: Factors perpetuating and hindering the continuance of female genital mutilation/cutting (FGM/C) summarized in a systematic review. *Health Care for Women International, 34*, 837–859.

Bhana, D., & Mayeza, E. (2016). We don't play with gays, they're not real boys they can't fight: Hegemonic masculinity and (homophobic) violence in the primary years of schooling. *International Journal of Educational Development, 51*, 36–42.

Bockting, W. O., Miner, M. H., Swinburne Romine, R. E., Hamilton, A., & Coleman, E. (2013). Stigma, mental health, and resilience in an online sample of the US transgender population. *American Journal of Public Health, 103*(5), 943–951. doi:10.2105/AJPH.2013.301241

Bogale, D., Markos, D., & Kaso, M. (2018). Intention toward the continuation of female genital mutilation in Bale Zone, Ethiopia. *International Journal of Women's Health, 7*, 85–93. doi:10.21747/IJWH.S74832

Bogale, D., Markos, D., & Kaso, M. (2019). Prevalence of female genital mutilation and its effect on women's health in bale zone, Ethiopia: A cross-sectional study. *BMC Public Health, 14*, 1076. doi:10.1186/1471-2458-14-1076

Bradford, J., Reisner, S. L., Honnold, J. A., & Xavier, J. (2013). Experiences of transgender-related discrimination and implications for health: Results from the Virginia transgender health initiative study. *American Journal of Public Health, 103*(10), 1820–1829. doi:10.2105/AJPH.2012.300796

Contreras, D., Elacqua, G., Martinez, M., & Miranda, Á. (2016). Bullying, identity and school performance: Evidence from Chile. *International Journal of Educational Development, 51*, 147–162.

Dey, A. (2019). Others within the 'others': An intersectional analysis of gender violence in India. *Gender Issues, 36*, 357–373. doi:10.1007/s12147-019-09232-4

Diop, N. J., & Askew, I. (2015). The effectiveness of a community-based education program on abandoning female genital mutilation/cutting in Senegal. *Studies in Family Planning, 40*, 307–318.

Dovlo, D. (2007). Migration of nurses from sub-saharan Africa: A review of issues and challenges. *Health Services Research, 42*, 1373–1388. doi:10.1111/j.1475-6773.2007.00712

Dye, C., Reeder, J. C., & Terry, R. F. (2020). Research for universal health coverage. *Science Translational Medicine, 5*(199). doi:10.1126/scitranslmed

Epundu, U. U., Ilika, A. L., Ibeh, C. C., Nwabueze, A. S., Emelumadu, O. F., & Nnebue, C. C. (2018). The epidemiology of female genital mutilation in Nigeria: A twenty-year review. *Africa Medical Journal, 6*(1), 1–10.

Ezenyeaku, C. C., Okeke, T. C., Chigbu, C. O., & Ikeako, L. C. (2017). Survey of women's opinions on female genital mutilation in South East Nigeria: Study of patients attending antenatal clinic. *Annals of Medical and Health Sciences Research, 1*(1), 15–20.

Fahmy, A., El-Mouelhy, M. T., & Ragab, A. R. (2016). Female genital mutilation/cutting and issues of sexuality in Egypt. *Reproductive Health Matters, 18*, 181–190. doi:10.2307/25767373

Fund, U. N. C., & Gupta, G. R. (2020). Female genital mutilation/cutting: A statistical overview and exploration of the dynamics of change. *Reproductive Health Matters, 21*, 184–190.

Galukande, M., Kamara, J., Ndabwire, V., Leistey, E., Valla, C., & Luboga, S. (2018). Eradicating female genital mutilation and cutting in Tanzania: An observational study. *BMC Public Health, 15*, 1147. doi:10.1186/s12889-015-2439-1

Garba, I. D., Muhammed, Z., Abubakar, I. S., & Yukasai, I. A. (2021). Prevalence of female genital mutilation among female infants in Kano, West Africa. *Archives of Gynaecology and Obstetrics, 286*(2), 173–178.

Geoffrey, T., Peter, G. O., Gatobu, C., & Pauline, T. (2018). Socio-cultural factors influencing the practice of female genital cut among the Maasai community of Kajiado central sub-county, Kenya. *International Journal of Innovation and Scientific Research, 13*(1), 186–192.

Integrated Regional Information Networks (IRIN). (2005). The controversy of female genital mutilation. U.N Office for the Coordination of Humanitarian Affairs. www.irinnews.org

IRIN. (2005). Female genital mutilation amongst the Maasai community of Kenya razor's Edge - the controversy of female genital mutilation/cut. http://www.irinnews.org/InDepthMain.aspx?in-depth =15andReportId=62470

Jacobson, D., Glazer, E., Mason, R., Duplessis, D., Blom, K., & Mont, J. D. (2018). The lived experience of female genital cutting (FGC) in Somali-Canadian women's daily lives. *PLoS One, 13*(11), e0206886. doi:10.1371/journal.pone.0206886

Kandala, N. B., & Komba, P. N. (2018). Geographic variation of female genital mutilation and legal enforcement in sub-saharan Africa: A case study of Senegal. *The American Journal of Tropical Medicine and Hygiene, 92*, 838–847. doi:10.4269/ajtmh.14-0074

Kaplan, A., Forbes, M., Bonhoure, I., Utzet, M., Martín, M., & Manneh, M. (2020). Female genital mutilation/cutting in the Gambia: Long-term health consequences and complications during delivery and for the newborn. *International Journal of Women's Health, 5*, 323–331. doi:10.21747/IJWH.S42064

Kaplan, A., Hechavarría, S. M., Martín, M., & Bonhoure, I. (2017). Health consequences of female genital mutilation/cutting in the Gambia, evidence into action. *Reproductive Health, 8*, 26.

Klomek, A. B., Sourander, A., & Elonheimo, H. (2015). Bullying by peers in childhood and effects on psychopathology, suicidality, and criminality in adulthood. *The Lancet Psychiatry, 2*(10), 930–941.

Koster, M., & Price, L. (2008). Rwandan female genital modification: Elongation of the Labia minora and the use of local botanical species. *Culture, Health and Sexuality, 10*(2), 191–204. doi:10.1080/13691050701775076

Ladan, S. Y. (2019). An analysis of contemporary security in Katsina state. *Direct Research Journal of Social Science and Education Studies, 6*(7), 95–102.

Mahmoud, M. I. H. (2016). Effect of female genital mutilation on female sexual function, Alexandria, Egypt. *Alexandria Journal of Medicine, 52*(1), 55–59.

Mboho, K. S., & Raphael, U. E. (2018). Gender and violence against women in Nigeria: A socio-psychological perspective. *International Journal of Sociology and Anthropology Research, 4*(5), 29–37.

Mshelia, I. H. (2021). Gender-based violence and violence against women in Nigeria: A sociological analysis. *International Journal of Research and Innovation in Social Science (IJRISS), V*(VIII).

Mwatsiya, I., & Rasool, S. (2021). We need to understand the whole story: A discursive analysis of the responses of informal support networks to help seeking by women experiencing abuse from men in a small South African Town. *Gender Issues.* doi:10.1007/s12147-021-09286-3

Myhill, A. (2017). Measuring domestic violence: Context is everything. *Journal of Gender-Based Violence, 1*(1), 33–44.

Nadama, M. U. (2019). Armed banditry and internal security in Zamfara. *International Journal of Scientific Engineering and Research, 10*(8).

National Bureau of Statistics. (2018). *Multiple indicator cluster survey 2016-2017, survey findings report.* National Bureau of Statistics.

Nigeria Demographic and Health Survey. (2019). *With the financial and technical assistance of ICF International.*

Nwankwo, O. C. (2020). *A practical guide to research writing: For students of research enterprise* (Revised 5th ed.). Uniport Publishing Ltd.

Obi, S. N. (2019). Female genital mutilation in south-east Nigeria. *International Journal of Gynecology and Obstetrician, 84*(2), 183–184.

Odu, B. K. (2008). The attitude of undergraduate females toward genital mutilation in a Nigerian University. *Research Journal of Medical Sciences, 2,* 295–299.

Ofor, M. (2018). Female genital mutilation: The place of culture and the debilitating effects on the dignity of the female gender. *European Scientific Journal, 11*(1), 112–121.

Ogbazi, J. N., & Opara, J. (2019). *Writing a research report: Guide for researcher in education the social and humanities.* Enugu.

Plo, K., Asse, K., Sei, D., & Yenan, J. (2019). Female genital mutilation in infants and young girls: Report of sixty cases observed at the General Hospital of Abobo (Abidjan, Cote D'Ivoire, West Africa). *International Journal of Pediatrics,* e837471. doi:10.1155/2019/837471

Rafferty, Y. (2020). International dimensions of discrimination and violence against girls: A human rights perspective. *Journal of International Women's Studies, 14,* 1–23.

Rasheed, S. M., Abd-Ellah, A. H., & Yousef, F. M. (2017). Female genital mutilation in Upper Egypt in the new millennium. *International Journal of Gynecology & Obstetrics, 114,* 47–50.

Rasool, S. (2022). Adolescent exposure to Domestic violence in a South African city: Implications for prevention and intervention. *Gender Issues, 39,* 99–121. doi:10.1007/s12147-021-09279-2

Rodriguez, M. I., Seuc, A., Say, L., & Hindin, M. J. (2016). Episiotomy and obstetric outcomes among women living with type 3 female genital mutilation: A secondary analysis. *Reproductive Health, 13,* 131. doi:10.1186/s12978-016-0242-9

Rosen, N. L., & Nofziger, S. (2019). Boys, bullying, and gender roles: How Hegemonic masculinity shapes bullying behavior. *Gender Issues, 36,* 295–318. doi:10.1007/s12147-018-9226-0

Rufa, I. M. A. (2017). Vigilante groups and rural banditry in Zamfara state: Excesses and contradictions. *International Journal of Humanities and Social Science Invention (IHSSI), 7*(6), 65–73.

Salihu, H., August, E., Salemi, J., Weldeselasse, H., Sarro, Y., & Alio, A. (2021). The association between female genital mutilation and intimate partner violence. *BJOG: An International Journal of Obstetrics and Gynaecology, 119,* 1597–1605. doi:10.1111/j.1471-0528.2021.03481

Serour, G. I. (2016). The issue of re-infibulation. *International Journal of Gynecology & Obstetrics, 109*(2), 93–96.

Sherif, M. A., Ahmed, Z. E., & Mostafa, A. A. (2018). Awareness and predictors of female genital mutilation/cutting among young health advocates in Nigeria. *International Journal of Women Health, 7*(2), 259–269.

Sipsma, H. L., Chen, P. G., Ofori-Atta, A., Ilozumba, U. O., Karfo, K., & Bradley, E. H. (2021). Female genital cutting: Current practices and beliefs in Western Africa. *Bulletin of the World Health Organization, 90,* 120–127, 8.

Smokowski, P. R., Evans, C. B., & Cotter, K. L. (2014). The differential impacts of episodic, chronic, and cumulative physical bullying and cyberbullying: The effects of victimization on the school experiences, social support, and mental health of rural adolescents. *Violence & Victims, 29*(6), 1029–1046.

UNICEF. (2022). *UNICEF warns FGM on the rise among young Nigerian girls.* Retrieved from https://www.unicef.org/nigeria/press-releases/unicef-warns-fgm-rise-among-young-nigerian-girls

United Nations International Children Educational Fund (UNICEF). (2018). *Children's and women rights in Nigeria: A wake-up call. Situation assessment and analysis of harmful traditional practice.* UNICEF Publication.

Vahida, N. (2022). Understanding the rise of sexual violence in India. *Journal of Gender and Violence Research, 6*(1), pp. 9–27.

WHO. (2016a). Study group on female genital mutilation and obstetric outcome: Female genital mutilation and obstetric outcome: WHO collaborative prospective study in six african countries. *Lancet, 367*(925), 1835–1841.

WHO. (2016b). *WHO Guidelines on the management of complications of female genital mutilation.* Retrieved from https://extranet.who.int/rhl/guidelines/who-guidelinesmanagement-health-complications-female-genital-mutilation

WHO. (2017). *Female genital mutilation: Fact sheet.* Retrieved from http://www.who.int/mediacentre/factsheets/fs241/en/

WHO. (2020). *Female genital mutilation: Economic costs of treating health complications of FGM.* Geneva.

Wolke, D., & Lereya, S. T. (2015). Long-term effects of bullying. *Archives of Disease in Childhood, 100*(9), 879–885.

World Health Organization (WHO). (2008). Eliminating female genital mutilation: An interagency statement. *OHCHR, UNAIDS, UNDP, UNECA, UNESCO, UNFPA, UNHCR, UNICEF, and UNIFEM.* http://whqlibdoc.who.int/publications/2008/9789241596442_eng.pdf

Yirga, W. S., Kassa, N. A., Gebremichael, M. W., & Aro, A. R. (2021). Female genital mutilation: Prevalence, perceptions, and effect on women's health in Kersa district of Ethiopia. *International Journal of Women's Health, 4*, 45–54. doi:10.21747/IJWH.S28805

Yoder, P. S., Noureddine, A., & Arlinda, Z. (2004). Female genital cutting in the demographic and health survey: A critical and comparative analysis. *DHS Comparative Reports, 7*(3), 300–301.

Zayed, A. A., & Ali, A. A. (2021). Abusing female children by circumcision is continued in Egypt. *Journal of Forensic and Legal Medicine, 19*, 196–200. doi:10.1016/j.jflm.2017.12.013

CHAPTER 5

GENDER-BASED VIOLENCE IN NORTH-WEST NIGERIA

Oluwadamisi Toluwalase Tayo-Ladega
and Joseph Olanrewaju Ilugbami

ABSTRACT

Northwest Nigeria is mostly populated by the Hausa and Fulani ethnic groups. Social inclusions and gender equality are listed among the fundamental rights. They are essential for human being to put up their best efforts in resolving all difficulties without restraint. Nonetheless, these rights are frequently withheld in many nations within the African continent, owing to ignorance, religion and custom fanaticism. In spite of these constraints, the northern Nigeria is faced with security issues such as persistent cattle rustling which ultimately evolved into armed banditry, which have exacerbated some lingering issues that revolves around children and women. This study attempts to examine the nature of the crisis that may relates to gender-based issues in Zamfara state. The article relied mostly on secondary literature. Evidences proved that security difficulties have worsened the living circumstances of women and girls in the understudied state, thereby espousing women and girls to dangerous attacks and hard living.

Keywords: Gender; violence; sexual; security challenges; Zamfara; North-west Nigeria

LIST OF ABBREVIATIONS

ECOWAS—Economic Community of West African Countries
FGM—Female Genital Mutilation
GBV—Gender Based Violence

Innovation, Social Responsibility and Sustainability
Developments in Corporate Governance and Responsibility, Volume 22, 99–115
Copyright © 2024 Oluwadamisi Toluwalase Tayo-Ladega and Joseph Olanrewaju Ilugbami
Published under exclusive licence by Emerald Publishing Limited
ISSN: 2043-0523/doi:10.1108/S2043-052320230000022005

1. BACKGROUND

Gender-based violence (GBV) is any form of the destructive act committed against a person or society based on their gender (Bauerband & Galupo, 2014; Bradford, Reisner, Honnold, & Xavier, 2013). According to empirical studies, the majority of rapists and other kinds of sexual assault are adults of age 18 and 25. The oldest among them (in the age bracket of 30 years) barely engage in this conduct, this is because of the ideology that enchantment would be neutralised if they engage in any form of sexual assault regardless of the gender; as a result, they refrain (Mwatsiya & Rasool, 2021). However, in certain cases, both seniors and mature people commit sexual assault while intoxicated by narcotics and alcoholic beverages (Elliott, 2012; Rosen & Nofziger, 2019). It is pertinent to note that there are reports of male being victims of bisexuality and homosexuality (Beasley, 2008; Dey, 2019); therefore it is not only children and women that are usually defenceless when faced with this assault (Berlan, Corliss, Field, Goodman, & Austin, 2010; Myhill, 2017; Omeiza, 2021).

It is essential to note that both man and woman can fall victim of domestic gender violence as a result of ignorance, and drug influence. Gender-based violence has emerged as a significant societal issue (Arseneault, 2017; Aseltine, 2009; Barlett & Coyne, 2014; Barzilay et al., 2017; Bhana & Mayeza, 2016), drawing the attention of professionals and researchers all around the world (Bockting, Miner, Swinburne Romine, Hamilton, & Coleman, 2013). Because of the phenomenon's varied nature and hazards, many specialists have launched a rigorous examination into the numerous indices causing gender-based violence, its frequency of occurrence, reoccurrence and difficulties (Klomek, Sourander, & Elonheimo, 2015). The effect of gender-based violence on girl-child is that they often end up in silence and weeping.

Although there are multiple scholarly works on the GBV (Rasool, 2022), it seems to be a general issue (Contreras, Elacqua, Martinez, & Miranda, 2016; Davis & Nixon, 2014). Some of which is influenced by socio-cultural believes which is the major suspect when identifying the factors that causes frequent gender sensitive violence in a specified jurisdiction (Pascoe & Bridges, 2016; Tukur, 2013). As a result, previous researchers have identified forms of abuse, frequently involving one or more forms of violence and brutality against girls and women (Butler, 2007; Card, Stucky, Sawalani, & Little, 2008). Some of these abuses that are more prevalent in Zamfara are kidnapping, killings and banditry.

The acts of GBV include rape, genital mutilation for females, forced marriages, modern domestic slavery, child trafficking, among others (Davis & Nixon, 2014; Olaiya, 2020). On the other hand, some of the existing studies on GBV such as Baiocco, Santamaria, Lonigro, and Laghi (2014), Paechter (2007), Hamburger, Basile, and Vivolo (2011) cannot provide a comprehensive picture of the problem or draw broad conclusions on a regional or national scale (Baldry, Farrington, & Sorrentino, 2017; Smokowski, Evans, & Cotter, 2014). Gender-based violence happens in several regions of Nigeria (World Bank Group, 2019), such as the violent extremism happening in the north-western

Nigeria. The case of kidnapping of Bethel Baptist High School student in Kaduna State, Nigeria is a clear evidence of gender based violence.

There are certain to be diverse origins, nature of the problem, and implications on society (Baiocco, Laghi, Di Pomponio, & Nigito, 2012; Wolke & Lereya, 2015). As a result, the essence of this study is to investigate cases of GBV in Zamfara State in-line with the various challenges happening in the 21st century. Because of its harmful consequences, rising pace, and prevalence, violence against girls and women is becoming a severe societal concern in recent times, and the fact that female population accounted for more than half of Nigerian population as accounted by Bakare, Asuquo, and Agomoh (2010), this study dwells only on GBV on females. This social crisis is exacerbated in locations where there are civil wars, political crises, community conflicts, banditry and so on.

Lethal armed banditry is dominant in the rural areas of Zamfara, these armed banditry has swept from the rural to the urban areas of Zamfara state including Zamfara which is the capital. They are faced with rapes, child abuse, abductions, among others which have lasted for more than 20 years. It is quite worrisome that little attention has been paid on its documentation of gender related issues, particularly on violence against girls and women. As a result, the need to investigate certain elements of the impact of violence on the girl child and women becomes necessary. This research will focus on some selected districts in Kaura Namoda local government areas (LGAs) in Zamfara state such as Dogon Kade, Kungurki, Kurya, and Sabon Gari, and Sakajiki districts. These districts were focused because of the high level of violence and attacks recorded.

The study is aimed at assessing the implication of insecurity on gender-based violence in Zamfara State with a view of proposing some mitigating measures to address this ugly trend. This research will assist academics, government and non-governmental organisations, parents and victims of gender-based violence, and other stakeholders on approaches to end gender-based violence in the region as it is being preached.

2. METHODS

The study took a multi-disciplinary approach because of the social and multi-dimensional characteristics of this research. The research dwelled more on review of relevant published documents on the subject matter.

3. STUDY AREA

Nigeria comprises 36 states and six geopolitical zones. One of the geopolitical zones is North West, which comprises seven states (Jigawa, Kaduna, Kano, Katsina, Kebbi, Sokoto and Zamfara) (Hassan, Steenstra, & Udo, 2013). The size of the North West zone, which is 216,065 sq. km, or 25.75% of the country's total land area, is comparable to the United Kingdom (International Crisis

Group, 2020). The Hausa and Fulani, two of its two largest ethnic groups, have long had close cultural links and are heavily intermingled with other, smaller ethnicities, particularly in Kaduna state (Adeniran & Owoeye, 2018). Based on data from the controversial 2006 census, the region's estimated 33 million inhabitants is mostly Muslim (Sunni). About 80% of the people work as farmers, pastoralists, agro-pastoralists or small business owners. There are significant solid mineral reserves in the area, including gold mined by artisanal miners in open pits (Adeniran & Owoeye, 2018; International Crisis Group, 2020).

The North West of Nigeria has Nigeria's highest rate of poverty despite its economic potential. As of 2019, all seven states in the zone have poverty rates higher than the national average of 40.1%, with Sokoto, Jigawa, and Zamfara having the highest rates (80.7, 87.7 and 74%, respectively) (Adagba, Ugwu, & Eme, 2012). Numerous people lack access to clean water and basic healthcare, and vaccination rates are substantially below government targets (Hassan et al., 2013). The region has a rich and proud heritage of Islamic and Arabic study, but throughout the years, there has been indifference towards and inadequate investment in formal education, which has resulted in a literacy rate of only 29.7% (International Crisis Group, 2020). The zone now has Nigeria's highest percentage of out-of-school children (Adeniran & Owoeye, 2018). Millions of children attend the underfunded and poorly monitored Quranic school system, known as almajiranci, which results in cohorts of youngsters with low skill levels in addition to those who do not attend school at all (International Crisis Group, 2020; Adagba et al., 2012). The region, like the rest of the nation, has very bad local government that is characterised by the improper use of public monies (International Crisis Group, 2020).

Federal and provincial authorities face significant obstacles as a result of the geology and climate of the area. Savannah makes up the majority of the North West, although there are also enormous woodlands scattered across the area, some of which are home to thousands of primarily Fulani herders (also known as pastoralists) (Mohammed, Abba, & Abba, 2016). These forests, which were once under the supervision of forestry officials, progressively turned into havens for criminals such as livestock rustlers, highway robbers, kidnappers and cannabis farmers. The Kamuku forest is now referred to as 'Sambisa' by people in Kaduna state, implying that it has become just as hazardous as the Borno state forests, where Boko Haram built its stronghold (Azazi, 2019). Additionally, the region shares almost two-thirds of Nigeria's 1,497 km of international border with the poorly governed Niger Republic (Siegle, 2020). Smugglers and criminals now have chances because to regional regulations on freedom of movement, historical and cultural linkages between communities on both sides, and these relationships. Numerous unauthorised crossings and widespread corruption of border guards allow the trafficking of illegal goods like weapons (Medina & Hepner, 2013).

The North West of Nigeria has seen waves of violence over the past 40 years, including sectarian battles, Islamist terrorism and election violence. Numerous Christian-Muslim and intra-Muslim clashes occurred there between 1980 and 2010 (Mohammed et al., 2016). Boko Haram carried out many bombings and killings in Kaduna and Kano states between 2011 and 2015, most notably the 20

January 2012 assaults in Kano city, which left over 185 people dead (Siegle, 2020). In 2011, protests in 14 northern states, including all seven north-western states, erupted into ethnic and sectarian riots that left over 1,000 people dead and 74,000 displaced after the incumbent, Goodluck Jonathan, a Christian from the Niger Delta, defeated then opposition candidate Muhammadu Buhari, a Muslim from the far northern Katsina state (Onapajo & Uzodike, 2021). Recurrent violence, often with considerable casualties, has arisen from a decades-long conflict between the Hausa and Fulani and a number of smaller ethnic groups in southern Kaduna state for political posts, financial resources and the benefits of government investment (Azazi, 2019).

The North West has also experienced a rise in violence more recently, beginning in 2011 and rising since 2014, between farmers supported by community and state-sponsored vigilantes and pastoralists and associated armed organisations commonly referred to as 'bandits' on the one side. The situation has been made worse by the growth of dangerous criminal gangs, which are prospering in an area that is overrun with weapons and that state security services are unable to control (Onapajo & Uzodike, 2021). The violence, which predominately affects rural regions, began in Zamfara state and has now expanded to Kano, Kaduna, Katsina, Kebbi, and Sokoto states in the North West as well as into Niger state in North Central Nigeria. Although accurate death toll statistics are not available, various accounts indicate that at least 8,000 people have been killed between 2011 and the present, largely in Zamfara state and mostly over the last five years (Adeniran & Owoeye, 2018). Jihadist organisations are gradually but steadily increasing their presence in the area, capitalising on the security problems and rise in crime (Elesin, 2019). This study dwelled mostly on gender-based violence in Zamfara State, Nigeria.

4. EMPIRICAL REVIEW

Adebayo (2003) conducted a comparative study of family violence against women in formal and informal business sectors in Ibadan metropolis. It was revealed that GBV affect women in all social classes but lower class women especially full-time housewives and those working in the informal sector are more prone to GBV than those in the middle and upper classes especially those working in the formal sector. This is agreed in the study of Ogunlade et al. (2023) which explored the meanings associated with family violence, the contexts for its occurrence, and the indigenous approaches to managing such conflicts among the Yoruba ethnic subgroup in southwest Nigeria.

Bakare et al. (2010) conducted an empirical review study on domestic violence and Nigeria women. It was revealed in their study that social injustices is domestic violence against women, and that religious belief influences the gender roles imposed on women by African culture and practices. Ibekwe, Kareem, Akpoti, and Ejiyooye (2022) conducted a study on the experience of violence against women and girls in southwest, Nigeria, and found that violence against women and girls was more among the older women than the younger women.

Ezeilo and Ohia (2006) sampled 2000 respondents, comprising 1,052 females and 948 males to study the impact of torture on female gender in Nigeria. They found that different forms of torture were used on females in Nigeria which include, beating, withholding of salary, need denial, suppression, sexual harassment, rape, forced widowhood practice, abusive speech, destructions of property, deprivation, threats and child abuse, to name a few.

Investigation on the socio-cultural superiority and inferiority of male and female genders were examined by Mboho and Raphael (2018). The study also investigates GBV against women in Akwa Ibom State, such as forced marriage, female genital mutilation, human trafficking, sexual harassment, physical torture, discrimination and so on. According to the study, there is growing evidence of the harmful influence on violence to children in the household.

Mshelia (2021) investigates GBV in Nigeria from the angle of FGM, rape, verbal abuse, early marriage, beating, humiliation, widowhood practices and sexual harassment, as well as the consequences of the acts. Zakariya (2021) is a global developmental catastrophe that affects both men and women regardless of race, class, culture or colour. Zakariya noted that the high occurrence of GBV in Nigeria is high and worrisome. He noted that rape has resulted in humiliation, mental harm, fear, sadness and guilt in rape victims, all of which have a detrimental impact on them.

Okech (2021) investigated forms and levels of maltreatment that is facing women and young girls by Boko Haram insurgents in Maiduguri, thereby revealing how women were forced to marry men among many issues. Impact of rehabilitation programs run by the public and private stakeholders was conducted. According to Aluko and Okunwa (2019), discrimination and limits are indications of systemic violence and inequality, both of which challenge the security of women. Despite the awareness and presence of human rights in the country, the rights of women and girl are widely undermined, as evidenced by the country's overall low Gender Development Index and exacerbated by the prevalence of early or forced, sexual and physical assault, marital rape, trafficking, marriage, and various stages of harrowing. Women's opportunities for advancement continue to elude them because of these practices.

The patterns of migration between Nigeria and Africa was examined by Olarinde (2021). The survey found that there are more than 500,000 Nigerian documented migrants living in other African nations, mostly in Cameroon, Chad and Niger, and suggested that the migration of people in 1960 was extremely high. Currently, female migrants outnumber male migrants. Since 2014, the issue of Boko Haram is a major factor that causes high number of migration into Cameroon and Chad. The study also revealed that 48% of Nigerian migrants in Africa were from Cameroon, Chad and Nigeria. Based on the distribution of migrants, 162,961 migrants were situated in the Republic of Niger, 115,774 migrants were situated in Cameroon, and 13,947 migrants were situated in the Republic of Chad. According to the survey, South Africa would have the biggest number of Nigerian migrants by 2021. The major factor influencing the surge of migration were unemployment, economic hardship, political instability and a lack of basic social amenities such as water and electricity.

Usman and Bawa (2021) conducted a study on migration in the Northwest geopolitical zone of Nigeria, and found that the region has an extensive history of cross-border migration dating back to the pre-colonial era. It was revealed that the migrations were motivated by demographic, religious, political, economic and security considerations. There were population shifts from the rural to urban whereby people seek for greener pastures. The study also demonstrated that economic and social variables play a significant role in informing these shifts.

Based on National Crimes Records Bureau records (NCRB), Nainar (2022) reported a dramatic increase in sexual assault against girls and women in India during the last 20 years, from 2015 to 2017, and revealed that the increase in sexually connected crimes in various Indian states is estimated to be between 30 to 95%. However, this work analogy did not demonstrate any link between these acts of violence and insecurity, which this work on Zamfara is planned to reveal over the research time. Ajayi, Chantler, and Radford (2022) investigated the form of sexual assault suffered by Nigerian women in both Nigeria and England. Their study found that sexual violence against women, sexual assaults, trafficking contributes significantly to migration.

Different scholarly ideas on why systems, organisations, and nations fail by combining economic, political, and historical perspectives to give a strong and persuasive approach to explaining wealth and poverty is conducted by Acemoglu and Robinson (2013). The study also looked at the disparities in wealth and living standards between countries like the United States, the United Kingdom and Germany and poor countries in Sub-Saharan Africa and South Asia. Acemoglu and Robinson's work has provided the foundation for investigating the system and institutional failures in Nigeria, as well as how public sensitisation would impact, transform, or promote values re-orientation towards involvement in nation-building, peace, and economic development in Nigeria.

Botha (2021) investigated the impact of terrorism on women, with a focus on Boko Haram. The study demonstrated that terrorism has gained global attention following the 11 September 2001 attack on the World Trade Centre in New York, New York, by Osama Bin Laden's Al-Qaeda terrorist organisation. Other economic losses include interruptions in commerce, local marketing, and cattle production. Tilewola's efforts have built a foundation for investigating the impact of insecurity on girls and women in the Zamfara areas under consideration in the study work. Emmanuela (2015) discussed how Boko Haram's renowned operations affect internal security and national unity. According to the works, the crisis has caused dread and distrust among numerous Nigerian ethnic groups, notably among the Christian faithful. As a result, the study revealed that the violence has hampered the free migration of Nigerians from the south to the north, notwithstanding the negative effects on the region's economic growth.

Daniel and Jiwul (2020) evaluated many elements that have contributed to Nigeria's underdevelopment, with a focus on security difficulties from 1967 to 2015, taking into consideration the fact that security and peace are Siamese twins for national growth and development. The research studied the setbacks caused by various terrorist organisations in Nigeria throughout the review period and concluded that corruption was the biggest factor affecting national stability in

Nigeria. However, the report did not investigate the influence of insecurity on gender-based abuses, which is the major subject of this research.

Anka (2020), Sadi and Maikwari (2020), Dauran (2020), and Abubakar (2020) discussed Zamfara state's security and development problems from 1996 to 2020. The studies looked at the state's development issues from its inception in 1996 to the present. These issues include ineffective administration, a lack of strategic planning, excessive salary bills, corruption, a misalignment of objectives, the expense of government, insufficient basic infrastructure, and, most importantly, armed banditry and general insecurity.

5. RESULTS

5.1 Rural Banditry in Zamfara State

The act of banditry began in northern Nigeria as a conflict between farmers and herders, which evolved into armed cattle rustling, abduction, and various types of brutality and sexual attacks (Yaba & Sadiq, 2020). Between 2010 and 2015, the local turmoil was transformed into armed banditry. Banditry, genocide, murder, agricultural product destruction, livestock rustling, and abduction have now become serious security concerns in Nigeria's North Western area, notably in Zamfara state (Ladan, 2019). There are several theories and explanations for the reasons and nature of the armed banditry problem in Zamfara state (Nganga, 2008). Some blamed the war on climate change, including declining rainfall quantities, and the 'scarcity' of arable land and pastures (Mande, 2022).

Zamfara is situated in northern Nigeria and shares common porous borders with the Republic of Niger via Kwashabawa and Gurbin Bore in Zurmi Local Government Area of Zamfara State (Mande, 2022). Similarly, some accounts link the war to a battle over 'gold resources', pitting illegal gold miners against residents. The state's mining conglomerates were accused of sponsoring and encouraging unrest in rural villages to deflect people's attention away from their illegal mining and dissuade other local and foreign investors in the Zamfara gold mining business.

Whatever the cause, politicians in the state are to blame, because it is claimed that the increase in rural banditry is the result of the nefarious machinations of the governing party's political opponents, who lost in the 2015 and 2019 elections. Some politicians viewed their defeat as an opportunity for vengeance, financing these criminals to commit various crimes throughout the state (Anka, 2020). In general, banditry has been portrayed as a battle between two groups: farmers and vigilantes on one side and herders and bandits on the other. Climate change, a scarcity of arable agricultural land, and the expropriation of pastoral grazing areas exacerbated competition for pasture and water supplies, resulting in confrontations between farmers and herders. The aftermath of the conflict is the growth of banditry and related crimes.

Other organisations affiliated with the Boko Haram insurgents came into the area and were able to exploit the Zamfara woodland and Katsina State regions to carry out their horrible acts of banditry. Banditry and abduction have grown more perilous as a result of the jihadist activity in the North West. The danger now is that the land will be transformed into a Jihadist base. Women are the primary targets in all circumstances, whether they are kidnapped for ransom or murdered on the scene. Women held in captivity are raped, and some are gang-raped (Adeniran et al., 2015; Ashimolowo & Otufale, 2012).

It is vital to highlight that almost 350,000 square kilometres of the already dry terrain have turned into a desert in the previous 60 years, diminishing agricultural land in Zamfara. Due to a lack of pasture, herders allowed their animals to graze on farmlands, resulting in confrontations between farmers and pastoralists (Mande, 2022). Similarly, the Zamfara civilian administration of 1999 assigned the grazing regions of Zamfara to elite farmers, disturbing the life cycle of the herders in the area, which extended back many decades. This situation gave rise to the actions of bandits who stole household animals for a living. To prevent robbers from stealing early in the crisis, vigilantes established a group to fight such activities, and innocent Fulani herders were ruthlessly slaughtered in the process.

On 7 July 2011, the crisis in Zamfara took a sad turn as vigilantes across the state slaughtered innocent Fulani. At the end of it all, 657 innocent Fulani and bandits were killed. The Fulani gathered together, bought an AK47 rifle and other sophisticated weapons, and started counter-attacks on villages that had participated in their brethren's killing (Nadama, 2019). The problem took on an ethnic dimension, with Hausa vigilantes killing Fulani and Fulani retaliating with attacks (vanguardngr.com, 29 May 2019). The battle had an impact on more than just the Fulani tribes. When their herds were stolen and butchered, some Fulani were victims of cattle rustling.

The Fulani Association of Herders in Nigeria (Miyetti Allah) stated that the bandits' operations had hurt them, since they had lost 30% of their livestock due to the crisis that had occurred (BBC news, 5 July 2020). The truth is that if you are a Fulani man or group with a flock of cattle, you must join or identify with a certain bandit syndicate for the safety of your animals, or you are considered an enemy of the movement (Namadinma, 2022; Rufa'I, 2017). The local bandits use their acquaintance with the environment to recruit foreign pastoralists to terrorise Zamfara. These activities were carried out effectively in Zamfara State since the territory is bordered by woods that extend and link to forests in Niger, Kaduna, Sokoto and the Kebbi States.

These woodlands received little or no government attention in the form of gazetting or monitoring against intruders, notably bandit gangs. Rugu, Rudunu, Dumburum, Dagwarwa, Kamara, Kunduma and Sububu forests, to name a few, have become popular hideouts for criminals (Garba, 2020). There are extensive claims of corruption against state security agents, police, judges, village chiefs, and even certain vigilante groups about the function of state security and other institutions. Due to logistical inadequacies, insufficient resources, and pervasive corruption, the official institutions in charge of providing safety and dispensing justice were unable or refused to bring bandits to justice. The bandits are so brazen that they warn towns of impending attacks and levy illegal fees on farmers seeking access to their farms during planting and harvest seasons.

The irony is that, despite huge investments in military and security operations, the security situation appears to be deteriorating. This is because the struggle against insecurity has been politicised and is being used to generate illegitimate profits, and the massive quantity of money pumped into the defence budget is not justified. Between January and April 2019, the Nigerian Army conducted a variety of operations, including Operation Harbin Kunama, Operation Diran Mikiya, and Operation Puff Adder, to combat banditry in the Northwest, despite informal efforts by security operatives known as vigilantes (Yan Banga and Yan Sakai).

5.2 The Situation of Women and Girl-Children Threatened

Banditry is connected with sexual-assault and kidnapping and on. Robbers attacking communities has now become the norm; bandits visit families and demand money from all members of a household. Finally, they rape ladies and grown-up girls in front of their parents (vanguardngr.com, 29th May 2019). Women and young girls are abducted and transported to the wilderness, where some are raped and others escape unscathed. Whatever predicament they were in, they were only released once the kidnappers were paid a ransom. Because there is little or no government authority in the jungles, they have become a haven for kidnappers.

Some people treat girls as though she was sexually abused, even if she was not. Bandits degrade women and young girls via physical assault, rape, child abuse, and, most horrifyingly, kidnapping across all of Zamfara's hamlets, villages, towns and cities (Bube, 2022). This act has caused students, particularly females, to drop out of school for fear of being assaulted and abducted by hoodlums because no one knows when or where they will strike (Yaba & Sadiq, 2020). It is now a habit for crops of Fulani bandits, hoodlums, and miscreants to visit homesteads in their neighbouring towns and hamlets to abduct matured and pre-matured juvenile girls aged 12–16 years to their jungles for rapes and other associated sexual crimes.

If the Girls become pregnant, the villagers are strongly advised not to attempt to abort the pregnancy. When the bandits' standing orders are disobeyed, impacted families are compelled to pay ransoms ranging from two hundred and fifty thousand to five hundred thousand Naira (₦250,000 to ₦500,000). All indicators point to the bandits' objective of creating a syndicate of children born out of marriage who will be conscripted into the criminal gangs run by the bandits (Bube, 2022; Mande, 2022; Okoli & Okpaleke, 2014). The villagers are also subject to annual mandatory charges for their protection and the right to develop their soil.

This fee often ranges between five and 10 million Naira, depending on the size of the acreage. 5,000,000 and 10,000,000, these taxes the villagers must pay by any means or be disallowed cultivation of their farmlands. These acts of intimidation and assault have been proven further by the United Nations Human Rights Commission Report (2022), which states that Nigeria, Somalia, Afghanistan and Syria are the worst in terms of taking over ungoverned territories, particularly wooded areas (Ladan, 2019). According to the survey, Nigeria is one of the nations with the highest number of internally displaced people as a result of deadly conflict, which has changed the demographics of the afflicted areas.

The categorisation is also based on officially documented cases, according to the paper. It is also assumed that the number of unreported instances is significantly more than the number of legally registered cases (Bube, 2022; Mande, 2022). The nature of settlements in rural Zamfara is centred on family lineages, with individuals settling close to blood relatives in their ancestral homelands near their farmlands. Religion, cultural ties, and occupation are minor influences. People cluster together to form hamlets and villages. These settlement patterns provide the bandits with an edge in committing terror and other sorts of violence against these populations. The villages were unable to mount a concerted response because they lacked contemporary fire guns.

All attempts to take alternative measures, such as ambushing the bandits, inviting Government security forces, or migrating out to safer hideouts, are revealed or reported to the bandits by a group of operatives known as informants. These gangs are commissioned agents that offer intelligence to the bandits on the movements and decisions of security personnel and citizens (Balatti, 2022; Ibrahim, 2021). As a result, rural residents became very exposed to bandit assaults and opted to relocate to nearby metropolitan areas for makeshift, temporary, and permanent housing.

This migration had a significant impact on rural, semi-rural, and urban demographics. Plots of land have become more costly, ranging from 150,000 to 250,000 per 50/50 foot of residential plots located close to Zamfara's semi-urban areas (Nagusau, 2022).

5.3 Impact of Kidnapping, Sexual Assaults and Rural Banditry

Another negative consequence of armed banditry, notably in rural Zamfara, has resulted in a severe socioeconomic setback, particularly in terms of settlement patterns and people's socioeconomic activities. People have been moving and relocating from their ancestral houses to safer regions near metropolitan centres. These migrations have had a significant impact on the affected victims' everyday economic activities (Mande, 2022; Zakari, 2020).

Animal thefts have caused an unprecedented deficit in animal traction since more than 96% of these animals were rustled by armed robbers. There are currently no animals available to plough the regions that cannot be farmed manually. Rural farmers cannot afford the recently imported Chinese land-tilling Machine (Anka, 2020). This dreadful condition has resulted to a significant decrease in food and cash crop output in Zamfara State. Table 5.1 contains case studies of sexual and other types of abuse that made people flee their homes and migrate to safer areas.

In a nutshell, the study found a prevalence of GBV in many forms against women and girls in Zamfara amidst worsened state of insecurity. It can be deduced that insecurity enhances the prevalence of GBV, and both have

Table 5.1. Trend of Sexual Assaults in the Study Areas in the Year 2021.

Female	Married	Gida Guwa/ Kungurki	24/1/21	A married woman was raped day and night by seven bandits. She was released after the payment of Five Hundred Thousand Xaira ransom on the 11th day.
Female	Widow	Kwaladawa/ Sakajiki	5/2/2021	A widow was kidnapped five times and raped several times in the forest after each kidnapped.
Female	Married	Sake/Kurya	26/2/2021	Married woman had always been raped by a group of teenagers who pretended to be bandits using toy guns but were later apprehended and reported to the police in Kasuwa Daji
Females	Splinter and her stepmother	Kwaladawa/ Sakajiki	22/3/21	A group of seven bandits raped the spinster and her step-mother after several injuries inflicted on them consequently to their resistance
Female	Married	Dokau/ Sakajiki	27/3/21	Two women were beaten to a coma, one adult slaughtered an infant and Balki was raped.
Female	Married	Dokau/ Sakajiki	14/7/21	A married woman was kidnapped and raped in the forest and released after 19 hours
Female	Married	Babbar Sabra/ Kungurki	21/7/21	The attempt to rape a married woman failed. Her sister was shot dead
Female	Single	Gidan Dan Kulodo/ Sakajiki	25/7/21	A young lady was kidnapped and taken to Yar-Rigadi bush, raped and released 21 hours later
Female	Widow	Dan Doguza/ Kungurki	17/9/21	Three armed bandits rustled a widow's cattle, raped and left her wounded at 2:37 p.m.

Source: Authors' collation.

undermined well-established moral standards and legal provisions. As a result, gender-based violence is detrimental to the victims' personal development, social coexistence and the general development of society at the local and national levels.

6. DISCUSSION

Following a lengthy period of endurance, suffering and social misery, a considerable number of rural residents were forced to flee to safer lands. These economic developments have resulted in demographic shifts in rural and semi-urban settlement patterns. Some of the men who were unable to evacuate for safety were living in fear and terror (Namadinma, 2022). During the rainy season, the majority of people abandon their homes at night to sleep in their farmlands or on top of trees. These occurrences have resulted in psychological trauma as a result of the terror of bandits' pistol shots, raids, indiscriminate killings, rapes, forced labour, daylight robbery, various types of molestation, obligatory levies and so on (Amusan & Ejoke, 2021).

In the district of Sakaji, there were 428 males and 657 females displaced from their locations; in the district of Kungurki 558 males and 889 females displaced from their locations; in the district of Sakajiki 175 males and 274 females displaced from their locations; in the district of Kurya 20 males and 57 females displaced from their locations; in the district of Galadima Dan Galadima 38 males and 44 females displaced from their locations; in the district of Yankaba37 males and 68 females displaced from their locations; and in the district of Gidan Duwa 28 males and 64 females displaced from their locations.

Other regions with high casualties are only a small percentage of the communities impacted. The cases are also a small sample of the big security assaults in the region (Garba, 2020). Vandalism, sexual assaults, mobile phone theft, horrific murder, kidnappings and unfair levies continue to occur before farmers may plough, till or harvest crops on their agricultural property. Members of the community are powerless, and security forces always arrive at the scene of the conflagration late, after harm has been done and bandits have fled to their enclaves in the forests (Bello, 2018). Food and cash crop output, population mobility and trading activity have all decreased significantly.

7. CONCLUSIONS

The North West has experienced a rise in violence more recently, beginning in 2011 and rising since 2014, between farmers supported by community and state-sponsored vigilantes and pastoralists and associated armed organisations commonly referred to as 'bandits' on the one side. The situation has been made worse by the growth of dangerous criminal gangs, which are prospering in an area that is overrun with weapons and that state security services are unable to control. The violence, which predominately affects rural regions, began in Zamfara state and has now expanded to other states in the North West. As a result of these violent acts, the prevalence of gender-based violence in many forms against women and girls is increasing, and has undermined both well-established moral standards and legal provisions under the Nigerian constitution. As a result, gender-based violence is detrimental to the victims' personal development, social coexistence, and the general development of society at the local and national levels. This research looked at how gender-based violence impacts the potential of women and girls in terms of their ability to contribute to the socio-political and economic development of their communities and the country as a whole. The report also examined the demographic implications of the current crisis.

Based on the findings, it was revealed that there is a need to implement more proactive steps to get to the bottom of these security concerns. The following are some suggestions: the necessity to lower the expense of democratic government in Nigeria; the integration of traditional and contemporary conflict management methods in Nigeria's security architecture by legally empowering traditional rulers; a request for the security system and defence strategy to be reformed in order to be more responsive to Nigeria's requirements and idiosyncrasies; development of existing grazing areas and livestock routes, and provision of rural infrastructure.

AUTHORS' CONTRIBUTION

OTL designed the manuscript and proofread; JOI designed the literature review. All authors have read and approved the manuscript.

REFERENCES

Abubakar, M. (2020). Securing the victims of violent conflicts in Zamfara state and the challenges of socio-political transformation from 1974 to 2019. In I. S. Maishanu, J. M. Kaura, & N. I. Abbas (Eds.), *Conference proceedings on the history of Zamfara kingdom* (pp. 565–569). Sokoto: A Publication of the Faculty of Arts and Islamic Studies, UDUS Press, Usmanu Danfodiyo University.

Acemoglu, D., & Robinson, J. A. (2013). Economics versus politics: Pitfalls of policy advice. *Journal of Economic Perspectives, American Economic Association, 27*(2), 173–192.

Adagba, O., Ugwu, S. C., & Eme, O. I. (2012). Activities of Boko Haram and insecurity question in Nigeria. *Arabian Journal of Business and Management Review, 1*(9), 77–99.

Adebayo, A. (2003). *Family violence against women: A comparative study of families in formal and informal business sectors in Ibadan metropolis.* Nigeria Institute of Social Economic Research.

Adeniran, A., Fawole, A., Balogun, O., Ijaiya, M., Adesina, K., & Adeniran, P. (2015). Female genital mutilation: Knowledge, practice and experiences of secondary schoolteachers in North Central Nigeria. *South African Journal of Obstetrics and Gynaecology, 21*(2), 39–43.

Adeniran, A. O., & Owoeye, A. S. (2018). Logistical study of Boko Haram terrorist in Nigeria: Lessons and way-out. *Journal of Industrial Engineering and Safety, 1*(1), 102. doi:10.0000/JIES.1000102

Ajayi, C. E., Chantler, K., & Radford, L. (2022). A feminist-intersectional analysis of sexual violence experienced by Nigerian human security: Perceptions and implications for development in Nigeria. *African Development, XLVI*(3), 1–9.

Aluko, Y. A., & Okunwa, O. B. (2019). Innovative solutions and women empowerment: Implications for sustainable development goals in Nigeria. *African Journal of Science, Technology, Innovation & Development: AJSTID, 10*(4), 441–449.

Amusan, L., & Ejoke, U. P. (2021). The psychological trauma inflicted by Boko Haram insurgency in the North Eastern Nigeria. *Aggression and Violence, 36*, 07. doi:10.1016/j.avb.2017.07.001

Anka, A. S. (2020). Twenty-three years of Zamfara journey to statehood. In I. S. Maishanu, J. M. Kaura, & N. I. Abbas (Eds.), *Zamfara and the challenges of socio-political transformation from 1974 to 2019, conference proceedings* (pp. 590–597). Sokoto: A Publication of the Faculty of Arts and Islamic Studies, UDUS Press, Usmanu Danfodiyo University.

Arseneault, L. (2017). The long-term impact of bullying victimization on mental health. *World Psychiatry, 16*(1), 27–28.

Aseltine, R. H. (2009). A reconsideration of parental and peer influences on adolescents deviance. *Journal of Health and Social Behavior, 36*(2), 103–121.

Ashimolowo, O. R., & Otufale, G. A. (2012). Assessment of domestic violence among women in Ogun state, Nigeria. *Greener Journal of Social Sciences, 2*(3), 102–114.

Azazi, A. (2019). *Responding to the emerging trends of terrorism in Nigeria, 5th policing executive forum conference proceedings organized by CLEEN foundation.*

Baiocco, R., Laghi, F., Di Pomponio, I., & Nigito, C. S. (2012). Self-disclosure to the best friend: Friendship quality and internalized sexual stigma in Italian lesbian and gay adolescents. *Journal of Adolescence, 35*(2), 381–387. doi:10.1016/j.adolescence.2011.08.002

Baiocco, R., Santamaria, F., Lonigro, A., & Laghi, F. (2014). Beyond similarities: Cross-gender and cross-orientation best friends in a sample of sexual minority and heterosexual young adults. *Sex Roles, 70*(3–4), 110–121. doi:10.1007/s11199-014-0343-2

Bakare, M. O., Asuquo, M. D., & Agomoh, A. O. (2010). Domestic violence and Nigeria women -A review of the present state. *Nigerian Journal of Psychiatry, 8*(2). doi:10.4314/njpsyc.v8i2.57620

Balatti, F. (2022). Age 58, Pastoralist *interviewed* in Kaura Namoda on 1 7th February 2022.

Baldry, A. C., Farrington, D. P., & Sorrentino, A. (2017). School bullying and cyberbullying among boys and girls: Roles and overlap. *Journal of Aggression, Maltreatment & Trauma, 26*(9), 937–951.

Barlett, C., & Coyne, S. M. (2014). A meta-analysis of sex differences in cyber-bullying behavior: The moderating role of age. *Aggressive Behavior, 40*(5), 474–488.

Barzilay, S., Klomek, A. B., Apter, A., Carli, V., Wasserman, C., & Hadlaczky, G. (2017). Bullying victimization and suicide ideation and behavior among adolescents in Europe: A 10-country study. *Journal of Adolescent Health, 61*(2), 179–186.

Bauerband, L. A., & Galupo, M. P. (2014). The gender identity reflection and rumination scale: Development and psychometric evaluation. *Journal of Counseling and Development, 92*(2), 219–231. doi:10.1002/j.1556-6676.2014.00151.x

Beasley, C. (2008). Rethinking hegemonic masculinity in a globalizing world. *Men and Masculinities, 11*(1), 86–103.

Bello, M. (2018). *A study of livestock economy in Zamfara Axis of the Rima Basin Region, 1903–2016.* An Unpublished PhD Thesis. Usmanu Danfodiyo University Sokoto.

Berlan, E. D., Corliss, H. L., Field, A. E., Goodman, E., & Austin, S. B. (2010). Sexual orientation and bullying among adolescents in the growing up today study. *Journal of Adolescent Health, 46*(4), 366–371.

Bhana, D., & Mayeza, E. (2016). We don't play with gays, they're not real boys they can't fight: Hegemonic masculinity and (homophobic) violence in the primary years of schooling. *International Journal of Educational Development, 51*, 36–42.

Bockting, W. O., Miner, M. H., Swinburne Romine, R. E., Hamilton, A., & Coleman, E. (2013). Stigma, mental health, and resilience in an online sample of the US transgender population. *American Journal of Public Health, 103*(5), 943–951. doi:10.2105/AJPH.2013.301241

Bradford, J., Reisner, S. L., Honnold, J. A., & Xavier, J. (2013). Experiences of transgender-related discrimination and implications for health: Results from the Virginia transgender health initiative study. *American Journal of Public Health, 103*(10), 1820–1829. doi:10.2105/AJPH. 2012.300796

Botha, S. (2021). The women and girls associated with Boko Haram: How has the Nigerian government responded? *South African Journal of International Affairs, 28*(2), 263–284.

Bube, A. (2022). Pastoralist, *Interviewed* in Gidan Gobirawa on 1st April 2022.

Butler, J. (2007). *Gender trouble.* New York, NY: Routledge.

Card, N. A., Stucky, B. D., Sawalani, G. M., & Little, T. D. (2008). Direct and indirect aggression during childhood and adolescence: A meta-analytic review of gender differences, intercorrelations, and relations to maladjustment. *Child Development, 79*(5), 1185–1229.

Contreras, D., Elacqua, G., Martinez, M., & Miranda, Á. (2016). Bullying, identity and school performance: Evidence from Chile. *International Journal of Educational Development, 51*, 147–162.

Daniel, A. A., & Jiwul, L. J. (2020). Nigerian security challenges and national unity: Analyzing the causes, impact and treatment. *Fuwukari Journal of Politics and Development, 4*(1), 1–15.

Dauran, A. B. M. (2020). Security and development challenges in Zamfara state: An overview of government efforts to establishment sustainable peaceful coexistence, in Zamfara and the Dey, A. (2019). Others within the 'Others': An intersectional analysis of gender violence in India. *Gender Issues. 36*, 357–373. doi:10.1007/s12147-019-09232-4

Davis, S., & Nixon, C. L. (2014). *Youth voice project: Student insights into bullying and peer mistreatment.* Champaign, IL: Research Press Publishers.

Dey, A. (2019). Others within the 'others': An intersectional analysis of gender violence in India. *Gender Issues, 36*, 357–373. doi:10.1007/s12147-019-09232-4

Elesin, A. M. J. (2019). Tackling the Nigeria security challenges: The islamic Panacea. *European Scientific Journal, 9*(8), 284–295.

Elliott, K. O. (2012). The right way to be gay: How school structures sexual inequality. In E. R. Meiners & T. Quinn (Eds.), *Sexualities in education: A reader* (pp. 158–166). New York, NY: Peter Lang Publishing.

Emmanuela, I. (2015). Insurgency and humanitarian crises in northern Nigeria: The case of Boko Haram. *African Journal of Political Science and International Relations, 9*(7), 284–296.

Ezeilo, J. N., & Ohia, O. E. (2006). *Tortue and the female gender: Report of National Survey on Tortue in Nigeria*. Enugu: Women's Aid Collective (WACOL).

Garba, A. (2020). Age 48, Civil Servant *interviewed* on Gender-Based Violence (GBV) in Shinkafi on 25th, December 2019.

Hamburger, M. E., Basile, K. C., & Vivolo, A. M. (2011). *Measuring bullying victimization, perpetration, and bystander experiences: A compendium of assessment experiences*. Atlanta, GA: Centers for Disease Control and Prevention, National Center for Injury Prevention and Control.

Hassan, M. R., Steenstra, F. A., & Udo, H. M. J. (2013). Benefits of donkeys in rural and urban areas in Northwest Nigeria. *African Journal of Agricultural Research, 8*(48), 6202–6212. doi:10.5897/AJAR12.1947

Ibekwe, O. C., Kareem, A. J., Akpoti, O. O., & Ejiyooye, T. (2022). The experience of violence against women and girls in Southwest, Nigeria. *International Journal of Community Medicine and Public Health, 9*(3), 1202. doi:10.18203/2394-6040.ijcmph20220676

Ibrahim, H. B. K. (2021). Banditry, kidnapping and women in Northern Nigeria. Paper presented at a conference on *Armed Banditry and National Security in Nigeria: Issues, Perspectives and the Way Forward Held at Federal University Gusau on 1st–3rd February 2021*.

International Crisis Group. (2020). Violence in Nigeria's North West: Rolling back the Mayhem. *Africa Report N 288*, 18 May 2020.

Klomek, A. B., Sourander, A., & Elonheimo, H. (2015). Bullying by peers in childhood and effects on psychopathology, suicidality, and criminality in adulthood. *The Lancet Psychiatry, 2*(10), 930–941.

Ladan, S. Y. (2019). An analysis of contemporary security in Katsina state. *Direct Research Journal of Social Science and Education Studies, 6*(7), 95–102.

Mande, A. (2022). Age 63 *interviewed* in SabonGari, KauraNamoda on 6th December 2022.

Mboho, K. S., & Raphael, U. E. (2018). Gender and violence against women in Nigeria: A socio-psychological perspective. *International Journal of Sociology and Anthropology Research, 4*(5), 29–37.

Medina, R. M., & Hepner, G. F. (2013). *The geography of international terrorism: An introduction to spaces and places of violent non-state groups*. Boca Raton, FL: CRC Press.

Mohammed, I., Abba, K., & Abba, I. M. (2016). Stemming the tide of insecurity imposed by the Boko Haraminsurgency on the north East Nigeria: A sociological view point. *Journal of Humanities and Social Science, 21*(12), 52–59.

Mshelia, I. H. (2021). Gender-based violence and violence against women in Nigeria: A sociological analysis. *International Journal of Research and Innovation in Social Science (IJRISS), V*(VIII).

Mwatsiya, I., & Rasool, S. (2021). We need to understand the whole story: A discursive analysis of the responses of informal support networks to help seeking by women experiencing abuse from men in a small South African town. *Gender Issues*. 10.1007/s12147-021-09286-3

Myhill, A. (2017). Measuring domestic violence: Context is everything. *Journal of Gender-Based Violence, 1*(1), 33–44.

Nadama, M. U. (2019). Armed banditry and internal security in Zamfara. *International Journal of Scientific Engineering and Research, 10*(8).

Nagusau, J. (2022). Age 71, Farmer *interviewed* in SabonGari, KauraNamoda on 15th January 2022.

Namadinma, M. (2022). Age 62, Pastoralist *interviewed* in Sabon Gari, KauraNamoda on 6th December 2022.

Nganga, C. F. (2008). *Effects of spread of small arms in Sub-Sahara Africa* (pp. 1–20). Strategy Research Project. Pennsylvania, PA: United States Army War College Carlise Barracks.

Ogunlade, O. B., Olowokere, A. E., Agunbiade, O. M., Olajubu, A. O., Oyelade, O. O., & Irinoye, O. O. (2023). Context and indigenous structures for managing family violence in a Yoruba community. *Qualitative Report, 28*(1), 177–199. doi:10.46743/2160-3715/2023.5310

Okech, A. (2021). *Governing gender: Violent extremism in northern Nigeria*. Reports of the Council for the Development of Social Science Research in Africa, 17th July 2021.

Okoli, C., & Okpaleke, F. N. (2014). Banditry and crisis of public safety in Nigeria: Issue in national security strategic. *European Scientific Journal, 10*(4), 350–362.

Olaiya, T. T. (2020). Killings, kidnapping, banditry hold sway amid covid-19 pandemic. www. researchgate.net. Accessed on 27th November, 2022.

Olarinde, O. (2021). Nigeria-Africa migration dynamics. In E. Obieju & I. A. A. Odimegwu (Eds.), *Nigerian migration dynamics and good governance* (pp. 106–111). Fab Education Books.

Omeiza, N. T. (2021). Banditry in northern Nigeria: An assessment of Kaduna state. paper presented at a conference on Armed Banditry and national security in Nigeria: Issues, Perspectives and the way forward held at Federal University Gusau on 1st - 3rd February Radio France International (2022): 7:00 - 7:330 am GMT News on United Nations Human Rights Commission Report on the Demographic Impact of Violence in the World and Increasing Rate of Internally Displaced Persons, 24th June 2021.

Onapajo, H., & Uzodike, U. O. (2021). Boko Haram terrorism in Nigeria. *African Security Review, 21*(3), 24–39.

Paechter, C. (2007). *Being boys; being girls: Learning masculinities and femininities: Learning masculinities and femininities*. London: McGraw-Hill Education.

Pascoe, C. J., & Bridges, T. (2016). *Exploring masculinities: Identity, inequality, continuity and change.* New York: Oxford University Press.

Rasool, S. (2022). Adolescent exposure to domestic violence in a South African city: Implications for prevention and intervention. *Gender Issues, 39,* 99–121. doi:10.1007/s12147-021-09279-2

Rosen, N. L., & Nofziger, S. (2019). Boys, bullying, and gender roles: How hegemonic masculinity shapes bullying behavior. *Gender Issues, 36,* 295–318. doi:10.1007/s12147-018-9226-0

Rufa, I. M. A. (2017). Vigilante groups and rural banditry in Zamfara state: Excesses and contradictions. *International Journal of Humanities and Social Science Invention (IHSSI), 7*(6), 65–73.

Sadi, S. A., & Maikwari, H. U. (2020). Shariah implementation and proliferation of armed banditry in Zamfara state: A reconnaissance. In I. S. Maishanu, J. M. Kaura, & N. I. Abbas (Eds.), *Zamfara and the challenges of socio-political transformation from 1974 to 2019, conference proceedings* (pp. 549–556). Sokoto: A Publication of the Faculty of Arts and Islamic Studies, UDUS Press, Usmanu Danfodiyo University.

Siegle, J. (2020). Boko Haram and the isolation of northern Nigeria: Regional and international implications. In I. Mantzikos (Ed.), *Boko Haram: Anatomy of a crisis* (pp. 85–91). Bristol, UK: e-International Relations.

Smokowski, P. R., Evans, C. B., & Cotter, K. L. (2014). The differential impacts of episodic, chronic, and cumulative physical bullying and cyberbullying: The effects of victimization on the school experiences, social support, and mental health of rural adolescents. *Violence & Victims, 29*(6), 1029–1046.

Tukur, B. (2013). Perspective on the conflict between farmers and transhumance pastoralists in Nigeria. *Paper Presented at a Conference on Pastoral Security and Development held at N'Djamena on 27–29 May 2013.*

Usman, A. F., & Bawa, A. (2021). Nigerian migration dynamics: North-west perspective. In E. Obieju & I. Odimegwu (Eds.), *Nigerian migration dynamics and good governance* (pp. 37–47). Aroma Awka Fab Education Books.

Vanguard. (2019). *Security in tatters: Government ignored warnings banditry, kidnapping killing will escalate, spread to Katsina, Kaduna, Sokoto* interviewed with Siddique Mohammed, 29th May 2019. Retrieved from vanguardngr.com

Wolke, D., & Lereya, S. T. (2015). Long-term effects of bullying. *Archives of Disease in Childhood, 100*(9), 879–885.

World Bank Group. (2019). *Gender-based violence: An analysis of the implications for Nigeria for women project.* Washington, DC: World Bank.

Yaba, M. I., & Sadiq, L. (2020). *Bandits kills 51 in Kaduna.* Retrieved from https://dailytrust.com/bandits-kills-51-in-kaduna/

Zakari, Y. A. (2020). In I. S. Maishanu, J. M. Kaura, & N. I. Abbas (Eds.), *An appraisal of state of poverty and insecurity in Zamfara state and the challenges of socio-political transformation from 1974 to 2019, conference proceedings.* Sokoto: A Publication of the Faculty of Arts and Islamic Studies, UDUS Press, Usmanu Danfodiyo University (pp. 467–469, 470).

Zakariya, R. I. (2021). An examination of gender-based violence in Africa: A critical analysis of rape culture in Nigeria, A B.Sc. Project submitted to the Department of International Relations and Diplomacy, Baze University "Zamfara state government spent 17 billion on security in seven years". *The Guardian.* Accessed on 18th September 2018.

CHAPTER 6

COVID-19 INDUCED SHIFT IN CSR: AN EMPIRICAL INVESTIGATION

Taral Pathak, Srushti Govilkar and Ruchi Tewari

ABSTRACT

Ample literature is available on the impact of socio-cultural and political conditions on corporate social responsibility (CSR), but the reverse has not been adequately studied. COVID-19 pandemic disrupted humankind and business, but CSR was resilient. COVID-19, an unprecedented crisis, developed into a disaster but had some positives too. In fact, it championed the businesses' role and relationships between businesses and regulators, society, stakeholders, environment at large. Some available literature analyses how CSR metamorphosised itself and disrupted and converged into all similar and associated phenomenon like philanthropy, charity, governance, sustainability, and as a regular business activity. The present research uses mixed methods to analyse the CSR data published by the government of India during COVID-19 years and refer to the firms' disclosures in the CSR reports. Findings offer a nuanced input to the understanding of the impact of COVID-19 on CSR by studying it in a regulated environment where firms emerged as responsible corporate citizens attending to the needs of all the stakeholders. Firms acts of responsibility transcended law and contributed in form of funds (PM relief funds) and other necessary health equipment like PPE kits, oxygen cylinders, masks, sanitizers, vaccines, etc. Interestingly, the government amended the law to include contributions to COVID-19 mitigation as a part of CSR. While the current study is based on a data from a limited time, it lays a ground for future studies analysing the nature of shift (short term or long term) and how changes have impacted the policies (public and organisational policies).

Keywords: CSR; COVID-19 impact; crisis; corporate citizenship; India; Nifty 50 companies

Innovation, Social Responsibility and Sustainability
Developments in Corporate Governance and Responsibility, Volume 22, 117–135
Copyright © 2024 Taral Pathak, Srushti Govilkar and Ruchi Tewari
Published under exclusive licence by Emerald Publishing Limited
ISSN: 2043-0523/doi:10.1108/S2043-052320230000022006

1. INTRODUCTION

The COVID-19 crisis unravelled itself as a devastating pandemic and the world made attempts to curb its ill effects, India as a nation responded with all its might by roping in the entire government machinery, citizens at large, social sector and also the corporates. While each of the agencies acted to the best of its capabilities, the government held charge to mobilise the best of each. The line of duty between businesses and governments is getting blurred and corporates are being asked to go beyond business responsibilities. Unlike what Scherer and Palazzo (2011) stated firms have begun to take up social and political responsibilities that go beyond legal mandates. Several countries around the world saw, the corporate channelize their corporate social responsibilities (CSR) towards COVID-19. In India, where CSR is mandatory, the Ministry of Corporate Affairs (MCA) which regulates and oversees the corporate activities, issued a statement which clarified that funds spent and activities carried out by corporates for COVID-19 would qualify as permissible CSR activity (MCA circular 23.3.2020). This marked a formal call to action for Indian corporates by the Government of India (GoI) during a catastrophic national event.

A crisis is defined as an abnormal situation which entails a high risk to business and may stimulate rapid public policy changes (Al-Dahash, Thayaparan, & Kulatunga, 2016; Alexander, 2003; Hanna Salman Sawalha, Eid Jraisat, & Al-Qudah, 2013; Shaluf, Ahmadun, & Mat Said, 2003). Lighthouse Readiness Group (2015) stated that a crisis is an event that is expected to lead to a dangerous situation, whether it is an emergency or a disaster and if an emergency is not treated in time, it can turn into a disaster (Jorgustin, 2012). Shaluf et al. (2003) argue that an unmanaged crisis could develop into a disaster. Applying the above understanding of crisis, to the COVID-19 situation, we can deduce that it was a crisis that led to a dangerous situation unfolding itself as an emergency and later on as a disaster. The International Federation of Red Cross and Red Crescent Societies (IFRC) defines disasters as 'serious disruptions to the functioning of a community that exceed its capacity to cope using its own resources. Disasters can be caused by natural, man-made and technological hazards, as well as various factors that influence the exposure and vulnerability of a community'. The term disaster has been differently defined by various researchers. Disasters are sudden unforeseen events with natural, technological or social causes that lead to destruction, loss and damage (Al-Dahash et al., 2016; Alexander, 2003; Iyer & Mastorakis, 2006; Jorgustin, 2012; Parker, 1992; UNISDR, 2009).

The GoI formalised the support of private firms by regulating CSR. In 2013, India mandated CSR through Section 135 of the Companies Act 2013. The mandate applied to every firm company (including its holding or subsidiary) with a net worth of ₹500 crores or more, OR turnover of ₹1,000 crores or more, OR a net profit of ₹5 crores or more during the immediately preceding financial year. The CSR law adopted the policy of comply or explain. Schedule VII of the Act listed out a set of activities which would help in an overall development of the nation (refer to Table A7). These activities aligned with the sustainable development goals (SDGs) as listed by UN. However, there was no reference to the role of the firms during a national crisis.

But in 2020, when the world experienced the COVID-19 pandemic, the GOI was quick to make changes to the CSR provisions of the Companies Act 2013. The GoI by modifying the CSR guidelines asked for the support of Indian corporates in managing the COVID-19 crisis. The involvement of the private sector in disaster management is not more than three decades old (Kanji & Agrawal, 2019). Earlier, corporates have responded during disasters like Hurricane Katrina in 2005, September 2011 terrorist attack on the World Trade Center, the 2004 Indian Ocean tsunami and many such instances (Johnson, Connolly, & Carter, 2011). The United Nations (UN) too has recognised private firms as important agents that partners with the government and aids in handling and managing humanitarian crisis. It has laid down guidelines and frameworks under UN Office Coordination of Humanitarian Affairs (OCHA) to foster cooperation and collaboration between the UN and the private sector. The private sector brings in efficiencies in terms of management skills, adequate financial and human resources and ability to engage into disaster mitigation, response as well as recovery activities (Berke, Kartez, & Wenger, 1993; Twigg, 2001).

Recognising the contribution of the corporates in the form of corporate social responsibility and its impact, the Government of India (GoI) introduced some changes in the CSR mandate of 2013, which was addressed by the Ministry of Corporate Affairs (MCA) in the form of FAQs (refer to Appendix 4). These changes were within the context of mitigating the COVID-19 crisis and encouraging the corporates' contribution based on their effectiveness in mitigating crisis. This led to variety of contributions in monetary and non-monetary forms like:

• Funds contributed to the PM-CARES Fund,
• Employees' salary contribution,
• Activities like arranging for healthcare facilities,
• Production of ventilators and PPE kits using the assets of the organisations,
• Employee volunteerism in the form of task forces, etc.

Vinod, Umesh, and Sivakumar (2022) talk about two models of crisis management, reactive and pro-active. They find CSR investments during COVID-19 pandemic move from being reactive to proactive as the pandemic progressed. Pandey (2022) analysed CSR expenditure by Indian companies and noted that COVID-19 has pushed CSR to the forefront in India. Similarly, Garg and Agarwal (2021) conducted an empirical study of CSR in India during the pre-COVID-19 and COVID-19 times and suggested that future research could be conducted to know if CSR policy was actually affected due to COVID-19.

Hence, the current paper aims to analyse the effect of COVID-19 on CSR activities in India. In order to identify any short term changes in CSR activities, we analyse the amount of expense incurred in the pre-COVID-19 times (2019–2020) with the COVID-19 times (2020–2021). We also study the changes in the CSR policies to find any long term shift in CSR due to COVID-19.

The findings of the study would help policy makers in understanding the role of private firms during crises. Whether the changes if any in CSR are at the policy level (long term) or only at the execution level (short term). The chapter adopts a mixed method approach, using both qualitative and quantitative research designs.

2. LITERATURE REVIEW

Business and society share a symbiotic relationship, and businesses are often known to have stepped up to mitigate any disaster related crisis. Johnson et al. (2011) study reveals that most corporations engaged in disaster-related activities because of their instrumental and ethical inclinations. The contribution of the corporates became even more pertinent when the governments failed to mitigate the crisis in emergencies high on management-related activities. These included recovery activities that were reactive and episodic and short-term relief activities, which included financial and in-kind activities for different stakeholder groups. In issues related to health that are comparatively predictable, reaching out to the broader stakeholder group for effective implementation, and collaborative partnerships with NGOs and governments are particularly beneficial. UN OCHA (Office of Humanitarian Affairs) identified the corporate sectors' key contribution and a vital agent along with different governmental and non-governmental bodies to mitigate the crisis. It also laid down a set of principle-based guidelines fostering effective partnerships amongst the corporate sector, government and non-government organisations. COVID-19 outbreak was one such disaster which affected global health, economic and social health. Everywhere people were trying to grapple with the situation while facing losses at the personal and the professional front. However, despite the challenging time, people worldwide remained committed to collectively work together and support each other (Mahmud, Ding, & Hasan, 2021).

3. DISASTER, CRISIS AND CSR

Wang (2008) in their research study claims that our environment is characterised by high uncertainty, risk and turbulence as a result of events called crisis or disasters. What makes them have far reaching and deep impact and implications is that most of the times they are unanticipated. Boin (2009), Robb (2007), Shrivastava, Mitroff and Alpaslan (2013) in their study share that, over time these adverse events experienced a shift in terms of cause, frequency, nature and consequences of the events. Consequently, new challenges have come up which have led to categorisation of these events into 'natural' as an outcome of natural forces like hurricanes, tsunamis, tornadoes, earthquakes, etc. and 'human induced' such as financial system implosion, terrorist attacks, technological failure, corporate scams and scandals, accidents like industrial, nuclear, etc., and health epidemics.

Johnson et al. (2011) conducted a content analysis of Fortune 100 companies' CSR reports, revealing that most corporations engaged in disaster-related activities because of their instrumental and ethical inclinations. The contribution of the corporates became even more pertinent when the governments failed to mitigate the crisis in emergencies high on management-related activities. These included recovery activities that were reactive and episodic and short-term relief activities, which included financial and in-kind activities for different stakeholder groups. In issues related to health that are comparatively predictable, reaching out to the broader stakeholder group for effective implementation, and collaborative partnerships with NGOs and governments are particularly beneficial.

Seeger (1995) attempts to look at crisis scope in terms of practice as well as theory. The research argues that crisis research is broadly guided by two thoughts – management evolved from bureaucracy and process involved in its resolution, and the other is embedded in the decision making process, concerned with the psychological aspects of crisis in term of what the event is being perceived, orientation and the perception of leaders and how it influences their decision making. The study further revealed crisis trends – how each crisis leaves a lesson revealing multiplicity of factors involved and affected within the domains of socio-economic-political, etc. In terms of the scope, crisis brings together practice and concepts together in the form of case based research which attempt to identify propositions, provide operational guideline for crisis and decision making and management.

Based on the argument of perception and decision making, culture does play a role in it. Wang, Anne, and McLean (2016) study explore the individual perceptions to the concept of crisis and strategies used to mitigate and manage the crisis events. It poses interesting questions – How do Indians define crisis? How do they manage it? And what are the implications of culture on their individual approaches to crisis management? As for the perceptions, the study revealed that Indians have a different perception and attitude towards crisis and usually take it as a philosophical way of testing one's resilience and paves the next subsequent path of life which gives strength and lessons to the individual. When it comes to what is considered as a 'crisis event' there are strong reflections of the impact of culture with the focus on family and relationships and performance in academics and in professional life. When it comes to the pertinent aspect of the paper in terms of strategies to handle crisis events, the research reveals three dominant categories – fighting, compromising and avoiding which consist of strategies like – seeking help through professional networks, investing in self-development, situational analysis using various tools like the fishbone analysis, and discussing with people; learning to accept and live the reality, adapting, identifying and living the expectations of the others; explaining the situation to any authority and trusting the authority to take the call, and depending and leaving the situation to God or any other Superpower. This revealed that approach of Indian culture is multi-faceted and has profound influence on individual behaviour and perceptions in crisis situations. The collectivist orientation of the country reflected the family orientation, the power distance reveals strong presence of hierarchy in the system, and a masculinist country driven by competition, achievement and success

Hofstede, Hofstede, and Minkov (2005). Another interesting finding of the study revealed the spiritual inclination as a resolve or approach towards crisis.

Extending the argument of the individual and the organisational connection, Udwadia and Mitroff (1991), in their study, attempt to understand the crisis behaviour and vulnerability of the organisations, and their mitigation by building models. By providing a set of criteria essential for mental activities, and providing a systematic approach of the mind-body problem, the study argues strong patterns of connections between an individual mind and the organisational mind. These patterns are further used to build and develop models which are embedded in the domain of psychoanalysis and interpersonal behaviour. The models of organisational mind are provided to obtain a deeper understanding of the crisis behaviour, and the organisational mind is more complex than the individual mind for the multiplicity of the individual in any organisations increases drastically. Highlighting the importance of multi-perspective model by providing an increased understanding of the organisational mind, it also impacts the predictive power of how the organisational mind reflect and would behave during a particular crisis. The models will further contribute in offering the understanding of the time-related, evolutionary dynamics of the circular and give insights on the profound recursive mental processes which go in an organisational mind related to the crisis and in its environmental interactions.

Pedersen, Ritter, and Di Benedetto (2020) in their study focused on the managerial implications of managing crisis in the context of a business to business. The study revealed five stage model for crisis – pre-crisis normality, emergence, occurrence, aftermath and post-crisis normality. Pre-crisis stage, which incorporates preventive approach based on the prediction and preparation based on the literature review. Emergence of crisis reflect prominent signs of crisis where stronger and focused attempts are in the direction of mitigation of crisis. Crisis aftermath involves rebuilding (recovery and remedy), focusing on extraordinary activities preceding new normality. Post-crisis is more focused on establishing normalcy in its day-to-day operations and functions. Managerial implications to crisis management are high for they are the key stakeholders to operationalise and implement the mitigating strategies. In the crisis phase, managers divide it into relevant sub-crisis with all the five phases. Salespeople have a crucial role to play in terms of crisis, for they can substantially change the perception during crisis with personal meetings and maintaining critical business relationships.

Research on crisis and its management has fragmented which poses a challenge in the domain. Bundy, Pfarrer, Short, and Coombs (2017) in their research attempt to address these issues by proposing an integrative framework for crises and crisis management which is developed from the domains of strategy, organisational theory and behaviour, public relations and corporate communication with the aim of making research in the domain coherent. The study identified two broad perspectives – focusing on the internal dynamics of crisis and focussing on the management of the external stakeholders. These perspectives (internal and external) are applied to three stages of crisis: (1) pre-crisis prevention, (2) crisis management and (3) post-crisis outcomes. Internal perspective for pre-crisis prevention includes organising for reliance, and the role of organisational structure, culture and devising strategy to prepare for a crisis; in the crisis management stage, it involves the essential role of leadership in the management of the crisis by taking the organisations' ability to adapt and change models in emergency situation which facilitates coordination and effective communication and in turn enhancing the efforts of the leadership in the crisis management. In the post-crisis stage, internal perspective is rooted in the organisational learning in order to balance out the social evaluations done by the external perspective. In order to effectively manage a crisis, focused efforts towards mitigation of specific pain points is paramount. External perspective in the pre-crisis stage is focused on fostering positive stakeholder relationships based on reasonable expectations and open communication. This helps to cushion the impact of the crisis to certain aspect given enough trust is being established. In the crisis management stage, external perspective involves stakeholder perceptions – how the stakeholders perceive and react to crisis, and how organisations can influence these perceptions. In order to create a positive perceptions of the stakeholders, it is essential to identify crisis response strategies which involve functional communication, and actions and include information which aid in avoiding harm to the stakeholders. In the post-crisis stage, social evaluations (external perspective) is essential and must prove to be critical to manage the process of social evaluations. Another key element is to take into cognisance the amount of responsibility attributed to the organisation, for higher the responsibility towards organisation deeper the damage.

4. CSR AND COVID-19

Crane and Matten, 2021 argued the need to relook at the value creation and stakeholder identification and prioritise them to look at how value is allocated and reassessed based on the economic resources. Disasters like COVID-19 immediately impact the social obligations of business and affect its operations especially supply chains.

Mahmud et al. (2021) explored the responses of the business towards the pandemic, and re-examined the company's voluntary role in society, during crisis and considered data of companies in the 100 Best Corporate Citizens – 2019 in the United States. Rooted in the stewardship model of CSR, these organisations predominantly responded to three major groups – employees, customers and community. For employees, extra pay for volunteerism, bonus packages for frontline workers, paid leaves and sick pay with healthcare benefits, health assessments and quarantine, PPE kits, work from home/remote working policy were provided. For customers various strategies were adopted to create a customer centric CSR, where the organisations adopted activities which were complementary to their mainstream business. This was reflected by companies like General Mills, Hasbro and 3M, where they began to make food that were required by the masses, tweaked their entertainment offering in order to engage children and families, and boosted their production of N95 respirators to maximum and subsequently increased their global output to double to the rate of

100 million per month, and committed to battle price extorting, fraud and fraudulent activities related to the products and the pandemic outbreak, respectively. Some organisations like Gap Inc., and Ford continued to work during the COVID-19 pandemic despite restrictions by using their existing resources for mitigation of the crisis by providing delivery services of urgent medical supplies like PPE, masks, protective gowns, etc. to the health professionals and hospital staff, and by engaging their researchers, engineers, and suppliers for the mass production of ventilators, masks, respirators, and other essential medical equipment for first responders, public health care professionals and patients battling COVID-19. Resources were also mobilised by Johnson & Johnson with its Janssen Pharmaceutical Companies by developing a potential preventive vaccine against COVID-19. Eighty percent of the companies engaged in relief efforts focused on the global community to tackle the challenges by offering direct relief efforts via cash and in-kind, creating funds, and donating to NFPOs. However, the future implications of the study revealed that there is a need for a new research framework to assess the impact of the pandemic, and the need to take broader stakeholder group into consideration.

Manuel and Herron (2020) study explored CSR and COVID-19 pandemic from an ethical perspective. Using the theories of utilitarianism and deontology, the business response to COVID-19 was categorised in three ways: philanthropic, transformational and negative. Philanthropic responses included medical support, food support to care workers and schools. Newer product innovations on masks, waiving costs of treatment, free technological support for education, health programs, free meals, and pay-cuts taken by the top management. Transformation involved changing traditional products and services to suffice requirements during pandemic, partnerships were fostered to produce or donate ventilators, respirators, increase production of the essential commodities. In the healthcare sector with virtual appointments and consultations, augmented the frequency of clearing and hygiene routines, altered waiting hours, etc. Local businesses transformed their operations by changing the hours of operation, arranged for curb side pickups, and offered delivery services. However, not every business response to COVID-19 was positive, negative responses included hoarding or jacking up prices of and tampering with the masks and PPE kits, promoting faux COVID-19 cures, constrained fund flow in the banking and finance sector, loans not being processed and applicants not communicated clearly. While public expectations and trust from the government in March 2020 was low, it significantly increased given their response and management of the crisis.

Most organisations put employee and community interests at the forefront, which reflected the deontological principles. The study presented different scope for future research by asking pertinent and sharp questions like: Does CSR responses to the pandemic affect the firms' value? Do certain external CSR responses create more value in a pandemic? Will the philanthropic bent of business continue post pandemic?

He and Harris, 2020 studied the impact of COVID-19 on CSR and its marketing philosophy. The study argues that the pandemic offers an opportunity to businesses to conduct genuine and authentic CSR by contributing to the critical global issues and its implications for the same. Using this opportunity, CSR activities can be catalysed for CSR development in the long run, by boosting consumer ethics. Furthermore, it revealed that initially consumers reacted to pandemic by stockpiling, and hoarding goods, while others exhibited altruistic behaviour which presented an interesting interplay between personal - situational and contextual factors. The study concludes by raising a pertinent question on exploring and assessing the long term opportunities and challenges for CSR in the long run, post pandemic.

However the above literature focus on the responses to COVID-19 portrays businesses independently mitigating the crisis, without mentioning or analysing the underlying partnerships and collaborations amongst, business, government, and the NFPOs and the NGOs in action. Raimo, Rella, Vitolla, Sánchez-Vicente, and García-Sánchez's (2021) study highlights the impact that these partnerships have on mitigating the pandemic, by analysing multiple 14 companies listed in the Madrid Stock Exchange. CSR was seen to be broadly contributing to offer food, health and technological support, which were operationalised with the support of NGOs. The NGOs helped to identifying the vulnerable communities, streamline resources offered and ensured that they receive the optimum support.

5. INDIA – CSR AND COVID-19

In 2014, India became one of the first countries worldwide to mandate corporate social responsibility (Mitra, Mukherjee, & Gaur, 2020; Singla, 2018). in their study, elucidate the dynamics of CSR in India within the mandate. The research provided some insights on the organisations' response to the mandate regarding resource allocation, the approach adopted, and what worked and did not. It was observed that the allocation of resources was carried out more efficiently with the focus on creating value for the organisation and society and was identified as voluntary. Furthermore, sporadic and voluntary CSR did not prove to be beneficial to the nation's development, hence the rationale behind the mandate.

Bhatia and Dhawan (2023) trace India's CSR from the traditional philanthropic bent which may have been the likely reason during the pre-mandate era to the post-mandate and how the pandemic impacted it. The study examined the pattern of CSR expenditure post 2013 (CSR mandate) and the change that COVID-19 pandemic brought in. With the policy shift and contributions towards mitigation of the Covid-19 pandemic were considered as CSR expenditure, including the research and development for vaccines and medicines for COVID-19 led to a shift in the CSR (Covid initiatives under CSR, 2021). Big corporates were proactive in announcing their COVID-19-relief contributions even before the amendment of the policy by the government. However, the research void lays in the long term impact of COVID-19 pandemic on CSR expenditure of Indian companies.

Building on the paradigm shift in CSR in India, it becomes important to re-analyse the CSR policy in the light of COVID-19 pandemic, and if the pandemic led to a diversification of CSR (Pandey, 2022). The shift can be charted as the partnerships that happened between the local state administration and organisations, large amounts of donations, surge in scientific research and overwhelming sense of solidarity between human beings. While some the CSR activities were reactive (donations, employee compensation), others were proactive which involved a long-term commitment like developing and adapting new technology (Vinod et al., 2022).

The CSR amendment gave a chance to the organisations, which had failed to do so earlier, to comply with the regulation. Arora, Sur, and Chauhan (2022) studied the impact of CSR on the shareholder value within the context of COVID-19 crisis. It revealed that firms who invested in more CSR activities in 2019 performed better and had better shareholder value than those who invested less. During crisis, investors provided premium valuation to those organisations who had strong corporate governance, and that firms' concerns and proactive response pays off during the distress period. Finally, it concluded that COVID-19 being an exogenous shock to equity value has had a positive relation between shareholder value and CSR activities.

6. DATA AND METHODOLOGY

In order to evaluate and analyse the individual and collective response of companies to COVID-19, we downloaded details of CSR expenditure as submitted to the GOI by Nifty 50 companies. The Government portal (csr.gov.in) provides details of expenditure incurred on different areas as specified by the Companies Act, 2013. We analysed the CSR expenditure of Nifty 50 companies for the year 2019–2020 and 2020–2021. The COVID-19 pandemic broke out in India in the month of March 2020 and hence the data and analysis for the year ended 31/3/2020 (2019–2020) should logically have little or no COVID-19-related CSR spend. The year is almost considered as pre-COVID-19. For tracing COVID-19-related CSR spend for both the years (2019–2020 and 2020–2021), we looked through the data for all the fifty companies and identified key words (refer to Table A5) related to expenses incurred towards COVID-19.

The amount of CSR expenditure incurred, was analysed through various lenses, viz. the sector of CSR investment, the geographical region of implementation and the mode of implementation. The analysis CSR expenditure for these two years will help determine whether CSR pivoted due to COVID-19 therefore establishing a short-term impact of COVID-19 on CSR.

The top five companies that pivoted due COVID-19 were shortlisted and their CSR policy was examined thoroughly for the pre (2019–2020) and post COVID-19 (2020–2021) period. The objective was to find out any shift in CSR at the policy level.

7. RESULTS AND DISCUSSION

The analysis of CSR expenses for both the years revealed that CSR expenditure of only 10 out of 50 companies were impacted in the year 2019–2020. Whereas, for the year 2020–2021 a total of 28 companies reported COVID-19-related expenses under their CSR spend. The total CSR spend and COVID-19-related spend for both the years is given in Table 1.

The involvement of only 10 companies for the year ended 2019–2020 is due to the fact that COVID-19 broke out in India during March 2020 accompanied with a national lock down, which gave very little time for companies to engage in any kind of COVID-19 relief activities before the year ended 31 March 2020. What is however surprising is that only 28 companies used the CSR route for engaging in COVID-19 relief, prevention or management activities. The Ministry of Corporate Affairs (MCA) issued the first clarification on expenditure for COVID-19 care facilities to be considered as CSR activities in January, 2021 and there was sufficient time for companies to revamp their CSR activities to include COVID-19-related outreach programs and awareness campaigns.

We do observe a sectoral impact of COVID-19 on CSR activities when we compare 2019–2020 and 2020–2021. Education was the top CSR-sectoral spend (at 24.06%), followed by Rural Development Projects (19.04%), Health care (13.60%) and contribution to Central Government funds (10.86%) for the year 2019–2020. However, education is replaced by health care as the top sector with health care garnering 27.29%, education comes in second with 24.70%, followed by contribution to Central Government funds (11.86%) and Rural Development Projects (5.83%). What comes out clearly is that COVID-19-related expenditure which was categorised under the sector of health care dominated the CSR activities for the year 2020–2021 and companies transferred funds meant for rural development projects to COVID-19. Table 2 summarises the sector wise allocation of CSR funds for both the years.

CSR activities are carried out directly by the companies, or by trusts and societies set up by the company itself, or by trusts and societies set up by the state or central government or by other implementing agencies. It is observed that the percentage of projects executed by other implementing agencies has shot up from 57.73% to 68.70% in 2020–2021. The usual partner agencies might not have been

Table 1. COVID-19-Related CSR Expenditure of Nifty 50 Companies.

Particulars	2019–2020	2020–2021
Number of companies with COVID-19-related CSR spend	10	28
Number of manufacturing companies	9	18
Number of service sector companies	1	10
Total CSR spend of the above companies (₹ in crores)	1,465	4,140
COVID-19-related CSR expenditure (₹ in crores)	359	1,021
Percentage of COVID-19 expenditure to total CSR expenditure	24.50%	24.66%

Table 2. Sectoral Allocation of Funds.

Particulars	2019–2020	2020–2021
Education	24.06%	24.70%
Rural development projects	19.04%	5.83%
Health care	13.60%	27.29%
Contribution to other central government funds	10.86%	11.86%

able to execute projects during local lock downs and hence companies may have got in touch with other agencies or direct help was rendered to hospitals, make shift medical facilities, etc.

The major geographical locations for CSR activities of companies have also been impacted due to COVID-19. In fact, we can clearly see CSR funds being diverted to those states where the impact of COVID-19 in terms of number of infections and deaths was higher. While the PAN India allocation of funds has reduced from 71.36% to 54.27%, we see that allocation to Uttar Pradesh and Andhra Pradesh doubling and allocations to Gujarat, Maharashtra, and Karnataka increasing incrementally. Details of CSR expenditures of major states is given in Table 3.

A closer look at the companies contributing to COVID-19 during the year 2020–2021 indicates that the top five companies account for 65% of the total funds spent on COVID-19-related CSR activities. Analysing the CSR policies of these five companies (List as per Table 4) will help understand if there is a policy shift due to COVID-19. While these companies contributed heavily for COVID, it is interesting to note that they donated a total of ₹386 crores out of ₹715 crores (amounts to 53.98%) to Prime Minister's Citizen Assistance and Relief in Emergency Situations Fund (PM Cares Fund). Only one company donated to the Chief Ministers Relief Fund. If more than 50% of the money is simply donated to the PM Cares Fund, it should be noted that technically no CSR activities are carried out but corporates are acting as providers of fund.

The top five companies donated a total of ₹386 crores to PM Cares Fund out of a total of ₹715 crores, indicating that 53.98% of the COVID-19-related

Table 3. Geographical Allocation of CSR Funds.

Particulars	2019–2020	2020–2021
PAN India	71.36%	54.27%
Andhra Pradesh	1.37%	7.83%
Uttar Pradesh	2.46%	5.82%
Gujarat	2.36%	3.44%
Karnataka	4.50%	5.09%
Maharashtra	8.63%	12.84%

Table 4. List of Top Five Companies.

Rank	Name of Company
1	Tata Consultancy Services Limited
2	Reliance Industries Limited
3	United Phosphorous Limited
4	Hindustan Unilever Limited
5	Adani Ports and Special Economic Zone

investment was donated to the central government fund. On the other hand, the amount spent directly by the company amounts to ₹283 crores and the amount spent through trusts, NGO'S and other implementing agencies amounted to ₹433 crores. Only one company donated to the CM Relief Fund.

Looking at the geographical spend, the numbers reveal that ₹624 crores were spent PAN India basis and the balance amount (₹91 crores) was spent by the top five companies across four different states, viz. Gujrat and Maharashtra ₹5 crores each, Andhra Pradesh 68 crores and Kerala 12.7 crores.

8. QUALITATIVE FINDINGS

The following themes emerge on analysing the CSR policy and reports of the top 5 companies.

8.1 Ingenuity and Innovation

Through innovative and committed efforts, solutions were found for the challenges raised by COVID-19. These included, converting nitrogen plants into oxygen plants and sharing this knowhow with other private and government organisations, companies with technical know-how and dealing with chemicals and dyes, diverted their mainstream production activities to manufacturing and distributing sanitizers free of cost, using in-company human resource for disinfecting and sanitising public areas through sprayers and sanitising solution and diverting manufacture facilities for manufacturing personal protective equipment (PPE) and distributing it free of cost to front line workers. Companies also offered to use their premises as makeshift hospitals with oxygen and other medical facilities and also using them as isolation centres thereby smartly leveraging corporate assets for the benefit of the society at large. The top 5 companies were large companies and many of them for the first time introduced the work from home option for their employees. They ensured the employee and their families well-being through regular communication and in case of any concerns or issues flagged by the employees the firms offered the support required, e.g., admission in hospitals, provision of oxygen cylinders, home-treatment, delivery of medicines and food packets.

8.2 Community Engagement

A common theme that emerged during COVID-19 was community engagement at various levels. Companies engaged with frontline workers – medical professionals, police officials, sanitation workers, migrant workers and other vulnerable sections of the society. Distribution of food packets, medicines and testing kits, setting up telemedicine centres, covering the cost of vaccination of the community at large and amplifying awareness of benefits of vaccination and creating large scale awareness about protective measures to prevent spread of the virus. Along with this firms also set-up camps to stay for the migrant workers. Providing part-time work like making masks and packing essential items at home was also done to ensure some source of income for the labourers. Several firms also distributed (free or subsidised) digital learning devices to the underprivileged sections of the society because several schools turned online, and a large chunk of the population did not access to learning devices.

8.3 Shift in CSR Focus Areas

For the top five corporates, there is a shift in the focus areas mentioned under Schedule VII of the Companies Act, 2013. Clause (xii) of Schedule VII which is disaster management, including relief, rehabilitation and reconstruction activities, features prominently in CSR policies of corporates post-COVID-19. Earlier CSR policies focused on education and skilling, water, sanitation & hygiene, rural transformation, promoting health and hygiene and nutrition along with environment, arts, heritage and culture. However, apart from the renewed emphasis on 'disaster management' and temporary shift in terms of higher allocation of funds to health care, we do not see shift at the policy level CSR. Table A6 tabulates the COVID-19 induced CSR activities.

9. CONCLUSION

The change in the Companies Act provisions related to CSR during COVID-19 was a call to action for corporates to contribute during the national calamity. This paper analyses the manner in which corporates responded to the call to action.

The findings of the study present the changes brought in CSR practices due to COVID-19. Because CSR was the one of the most positive ways in which businesses presence was felt the results of the quantitative and qualitative analysis reveal that CSR activities had gathered pace. CSR expenditure towards COVID-19 doubled from the previous year and was the highest among all the CSR activities as mentioned under Schedule VII of the Companies Act, 2013. This pivot in CSR activities was a short-term change since a qualitative analysis of the CSR policies revealed no change at a strategic level. Thus, the call to action resulted into a short-term change rather than a long-term shift.

The CSR policy of a few firms also saw the inclusion of 'disaster response', as a head within their CSR purview. But CSR policy of most firms had 'disaster' included earlier which saw action during COVID-19 times. While health became the leading head for CSR expenditure during the COVID-19 year (2020–2021), this was only temporary. As the government machinery gathered its act and was able to make provision of adequate hospitals, medical equipment, vaccines etc. the firms moved back to areas of pre-COVID-19 CSR focus trends.

The response of corporates to the call to action by the government during COVID-19 has implications for governments across the globe. The fact that governments would get support from the corporate sector during an emergency is encouraging, but at the same time, a long-term shift would require more than a change in regulation. A well thought out consultative approach involving all key stakeholders is more likely to result into long term shift in corporate policy.

The long-lasting change which COVID-19 brought for leading firms was the ability to innovate, reengineer and stand up as leaders. Their CSR spending beyond the government set mandate, and support to all the stakeholders was irrespective of their core area of business focus reflected a normative CSR spirit. CSR literature over the last years has been heavily debating the 'instrumental' and 'normative' view, where researchers have found CSR activities being focused on outcome and measurement than being driven by normative goals. The COVID-19 pandemic certainly showed a reflection of normative CSR. The long-term impact of COVID-19 on CSR still needs to be investigated through a longitudinal study.

The analysis reveals a much deeper insight into the resilience of companies and their commitment towards CSR. India experienced one of the most stringent lockdowns in the world for a very long time period, which was implemented by the Centre and the states. With multiple lockdowns across several regions, spanning across different time periods, companies experienced irregular operating patterns, disruptions in supply chain and decline in consumer footfalls. The COVID-19-related CSR spend in India during times of severe financial crunch re-establishes that CSR is well rooted in the Indian ethos of trusteeship model embedded in the Gandhian philosophy and social responsibility model based on the Nehruvian philosophy. This also corroborated by the CRISIL CSR Yearbook 2020, which states that the average CSR spend by the Indian companies was 2.12% of profits with more than half of the companies across sectors spending more than the mandated 2% of profits during fiscal 2020.

REFERENCES

Al-Dahash, H., Thayaparan, M., & Kulatunga, U. (2016, August). Understanding the terminologies: Disaster, crisis and emergency. In *Proceedings of the 32nd annual ARCOM conference*, ARCOM (pp. 1191–1200).

Alexander, D. (2003). Towards the development of standards in emergency management training and education. *Disaster Prevention and Management: An International Journal, 12*(2), 113–123.

Arora, S., Sur, J. K., & Chauhan, Y. (2022). Does corporate social responsibility affect shareholder value? Evidence from the COVID-19 crisis. *International Review of Finance, 22*(2), 325–334.

Berke, P. R., Kartez, J., & Wenger, D. (1993). Recovery after disaster: Achieving sustainable development, mitigation and equity. *Disasters, 17*(2), 93–109.

Bhatia, A., & Dhawan, A. (2021). A paradigm shift in corporate social responsibility: India's transition from mandatory regime to the COVID-19 era. *Social Responsibility Journal, 19*(1), 166–183.

Boin, A. (2009). The new world of crises and crisis management: Implications for policymaking and research. *The Review of Policy Research, 26*(4), 367–377.

Bundy, J., Pfarrer, M. D., Short, C. E., & Coombs, W. T. (2017). Crises and crisis management: Integration, interpretation, and research development. *Journal of Management, 43*(6), 1661–1692.

Covid initiatives under CSR. (2021). KSR & Co - Company Secretaries. Retrieved from https://ksrandco.in/publications/covid-initiatives-under-csr/. Accessed December 8, 2022.

Crane, A., & Matten, D. (2021). COVID-19 and the future of CSR research. *Journal of Management Studies, 58*(1), 280.

CRISIL. (2020). *Doing good in bad times.* CRISIL An S&P Global Company. Retrieved from https://www.crisil.com/en/home/our-analysis/reports/2020/06/doing-good-in-bad-times.html. Accessed December 14, 2022.

Garg, V., & Agarwal, S. (2021). An empirical study on the corporate social responsibility regime in India: Pre-COVID and COVID times. *Review of Market Integration.* doi:10.1177/09749292221093835.

Hanna Salman Sawalha, I., Eid Jraisat, L., & Al-Qudah, K. A. (2013). Crisis and disaster management in Jordanian hotels: Practices and cultural considerations. *Disaster Prevention and Management: An International Journal, 22*(3), 210–228.

He, H., & Harris, L. (2020). The impact of covid-19 pandemic on corporate social responsibility and marketing philosophy. *Journal of Business Research, 116*, 176–182.

Hofstede, G., Hofstede, G. J., & Minkov, M. (2005). *Cultures and organizations: Software of the mind* (Vol. 2). New York, NY: McGraw-Hill.

Iyer, V., & Mastorakis, N. E. (2006). Important elements of disaster management and mitigation and design and development of a software tool. *WSEAS Transactions on Environment and Development, 2*(4), 263–282.

Johnson, B. R., Connolly, E., & Carter, T. S. (2011). Corporate social responsibility: The role of fortune 100 companies in domestic and international natural disasters. *Corporate Social Responsibility and Environmental Management, 18*(6), 352–369.

Jorgustin, K. (2012). Disaster and emergency, What's the difference. *Modern Survival Blog.*

Kanji, R., & Agrawal, R. (2019). Building a society conducive to the use of corporate social responsibility as a tool to develop disaster resilience with sustainable development as the goal: An interpretive structural modelling approach in the Indian context. *Asian Journal of Sustainability and Social Responsibility, 4*(1), 1–25.

Lighthouse Readiness Group. (2015). The difference between a crisis, emergency, and disaster. Retrieved from http://lighthousereadiness.com/lrg/difference-crisis-emergency-disaster/. Accessed May 6, 2015.

Mahmud, A., Ding, D., & Hasan, M. M. (2021). Corporate social responsibility: Business responses to Coronavirus (COVID-19) pandemic. *Sage Open, 11*(1). doi:10.1177/2158244020988710.

Manuel, T., & Herron, T. L. (2020). *An ethical perspective of business CSR and the COVID-19 pandemic.* Society and Business Review.

MCA General Circular. (2020). Ministry of Corporate Affairs. Retrieved from https://www.mca.gov.in/Ministry/pdf/Covid_23032020.pdf. Accessed November 5, 2022.

Mitra, N., Mukherjee, D., & Gaur, A. S. (2020). Mandated CSR in India: Opportunities, constraints, and the road ahead. In *Rethinking business responsibility in a global context* (pp. 193–217). Cham: Springer.

Pandey, A. (2022). Remodelling of corporate social responsibility in India during Covid-19. *International Journal of Law Management & Humanities, 5*(1), 1626.

Parker, D. J. (1992). Flood disasters in Britain: Lessons from flood hazard research. *Disaster Prevention and Management: An International Journal, 1*(1).

Pedersen, C. L., Ritter, T., & Di Benedetto, C. A. (2020). Managing through a crisis: Managerial implications for business-to-business firms. *Industrial Marketing Management, 88*, 314.

Raimo, N., Rella, A., Vitolla, F., Sánchez-Vicente, M. I., & García-Sánchez, I. M. (2021). Corporate social responsibility in the COVID-19 pandemic period: A traditional way to address new social issues. *Sustainability, 13*(12), 6561.

Robb, J. (2007). *Brave new war: The next stage of terrorism and the end of globalization.* Hoboken, NJ: John Wiley & Sons.

Scherer, A. G., & Palazzo, G. (2011). The new political role of business in a globalized world: A review of a new perspective on CSR and its implications for the firm, governance, and democracy. *Journal of Management Studies, 48*(4), 899–931.

Seeger, J. C. (1995). Crisis research: The state of the field. In *International Studies Notes* (pp. 17–22).

Shaluf, I. M., Ahmadun, F. L. R., & Mat Said, A. (2003). A review of disaster and crisis. *Disaster Prevention and Management: An International Journal, 12*(1), 24–32.

Shrivastava, P., Mitroff, I., & Alpaslan, C. M. (2013). Imagining an education in crisis management. *Journal of Management Education, 37*(1), 6–20.

Singla, A. (2018). Corporate social responsibility (CSR) as per companies act, 2013, TaxGuru. Tax Guru. Retrieved from https://taxguru.in/company-law/corporate-social-responsibility-csr-companies-act-2013.html. Accessed December 8, 2022.

Twigg, J. (2001). *Sustainable livelihoods and vulnerability to disasters.*

Udwadia, F. E., & Mitroff, I. I. (1991). Crisis management and the organizational mind: Multiple models for crisis management from field data. *Technological Forecasting and Social Change, 40*(1), 33–52.

UNISDR terminology on Disaster Risk Reduction. (2009). *UNDRR.* Retrieved from https://www.undrr.org/quick/10973. Accessed February 04, 2023.

Vinod, M. S., Umesh, P., & Sivakumar, N. (2022). Impact of COVID-19 on corporate social responsibility in India–a mixed methods approach. *International Journal of Organizational Analysis.* (ahead-of-print).

Wang, J. (2008). Developing organizational learning capacity in crisis management. *Advances in Developing Human Resources, 10*(3), 425–445.

Wang, J., Anne, M., & McLean, G. N. (2016). Understanding crisis and crisis management: An Indian perspective. *Human Resource Development International, 19*(3), 192–208.

APPENDIX 1: KEYWORDS SEARCHED ON THE COMPANY DATABASE

Sr. No.	Keywords
1	Masks
2	PPE
3	COVID-19
4	Corona
5	Isolation centres
6	Food relief for COVID-19
7	Lockdown
8	Sanitiser
9	Sanitisation
10	Oxygen
11	Hospitals
12	Ventilators
13	Food relief
14	Lockdown

APPENDIX 2: BELOW SHOWS THE COVID-19 RESPONSE OF THE DIFFERENT COMPANIES

#	Company	CSR Activity Due to COVID	CSR Policy
1	United Phosphorous Limited (UPL)	Converted the nitrogen plant into an oxygen plant. Knowledge sharing of setting up an oxygen plant through webinars Distributed 50,000 litres of sanitizers, PPE kits Disinfected 7,000 plus villages	CSR policy recognises and states the shift towards contribution to rebuild or provide relief during natural calamities
2	Reliance Industries Limited	Support to community and employees in the form of COVID-19-related health support	No change on the CSR policy. Disaster response was included in the pre-COVID-19 CSR policy as well, but it was found to be operationalised only during COVID
3	Hindustan Unilever Limited		No change on the CSR policy. Disaster response was included in the pre-COVID-19 CSR policy as well, but it was found to be operationalised only during COVID
4	Tata Consultancy Services Limited	Extensive push to work from home for employees. Education and skilling Basic health and wellness Water, Sanitation & hygiene	No change on the CSR policy. Disaster response was included in the pre-COVID-19 CSR policy as well, but it was found to be operationalised only during COVID
5	Adani Ports and Special Economic Zone		CSR policy is not available

APPENDIX 3: SCHEDULE VII

Activities which may be included by companies in their Corporate Social Responsibility Policies relating to:

- Eradicating hunger, poverty and malnutrition, promoting health care including preventive health care and sanitation including contribution to the Swachh Bharat Kosh set-up by the Central Government for the promotion of sanitation and making available safe drinking water.
- Promoting education, including special education and employment enhancing vocation skills especially among children, women, elderly and the differently abled and livelihood enhancement projects.
- Promoting gender equality, empowering women, setting up homes and hostels for women and orphans; setting up old age homes, day care centres and such other facilities for senior citizens and measures for reducing inequalities faced by socially and economically backward groups.

- Ensuring environmental sustainability, ecological balance, protection of flora and fauna, animal welfare, agroforestry, conservation of natural resources and maintaining quality of soil, air and water including contribution to the Clean Ganga Fund set-up by the Central Government for rejuvenation of river Ganga.
- Protection of national heritage, art and culture including restoration of buildings and sites of historical importance and works of art; setting up public libraries; promotion and development of traditional art and handicrafts.
- Measures for the benefit of armed forces veterans, war widows and their dependants.
- Training to promote rural sports, nationally recognised sports, paralympic sports and Olympic sports.
- Contribution to the Prime Minister's national relief fund or any other fund set up by the central govt. for socio economic development and relief and welfare of the schedule caste, tribes, other backward classes, minorities and women.
- Contributions or funds provided to technology incubators located within academic institutions, which are approved by the central govt.
- Rural development projects.
- Slum area development.

(https://www.mca.gov.in/Ministry/pdf/InvitationOfPublicCommentsHLC_18012019.pdf)

APPENDIX 4: MCA CLARIFICATIONS VIA FAQS AS ON 10TH APRIL 2020

- Contribution made to 'PM CARES Fund' shall qualify as CSR expenditure.
- Contribution to 'Chief Minister's Relief Fund' or 'State Relief Fund for COVID-19' shall not qualify as admissible CSR expenditure, as its not included in Schedule VII of the Companies Act, 2013 ('the Act').
- Contribution made to State Disaster Management Authority shall qualify as CSR expenditure under Item No (xii) of Schedule VII of the Act.
- Funds may be spent for various activities related to COVID-19 under Items Nos.(i) and (xii) of Schedule VII of the Act.
- Payment of salary/wages to employees and workers during the lockdown period is a moral obligation of the employers. Hence, such payment shall not qualify as an admissible CSR expenditure.
- Ex-gratia payment made to temporary/casual workers/daily wage workers over and above the disbursement of wages, specifically for the purpose of fighting COVID-19, shall be admissible towards CSR expenditure as a onetime exception, provided there is an explicit declaration to that effect by the Board of the Company, which is duly certified by the statutory auditor.

(https://pib.gov.in/PressReleasePage.aspx?PRID=1613404)

PART 2

DEVELOPING SUSTAINABILITY

CHAPTER 7

HARNESSING THE POWER OF MAURITIUS HEMP FIBRES FOR POLYHYDROXYBUTYRATE BIOPOLYMER SYNTHESIS

Nausheen Bibi Jaffur, Pratima Jeetah and Gopalakrishnan Kumar

ABSTRACT

The increasing accumulation of synthetic plastic waste in oceans and landfills, along with the depletion of non-renewable fossil-based resources, has sparked environmental concerns and prompted the search for environmentally friendly alternatives. Biodegradable plastics derived from lignocellulosic materials are emerging as substitutes for synthetic plastics, offering significant potential to reduce landfill stress and minimise environmental impacts. This study highlights a sustainable and cost-effective solution by utilising agricultural residues and invasive plant materials as carbon substrates for the production of biopolymers, particularly polyhydroxybutyrate (PHB), through microbiological processes. Locally sourced residual materials were preferred to reduce transportation costs and ensure accessibility. The selection of suitable residue streams was based on various criteria, including strength properties, cellulose content, low ash and lignin content, affordability, non-toxicity, biocompatibility, shelf-life, mechanical and physical properties, short maturation period, antibacterial properties and compatibility with global food security. Life cycle assessments confirm that PHB dramatically lowers CO_2 emissions compared to traditional plastics, while the growing use of lignocellulosic biomass in biopolymeric applications offers renewable and readily available resources. Governments worldwide are increasingly inclined to develop comprehensive

Innovation, Social Responsibility and Sustainability
Developments in Corporate Governance and Responsibility, Volume 22, 139–171
Copyright © 2024 Nausheen Bibi Jaffur, Pratima Jeetah and Gopalakrishnan Kumar
Published under exclusive licence by Emerald Publishing Limited
ISSN: 2043-0523/doi:10.1108/S2043-052320230000022007

bioeconomy policies and specialised bioplastics initiatives, driven by customer acceptability and the rising demand for environmentally friendly solutions. The implications of climate change, price volatility in fossil materials, and the imperative to reduce dependence on fossil resources further contribute to the desirability of biopolymers. The study involves fermentation, turbidity measurements, extraction and purification of PHB, and the manufacturing and testing of composite biopolymers using various physical, mechanical and chemical tests.

Keywords: Lignocellulosic biomass; polyhydroxyalkanoate; batch fermentation; Plackett Burman; Box-Behnken design; Mauritius hemp

1. INTRODUCTION

The main materials employed by the packaging industry are based on glass, aluminium, tin and fossil-derived synthetic plastics. Due to the intensifying economic and environmental concerns of these particular materials, eco-friendly substitutes such as cellulose reinforcement are being contemplated. The prolonged adoption of agricultural residues could help solve the unsustainability, costs and disposal challenges that the island is currently facing. Moreover, the incorporation of cellulosic particles into polymer films and bioplastics to control microbial surface contamination of foods, improving food quality and extending shelf-life has gained much attention due to the increasing consumer demand for minimal processed and preservative-free products. Moreover, superior combination of sustainability and safety, design as well as end-use performance improvements make cellulosic reinforced bioplastics an ideal material in applications such as eye glass frames, headphones, covers, lenses, electronics, housings, cosmetic accessories and automotive interior components (Ferrer, Pal, & Hubbe, 2017; Pérez-Arauz et al., 2019). Moreover, products with eco-friendly attributes have gained much recognition during the last decade owing to the consumption of less environmental resources (water and energy), less pollution emission, and effective resource recovery from agro-waste while offering good mechanical properties. Polymer composites with cellulose fibres are being adopted as substitutes for composites containing glass fibres in important applications which include automotive or construction and have found viable applications in biomedical and cosmetic industries, electrical and electronic field, and the paper, and packaging industries. Plant fibres originate from a vast variety of sources and the most common plant fibres that exist in Mauritius are raffia palm, cotton, Mauritius hemp, coconut, Vacoas, pineapple, sisal, flax amongst others (Jaffur & Jeetah, 2019; Jeetah & Jaffur, 2021; Senthilkumar, Siva, Rajini, Jappes, & Siengchin, 2018). This research can significantly contribute to solving environmental pollution problems particularly global warming and greenhouse gas effects, solid waste management challenges, exhaustible reserve supply, intermittent economic rates, unstable geopolitical trends and formation of micro-plastics that induce the death of millions of aquatic animals generated by petrochemical plastics. In addition, the resilience and durability of traditional plastics consist of one major drawback which is its persistence in the environment and thus, rendering it immune to biodegradation. Hence, the production of bioplastic materials such as polyhydroxyalkanoate (PHA) is emphasised as critical to finding solutions to our worldwide environmental concerns and restoring our planet's well-being. Moreover, owing to its potential to breakdown naturally in the environment, the use of PHA is a step closer to a greener environment, intending to reduce reliance on non-biodegradable synthetic plastic. PHAs are compostable, 100% bio-based and biodegradable in anaerobic conditions, soil, freshwater and marine environments. It can be processed with food waste and other organic wastes in composting facilities. Hence, there is a decrease in landfill stress and waste dumping since low-cost non-edible carbon substrate from lignocellulosic biomass are being exploited to create value-added products replacing conventional plastics. Bio-based plastics offer the distinct benefit of reducing reliance on fossil resources, lowering greenhouse gas (GHG) emissions and improving resource efficiency. Furthermore, biodegradable plastics are an important component of the bio-economy. Whilst bioplastics output is relatively minimal in comparison to conventional plastics (approximately 1-2 percent of total world plastics production), the potential for expansion and future innovation and development is considerable. When considering the environmental impact of bioplastics – especially when compared to established conventional plastics – these yet unexplored potentials of the bioplastics sector, as well as the positive environmental and socioeconomic benefits, must be addressed. Since they are based on standardised procedures and standards, ASTM 68636 (biobased/renewable content) and ISO/TS 14067 (reduction of greenhouse gas emissions) are now two important metrics that should be prioritised in sustainability analyses of biopolymers.

The viability of petroleum feedstocks is in jeopardy due to depletable reserve supplies, fluctuating economic rates, uncertain geopolitical tendencies and the hazardous discharge of chemicals such as phthalates and bisphenol A, which have negative effects on human health, the ecosystem and animals. Furthermore, plastics, which are formed of synthetic organic polymers with a high molecular mass originating from hydrocarbons, are key precursors of environmental destruction, particularly global warming and greenhouse gas (GHG) consequences. In addition, a deeper comprehension and awareness of costs and dangers associated with environmental disequilibrium caused by plastic waste products has substantially affected consumer views and behaviours regarding bio-based polymers. To guarantee a risk-free accessibility of resources, there is an increasing need for various kinds of biocomposite products derived from renewable and sustainable ingredients. It is consequently essential to switch to other strategies and resources that are not dependent on fossil fuels, such as the abundant lignocellulosic biomass resources on the island. Straw, bagasse, wasted coffee grounds and wheat bran are emerging as promising for the synthesis of biopolymers such polyhydroxybutyrate (PHB) and polylactic acid (PLA) (PLA). Bio-based polymers may replace standard polymers with comparable physical, chemical, thermal and mechanical qualities, such as polypropylene (PP) and low-density polyethylene (LDPE) (LDPE). Biopolymers significantly enhance characteristics, such as high tensile strength, durability, flexibility, biodegrad-ability, biocompatibility and simplicity of processing, in addition to the possi-bility of building a sustainable polymer business. To achieve ethical compliance, the feedstocks used in biopolymer manufacturing must not interfere with the food supply intended for living beings and must be capable of evolving to accessible carbon matter through upstream cell culture.

2. POLYHYDROXYALKANOATES (PHAS)

Microbial PHA is mainly composed of hydroxyalkanoate monomers linked together through ester linkages. It is biosynthesised as intracellular granular aggregates in response to nutritional imbalances such as nitrogen, phosphate, oxygen, and carbon shortages and surpluses (Berezina, 2013; Dietrich, Dumont, Del Rio, & Orsat, 2019; Jaffur, Jeetah, & Kumar, 2021). The thermoplasticity and biodegradability of microbial PHA are both impressive qualities that it exhibits as a natural macromolecule. Hence, it is regarded to be one of the most promising materials for the development of biodegradable polymers. Multiple substrates, notably monosaccharides, lignocellulosic biomass, sewage sludge and municipal solid wastes, spent coffee beans may be used to create microbial PHA. In recent decades, scientists have discovered that some bacteria can extract PHA from cellulose and hemicellulose, that not only decreases the price of PHA manufacturing but also enables the efficient exploitation of lignocellulosic biomass (Berezina, 2013; Ribeiro Lopes, Azevedo dos Reis, & Almeida, 2017). Fig. 7.1 illustrates the different features and potential applications of PHAs.

3. LIGNOCELLULOSIC BIOMASS

Lignocellulose, which is made up of cellulose, hemicellulose, lignin and other extractives including pectin, ash and protein, is the most commonly accessible resource on the planet. As a result, they are recognised as valuable bioresources for the manufacture of diverse bio-based and value-added products. The per-centage composition of cellulose (40–80%), hemicellulose (10–40%) and lignin (5%–25%) in various plant species varies according to the type of biomass feedstocks such as soft wood, hard wood and straw materials. Cellulose makes up between 40 and 80% of the total mass of the plant, while hemicellulose makes up between 10 and 40% (Chandel & Singh, 2011; Obruca, Benesova, Marsalek, & Marova, 2015; Sánchez, 2009). A prospective source of raw material for the synthesis of biopolymers is waste streams from lignocellulosic-based substrates, which are generated in huge amounts from the agricultural and food industries. Bagasse, being the fibrous residue left behind after the juice has been extracted from sugarcane stalks, has the potential to be a useful waste substrate. This by-product is readily accessible in many parts of the globe, and efforts have been undertaken to convert sugars produced from bagasse into polyhydroxybutyrates (PHBs), the most prevalent form of PHA with a short chain length (Chen, Chen,

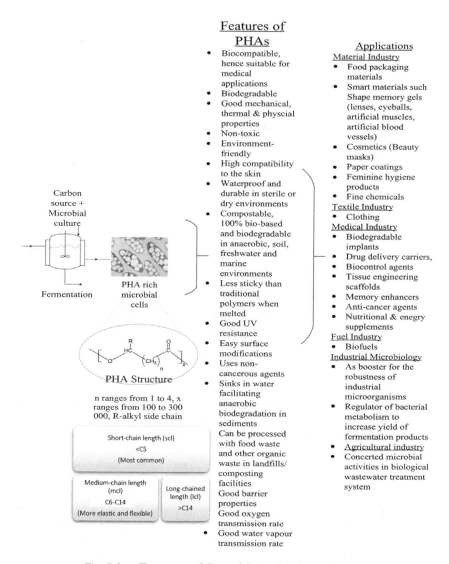

Fig. 7.1.   Features and Potential Applications of PHAs.

Wu, & Chen, 2020). Chemical properties such as cellulose, hemicellulose, lignin, α-cellulose, pectins, fats and wax content, crystallinity indexes, lateral order indexes, hydrogen bonding indexes (Dietrich et al., 2019; Sfiahi, Joshi, & Min, 2020) as well as physical and mechanical properties notably fibre length, fibre fineness, fibre density, tensile strength, young's modulus, specific strength, elongation at break, elongation at failure, moisture absorption in the plant biomass are necessary characteristics for estimating the quality of the carbon source to be fed to the microorganisms for the development of PHB biopolymers. Moreover, criteria such as availability, abundancy, accessibility, shelf-life, growth rate; fast-growing plant with a short maturation period, anti-bacterial attributes (Lobo, Franco, Fernandes, & Reis, 2021), low abrasive and non-toxic nature, biocompatibility, current uses in local context along with cost of extraction are important aspects to consider prior to the adoption of a particular biomass for exploitation in the manufacture of value-added green products (Dietrich et al., 2019; Lobo et al., 2021). In addition, perennial fibres are preferred LCB over annual crops since they are not susceptible to pests and diseases, requires little to no attention from the grower in terms of additional nutrient requirement, fertilisation, pesticides, energy input and financial investment as well as being resilient to changes in weather conditions are desirable criteria to produce good quality and economical products through bioconversion processes (Berg & Steinberger, 2012; Dahmen, Lewandowski, Zibek, & Weidtmann, 2019; Vico & Brunsell, 2018; Visconti et al., 2020). Some commonly available local lignocellulosic biomass are *Cocos Nucifera* husks (coconut husk), *Pandanus Utilis* leaves, Mauritius Hemp leaves, maize husk and leaves, *Arundo Donax* leaves and stalks, and bamboo stalks.

Furcraea Foetida (Aloes in Mauritius) also known as Mauritius hemp or green aloe or giant cabuya is an invasive species that was initially utilised to manufacture ropes, sacks, clothes as well as papers. Other uses involve planting for decorative purposes, as prevention for soil erosion and for medicinal purposes wherein their roots are employed in concoctions for blood purification (Francis, 2004). Nonetheless, the employment of Mauritius Hemp is currently restricted to only artisanal products and decorative purposes. Around 93 tonnes of Mauritius Hemp tow and waste was generated in 2019 in Mauritius which corresponds to 11,204 US$/capita and ended its path at the landfill. Worlwide, 274,603 tonnes of *Furcraea Foetida* fibre was generated. The *Cocos Nucifera* L. plant which is widely available in Mauritius offers various products such as coconut oil, cream, copra, tender meat, coconut water, vinegar, jaggery, syrup, coconut shell-based artisanal products, charcoal and activated carbon. Nonetheless, once the coconut fruit and water are consumed, the husks of these tropical fruits from fruit vendors operating around the island are normally discarded as agricultural or food wastes. These husks can also be found in large quantities at beaches around the island and near the markets. Most of the mentioned plants have limited functions in the control of soil erosion, manufacture of artisanal products such as baskets and souvenirs by a handful of craftsperson while the majority of the leaves which keep on falling on the ground are discarded as agricultural wastes.

4. MARKET PRICE

Production methods, feedstock employed as raw materials, microbial consortia deployed and downstream processing all have significant impacts on the economic value and market price of the completed product. Large-scale commercialisation and extensive industrial expansion of PHAs remain complex due to the increased production costs associated with biopolymers, resulting in considerably larger prices than conventional polymeric materials. Polyhydroxyalkanoates (PHAs) are anticipated to cost between $2.25 and $2.75 per pound, or almost four times as much as more conventional plastics (Kourmentza et al., 2017). However, the rising need for eco-friendly products in the packaging and food markets has prompted an upturn in manufacturing of such items from more cost-effective sources such as biocompostable and biodegradable bioplastics used for a variety of purposes. The expanding PHA industry in the packaging, food, cosmetic, vehicle and biomedical industries is expected to benefit from the rising market demand for bio-based polymers, the implementation of Green Public Procurement (GPP), and circular economy policies. The worldwide PHA market is likely to increase by 11.20% from its current valuation of US$57 million to a projected valuation of US$98 million by 2024, according to market research estimates. The rapid expansion of the bio-based plastic market may be traced back to the rising number of people who are becoming politically and socially active in opposition to the use of conventional plastic goods. Consumers' views and actions towards bio-based polymers have been profoundly impacted by an increased awareness of the dangers posed by plastic waste to the natural world (Bugnicourt, Cinelli, Lazzeri, & Alvarez, 2014; Cinelli, Coltelli, Signori, Morganti, & Lazzeri, 2019; Markets, 2019).

5. PRETREATMENT OF BIOMASS

A number of innovative thermochemical techniques and catalysts have been developed in recent years to depolymerise lignin to various value-added compounds, which has significantly increased the valorisation of lignin (Xu, Xu, Cai, Chen, & Jin, 2021) In spite of this, it is challenging to extract and purify desired components from the hydrolysed lignin solution owing to the variability of lignin. Pretreatment process is an essential method for altering the cellulosic substrate framework into a form that is readily available to be transformed into fermentable sugars by hydrolysis and enzymes. Since lignocellulosic biomass has a recalcitrant nature which renders it very resistant to the release of sugars for fermentation owing to biological degradation, a pretreatment phase is necessary prior to the hydrolysis stage for its transformation into fermentable sugars (Coz et al., 2016; Govil et al., 2020; Gunny, Arbain, & Jamal, 2017; Moreno, Ibarra, Alvira, Tomás-Pejó, & Ballesteros, 2015; Tomás-Pejó, Alvira, Ballesteros, & Negro, 2011). Pretreatment processes have the possibility of improving sugar yields from feedstocks by more than 90% of its theoretical yield and thus preventing the development of sugars inhibitors for following phases of enzymatic hydrolysis or fermentation while also being economical (Brodeur et al., 2011; Foston & Ragauskas, 2012; Hassan, Williams, & Jaiswal, 2018; Pielhop, Amgarten, Von Rohr, & Studer, 2016; Zhang et al., 2019). The aim of this process is to rupture the lignin seal in order to destabilise the crystalline cellulose network (Coz et al., 2016; Dussán, Silva, Moraes, Arruda, & Felipe, 2014; Mosier, Hendrickson, Ho, Sedlak, & Ladisch, 2005; Viikari, Vehmaanperä, & Koivula, 2012). The most suitable approach for the synthesis of sugars is the exploitation of the non-edible part of widely available lignocellulosic fibres to be utilised as feedstock comprising polysaccharides which normally have 25% cellulose and 25% hemicellulose by composition. Nonetheless, complex intermolecular and intramolecular hydrogen bonding present between the cellulose along with lignin and other inter-bonding between the components in the lignocellulosic material renders the direct transformation of lignocelluloses into sugars complex (Azizi, Najafpour, & Younesi, 2017; Dussán et al., 2014; Mosier et al., 2005; Pielhop et al., 2016; Tomás-Pejó et al., 2011). Furthermore, these particular processes operate by making use of additives and energy to extract or discard desired solids such as cellulose, hemicellulose which are far more receptive than the original biomass feedstock while also producing liquid compounds such as oligosaccharides (Mosier et al., 2005; Parawira & Tekere, 2011; Rabemanolontsoa & Saka, 2016; Raghavi, Sindhu, Binod, Gnansounou, & Pandey, 2016) as depicted in Fig. 7.2. Some features of an effective pretreatment process involve optimising of the sugar output from both the cellulose and hemicellulose, preventing the deterioration as well as loss of carbohydrates, and preventing the development of inhibitors for following phases of enzymatic hydrolysis or fermentation while also being economical (Cantarella, Cantarella, Gallifuoco, Spera, & Alfani, 2004; Ingram et al., 2011; Kumar & Sharma, 2017; Pielhop et al., 2016). This chapter explores process specifications and essential mechanisms for some effective pretreatment processes. A good and efficient pretreatment process is distinguished by certain requirements such that it eliminates the necessity to decrease the dimensions of the biomass, upholds the portion of hemicellulosic materials, prevents the development of degradation materials that hinder the activity of microorganisms responsible for fermentation, lessens energy requirements and drives down prices (Chang & Holtzapple, 2000; Govil et al., 2020; Gunny et al., 2017; Lynd, Elander, & Wyman, 1996; Mosier et al., 2005; Tomás-Pejó et al., 2011).

6. PHYSICAL PRETREATMENT OF BIOMASS

The primary objective of the physical pretreatment of lignocellulose is to cause a reduction in the particle size as well as the cellulose crystallinity of the biomass

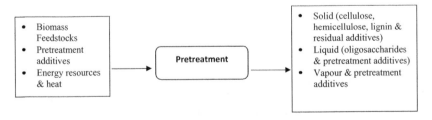

Fig. 7.2.   Schematic Representation for Pretreatment Process.

feedstock (Coz et al., 2016; Dussán et al., 2014; Hu & Ragauskas, 2012; Mtui, 2009; Tomás-Pejó et al., 2011). Physical pretreatment methods include grinding, chipping and milling such as ball milling, two-roll milling, hammer milling, colloid milling and vibro energy milling (Bhaumik & Dhepe, 2016; He, Miao, Jiang, Xu, & Ouyang, 2010; Kourmentza et al., 2017; Liu et al., 2016; Taherzadeh & Karimi, 2008; Yabushita, Kobayashi, Hara, & Fukuoka, 2014; Yuan et al., 2015). Irradiation is also a common technique of physical pretreatment which consists of gamma-ray irradiation, electron beam irradiation and microwave irradiation. Furthermore, some other processes to yield biogas and ethanol as end products are also high pressure, high-temperature hydrothermal, expansion, extrusion, pyrolysis and ultrasonication techniques to enhance the biodegradability of the lignocellulosic biomass (Bhaumik & Dhepe, 2016; Chen, Hong, Yang, & xia, 2013; Coz et al., 2016; Karimi & Taherzadeh, 2016; Kourmentza et al., 2017; Taherzadeh & Karimi, 2008; Yuan et al., 2015). Milling and other types of grinding techniques allow a reduction in the dimension of the lignocellulosic materials. For instance, the size of biomass compounds in the range of 10–30 mm can be reduced to 0.2–2 mm. The decrease in the dimension of lignocellulosic fibres is attributed to the amount of energy consumed as well as the residence time needed for the pretreatment method (Chang & Holtzapple, 2000; Huang, Wu, Kuga, & Huang, 2013; Kourmentza et al., 2017; Liu et al., 2016; Taherzadeh & Karimi, 2008; Zhang, Tsuzuki, & Wang, 2015). Schwanninger, Rodrigues, and Fackler (2011) and Yabushita et al. (2014) reported that ball milling revealed a decrease in cellulosic size, crystallinity, and degree of polymerisation and thus improving the performance and rate of the hydrolysis. In terms of expenditure reduction, milling/grinding was considered to be a good option. Nevertheless, chemical as well as physical pretreatment processes are necessary to achieve better effectiveness.

7. CHEMICAL PRETREATMENT

Chemical pretreatment of lignocellulosic materials is the most effective technique for increasing the cellulose accessibility through the elimination of lignin as well as hemicellulose while also reducing the crystallinity and degree of polymerisation of the cellulosic fraction of the biomass matrix (Agbor, Cicek, Sparling, Berlin, & Levin, 2011; Coz et al., 2016; Dussán et al., 2014; Isaac et al., 2018; Rabemanolontsoa & Saka, 2016). This process has been widely employed in the pulp and paper industry for delignifying lignocellulosic fibres for the production of packaging, writing materials, cups, plates amongst others (Amode & Jeetah, 2020; Buxoo & Jeetah, 2020; Jaffur & Jeetah, 2019; Ramdhonee & Jeetah, 2017). Furthermore, certain chemical substances that were identified to depict no negative impact when interacted with the natural framework of lignocellulosic biomass were observed to also not generate any harmful compounds for subsequent post-pretreatment processes and would react at ambient conditions (Behera, Arora, Nandhagopal, & Kumar, 2014; Mtui, 2009). Chemical pretreatment can be achieved by using acid, alkali, ozone, or other organic solvents

(Baruah et al., 2018; Bhaumik & Dhepe, 2016; Dussán et al., 2014; Mosier et al., 2005).

7.1 Alkaline Pretreatment

Alkaline or lime pretreatment can be accomplished through chemicals such as sodium hydroxide (Silverstein, Chen, Sharma-Shivappa, Boyette, & Osborne, 2007; Wang, Keshwani, Redding, & Cheng, 2010), potassium hydroxide, hydrogen peroxide, sodium hypochlorite, calcium hydroxide, and ammonium hydroxide at low temperature and pressure (Banerjee et al., 2012; Bhaumik & Dhepe, 2016; Wanitwattanarumlug, Luengnaruemitchai, & Wongkasemjit, 2012). The dominant outcome of this particular pretreatment is lignin elimination from the raw material, thereby increasing the responsiveness of the resulting polysaccharides. Furthermore, lime pretreatment processes eliminate acetyl as well as numerous uronic acid substitutions on hemicellulosic fibres leading to a reduction the enzyme's availability to hemicellulose and cellulose (Chang, Burr, & Holtzapple, 1997; Mosier et al., 2005). Throughout this process, the biomass fibres are swollen leading to a reduction in the degree of crystallinity and polymerisation of the pretreated fibres. Moreover, the fibres are observed to experience a higher internal surface area along with a displacement in the lignin framework and a split in the bonding between lignin and other components in the matrix (Behera et al., 2014; Taherzadeh & Karimi, 2008). Sun, Lawther, and Banks (1995) observed that a favourable environment of 20°C for a residence time of 144 h and sodium hydroxide concentration of 1.5% was deemed ideal for delignifying and dissolving the hemicellulose in the biomass matrix. The lime pretreatment can also be carried out for a shorter contact period but the process needs to be monitored at higher temperatures, for instance, alkali can be used to treat wheat straws for 3 hours at a temperature of 85°C and perennial plants for 2 hours at 100°C (Chang et al., 1997; Mosier et al., 2005). A glucose yield of 30% was observed when lignocellulosic fibres were subjected to alkaline hydrolysis at 100°C for 1 h in 18%wt NaOH. Despite the high reaction rate of this technology, low sugar yield was observed and the sugar was exposed to alkali attack which led to its decomposition (Devi et al., 2016).

7.2 Acid Pretreatment

The acid pretreatment of lignocellulosic biomass is a viable and prevailing method for achieving a framework appropriate for further hydrolysis treatments to synthesise sugars. Acidic pretreatment relies on specifications in particular the nature, solute/solvent ratio, solid/liquid ratio as well as temperature of the acid (Behera et al., 2014; Saratale, 2012). Pretreatment with acid involves elevated temperatures and pressures for adequate pretreatment. In addition, dilute acid pretreatment is by far the most efficient method for lignocellulosic materials since it engenders little deterioration in products when compared to concentrated acid pretreatment (Behera et al., 2014; Wyman et al., 2005). It could be employed both as a pretreatment prior to enzymatic hydrolysis of lignocellulosic materials and as a technique for hydrolysing and synthesising lignocellulosic biomass into fermentable sugars in a two-stage acid hydrolysis. López-Arenas, Rathi, Ramírez-Jiménez, and Sales-Cruz (2010) reported that dilute acids having concentration varying between 0.1 to 2 w/v% are typically utilised for a proper acid pretreatment. Devi et al. (2016) reported that a glucose yield of 50–70% can be recovered from LCM when the latter is subjected to <1% sulphuric acid at high temperatures of 215°C for 3 mins. Concentrated acid hydrolysis is based on the foundation that the crystalline cellulosic part of the biomass can be fully hydrolysed within short period of time at low temperatures using 72wt% H_2SO_4, 42wt% HCl or 83wt% H_3PO_4 giving rise to a homogeneous cellulose hydrolysis mechanism (Chen, 2015). Cellulose can be transformed into multiple oligosaccharides throughout the treatment, consisting of mainly cellobiose which is a 4-glucose polymer, glucose oxidase, piranose oxidase and oxy-reductase (Chen, 2015; Kucharska, Rybarczyk, Hołowacz, Łukajtis Rafałand Glinka, & Kamiński, 2018). The first hydrolysis with concentrated acid decrystallises the cellulose in the biomass and when the solution is further diluted with water and the reaction is allowed for a period of time, the oligosaccharides are hydrolysed to reducing sugars, mainly glucose. Wijaya et al. (2014) reported that xylose production decreases with increasing acid concentration while glucose production increases when acid concentration is increased in the range of 70–75 wt%. The most evident advantage of the concentrated acid hydrolysis is the high sugar recovery of approximately 90% can be achieved (Chen, 2015). Acid pretreatment enables xylan (a group of hemicellulose) hydrolysation in lignocellulosic biomass into compounds such as glucose, galactose, mannose as well as acetic acid (Behera et al., 2014; Davies, Linforth, Wilkinson, Smart, & Cook, 2011). The hydrolysed compounds can be further processed into products like furfural and hydroxymethyl furfural at higher pressure and temperature (Behera et al., 2014; Mosier et al., 2005; Zeitsch, 2000). Nonetheless, this process requires high concentrations of chemicals which are difficult to recycle and reuse. Moreover, additional degradation yields phenolic compounds, formic acid and levulinic acid which have adverse impacts on subsequent operations and are necessary to be eliminated. Hence, contributing to increasing expenditure (Chiaramonti et al., 2012; Davies et al., 2011; Kootstra, Beeftink, Scott, & Sanders, 2009).

7.2.1 Two-step Thermochemical Cellulose Hydrolysis With Partial Neutralisation
The hydrolysis of lignocellulosic materials to release fermentable sugars is an essential step that eventually influences the overall efficiency, performance, and yield of the process (Binod, Janu, Sindhu, & Pandey, 2011; Moe et al., 2012). The utilisation of concentrated acid for the development of sugars from lignocellulosic materials has been around for a long period of time. The concentrated acid allows the disruption of hydrogen bonds between the polysaccharide comprising cellulosic linear chains transforming it from a crystalline structure into an amorphous solid. The breakdown of the crystalline structure develops a gelatinous material in the acid (Binod et al., 2011; Shahbazi & Zhang, 2010). Since at this stage, cellulose is highly receptive to hydrolysis, water dilution is carried out at

moderate temperatures in order to ensure optimum and quick hydrolysis to glucose with the least deterioration of simple sugars possible (Binod et al., 2011; Shahbazi & Zhang, 2010; Wijaya et al., 2014). Inorganic acids such as sulphuric acid, phosphoric acid, and hydrochloric acid can be employed in the acid pretreatment. Nonetheless, sulphuric acid has primarily been used as an effective chemical pretreatment for hemicellulose elimination before acid hydrolysis, to improve cellulose digestion into glucose and other components (Goldstein & Easter, 1992; Kim, Lee, & Park, 2000; Mosier et al., 2005; Torget, Werdene, Himmel, & Grohmann, 1990). Hydrolysis employing concentrated acid generally entails two stages to achieve a significant degree of glucose yield. During the first stage which is the pretreatment process, cellulose is decrystallised while in the second stage (post-hydrolysis), cellulose is transformed into glucose as well as other sugars. Requirements include pretreatment of lignocellulosic biomass at a low temperature of 30°C alongside concentrated sulphuric acid having a concentration of 60–72 wt% in sulphuric acid to biomass ratio of 36:1 for a period of 60–120 mins. The mixture is then partially neutralised with 20 wt% sodium hydroxide with an H^+/OH^- molar ratio varying between 2.3 and 2.5 or the acid concentration is diluted to 4wt% at an optimum temperature of 121°C for a period of 0.25 h or at boiling temperature for 3 h (Chang, Duret, Berberi, Zahedi-Niaki, & Lavoie, 2018; Chin, H'ng, Wong, Tey, & Paridah, 2011; Chu et al., 2018). Devi et al. (2016) reported a glucose yield of 90% from lignocellulosic biomass (LCB) when concentrated sulphuric acid between 30 to 70wt% was employed at a mild temperature of 40°C while Cheng et al. (2015) declared that 78–82% sugar could be recovered from water hyacinth treated at 100°C for 0.25 h–2 h. Hence, it can be established that concentrated acid hydrolysis has a high reaction rate, operates at mild temperatures, and provide high sugar recovery from biomass.

7.3 Wet Oxidation

Wet oxidation is an oxidative pretreatment technique whereby oxygen is used as a catalyst to degrade lignin and hemicellulose via the generation of organic acids in a vessel containing 1 L of water for each 6 g of lignocellulosic material at temperatures varying between 148 to 200°C for a time period of 30 minutes. During the process, hemicellulose is dissolved while lignin is degraded into carboxylic acid as well as water and carbon dioxide. It is a very efficient process for isolating cellulose from the other components in the substrate matrix (Brodeur et al., 2011; Coimbra et al., 2016; Palonen, Thomsen, Tenkanen, Schmidt, & Viikari, 2004; Taherzadeh & Karimi, 2008; Varga, Klinke, Réczey, & Thomsen, 2004). Palonen et al. (2004) reported a sugar yield of 79% when wet oxidation was used as pretreatment of LCM followed by enzymatic hydrolysis conducted for 72 h.

7.4 Ozonolysis

Efficient delignification of lignocellulose from biomass feedstocks can be accomplished via ozonolysis process which is the utilisation of ozone to transform the biomass at ambient conditions. This procedure comprises only a slight impact on the hemicellulosic fraction of the biomass matrix (Capolupo & Faraco, 2016;

Neely, 1984; Taherzadeh & Karimi, 2008; Travaini, Otero, Coca, Da-Silva, & Bolado, 2013). In addition, no harmful substances are produced throughout the pretreatment process (Capolupo & Faraco, 2016; Taherzadeh & Karimi, 2008; Travaini, Barrado, & Bolado-Rodríguez, 2016). Following environmental considerations, ozonolysis is a safer approach owing to the quick catalytic decomposition of the ozone at higher temperatures. Nevertheless, the need for a considerable volume of expensive ozone renders the procedure unaffordable (Bhattarai et al., 2015; Bhaumik & Dhepe, 2016; Travaini et al., 2013). Orduña Ortega et al. (2020) reported a maximum yield of 71% when sugarcane straw was subjected to ozonolysis at 80°C for 8 h.

7.5 Organosolv Process

Bond-breaking between hemicellulose and lignin in the biomass matrix can be achieved through organosolvation method whereby various organic solvents (ethanol methanol, acetone, glycerol, aqueous phenol, and triethylene glycol) and inorganic acids (hydrochloric acid, sulphuric acid, lewis acids along with water) are employed to degrade lignin from various lignocellulosic wastes (Behera et al., 2014; Taherzadeh & Karimi, 2008; Zhao, Cheng, & Liu, 2009). Moreover, organic acids such as oxalic acid and salicylic acid are employed as catalysts in the process, and solvents such as ethanol and methanol having lower boiling points are preferred to those having higher boiling points for instance ethylene glycol owing to lower prices (Behera et al., 2014; Capolupo & Faraco, 2016; Mosier et al., 2005; Zhao et al., 2009). In order to render the approach cost-effective, recovery of the organic additives ought to be practicable. Furthermore, organosolvation generates lignin bearing a good which in turn can be utilised to manufacture different useful chemical products. The optimum working temperatures of organosolvation method range between 150 and 200°C. Solvent spent is discharged from the reacting vessel and in order to minimise running costs, the solvent undergoes condensation, evaporation or recovery processes (Borand & Karaosmanoglu, 2018; Capolupo & Faraco, 2016; Pérez-Merchán et al., 2022; Zhao et al., 2009). A maximum glucose concentration of 47.6 mg/L was observed when cassava peels was soaked in 100 ml methanol catalysed by sodium acetate at atmospheric conditions (Olanbiwoninu & Odunfa, 2015).

8. PHYSICO-CHEMICAL PRETREATMENT OF BIOMASS

Physico-chemical pretreatment incorporates both physical and chemical methods that are essential for disintegrating hemicellulose and altering the configuration of lignin in order to increase the cellulose availability for subsequent hydrolysis processes (Behera et al., 2014; Kootstra et al., 2009; Mosier et al., 2005). This pretreatment technique encompasses overwhelming types of pretreatment processes particularly steam explosion, liquid hot water, wet explosion, ammonia fibre or freeze explosion, aqueous ammonia, ammonia recycle percolation, green solvents/organosolv and carbon dioxide explosion (Brodeur et al., 2011; Mosier et al., 2005).

8.1 Steam Explosion

Steam explosion is one of the most effective and commonly employed physico-chemical biomass treatment technique necessary for the fragmentation of lignocellulosic materials. This process is focused on a variation of mechanical, chemical as well as thermal influences interacting with the biomass feedstock in order to break the bonds between the lignocellulosic fibres to modify the cellulose crystallinity as well as to prompt the conversion of lignin in the substrate (Alvira, Tomás-Pejó, Ballesteros, & Negro, 2010; Sassner, Mårtensson, Galbe, & Zacchi, 2008). Steam explosion treatment in particular provides many benefits, notably relatively minimal environmental consequences than other pretreatment methods, reduced capital cost and it does not involve any usage of dangerous chemical reagents. Moreover, the vessel can cater to different types of raw feedstocks(Cara, Ruiz, Ballesteros, Negro, & Castro, 2006). Furthermore, this pretreatment technique results in greater fermentable sugar yields, provides pretreated biomass feedstocks with strong enzymatic digestibility, and has exhibited huge potential for commercial upscale. When compared to the mechanical pretreatment process, the steam explosion vessel utilises fewer resources and when contrasted with the chemical pretreatment, the physico-chemical process prevents contamination and mitigates costs related to environmental degradation (Alvira et al., 2010; Coimbra et al., 2016).

In the vessel, the raw feedstock is processed with saturated steam in the range of 6.9–48.3 bars at an elevated temperature varying from 160 to 260°C for an optimum period of time (Bhaumik & Dhepe, 2016). The pressure is instantly lowered to ambient one causing the feedstock to undergo a rapid explosive decompression. This mechanism allows the extraction of hemicellulose and reallocate the amount of lignin initially present in the biomass (Chiaramonti et al., 2012; Duque, Manzanares, Ballesteros, & Ballesteros, 2016; Shi, Li, Li, Cheng, & Zhu, 2019; Steinbach, Kruse, Sauer, & Storz, 2020). Numerous variables notably the volume of the biomass, the amount of moisture in the raw material, temperature as well as the residence time are crucial for the development of an efficient steam explosion biomass pretreatment process. Furthermore, the incorporation of dilute hydrochloric acid having a concentration varying between 0.3 to 3 w/w% in the steam explosion vessel helps to increase the performance of the process through a reduction in the residence time desired as well as the temperature. This physico-chemical treatment process has several merits such that it requires at least 70% less energy than the mechanical treatment process. Hence, it is 70% less costly (Pielhop et al., 2016; Shi et al., 2019; Steinbach et al., 2020). Moreover, the steam explosion treatment has a reduced environmental impact enabling efficient processes on large commercial levels. The lignocellulose pretreatment process is commonly conducted in a bath of water at a relatively high temperature ranging between 200 to 230°C instead of using steam in either a co-current reactor, a counter-current reactor or a flow-through reactor for a specific pre-determined residence time (Bhaumik & Dhepe, 2016; Capolupo & Faraco, 2016; Coimbra et al., 2016; Jacquet, Maniet, Vanderghem, Delvigne, & Richel, 2015; Pielhop et al., 2016; Zhao, Li, Zheng,

Wang, & Yu, 2018). Hu et al. (2013) reported a sugar and glucose yield of 36.14% and 15.35% correspondingly when reed straw was pretreated via steam explosion at 220°C for 5 min followed by enzymatic hydrolysis for 60 h. Nonetheless, a study conducted by Amores et al. (2013) revealed a high glucose yield of around 85% when sugarcane bagasse was pretreated via steam explosion at a temperature of 215°C for 5 mins.

8.2 Liquid Hot Water Pretreatments

Liquid hot water (LHW) pretreatment utilises pressure for keeping water in the normal flowable form at high temperatures in the absence of chemical reagents. It is a highly desirable solution to the pretreatment of lignocellulosic materials owing to decreased health and environmental risks as well as the reasonably low price associated with it (Kim, Kreke, Hendrickson, Parenti, & Ladisch, 2013; Mosier et al., 2005; Yan, Ma, Li, & Fu, 2016). LHW functions in a similar manner as the steam explosion process apart from the employment of water at high temperatures varying between 160 to 240°C rather than steam (Behera et al., 2014; Brandon et al., 2008). This procedure can be conducted in reactors operating co-currently, counter-currently as well as in a flow-through reactor (Behera et al., 2014). To ensure an effective pretreatment, the biomass feedstock is immersed in water for an optimum residence time period of 15–20 mins (Behera et al., 2014; Mosier et al., 2005). LHW leads to material hydrolysis while eliminating lignin from the compound matrix. Hence, causing the cellulosic fibres to be more available and preventing the production of inhibitory materials which are formed at greater temperatures. Nevertheless, the absolute delignification of the biomass by solely hot water is not achievable owing to the re-condensation of lignin-derived soluble substances (Brandon et al., 2008; Ingram et al., 2011; Mosier et al., 2005; Xiao, Sun, Shi, Xu, & Sun, 2011). The hot water inside the vessel splits hemiacetal bonds to release during biomass processing which stimulates the rupture of ether bonds in biomass (Behera et al., 2014; Capolupo & Faraco, 2016; Ingram et al., 2011; Kim et al., 2013; Mosier et al., 2005). The separation of the O-acetyl groups and the replacement of uronic acids in the matrix can aid or impede the pretreatment process owing to acid being liberated. These acids serve as catalysts in the synthesis and elimination of oligosaccharides and further hydrolysing hemicellulose to monomeric sugars which has the possibility of degrading into aldehydes. The production and degradation of monosaccharides act as a catalyst in the cellulose hydrolysis (Behera et al., 2014; Capolupo & Faraco, 2016; Mosier et al., 2005; Xiao et al., 2011). Sugar yields ranging between 1.9 to 52.2% could be attained when corn stover was pretreated by liquid hot water at 180°C for 4 min and when the fibre was subordinated while 47.7–79.1% glucose yield could be achieved when the fibre was post-treated by disk milling (Kim, Dien, Tumbleson, Rausch, & Singh, 2016).

8.3 Wet Explosion

An alternative approach to the steam explosion method is a wet explosion (WEx). This process is a blend of other techniques namely steam explosion, thermal hydrolysis and wet oxidation to accomplish greater efficient lignin solubilisation relative to the traditional steam explosion method (Biswas & Ahring, 2016; Biswas, Uellendahl, & Ahring, 2015). The driving agent for wet explosion is attributable to the utilisation of an oxidising agent whereby hemicellulose is thoroughly solubilised (Biswas, Uellendahl, & Ahring, 2014; Duque et al., 2016; Mosier et al., 2005). 152 g/L of glucose and 67 g/L of xylose (286 g/L of total carbohydrates) could be retrieved when loblolly pine was pretreated via wet explosion at pressures of 6.5–7.2 bar, temperatures of 170–175°C and residence time from ranging from 20 to 22.5 min (Rana, Rana, & Ahring, 2012).

8.4 Ammonia Fibre Explosion (AFEX)

Another method to achieve this pretreatment process is via the use of high-pressure liquid anhydrous ammonia in a process called ammonia fibre explosion or freeze-explosion. This particular system is observed to produce more favourable results for lignocellulosic fibres consisting of more cellulosic and hemicellulosic content and less lignin percentage such as sugarcane leaves, Napier grass, *Eucalyptus Saligna* as well as bagasse (Alizadeh, Teymouri, Gilbert, & Dale, 2005; Baral & Shah, 2017; Holtzapple, Lundeen, Sturgis, Lewis, & Dale, 1992; Kim, 2018; Taherzadeh & Karimi, 2008; Wyman et al., 2005). Liquid ammonia is allowed to interact with the lignocellulosic biomass for a pre-determined residence time in a biomass to ammonia ratio of 1:1 to 1:2 under elevated pressures fluctuating between 17 to 21 bars and temperatures of 60–100°C. The decrease in pressure in the vessel allows the explosion to occur (Bhaumik & Dhepe, 2016; Stelte, 2013). a maximum sugar yield of 65.6% (385 g/kg biomass) could be retrieved when switchgrass was allowed to interact in 0.9 g NH_3/g biomass and 0.4 g NH_3/g biomass at 80°C for a residence time of 20 mins (Bals, Rogers, Jin, Balan, & Dale, 2010).

8.5 Ammonia Recycled Percolation (ARP)

Ammonia recycle percolation is a pretreatment technique whereby aqueous ammonia around 5 to 15 wt % is allowed in a packed bed reactor which in turn triggers swelling and delignification of the lignocellulosic fibres at temperatures ranging between 140 to 210°C (Brodeur et al., 2011; Menon & Rao, 2012). The ARP process causes half of the xylan fraction present to be solubilised while 92% of the cellulosic fraction is withheld. When the cycle is completed, carbon dioxide is liberated which allows a disintegration in the cellulosic fraction of the substrate (Brodeur et al., 2011; Kim & Lee, 1986; Menon & Rao, 2012; Tae & Lee, 2005). Glucose yields fluctuating between 17.98 and 50.98% were ascertained when rye straw was pretreated in 2% aqueous ammonia for 0–8 h at temperatures ranging between 60 and 90°C (Domanski, Borowski, Marchut-Mikolajczyk, & Kubacki, 2016).

8.6 Supercritical Fluid (SCF) or Carbon Dioxide Explosion (Supercritical Carbon Dioxide, Sc-CO$_2$)

Supercritical fluid pretreatment is a process whereby a fluid is employed in a condition beyond critical temperature and pressure. The fluid can be in the liquid or gaseous state. Conditions for supercritical water are achieved at 374°C and 221 bars (Capolupo & Faraco, 2016; Daza Serna, Orrego Alzate, & Cardona Alzate, 2016; Escobar, da Silva, Pirich, Corazza, & Pereira Ramos, 2020). Carbon dioxide being a supercritical fluid is the most commonly utilised fluid under high pressure in the pretreatment of lignocellulosic materials whereby the biomass is digested and lignin is efficiently disintegrated (Capolupo & Faraco, 2016; Narayanaswamy, Faik, Goetz, & Gu, 2011; Srinivasan & Ju, 2010). As carbon dioxide dissolves in water, carbonic acid is produced which acts as a catalyst to hydrolyse hemicellulosic materials in the substrate. As soon as pressurised gas is liberated in the reactor vessel, the biomass framework is disrupted thereby providing a higher surface area attainability to enzymes (Akhtar, Gupta, Goyal, & Goyal, 2016; Behera et al., 2014; Capolupo & Faraco, 2016; Escobar et al., 2020; Narayanaswamy et al., 2011). In addition, the vessel operates at a low temperature of around 31°C to avoid sugar degradation along with a critical temperature of approximately 7.4 MPa (Schacht, Zetzl, & Brunner, 2008). Tan et al. (2021) reported that the total reducing sugar yields of 50 and 29.8% could be achieved from straw biomass solely by Sc-CO$_2$ treatment from corn cob and corn stalk respectively while the yield could be increased to 75% when combined ultrasound pretreatment was employed.

9. BIOLOGICAL PRETREATMENT

Biological pretreatment is correlated with the activity of fungi designed to produce enzymes such as Laccases that dissolve/eliminate lignin, hemicelluloses as well as polyphenols contained in biomass by oxidation using O$_2$. Laccases can be isolated from plants such as cabbages, potatoes, apples, and also from bacteria as well as insects (Eggert, Temp, Dean, & Eriksson, 1996; Shraddha, Shekher, Sehgal, Kamthania, & Kumar, 2011). Biological pretreatment offers competitive merits over physico-chemical pretreatments notably substrate specificity, reaction specificity, energy efficiency, zero toxic emissions and high throughput and yield of end commodities (Behera et al., 2014; Capolupo & Faraco, 2016; Isroi et al., 2011; Mtui, 2009; Rabemanolontsoa & Saka, 2016; Saritha, Arora, & Lata, 2012). Nevertheless, its drawbacks are as evident as its strengths owing to the fact that biological pretreatment is an extremely time-consuming undertaking that involves close monitoring of growth environments and a significant amount of volume for proper functioning. Moreover, some of the lignolytic enzymes that are employed degrade both the lignin as well as the desired hemicellulose (Behera et al., 2014; Cardona & Sánchez, 2007; Kuhar, Nair, & Kuhad, 2008; Singh, 2018). A glucose yield varying between 75 to 95% was reported when LCB was allowed to interact with cellulase at 70°C for >1.

10. MATERIALS AND METHODS

This research study comprises two phases. In the first phase, 15 widely available local lignocellulosic biomass feedstocks were characterised in terms of their physico-chemical attributes (Cellulose %, hemicellulose %, lignin %, ADF, NDF, Fibre length, moisture content, ash and volatile solid content), elemental analysis (C%, H%, N%, S%), proximate analysis (GCV) as well as their accessibility, abundancy, strength properties and current uses around the island. One biomass with the most favourable attributes was opted to further undergo hydrolysis via four different processes such as two-stage concentrated acid hydrolysis (CAH), dilute acid hydrolysis (DAH), alkaline hydrolysis (AH) and thermal treatment (TT) under various conditions to yield fermentable sugars. Taguchi design of experiment (9 levels) was employed to determine the optimum values of the parameters while ensuring no damaging effect on the cellulosic framework. Taguchi analysis aided in exploring the individual effect of each parameter as well as in confirming the anticipated result at optimum conditions. The optimal operating conditions to yield maximum fermentable sugars for each technology were determined and eventually the most efficient technology and fibre yielding maximum sugars were adopted for further processing. The second phase consisted of utilising fermentable sugars from the lignocellulosic material opted to produce polyhydroxybutyrate (PHB) biopolymer with the aid of a culture of *Ralstonia Eutropha(Cupriavidus Necator* H16*)* which is a non-pathogenic microorganism. The optimisation of the PHB production from lignocellulosic biomass will be achieved by Plackett-Burman on Minitab to construct the experimental design, to perform the experiments and to analyse the experimental observations for optimisation purposes by two-level factorial. 12 experimental runs will be performed on each type of carbon source rich in reducing sugars which are the hydrolysates and the residual mass from CAH hydrolysis.

Trials for sugar extraction were also conducted for the pretreatment of the different fibres via steam explosion (SE) followed by DAH and also by soaking in fly ash water, an alkaline water obtained from a pizza restaurant which was eventually discarded due to significantly lower amount of sugar obtained per ml of hydrolysate than in total acid hydrolysis as well as the high temperature and residence time required for SE.

11. ANALYSIS

11.1 Taguchi Analysis for Sugar Content Determination

Taguchi method is based on the study of response variations employing the Signal to Noise ratio (S/N). It targets to minimise variations as a consequence of noise factors which are uncontrollable parameters and also, to maximise the quality characteristic variations in response to the signal factors. The quality characteristic chosen was the sugar yield (Rao, Kumar, Prakasham, & Hobbs, 2008; Tjantelé, 1991). The aim is to identify which optimal treatment parameters would lead to higher sugar content with complete hemicellulose hydrolysation and partial lignin removal. Since a higher sugar yield is favoured as a key factor of the bioconversion process of LCM, the sugar yield was considered the key quality characteristic. Hence, the signal to noise (S/N) ratio was conducted in accordance to 'The larger the better' method for each technological process and experiment run on Minitab as shown in Eq. (1).

$$S\Big/N \text{ ratio} = -10 \times \text{Log}_{10}\left[\frac{1}{n}\sum\frac{1}{Y^2}\right] \tag{1}$$

where Y is the measured values (responses) for the factor level combination and, n is the number of measurements in the factor level combination.

The analysis of mean (ANOM) and analysis of variance (ANOVA) were also performed to determine the optimum level of process conditions which will eventually yield the highest sugar content.

Taguchi method is a statistical approach that has been used primarily for evaluating the optimal processing parameter without the need for rigorous analytical investigations (Athreya & Venkatesh, 2012; Fei, Mehat, & Kamaruddin, 2013). By employing orthogonal arrays to execute matrix experiments, the number of tests that can be conducted to determine optimum parameters is drastically decreased (Athreya & Venkatesh, 2012). The performance characteristics that differ significantly from the target response are then evaluated using the loss function value which is eventually converted into the signal to noise ratio (S/N) (Athreya & Venkatesh, 2012; Yang & Tarng, 1998).

Taguchi analysis (Fig. 7.3) was conducted:

i. To determine optimum parameter conditions for concentrated acid hydrolysis of biomass feedstocks that give maximum sugar yield.
ii. To analyse and evaluate the effect of each parameter individually which were sulphuric acid concentration, time and temperature.
iii. To substantiate expected results at optimum conditions.

11.2 Taguchi Analysis for Acid Hydrolysis of Fibres

First-stage acid hydrolysis requirements include pretreatment of lignocellulosic biomass at a low temperature of 30°C alongside dilute sulphuric acid having concentration ranging from 60–72 wt% in a sulphuric acid to biomass ratio of 36: 1 for a period of 60–120 mins. During the second stage hydrolysis, the concentrated sulphuric acid is diluted to 4wt% and the range of conditions depicting feasible conversion to fermentable sugars include 4wt% H_2SO_4, duration of 0.25–3 h and temperatures ranging from 80 to 121°C (Chang et al., 2018; Chen, 2015; Håkansson & Ahlgren, 2005; Kumar, Dheeran, Singh, Mishra, & Adhikari, 2015; Lavarack, Griffin, & Rodman, 2002; Shahbazi & Zhang, 2010; Wijaya et al., 2014).

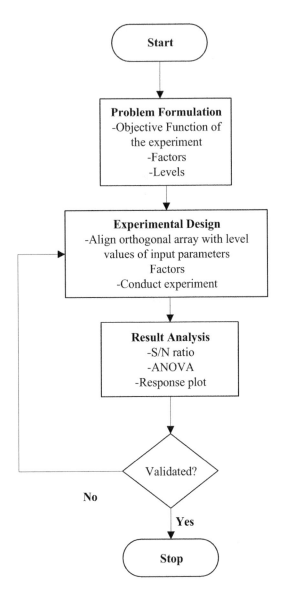

Fig. 7.3.   Flowchart for Taguchi Method.

12. PLACKETT-BURMAN AND BOX-BEHNKEN DESIGN OF EXPERIMENT

Plackett-Burman design of the experiment on Minitab will be employed to analyse the effect of the variables, 'one variable at a time' in order to optimise the process and screen out factors that are not contributing to the optimisation of the PHB. Some variables identified are:

(1) Inoculum Age.
(2) Inoculum size.
(3) Incubation time.
(4) Substrate concentration (1–4%)-hydrolysate.
(5) Substrate concentration using solid fraction.
(6) Effect of Complex nitrogen source such as beef extract, peptone on the process.
(7) Effect of Inorganic nitrogen source such as ammonium sulphate on the process.
(8) Effect of phosphate such as M9 minimal salt on the process.
(9) Effect of trace element on the process.
(10) Stirring speed.

Using the Plackett-Burman design ($+1$, -1), the media and environmental conditions will be randomised. The mean of the $+1$ experiment will be determined using the formula $\frac{(\Sigma + 1)}{n(+1)}$.

The mean of the -1 experiment will be determined using the formula $\frac{(\Sigma - 1)}{n(-1)}$.

In order to assess the correlation between the variables at a 90% or greater level of confidence, an ANOVA test will be implemented for each response.

13. INOCULUM PREPARATION

13.1 Serial Dilution and Plating

  i. A loop inoculated with cells from a 24-hour old agar slant was transferred to 50 ml of M9 minimal salt in a 250 mL Erlenmeyer flask.
 ii. The flask was incubated on a rotary shaker at 30°C and 200 rpm for 18 hours.
iii. After 18 hours, 1 ml of the culture was transferred in a glass vial by a sterilised 1,000 µL micropipettor and vortexed.
iv. Serial dilution and plating were performed on the 1 ml microbial culture to determine the mean number of viable colonies in each inoculum as shown in Fig. 7.4.

The number of viable colonies in the 1 ml culture was determined to be 8×10^8 CFU/mL.

The following formula was adopted to determine the concentration of the undiluted sample:

$$\frac{CFU}{ml} = ANC \times 50 \times \frac{1}{df} \qquad (2)$$

where,

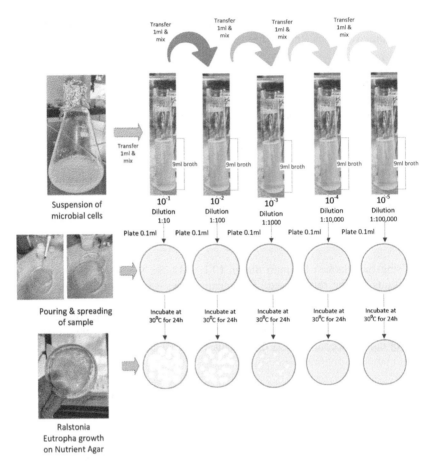

Fig. 7.4. Serial Dilution and Plating of Ralstonia Eutropha.

$\frac{CFU}{ml}$ = colony forming unit per volume
ANC = Average number of colonies
df = dilution factor

14. SUBMERGED FERMENTATION

Polyhydroxybutyrate samples and blends with other materials such as PLA, cellulose derivatives, and lignin shall be produced and tested. The samples produced from the cheap lignocellulosic materials will be compared and contrasted with commercial **PHB** generated from pure carbon sources. Continuous fermentation shall be run in bioreactors at University of Stavanger to assess the feasibility of upscaling the process. 1%, 2%, 3%, and 4% reducing sugar per 100 ml accordingly will be filter-sterilised reducing sugar as carbon source was added to the inoculated shake flasks and the latter was maintained in a shaking incubator with the temperature monitored at 30°C for 48 hours at a rotation speed of 300 rpm. The clear broth turned more turbid as the fermentation process continued. Three types of carbon sources were used one at a time as follows:

(1) Hydrolysate from acid hydrolysis which consisted of reducing sugar from the hemicellulosic part of the Furcraea Foetida (FF) fibre.
(2) Cellulosic part of the FF fibre.
(3) 1%, 2%, 3% and 4% glucose solution.

15. EXPECTED OUTCOME

The expected outcomes of this study are (1) to create a product that not only addresses the requirements of producers and customers, but also actively lowers environmental pollution problems, (2) production of good quality biodegradable polymers from lignocellulosic biomass to reduce the use of fossil fuels and the reliance on non-renewable resources, (3) job creation prospects, (4) possibility to provide improved recovery and recycling solutions than synthetic plastics, especially strong biodegradability or compostability and (5) to boost industrial competitiveness by introducing novel eco-efficient bio-based products and applications.

15.1 Policy and Practice

Bioplastics are efficient and technologically advanced materials on the inside. They can optimise the balance of environmental advantages and environmental harm of plastics. According to life cycle assessments, PHAs can dramatically lower CO_2 emissions when compared to traditional plastics. Furthermore, the growing use of lignocellulosic biomass in biopolymeric applications offers two distinct advantages: renewability and availability. Many governments throughout the world are becoming more willing to develop comprehensive bioeconomy policies, with prospects for specialised bioplastics initiatives.

15.2 Target Groups

• Industries

Beverage industries that have a pressing need to substitute their plastic bottles since the latter will be prohibited completely soon along with the packaging industries including plates, bowls, straws, beverage stirrers, lids, trays/barquettes, cups, forks, spoons, receptacles to hold food for immediate consumption, plastic trays utilised to package fresh, pre-cooked and cooked meat products, cheese and seafood as well as the yogurt and ice cream industry will definitely benefit from this research.

• Government agencies

This research will help the government to devise better plans to implement waste management strategy since PHA polymers will definitely ease the challenges of waste management and the issue of our landfill being packed to capacity.

• Society

Since single-use plastic products have already been prohibited in Mauritius and other plastic based products are soon to be banned, PHA biopolymers will serve as an eco-friendly alternative to consumers and industries alike.

16. CONCLUSION

PHAs may be composted, are entirely biodegradable, and can break down in soil, freshwater, and the ocean. Since low-cost non-consumable carbon substrate from lignocellulosic biomass is being used to manufacture value-added products in lieu of conventional plastics, there is a significant decline in landfill stress and waste discharge. Hence, bio-based plastics have the undeniable advantage of reducing reliance on fossil fuels, reducing emissions of greenhouse gases (GHG), and improving asset efficiency. This research examined the feasibility of extracting reducing sugar from locally accessible lignocellulosic biomass for biopolymer synthesis. The principal method hydrolysed cellulose and hemicellulose into monomer units that bacteria might use for polymer formation. *Furcraea Foetida*, a perennial plant found across the island, has the best characteristics: high cellulose content, low lignin, low ash and low cost was selected for sustainable biopolymer manufacturing. Several pretreatment methods have been tested to maximise fermentable sugars from *Furcraea Foetida*. In this paper, Taguchi analysis and Plackett-Burman coupled with Box-Behnken design of experiments were proposed to determine optimum parameter conditions, to analyse and evaluate the effect of each parameter individually which were reagent concentration, time and temperature and also to evaluate an experiment and determine the most significant model terms and their interactions that can influence the response. The response surface methodology will be employed to further optimise the most influential parameter. Once the most favourable conditions are determined, polyhydroxybuyrate (PHB) films will be produced using these exact parameters and blending with other biopolymers will be done. Composite biopolymers consisting of PHB-PLA, PHB-lignin, PHB-starch, PHB-PEG, PHB-cellulose acetate will be manufactured and tested physically, mechanically and chemically. Tests such as tensile strength, shear stress, elongation at break, abrasion, scanning electron microscopy, biodegradation as per ASTM, high performance liquid chromatography, thermogravimetric analysis and BET analysis will be determined against standard PHB which will be used as control.

This study has the potential to make a significant contribution to the tackling of environmental pollution issues such as global warming and greenhouse gas effects and, solid waste management challenges. Furthermore, the resistance and durability of conventional plastics have one important limitation: their permanence in the environment, making them impervious to biodegradation. As a result, the manufacturing of biodegradable polymers is stressed as important to finding answers to our global environmental challenges and re-establishing our planet's well-being.

AUTHORS' CONTRIBUTIONS

NJ carried out the production of samples and draughted the manuscript. PJ and GK participated in the design of the study, coordinated the study and did the sequence alignment. All authors read and approved the final manuscript.

COMPETING INTERESTS

The authors declare that they have no competing interests and the paper has not been sent elsewhere for publication. The data, tables and figures are also our own and have not been published yet.

ACKNOWLEDGEMENTS

The authors would like to acknowledge the University of Mauritius, the Higher Education Commission and UNESCO-L'Oréal For Women in Science for funding this research project.

REFERENCES

Agbor, V. B., Cicek, N., Sparling, R., Berlin, A., & Levin, D. B. (2011). Biomass pretreatment: Fundamentals toward application. *Biotechnology Advances, 29*, 675–685.

Akhtar, N., Gupta, K., Goyal, D., & Goyal, A. (2016). Recent advances in pretreatment technologies for efficient hydrolysis of lignocellulosic biomass. *Environmental Progress & Sustainable Energy, 35*, 489–511.

Alizadeh, H., Teymouri, F., Gilbert, T. I., & Dale, B. E. (2005). Pretreatment of switchgrass by ammonia fiber explosion (AFEX). *Applied Biochemistry and Biotechnology - Part A Enzyme Engineering and Biotechnology, 124*, 1133–1141.

Alvira, P., Tomás-Pejó, E., Ballesteros, M., & Negro, M. J. (2010). Pretreatment technologies for an efficient bioethanol production process based on enzymatic hydrolysis: A review. *Bioresource Technology, 101*(13), 4851–4861.

Amode, N. S., & Jeetah, P. (2020). Paper production from hemp fibres. *Waste and Biomass Valorization, 12*(4), 1781–1802.

Amores, I., Ballesteros, I., Manzanares, P., Sáez, F., Michelena, G., & Ballesteros, M. (2013). Ethanol production from sugarcane bagasse pretreated by steam explosion. *Electronic Journal of Energy and Environment, 1*(1).

Athreya, S., & Venkatesh, Y. D. (2012). Application of Taguchi method for optimization of process parameters in improving the surface roughness of Lathe facing operation. *International Refereed Journal of Engineering and Science, 1*(3), 13–19.

Azizi, N., Najafpour, G., & Younesi, H. (2017). Acid pretreatment and enzymatic saccharification of brown seaweed for polyhydroxybutyrate (PHB) production using Cupriavidus necator. *International Journal of Biological Macromolecules, 101*, 1029–1040.

Bals, B., Rogers, C., Jin, M., Balan, V., & Dale, B. (2010). Evaluation of ammonia fibre expansion (AFEX) pretreatment for enzymatic hydrolysis of switchgrass harvested in different seasons and locations. *Biotechnology for Biofuels, 3.*

Banerjee, G., Car, S., Liu, T., Williams, D. L., Meza, S. L., Walton, J. D., & Hodge, D. B. (2012). Scale-up and integration of alkaline hydrogen peroxide pretreatment, enzymatic hydrolysis, and ethanolic fermentation. *Biotechnology and Bioengineering, 109*(4), 922–931.

Baral, N. R., & Shah, A. (2017). Comparative techno-economic analysis of steam explosion, dilute sulfuric acid, ammonia fiber explosion and biological pretreatments of corn stover. *Bioresource Technology, 232*, 331–343.

Baruah, J., Nath, B. K., Sharma, R., Kumar, S., Deka, R. C., Baruah, D. C., & Kalita, E. (2018). Recent trends in the pretreatment of lignocellulosic biomass for value-added products. *Frontiers in Energy Research.*

Behera, S., Arora, R., Nandhagopal, N., & Kumar, S. (2014). Importance of chemical pretreatment for bioconversion of lignocellulosic biomass. *Renewable and Sustainable Energy Reviews, 36*, 91–106.

Berezina, N. (2013). Novel approach for productivity enhancement of polyhydroxyalkanoates (PHA) production by Cupriavidus necator DSM 545. *Nature Biotechnology, 30*(2), 192–195.

Berg, N., & Steinberger, Y. (2012). The role of perennial plants in preserving annual plant complexity in a desert ecosystem. *Geoderma, 185–186*, 6–11. doi:10.1016/j.geoderma.2012.03.023

Bhattarai, S., Bottenus, D., Ivory, C. F., Gao, A. H., Bule, M., Garcia-Perez, M., & Chen, S. (2015). Simulation of the ozone pretreatment of wheat straw. *Bioresource Technology, 196*, 78–87.

Bhaumik, P., & Dhepe, P. L. (2016). Conversion of biomass into sugars. In *RSC Green Chemistry* (Vol. 2016-January, pp. 1–53). Royal Society of Chemistry.

Binod, P., Janu, K. U., Sindhu, R., & Pandey, A. (2011). Hydrolysis of lignocellulosic biomass for bioethanol production. *Biofuels: Alternative Feedstocks and Conversion Processes*, 229–250.

Biswas, R., & Ahring, B. K. (2016). Fractionation of lignocellulosic biomass materials with wet explosion pretreatment. *Biomass fractionation technologies for a lignocellulosic feedstock based biorefinery.*

Biswas, R., Uellendahl, H., & Ahring, B. K. (2014). Wet explosion pretreatment of sugarcane bagasse for enhanced enzymatic hydrolysis. *Biomass and Bioenergy, 61*, 104–113.

Biswas, R., Uellendahl, H., & Ahring, B. K. (2015). Wet explosion: A universal and efficient pretreatment process for lignocellulosic biorefineries. *Bioenergy Research, 8*, 1101–1116.

Borand, M. N., & Karaosmanoğlu, F. (2018). Effects of organosolv pretreatment conditions for lignocellulosic biomass in biorefinery applications: A review. *Journal of Renewable and Sustainable Energy, 10*(3).

Brandon, S. K., Eiteman, M. A., Patel, K., Richbourg, M. M., Miller, D. J., Anderson, W. F., & Peterson, J. D. (2008). Hydrolysis of Tifton 85 bermudagrass in a pressurized batch hot water reactor. *Journal of Chemical Technology & Biotechnology, 83*(4), 505–512.

Brodeur, G., Yau, E., Badal, K., Collier, J., Ramachandran, K. B., & Ramakrishnan, S. (2011). Chemical and physicochemical pretreatment of lignocellulosic biomass: A review. *Enzyme Research.*

Bugnicourt, E., Cinelli, P., Lazzeri, A., & Alvarez, V. (2014). Polyhydroxyalkanoate (PHA): Review of synthesis, characteristics, processing and potential applications in packaging. *Express Polymer Letters, 8*(11), 791–808. doi:10.3144/expresspolymlett.2014.82

Buxoo, S., & Jeetah, P. (2020). Feasibility of producing biodegradable disposable paper cup from pineapple peels, orange peels and hemp leaves with beeswax coating. *SN Applied Sciences, 2*(8).

Cantarella, M., Cantarella, L., Gallifuoco, A., Spera, A., & Alfani, F. (2004). Comparison of different detoxification methods for steam-exploded poplar wood as a substrate for the bioproduction of ethanol in SHF and SSF. *Process Biochemistry, 39*(11), 1533–1542.

Capolupo, L., & Faraco, V. (2016). Green methods of lignocellulose pretreatment for biorefinery development. *Applied Microbiology and Biotechnology*, *100*, 9451–9467.

Cara, C., Ruiz, E., Ballesteros, I., Negro, M. J., & Castro, E. (2006). Enhanced enzymatic hydrolysis of olive tree wood by steam explosion and alkaline peroxide delignification. *Process Biochemistry*, *41*(2), 423–429.

Cardona, C. A., & Sánchez, Ó. J. (2007). Fuel ethanol production: Process design trends and integration opportunities. *Bioresource Technology*, *98*, 2415–2457.

Chandel, A. K., & Singh, O. V. (2011). Weedy lignocellulosic feedstock and microbial metabolic engineering: Advancing the generation of "Biofuel". *Applied Microbiology and Biotechnology*, *89*, 1289–1303.

Chang, J. K. W., Duret, X., Berberi, V., Zahedi-Niaki, H., & Lavoie, J. M. (2018). Two-step thermochemical cellulose hydrolysis with partial neutralization for glucose production. *Frontiers in Chemistry*, *6*(APR).

Chang, V. S., Burr, B., & Holtzapple, M. T. (1997). Lime pretreatment of switchgrass. *Applied Biochemistry and Biotechnology - Part A Enzyme Engineering and Biotechnology*, *63–65*(1), 3–19.

Chang, V. S., & Holtzapple, M. T. (2000). Fundamental factors affecting biomass enzymatic reactivity, *Applied Biochemistry and Biotechnology - Part A Enzyme Engineering and Biotechnology*, *84*, 5–37.

Chen, G.-Q., Chen, X.-Y., Wu, F.-Q., & Chen, J.-C. (2020). Polyhydroxyalkanoates (PHA) toward cost competitiveness and functionality. *Advanced Industrial and Engineering Polymer Research*, *3*, 1–7. doi:10.1016/j.aiepr.2019.11.001

Chen, H. (2015). Lignocellulose biorefinery feedstock engineering, *Biorefinery Engineering*, 37–86.

Chen, L., Hong, F., Yang, X.-x., & Han, S.-f. (2013). Biotransformation of wheat straw to bacterial cellulose and its mechanism. *Bioresource Technology*, *135*, 464–468.

Cheng, J., Lin, R., Song, W., Xia, A., Zhou, J., & Cen, K. (2015). Enhancement of fermentative hydrogen production from hydrolyzed water hyacinth with activated carbon detoxification and bacteria domestication. *International Journal of Hydrogen Energy*, *40*(6), 2545–2551.

Chiaramonti, D., Prussi, M., Ferrero, S., Oriani, L., Ottonello, P., Torre, P., & Cherchi, F. (2012). Review of pretreatment processes for lignocellulosic ethanol production, and development of an innovative method. *Biomass and Bioenergy*, *46*, 25–35.

Chin, K. L., H'ng, P. S., Wong, L. J., Tey, B. T., & Paridah, M. T. (2011). Production of glucose from oil palm trunk and sawdust of and mixed hardwood. *Applied Energy*, *88*(11), 4222–4228.

Chu, Q., Song, K., Bu, Q., Hu, J., Li, F., Wang, J., . . . Shi, A. (2018). Two-stage pretreatment with alkaline sulphonation and steam treatment of Eucalyptus woody biomass to enhance its enzymatic digestibility for bioethanol production. *Energy Conversion and Management*, *175*, 236–245.

Cinelli, P., Coltelli, M. B., Signori, F., Morganti, P., & Lazzeri, A. (2019). Cosmetic packaging to save the environment: Future perspectives. *Cosmetics*, *6*.

Coimbra, M. C., Duque, A., Saéz, F., Manzanares, P., Garcia-Cruz, C. H., & Ballesteros, M. (2016). Sugar production from wheat straw biomass by alkaline extrusion and enzymatic hydrolysis. *Renewable Energy*, *86*, 1060–1068.

Coz, A., Llano, T., Cifrián, E., Viguri, J., Maican, E., & Sixta, H. (2016). Physico-chemical alternatives in lignocellulosic materials in relation to the kind of component for fermenting purposes. *Materials (Basel)*, *9*.

Dahmen, N., Lewandowski, I., Zibek, S., & Weidtmann, A. (2019). Integrated lignocellulosic value chains in a growing bioeconomy: Status quo and perspectives. *GCB Bioenergy*, *11*(1), 107–117. doi:10.1111/gcbb.12586

Davies, S. M., Linforth, R. S., Wilkinson, S. J., Smart, K. A., & Cook, D. J. (2011). Rapid analysis of formic acid, acetic acid, and furfural in pretreated wheat straw hydrolysates and ethanol in a bioethanol fermentation using atmospheric pressure chemical ionisation mass spectrometry. *Biotechnology for Biofuels*, *4*.

Daza Serna, L. V., Orrego Alzate, C. E., & Cardona Alzate, C. A. (2016). Supercritical fluids as a green technology for the pretreatment of lignocellulosic biomass. *Bioresource Technology*, *199*, 113–120.

Devi, Dhaka, & Singh (2016). Acid and alkaline hydrolysis technologies for bioethanol production : An overview. *International Journal of Advanced Technology in Engineering and Science*, *4*(6), 94–106.

Dietrich, K., Dumont, M. J., Del Rio, L. F., & Orsat, V. (2019). Sustainable PHA production in integrated lignocellulose biorefineries. *Nature Biotechnology*, *49*, 161–168.

Domanski, J., Borowski, S., Marchut-Mikolajczyk, O., & Kubacki, P. (2016). Pretreatment of rye straw with aqueous ammonia for conversion to fermentable sugars as a potential substrates in biotechnological processes. *Biomass and Bioenergy*, *91*, 91–97.

Duque, A., Manzanares, P., Ballesteros, I., & Ballesteros, M. (2016). Steam explosion as lignocellulosic biomass pretreatment, *Biomass fractionation technologies for a lignocellulosic feedstock based biorefinery*, 349–368.

Dussán, K. J., Silva, D. D. V., Moraes, E. J. C., Arruda, P. V., & Felipe, M. G. A. (2014). Dilute-acid hydrolysis of cellulose to glucose from sugarcane bagasse. *Chemical Engineering Transactions*, *38*, 433–438.

Eggert, C., Temp, U., Dean, J. F. D., & Eriksson, K. E. L. (1996). A fungal metabolite mediates degradation of non-phenolic lignin structures and synthetic lignin by laccase. *FEBS Letters*, *391*(1–2), 144–148.

Escobar, E. L. N., da Silva, T. A., Pirich, C. L., Corazza, M. L., & Pereira Ramos, L. (2020). Supercritical fluids: A promising technique for biomass pretreatment and fractionation. *Frontiers in Bioengineering and Biotechnology*.

Fei, N. C., Mehat, N. M., & Kamaruddin, S. (2013). Practical applications of Taguchi method for optimization of processing parameters for plastic injection moulding: A retrospective review. *ISRN Mechanical Engineering*, *2013*, 1–11.

Ferrer, A., Pal, L., & Hubbe, M. (2017). Nanocellulose in packaging: Advances in barrier layer technologies. *Industrial Crops and Products*, *95*, 574–582.

Foston, M., & Ragauskas, A. J. (2012). Biomass characterization: Recent progress in understanding biomass recalcitrance. *Industrial Biotechnology*, *8*, 191–208.

Francis, J. K. (2004). *Wildland shrubs of the Unites States and its territories: Thamnic descriptions: Volume 1*. General Technical Reports IITF-GTR-26. USDA, Forest Service. International Institute of Tropical Forestry and Shrub Sciences Laboratory.

Goldstein, I., & Easter, J. (1992). An improved process for converting cellulose to ethanol. *Tappi Journal*, *75*(8), 135–140.

Govil, T., Wang, J., Samanta, D., David, A., Tripathi, A., Rauniyar, S., ... Sani, R. K. (2020). Lignocellulosic feedstock: A review of a sustainable platform for cleaner production of nature's plastics. *Journal of Cleaner Production*, *270*.

Gunny, A. A. N., Arbain, D., & Jamal, P. (2017). Effect of structural changes of lignocelluloses material upon pre-treatment using green solvents. *AIP Conference Proceedings*, *1835*.

Håkansson, H., & Ahlgren, P. (2005). Acid hydrolysis of some industrial pulps: Effect of hydrolysis conditions and raw material. *Cellulose*, *12*, 177–183.

Hassan, S. S., Williams, G. A., & Jaiswal, A. K. (2018). Emerging technologies for the pretreatment of lignocellulosic biomass. *Bioresource Technology*, *262*, 310–318.

He, X., Miao, Y., Jiang, X., Xu, Z., & Ouyang, P. (2010). Enhancing the enzymatic hydrolysis of corn stover by an integrated wet-milling and alkali pretreatment. *Applied Biochemistry and Biotechnology*, *160*(8), 2449–2457.

Holtzapple, M. T., Lundeen, J. E., Sturgis, R., Lewis, J. E., & Dale, B. E. (1992). Pretreatment of lignocellulosic municipal solid waste by ammonia fiber explosion (AFEX). *Applied Biochemistry and Biotechnology*, *34–35*(1), 5–21.

Hu, F., & Ragauskas, A. (2012). Pretreatment and lignocellulosic chemistry. *Bioenergy Research*, *5*, 1043–1066.

Hu, Q., Su, X., Tan, L., Liu, X., Wu, A., Su, D., ... Xiong, X. (2013). Effects of a steam explosion pretreatment on sugar production by enzymatic hydrolysis and structural properties of reed straw. *Bioscience Biotechnology & Biochemistry*, *77*(11), 2181–2187.

Huang, P., Wu, M., Kuga, S., & Huang, Y. (2013). Aqueous pretreatment for reactive ball milling of cellulose. *Cellulose*, *20*(4), 2175–2178.

Ingram, T., Wörmeyer, K., Lima, J. C. I., Bockemühl, V., Antranikian, G., Brunner, G., & Smirnova, I. (2011). Comparison of different pretreatment methods for lignocellulosic materials. Part I: Conversion of rye straw to valuable products. *Bioresource Technology, 102*(8), 5221–5228.

Isaac, A., Antunes, F. A. F., Conti, R., Montoro, L. A., Malachias, A., Massara, P., ... da Silva, S. S. (2018). Unveiling 3D physicochemical changes of sugarcane bagasse during sequential acid/ alkali pretreatments by synchrotron phase-contrast imaging. *Industrial Crops and Products, 114*, 19–27.

IsroiMillati, R., Syamsiah, S., Niklasson, C., Cahyanto, M. N., Lundquist, K., & Taherzadeh, M. J. (2011). Biological pretreatment of lignocelluloses with white-rot fungi and its applications: A review. *Bioresources, 6*, 5224–5259.

Jacquet, N., Maniet, G., Vanderghem, C., Delvigne, F., & Richel, A. (2015). Application of steam explosion as pretreatment of lignocellulosic material: A review. *Industrial & Engineering Chemistry Research, 54*, 2593–2598.

Jaffur, N., & Jeetah, P. (2019). Production of low cost paper from Pandanus utilis fibres as a substitution to wood. *Sustainable Environment Research, 1*(1).

Jaffur, N., Jeetah, P., & Kumar, G. (2021). A review on enzymes and pathways for manufacturing polyhydroxybutyrate from lignocellulosic materials. *3 Biotech, 11*.

Jeetah, P., & Jaffur, N. (2021). Coconut husk, a lignocellulosic biomass, as a promising engineering material for non-wood paper production. *Journal of Natural Fibers, 19*(13), 5622–5636.

Karimi, K., & Taherzadeh, M. J. (2016). A critical review on analysis in pretreatment of lignocelluloses: Degree of polymerization, adsorption/desorption, and accessibility. *Bioresource Technology, 203*, 348–356.

Kim, D. (2018). Physico-chemical conversion of lignocellulose: Inhibitor effects and detoxification strategies: A mini review. *Molecules, 23*.

Kim, J. S., Lee, Y. Y., & Park, S. C. (2000). Pretreatment of wastepaper and pulp mill sludge by aqueous ammonia and hydrogen peroxide. *Applied Biochemistry and Biotechnology – Part A Enzyme Engineering and Biotechnology, 84–86*, 129–139.

Kim, S. B., & Lee, Y. Y. (1986). Kinetics in acid-catalyzed hydrolysis of hardwood hemicellulose. *Biotechnology and Bioengineering Symposium, 17*, 71–84.

Kim, S. M., Dien, B. S., Tumbleson, M. E., Rausch, K. D., & Singh, V. (2016). Improvement of sugar yields from corn stover using sequential hot water pretreatment and disk milling. *Bioresource Technology, 216*, 706–713.

Kim, Y., Kreke, T., Hendrickson, R., Parenti, J., & Ladisch, M. R. (2013). Fractionation of cellulase and fermentation inhibitors from steam pretreated mixed hardwood. *Bioresource Technology, 135*, 30–38.

Kootstra, A. M. J., Beeftink, H. H., Scott, E. L., & Sanders, J. P. M. (2009). Comparison of dilute mineral and organic acid pretreatment for enzymatic hydrolysis of wheat straw. *Biochemical Engineering Journal, 46*(2), 126–131.

Kourmentza, C., Plácido, J., Venetsaneas, N., Burniol-Figols, A., Varrone, C., Gavala, H. N., & Reis, M. A. M. (2017). Recent advances and challenges towards sustainable polyhydroxyalkanoate (PHA) production. *Bioengineering, 4*.

Kucharska, K., Rybarczyk, P., Hołowacz, I., Łukajtis Rafałand Glinka, M., & Kamiński, M. (2018). Pretreatment of lignocellulosic materials as substrates for fermentation processes. *Molecules, 23*.

Kuhar, S., Nair, L. M., & Kuhad, R. C. (2008). Pretreatment of lignocellulosic material with fungi capable of higher lignin degradation and lower carbohydrate degradation improves substrate acid hydrolysis and the eventual conversion to ethanol. *Canadian Journal of Microbiology, 54*(4), 305–313.

Kumar, A. K., & Sharma, S. (2017). Recent updates on different methods of pretreatment of lignocellulosic feedstocks: A review. *Bioresources and Bioprocessing, 4*.

Kumar, S., Dheeran, P., Singh, S. P., Mishra, I. M., & Adhikari, D. K. (2015). Kinetic studies of two-stage sulphuric acid hydrolysis of sugarcane bagasse. *Renewable Energy, 83*, 850–858.

Lavarack, B. P., Griffin, G. J., & Rodman, D. (2002). The acid hydrolysis of sugarcane bagasse hemicellulose to produce xylose, arabinose, glucose and other products. *Biomass and Bioenergy, 23*(5), 367–380.

Liu, Q., Li, W., Ma, Q., An, S., Li, M., Jameel, H., & Chang, H. M. (2016). Pretreatment of corn stover for sugar production using a two-stage dilute acid followed by wet-milling pretreatment process. *Bioresource Technology*, *211*, 435–442.

Lobo, F. C. M., Franco, A. R., Fernandes, E. M., & Reis, R. L. (2021). An overview of the antimicrobial properties of lignocellulosic materials. *Molecules*, *26*.

López-Arenas, T., Rathi, P., Ramírez-Jiménez, E., & Sales-Cruz, M. (2010). Factors affecting the acid pretreatment of lignocellulosic biomass: Batch and continuous process. *Computer Aided Chemical Engineering*, *28*(C), 979–984.

Lynd, L. R., Elander, R. T., & Wyman, C. E. (1996). Likely features and costs of mature biomass ethanol technology. *Applied Biochemistry and Biotechnology - Part A Enzyme Engineering and Biotechnology*, *57–58*, 741–761.

Markets, M. (2019). *Polyhydroxyalkanoate (PHA) market*. Marketsandmarkets.

Menon, V., & Rao, M. (2012). Trends in bioconversion of lignocellulose: Biofuels, platform chemicals {\&} biorefinery concept. *Progress in Energy and Combustion Science*, *38*, 522–550.

Moe, S. T., Janga, K. K., Hertzberg, T., Hägg, M. B., Øyaas, K., & Dyrset, N. (2012). Saccharification of lignocellulosic biomass for biofuel and biorefinery applications A renaissance for the concentrated acid hydrolysis?. *Energy Procedia*, *20*, 50–58.

Moreno, A. D., Ibarra, D., Alvira, P., Tomás-Pejó, E., & Ballesteros, M. (2015). A review of biological delignification and detoxification methods for lignocellulosic bioethanol production. *Critical Reviews in Biotechnology*, *35*, 342–354.

Mosier, N., Hendrickson, R., Ho, N., Sedlak, M., & Ladisch, M. R. (2005). Optimization of pH controlled liquid hot water pretreatment of corn stover. *Bioresource Technology*, *96*(18), 1986–1993.

Mosier, N., Wyman, C., Dale, B., Elander, R., Lee, Y. Y., Holtzapple, M., & Ladisch, M. (2005). Features of promising technologies for pretreatment of lignocellulosic biomass. *Bioresource Technology*, *96*(6), 673–686.

Mtui, G. Y. S. (2009). Recent advances in pretreatment of lignocellulosic wastes and production of value added products. *African Journal of Biotechnology*, *8*, 1398–1415.

Narayanaswamy, N., Faik, A., Goetz, D. J., & Gu, T. (2011). Supercritical carbon dioxide pretreatment of corn stover and switchgrass for lignocellulosic ethanol production. *Bioresource Technology*, *102*(13), 6995–7000.

Neely, W. C. (1984). Factors affecting the pretreatment of biomass with gaseous ozone. *Biotechnology and Bioengineering*, *26*(1), 59–65.

Obruca, S., Benesova, P., Marsalek, L., & Marova, I. (2015). Use of lignocellulosic materials for PHA production. *Chemical and Biochemical Engineering Quarterly*, *29*, 135–144.

Olanbiwoninu, A. A., & Odunfa, S. A. (2015). Production of fermentable sugars from organosolv pretreated cassava peels. *Advances in Microbiology*, *5*(2), 117–122.

Orduña Ortega, J., Mora Vargas, J. A., Perrone, O. M., Metzker, G., Gomes, E., da Silva, R., & Boscolo, M. (2020). Soaking and ozonolysis pretreatment of sugarcane straw for the production of fermentable sugars. *Industrial Crops and Products*, *145*.

Palonen, H., Thomsen, A. B., Tenkanen, M., Schmidt, A. S., & Viikari, L. (2004). Evaluation of wet oxidation pretreatment for enzymatic hydrolysis of softwood. *Applied Biochemistry and Biotechnology - Part A Enzyme Engineering and Biotechnology*, *117*(1), 1–17.

Parawira, W., & Tekere, M. (2011). Biotechnological strategies to overcome inhibitors in lignocellulose hydrolysates for ethanol production: Review. *Critical Reviews in Biotechnology*, *31*, 20–31.

Pérez-Arauz, A. O., Aguilar-Rabiela, A. E., Vargas-Torres, A., Rodríguez-Hernández, A. I., Chavarría-Hernández, N., Vergara-Porras, B., & López-Cuellar, M. R. (2019). Production and characterization of biodegradable films of a novel polyhydroxyalkanoate (PHA) synthesized from peanut oil. *Food Packaging and Shelf Life*, *20*.

Pérez-Merchán, A. M., Rodríguez-Carballo, G., Torres-Olea, B., García-Sancho, C., Maireles-Torres, P. J., Mérida-Robles, J., & Moreno-Tost, R. (2022, August 1). Recent advances in mechanochemical pretreatment of lignocellulosic biomass. *Energies*, *15*. doi:10.3390/en15165948

Pielhop, T., Amgarten, J., Von Rohr, P. R., & Studer, M. H. (2016). Steam explosion pretreatment of softwood: The effect of the explosive decompression on enzymatic digestibility. *Biotechnology for Biofuels*, *9*(1).

Rabemanolontsoa, H., & Saka, S. (2016). Various pretreatments of. *Bioresource Technology, 199*, 83–91.

Raghavi, S., Sindhu, R., Binod, P., Gnansounou, E., & Pandey, A. (2016). Development of a novel sequential pretreatment strategy for the production of bioethanol from sugarcane trash. *Bioresource Technology, 199*, 202–210.

Ramdhonee, A., & Jeetah, P. (2017). Production of wrapping paper from banana fibres. *Journal of Environmental Chemical Engineering, 5*(5), 4298–4306.

Rana, D., Rana, V., & Ahring, B. K. (2012). Producing high sugar concentrations from loblolly pine using wet explosion pretreatment. *Bioresource Technology, 121*, 61–67.

Rao, R. S., Kumar, C. G., Prakasham, R. S., & Hobbs, P. J. (2008). The Taguchi methodology as a statistical tool for biotechnological applications: A critical appraisal. *Biotechnology Journal, 3*, 510–523.

Ribeiro Lopes, J., Azevedo dos Reis, R., & Almeida, L. E. (2017). Production and characterization of films containing poly(hydroxybutyrate) (PHB) blended with esterified alginate (ALG-e) and poly(ethylene glycol) (PEG). *Journal of Applied Polymer Science, 134*(1).

Sánchez, C. (2009). Lignocellulosic residues: Biodegradation and bioconversion by Fungi. *Biotechnology Advances, 27*, 185–194.

Saratale, G. D. (2012). Lignocellulosics to ethanol: The future of the chemical and energy industry. *African Journal of Biotechnology, 11*(5).

Saritha, M., Arora, A., & Lata (2012). Biological pretreatment of lignocellulosic substrates for enhanced delignification and enzymatic digestibility. *Indian Journal of Microbiology, 52*, 122–130.

Sassner, P., Mårtensson, C. G., Galbe, M., & Zacchi, G. (2008). Steam pretreatment of H_2SO_4-impregnated Salix for the production of bioethanol. *Bioresource Technology, 99*(1), 137–145.

Schacht, C., Zetzl, C., & Brunner, G. (2008). From plant materials to ethanol by means of supercritical fluid technology. *The Journal of Supercritical Fluids, 46*, 299–321.

Schwanninger, M., Rodrigues, J. C., & Fackler, K. (2011). A review of band assignments in near infrared spectra of wood and wood components. *Journal of Near Infrared Spectroscopy, 19*, 287–308.

Senthilkumar, K., Siva, I., Rajini, N., Jappes, J. T. W., & Siengchin, S. (2018). Mechanical characteristics of tri-layer eco-friendly polymer composites for interior parts of aerospace application. *Sustainable Composites for Aerospace Applications*, 35–53.

Sfiahi, N., Joshi, G., & Min, B. (2020). Potential sustainable biomaterials derived from cover crops. *BioResources, 15*(3), 5641–5652. doi:10.15376/biores.15.3.5641-5652

Shahbazi, A., & Zhang, B. (2010). *Bioalcohol production: Biochemical conversion of lignocellulosic biomass* (pp. 143–158). Woodhead Publishing Series in Energy.

Shi, Q., Li, Y., Li, Y., Cheng, Y., & Zhu, W. (2019). Effects of steam explosion on lignocellulosic degradation of, and methane production from, corn stover by a co-cultured anaerobic fungus and methanogen. *Bioresource Technology, 290*.

ShraddhaShekher, R., Sehgal, S., Kamthania, M., & Kumar, A. (2011). Laccase: Microbial sources, production, purification, and potential biotechnological applications. *Enzyme Research*. doi:10.4061/2011/217861

Silverstein, R. A., Chen, Y., Sharma-Shivappa, R. R., Boyette, M. D., & Osborne, J. (2007). A comparison of chemical pretreatment methods for improving saccharification of cotton stalks. *Bioresource Technology, 98*(16), 3000–3011.

Singh, S. (2018). Designing tailored microbial and enzymatic response in ionic liquids for lignocellulosic biorefineries. *Biophysical Reviews, 10*, 911–913.

Srinivasan, N., & Ju, L. K. (2010). Pretreatment of guayule biomass using supercritical carbon dioxide-based method. *Bioresource Technology, 101*(24), 9785–9791.

Steinbach, D., Kruse, A., Sauer, J., & Storz, J. (2020). Is steam explosion a promising pretreatment for acid hydrolysis of lignocellulosic biomass? *Processes, 8*(12), 1–12.

Stelte, W. (2013). *Steam explosion for biomass pre-treatment* (pp. 1–15). Danish Technological Institute.

Sun, R., Lawther, J. M., & Banks, W. B. (1995). Influence of alkaline pre-treatments on the cell wall components of wheat straw. *Industrial Crops and Products, 4*(2), 127–145.

Tae, H. K., & Lee, Y. Y. (2005). Pretreatment and fractionation of corn stover by ammonia recycle percolation process. *Bioresource Technology, 96*(18), 2007–2013.

Taherzadeh, M. J., & Karimi, K. (2008). Pretreatment of lignocellulosic wastes to improve ethanol and biogas production: A review. *International Journal of Molecular Sciences, 9*, 1621–1651.

Tan, J., Li, Y., Tan, X., Wu, H., Li, H., & Yang, S. (2021). Advances in pretreatment of straw biomass for sugar production. *Frontiers in Chemistry, 9*.

Tjantelé, M. (1991). Parameter design using the Taguchi methodology. *Microelectronic Engineering, 10*(3–4), 277–286.

Tomás-Pejó, E., Alvira, P., Ballesteros, M., & Negro, M. J. (2011). Pretreatment technologies for lignocellulose-to-bioethanol conversion. *Biofuels,* 149–176.

Torget, R., Werdene, P., Himmel, M., & Grohmann, K. (1990). Dilute acid pretreatment of short rotation woody and herbaceous crops. *Applied Biochemistry and Biotechnology, 24–25*(1), 115–126.

Travaini, R., Barrado, E., & Bolado-Rodríguez, S. (2016). Effect of ozonolysis pretreatment parameters on the sugar release, ozone consumption and ethanol production from sugarcane bagasse. *Bioresource Technology, 214*, 150–158.

Travaini, R., Otero, M. D. M., Coca, M., Da-Silva, R., & Bolado, S. (2013). Sugarcane bagasse ozonolysis pretreatment: Effect on enzymatic digestibility and inhibitory compound formation. *Bioresource Technology, 133*, 332–339.

Varga, E., Klinke, H. B., Réczey, K., & Thomsen, A. B. (2004). High solid simultaneous saccharification and fermentation of wet oxidized corn stover to ethanol. *Biotechnology and Bioengineering, 88*(5), 567–574.

Vico, G., & Brunsell, N. A. (2018). Tradeoffs between water requirements and yield stability in annual vs. perennial crops. *Advances in Water Resources, 112*, 189–202. doi:10.1016/j.advwatres.2017. 12.014

Viikari, L., Vehmaanperä, J., & Koivula, A. (2012). Lignocellulosic ethanol: From science to industry. *Biomass and Bioenergy, 46*, 13–24.

Visconti, D., Fiorentino, N., Cozzolino, E., Mola, I. Di, Ottaiano, L., Mori, M., … Fagnano, M. (2020). Use of giant reed (*Arundo Donax* L.) to control soil erosion and improve soil quality in a marginal degraded area. *Italian Journal of Agronomy, 15*(4), 332–338. doi:10.4081/ija.2020. 1764

Wang, Z., Keshwani, D. R., Redding, A. P., & Cheng, J. J. (2010). Sodium hydroxide pretreatment and enzymatic hydrolysis of coastal Bermuda grass. *Bioresource Technology, 101*(10), 3583–3585.

Wanitwattanarumlug, B., Luengnaruemitchai, A., & Wongkasemjit, S. (2012). Characterization of corn cobs from microwave and potassium hydroxide pretreatment. *International Journal of Chemical and Biomolecular Engineering, 6*(November 2015), 354–358.

Wijaya, Y. P., Putra, R. D. D., Widyaya, V. T., Ha, J. M., Suh, D. J., & Kim, C. S. (2014). Comparative study on two-step concentrated acid hydrolysis for the extraction of sugars from lignocellulosic biomass. *Bioresource Technology, 164*, 221–231.

Wyman, C. E., Dale, B. E., Elander, R. T., Holtzapple, M., Ladisch, M. R., & Lee, Y. Y. (2005). Coordinated development of leading biomass pretreatment technologies. *Bioresource Technology, 96*(18), 1959–1966.

Xiao, L. P., Sun, Z. J., Shi, Z. J., Xu, F., & Sun, R. C. (2011). Impact of hot compressed water pretreatment on the structural changes of woody biomass for bioethanol production. *Bioresources, 6*(2), 1576–1598.

Xu, Z., Xu, M., Cai, C., Chen, S., & Jin, M. (2021). Microbial polyhydroxyalkanoate production from lignin by Pseudomonas putida NX-1. *Bioresource Technology, 319*.

Yabushita, M., Kobayashi, H., Hara, K., & Fukuoka, A. (2014). Quantitative evaluation of ball-milling effects on the hydrolysis of cellulose catalysed by activated carbon. *Catalysis Science and Technology, 4*(8), 2312–2317.

Yan, L., Ma, R., Li, L., & Fu, J. (2016). Hot water pretreatment of lignocellulosic biomass: An effective and environmentally friendly approach to enhance biofuel production. *Chemical Engineering & Technology, 39*, 1759–1770.

Yang, W. H., & Tarng, Y. S. (1998). Design optimization of cutting parameters for turning operations based on the Taguchi method. *Journal of Materials Processing Technology, 84*(1–3), 122–129.

Yuan, Z., Long, J., Wang, T., Shu, R., Zhang, Q., & Ma, L. (2015). Process intensification effect of ball milling on the hydrothermal pretreatment for corn straw enzymolysis. *Energy Conversion and Management, 101,* 481–488.

Zeitsch, K. J. (2000). *The chemistry and technology of furfural and its many by-products.* Amsterdam: Elsevier, 13. Sugar Series.

Zhang, L., Tsuzuki, T., & Wang, X. (2015). Preparation of cellulose nanofiber from softwood pulp by ball milling. *Cellulose, 22*(3), 1729–1741.

Zhang, Y., Huang, M., Su, J., Hu, H., Yang, M., Huang, Z., ... Feng, Z. (2019). Overcoming biomass recalcitrance by synergistic pretreatment of mechanical activation and metal salt for enhancing enzymatic conversion of lignocellulose. *Biotechnology for Biofuels, 12*(1).

Zhao, S., Li, G., Zheng, N., Wang, J., & Yu, Z. (2018). Steam explosion enhances digestibility and fermentation of corn stover by facilitating ruminal microbial colonization. *Bioresource Technology, 253,* 244–251.

Zhao, X., Cheng, K., & Liu, D. (2009). Organosolv pretreatment of lignocellulosic biomass for enzymatic hydrolysis. *Applied Microbiology and Biotechnology, 82,* 815–827.

CHAPTER 8

BUT WHAT DOES SUSTAINABILITY MEAN? THE GROUNDWORK FOR KNOWLEDGE *ABOUT* SUSTAINABILITY AND KNOWLEDGE *FOR* SUSTAINABILITY

Florian Kragulj, Anna Katharina Grill, Raysa Geaquinto Rocha and Arminda do Paço

ABSTRACT

Sustainable management requires companies to build up new knowledge to acquire the competencies needed for action. This chapter aims to deliver knowledge about sustainability and knowledge for sustainability. Firstly, we systematically analyse the sustainability literature in the social sciences through a bibliographic analysis and topic modelling using VOSviewer and Mallet software. We outline research directions, themes and critical contributions for each research cluster identified. Additionally, we categorise over 30 definitions of sustainability identified by Meuer, Koelbel, and Hoffmann (2020). Secondly, we enumerate knowledge types needed for effective sustainability transitions of organisations. We trace typologies of sustainable business models and their distinct evaluations of sustainability. In this chapter, we argue that integrating the triad of social, ecological and economic goals is central for sustainability attempts as well as long-term thinking. Therefore, our research offers a comprehensive overview of sustainability in the social sciences supporting researchers and practitioners to navigate this miscellaneous and scattered field. Accordingly, our study is precious to young scholars

Innovation, Social Responsibility and Sustainability
Developments in Corporate Governance and Responsibility, Volume 22, 173–206
ISSN: 2043-0523/doi:10.1108/S2043-052320230000022008

researching sustainability who want to use the term in an informed and meaningful way.

Keywords: Sustainability; sustainable management; competencies; knowledge; corporate social responsibility; systematic review

1. INTRODUCTION

Due to the climate crisis, sustainability has become a social and political imperative that companies must address to succeed. Economic considerations have to take into account limitations of natural resources, as well as human working and living conditions. The interdependence of these three areas is crucial, as there can be no profit on a dead planet. Neither is economic profit possible without human involvement. Consequently, actors aiming for success should not perceive sustainability as a source of exogenous costs but rather as a strategic opportunity that can be exploited (Lubin & Esty, 2010; Porter & Kramer, 2011).

The importance of the sustainability imperative has increased significantly in the last decade, both politically and socially. The sustainable development goals (SDGs) of the United Nations, which were published in 2015 (Hák, Janoušková, & Moldan, 2016), as well as the 'Green Deal' (European Commission, 2022)[1] demonstrate, among other initiatives, the political centrality of the issue. The European community focuses on environmental and social sustainability in their efforts to become the first climate-neutral continent. Furthermore, figures from a recent market study by McKinsey and Company (2021, p. 89f) indicate that consumers are showing an increased awareness for sustainability in their purchasing behaviour. As a result, social expectations towards organisations and companies to act sustainably are intensifying.

But what does sustainability mean? Sustainability is an abstract concept. Sometimes it is a buzzword rather than a meaningful concept. It is viewed inconsistently, as Grunert, Hieke, and Wills have shown (2014, p. 183). However, their results indicate that sustainability is generally more associated with environmental issues (e.g., 'environmental impact of use of land and water, environmental impact of food production') rather than ethical issues (e.g., 'working conditions in food, child labour in food, world food supply'). Interestingly, the authors claim that linguistic-cultural differences exist internationally in translating the concept. While in Germany, France, Spain and the United Kingdom, the term sustainability is primarily associated with 'environmental protection', most respondents in Poland associated it with 'maintaining the standard of living', and in Sweden (for linguistic reasons), a temporal dimension (e.g. the shelf life of products) is associated with it. Consequently, we aim to address this diversity of perceptions by mapping the social science sustainability research field.

We intent to answer the following question: *What knowledge is necessary to implement sustainability principles in practice?* In the process of providing a

[1]Proclaimed by the European Commission at the end of 2019 (Ossewaarde and Ossewaarde-Lowtoo, 2020).

systematic response to it, the paper differentiates knowledge *about* sustainability and knowledge *for* sustainability. The former refers to dimensions and definitions that contribute to an overall understanding crucial for sustainable management research and practices. Their basic assumptions are situated in dominant or green growth framings (Grill, 2021). These framings of sustainability argue that (more) sustainable business practices are possible without radical change. The latter is increasingly important for building new knowledge and competencies to act sustainably.

2. KNOWLEDGE ABOUT SUSTAINABILITY

In order to gain what we coin 'knowledge *about* sustainability' in different social science disciplines, this chapter examines several concepts and definitions and maps the field. It does not, however, critically discuss their epistemological and ontological assumptions that might be incompatible. First, the chronological development of the concept is traced along major contributions. Then, a broad literature review identifies distinct research directions and contributions representative of the respective research direction (and themes). Additionally, based on a recent literature review by Meuer et al. (2020), we identify characteristic patterns in definitions of corporate sustainability.

2.1 Central Concepts and Definitions

The idea of sustainability can be found very early in the work of Hans Carl von Carlowitz, who advocated sustainable resource use ('Nachhaltende Nutzung', cited in Gottschlich & Friedrich (2014, p. 25)) and made this a principle of forestry action: more forest should grow back than wood is consumed. To ensure this ratio, he described three ways: reduction of wood consumption, substitution by other materials and controlled reforestation (in Gottschlich & Friedrich (2014, p. 25)). If consumption remains below the natural regeneration capacity, the long-term usability of wood can be ensured. While this does not maximise profit in the short term, it avoids shortages and the associated social and economic consequences in the long term (Grober (2001) in Reidegeld (2014)).

In their report 'The Limits to Growth', Meadows, Meadows, Randers, and Behrens, (1972) showed already in 1972 by computer simulations that with then (!) continuing growth of population, production, resource use and pollution the natural absorption capacity of the earth would be exceeded within 100 years. In subsequent updates of the report and its data basis (1992, 2004, 2012, 2020), the forecasts in this regard became gloomier, and a recent study (Herrington, 2021) empirically corroborated. This empirical data suggests a slowdown and eventual stalling of growth (welfare, food and industrial production) within the next decade. To counter this trend, Meadows, Randers, and Meadows (2005, p. 259f) propose 'general guidelines for restructuring any system toward sustainability' (e.g., households, businesses, economies):

- 'Extend the planning horizon': decisions should be made based on long-term cost and benefit estimates rather than short-term expectations.
- 'Improve the signals': What constitutes prosperity and how can it best be measured? Environmental and social costs should be included in the analysis.
- 'Speed up response times': Negative social and environmental developments should be recognised or anticipated early so that technological and institutional changes can counteract them. Flexibility, creativity, critical and systemic thinking, and the necessary will to change are crucial.
- 'Minimize the use of nonrenewable resources'.
- 'Prevent the erosion of renewable resources'.
- 'Use all resources with maximum efficiency'.
- 'Slow and eventually stop exponential growth of population and physical capital'.

Another milestone in the sustainability discourse is the UN report 'Our common future', published in 1987 and commonly known as the 'Brundtland Report' (named after the then chairwoman of the relevant UN commission and Norwegian prime minister) (United Nations, 1987). This report defines sustainable development as 'development that meets the needs of the present without compromising the ability of future generations to meet their own needs'. Essential in this definition is the concept of needs and the orientation towards the future. Basic needs enjoy priority, and needs beyond that are subject to the limits of ecological (regeneration) capacities (United Nations, 1987, chap. 2/I).

The 'Triple Bottom Line, 3Ps - People, Planet, Profit' model (Elkington, 1997) or 'three pillars model' (Deutscher Bundestag, 1998) present an alternative view of the concept of sustainability. They reflect the target variables of sustainable development that must be balanced: economic prosperity, environmental quality and social justice (Elkington, 1997). The Enquete Commission of the Deutscher Bundestag (1998, p. 18, translated) emphasises that 'sustainability policy [is] to be interpreted as social policy that, in principle and in the long term, treats all of the aforementioned dimensions [ecological, economic and social goals] on an equal footing and with equal value'. However, politics must recognise 'that economic development and thus social welfare are only possible to the extent that nature as the basis of life is not endangered'.

In 2000, the United Nations adopted the Millennium Development Goals (MDGs). The original eight SDGs, which were to be achieved by 2015, were replaced in 2015 by the 17 SDGs (Hák et al., 2016). In these 17 target areas (concretised in 169 sub-targets and 303 indicators), it is evident that sustainability has become a global issue (Sachs, 2012). However, precisely this 'breadth' led to the SDGs being regarded by some as 'vague, weak, or meaningless' (Holden, Linnerud, & Banister, 2017, p. 213).

So far, the perspectives on sustainability and sustainable development originate primarily from a macro perspective – one of the most prominent approaches (Wieland, 2017). Michael Porter and Mark Kramer (2006, 2011) prominently transfer sustainability to the micro-level of business. Based on the insight that companies and their social and ecological environment are interdependent, the authors argue that value creation must be viewed more holistically and understood beyond the exclusive pursuit of profit. Thus, long-term success factors, such as customer needs, social impact, ecological resources management and supplier relationship quality, are considered and addressed. They define their idea of 'Creating Shared Value' (CSV) as 'policies and operating practices that enhance the competitiveness of a company while simultaneously advancing the economic and social conditions in the communities in which it operates' (Porter & Kramer, 2011, p. 66). CSV can be seen as an evolution of 'corporate social responsibility' and states that corporate sensitivity to the social and environmental surroundings is not philanthropy (i.e., costs that reduce profitability) but a source of growth and innovation. Satisfying social and environmental needs both opens new markets and secures companies' strategic resources in the long term (e.g., well-trained employees and steady consumption). It is, therefore, a matter of combining sustainable and responsible action with the achievement of economic success. Nevertheless, Porter and Kramer's win-win perspective has been questioned. Crane, Palazzo, Spence, and Matten (2014) criticise the concept of CSV as 'wishful thinking' because it fundamentally fails to recognise tensions between social, environmental and economic goals. Furthermore, Dembek, Singh, and Bhakoo (2016) argue that the concept is vague and that it resembles a 'management buzzword' that needs concretisation (e.g., by focussing on common needs; cf. Kragulj, 2023).

2.2 Methods and Results of Bibliographic Analysis and Topic Modelling

In this section, we analyse the current discourse on sustainability. We identify distinct research directions/themes as research strands on sustainability in the social sciences (Safón & Docampo, 2020) and point to central contributions that are representative of the respective research direction (and themes). To this end, we adopted a two-stage mixed-methods approach, combining bibliographic analysis and topic modelling based on natural language processing. The bibliographic analysis identified research clusters based on bibliographic data. The subsequent topic modelling approach detected common themes within a given text data set (i.e., abstracts of articles).

In July 2021, we searched in the *Web of Science* database for publications on sustainability that were listed in the SSCI-index. We chose all social science articles published between 2010 and 2020. Accordingly, our inclusion criteria were that 'sustainability' was mentioned either in the title, abstract, or as a keyword of the articles. Moreover, we restricted the search to English language papers and social sciences. The search resulted in 19,291 records. We analysed this large sample iteratively in two steps.

a. Firstly, we started with the *identification of research directions.* In order to make sense of the interrelations and cross-citations between all the papers in our sample we conducted a bibliographic analysis. This technique assumes that articles that refer to the same sources are similar in terms of content and thus belong to a common research direction or 'cluster', how we named them. Clusters are thus created by statistical correlations of the sources used for current contributions. More specifically, we conducted a bibliographic coupling analysis with the software VOSviewer 1.6.16 (van Eck & Waltman, 2010). In this way, we mapped the current state of the research landscape on sustainability-related social science research in eight clusters.

b. Building on that groundwork, *we identified themes per research direction.* Within each of our clusters, we explored three distinct themes. Towards that end, we used an algorithm for topic clustering analysis, specifically the software Mallet 2.0.8 (Graham, Weingart, & Milligan, 2012; McCallum, 2002). It analysed the abstracts of all papers per cluster automatically and examined for their similarity. The more words two contributions had in common in their abstract, the more 'related in content' they are according to this logic. Furthermore, the more frequently terms were detected (signal words), the more characteristic they were for the topic. This second step enabled us to dive deeper into the keywords and content of the respective clusters.

Fig. 8.1 shows the eight identified clusters represented by different colours. It is the outcome of our first step, the bibliographic analysis. The circles symbolise the papers belonging to the respective cluster (common colour). The size of these circles reflects how often an article has been cited, and their position reflects the interconnectedness with other cluster sources.

Table 8.1 lists and describes the eight research directions (clusters) that resulted from the bibliographic analysis. We assigned the respective names and

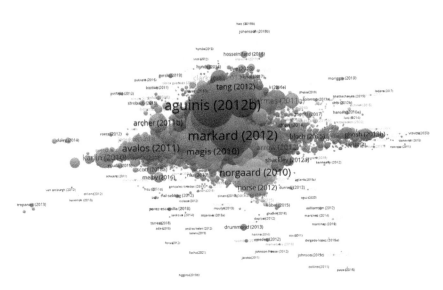

Fig. 8.1.   Cluster Analysis of Sustainability Papers (Bibliographic Coupling in VOSviewer 1.6.16).

Table 8.1. Research Directions (Clusters), Themes (Signal Words) and Representative Contributions.

Research Direction (Cluster)	Description	Descriptive Signal Words of the Three Themes per Cluster	Top Three Articles per Theme
1. CSR, stakeholder management and sustainability *Red* in Fig. 8.1	The top articles in this cluster were mainly published in management journals and thus represent a business perspective on 'sustainability'. CSR (corporate social responsibility) often appears as a keyword. The article by Aguinis and Glavas (2012), a literature review concerning CSR, is the most cited one in our selection.	CSR, corporate, firms, companies, performance, environmental, reporting, social, financial, disclosure, reports, responsibility, assurance, find, governance, market, stakeholder, firm, countries, quality	Cheng, Ioannou, and Serafeim (2013), *Strategic Management Journal*; Eccles, Ioannou, and Serafeim (2014), *Management Science*; Schaltegger, Hansen, and Lüdeke-Freund (2016), *Organization and Environment*
		Business, social, accounting, development, corporate, practice, stakeholders, systems, case, change, future, authors, understanding, field, challenges, review, institutional, society, local, public	Smith and Lewis (2011), *Academy of Management Review*; Doherty, Haugh, and Lyon (2014) and Adams, Jeanrenaud, Bessant, Denyer, and Overy (2015), *International Journal of Management Reviews*
		Environmental, organisational, green, innovation, practices, organisations, performance, social, employees, managers, role, environment, knowledge, development, business, leadership, resources, implementation, support, orientation	Aguinis and Glavas (2012), *Journal of Management*; Schaltegger and Wagner (2011), *Business Strategy and the Environment*; van Dierendonck (2010), *Journal of Management*
2. Sustainability transitions (policy) *Green* in Fig. 8.1	Contributions in this research direction go beyond purely descriptive analyses and deal normatively with how the transition to more sustainable forms of economy and society can succeed. Most assume that the economy is embedded in society and the environment. Measures for change towards greater sustainability are examined based on central topics such as mobility, energy and innovation.	Urban, system, transport, policy, development, systems, public, future, indicators, planning, city, performance, assessment, case, areas, social, time, policies, potential, cities	Egbue and Long (2012), *Energy Policy*; Greco, Ishizaka, Tasiou, and Torrisi (2018), *Social Indicators Research*; Kivimaa and Kern (2016), *Research Policy*
		Energy, economic, environmental, growth, development, countries, policy, policies, renewable, production, emissions, capital, resources, consumption, water, sector, green, power, electricity, resource	Geels et al. (2016), *Research Policy*; Zhang and Anadon (2014), *Ecological Economics*; Arrow, Dasgupta, Goulder, Mumford, and Oleson (2012), *Environment and Development Economics*

(Continued)

Table 8.1. (*Continued*)

Research Direction (Cluster)	Description	Descriptive Signal Words of the Three Themes per Cluster	Top Three Articles per Theme
		Social, policy, change, innovation, environmental, development, climate, political, governance, local, transition, knowledge, transitions, challenges, ecological, public, actors, systems, role, community	Markard, Raven, and Truffer (2012), *Research Policy*; Martin (2016), *Ecological Economics*; Smith and Raven (2012), *Research Policy*
3. Health, education and economic analysis *Blue* in Fig. 8.1	Sustainability in this cluster refers primarily to the time dimension, in the sense of 'in the long term'. Accordingly, articles from scientific journals in the fields of health and education are found here. From a 'global health' perspective, these issues are relevant to sustainability research: Health is not only the absence of disease, but also a socioeconomic factor. Moreover, the effects of climate change are addressed.	Education, social, development, policy, environmental, systems, change, community, global, economic, critical, role, practices, challenges, nature, public, work, educational, ways, local	Watermeyer, Crick, Knight, and Goodall (2020), *Higher Education*; Gonzales (2015), *Information Communication & Society*; Helsper (2012), *Communication Theory*
		Students, education, learning, development, university, higher, teachers, environmental, knowledge, universities, teaching, design, curriculum, student, institutions, design/ methodology/approach, originality/value, engineering, practical, change	Avalos (2011), *Teaching and Teacher Education*; Rieckmann (2012), *Futures*; Brundiers, Wiek, and Redman (2010), *International Journal of Sustainability in Higher Education*
		Health, implementation, programme, intervention, care, support, school, community, programs, training, schools, interventions, outcomes, children, services, quality, treatment, practice, years, clinical	Panter-Brick, Burgess, Eggerman, McAllister, Pruett, & Leckman, (2014), *Journal of Child Psychology and Psychiatry*; Karlin et al. (2010), *Journal of Traumatic Stress*; Doren et al. (2018), *European Child & Adolescent Psychiatry*
4. Green supply chain management and technology *Yellow* in Fig. 8.1	This cluster includes research on logistics topics such as the sustainable design of supply chains and production technologies. A focus of the third sub-cluster is also on the concept of the circular economy. This is an economic concept in which the use of new materials and resources as well as energy and waste should be minimised as much as	Supply, chain, performance, environmental, practices, green, social, firms, chains, supplier, suppliers, companies, logistics, managers, role, manufacturing, design/ methodology/approach, firm, corporate, case	Hong and Guo (2019), *Omega-International Journal of Management Science*; Kamble, Gunasekaran, and Dhone (2019), *International Journal of Production Research*; Green, Zelbst, Meacham, and Bhadauria (2012), *Supply Chain Management – An International Journal*

Cluster	Description	Keywords	References
	possible; using products and materials for as long as possible promotes regenerative natural systems.	Environmental, efficiency, economic, production, energy, performance, financial, cost, policy, products, product, emissions, show, waste, costs, transportation, proposed, carbon, problem, decisions	Chaabane, Ramudhin, and Paquet (2012), *International Journal of Production Economics*; Sueyoshi, Yuan, and Goto (2017), *Energy Economics*; Gebler, Uiterkamp, and Visser (2014), *Energy Policy*
		Development, business, industry, future, review, project, identify, identified, social, challenges, systems, key, manufacturing, construction, barriers, proposed, economy, implementation, projects, circular	Korhonen, Honkasalo, and Seppälä (2018), *Ecological Economics*; Saberi, Kouhizadeh, Sarkis, and Shen (2018), *International Journal of Production Research*; Murray, Skene, and Haynes (2015), *Journal of Business Ethics*
5. Environmental Ecosystem Services *Purple* in Fig. 8.1	Based on the fundamental need for a healthy ecosystem that ensures the survival of humanity, the top articles in this cluster deal with the preservation of the natural environment. The approach to sustainability is mostly a holistic one.	Fisheries, fishing, marine, resources, economic, fishery, resource, conservation, communities, ecosystem, ecological, fish, species, coastal, areas, stakeholders, policy, fishermen, natural, local	Singh et al. (2018), *Marine Policy*; Long, Charles, and Stephenson (2015), *Marine Policy*; Farley and Costanza (2010), *Ecological Economics*
	In particular, the cluster addresses topics such as maritime ecosystems and fisheries as well as agriculture and their potential for improvement for sustainable food security is highlighted. Accordingly, problems related to land use are also an important topic.	Governance, food, social, policy, global, environmental, development, local, systems, case, public, private, system, international, challenges, actors, change, institutional, political, role	Norgaard (2010), *Ecological Economics*; Magis (2010), *Society & Natural Resources*; Béné et al. (2019), *World Development*
		Production, forest, farmers, land, agricultural, water, economic, market, rural, environmental, show, countries, certification, markets, products, producers, higher, supply, b.v, food	Harvey and Pilgrim (2011), *Food Policy*; Powlson et al. (2011), *Food Policy*; Aker (2011), *Agricultural Economics*
6. Green consumption marketing *Turquoise* in Fig. 8.1	This research cluster focuses on the psychology of individual consumption decisions and sustainable marketing. For example, the labelling of sustainable products in the food sector is being researched. Or practices of the 'sharing economy' are considered, including the motivations underlying these practices and their implications for new service business models.	Food, consumption, environmental, behaviour, energy, change, health, pro-environmental, participants, behaviour, meat, waste, students, behaviours, water, attitudes, environment, norms, climate, production	Gifford (2011), *American Psychologist*; Garnett (2011), *Food Policy*; Benjaafar, Kong, Li, and Courcoubetis (2019), *Management Science*
		Consumers, consumer, green, products, environmental, product, perceived, social, purchase, brand, ethical, fashion, intention,	Paul, Modi, and Patel (2016), *Journal of Retailing and Consumer Services*; Grunert et al. (2014), *Food Policy*; Peloza and Shang

(Continued)

Table 8.1. *(Continued)*

Research Direction (Cluster)	Description	Descriptive Signal Words of the Three Themes per Cluster	Top Three Articles per Theme
		intentions, perceptions, attributes, organic, choice, quality, behaviour	(2010), *Journal of the Academy of Marketing Science*
		Social, marketing, practices, sharing, consumption, development, service, public, community, future, practice, economic, business, economy, users, knowledge, systems, system, key, understanding	Hamari, Sjöklint, and Ukkonen (2015), *Journal of the Association for Information Science and Technology*; Vargo and Lusch (2017), *International Journal of Research in Marketing*; Cheng (2016), *International Journal of Hospitality Management*
7. Sustainable tourism *Orange* in Fig. 8.1	The thematic focus of this cluster is on sustainable tourism. For example, the environmental impact of tourism is examined. Papers in this cluster investigate 'over tourism' and its social impacts from the perspective of the local population. They analyse mechanisms of tourism. The shock induced by the COVID-19 pandemic is already addressed by some articles.	Tourism, development, social, local, community, economic, stakeholders, communities, cultural, rural, destination, interviews, growth, heritage, governance, planning, destinations, case, knowledge, policy	Bornhorst, Ritchie, and Sheehan (2010), *Tourism Management*; Gonzalez, Coromina, and Gali (2018), *Tourism Review*; Bramwell (2011), *Journal of Sustainable Tourism*
		Tourists, environmental, tourist, destination, residents, economic, destinations, tourism, visitors, indicators, marketing, quality, ecotourism, perceptions, perceived, importance, experience, activities, hotel, performance	Tian, Peng, Zhang, Zhang, and Wang (2019), *Technological and Economic Development of the Economy*; Lee and Jan (2019), *Tourism Management*; Ramkissoon, Smith, and Weiler (2013), *Tourism Management*
		Industry, change, tourism, practices, climate, future, environmental, global, events, business, potential, sector, hospitality, sport, water, critical, travel, systems, policy, related	Hall, Scott, and Gössling (2020), *Tourism Geographies*; Seraphin, Sheeran, and Pilato (2018), *Journal of Destination Marketing & Management*; Jiang and Wen (2020), *International Journal of Contemporary Hospitality Management*
8. Innovative financial and fiscal development *Brown* in Fig. 8.1	While the most cited articles in the first two thematic sub-clusters (topics) deal with the sustainable (in the sense of long-term) development of economic topics such as taxes and debt, the focus in this cluster is	Fiscal, debt, countries, public, policy, government, rate, crisis, account, ratio, tax, budget, show, GDP, interest, monetary, deficit, rates, risk, find	Elliot (2011), *MIS Quarterly*; Ghosh, Kim, Mendoza, Ostry, and Qureshi (2013), *Economic Journal*; Baum, Checherita-Westphal, and Rother (2013), *Journal of International Money and Finance*

otherwise more on the area of environmental sustainability. Topics include, for example, the substitution of fossil fuels or renewable energy consumption	Pension, financial, system, social, health, policy, public, welfare, political, population, state, local, economic, reform, care, reforms, government, long-term, retirement, policies	van Barneveld et al. (2020), *Economic and Labour Relations Review*; Faguet (2014), *World Development*; Bonsang, Adam, and Perelman (2012), *Journal of Health Economics*
	Growth, economic, countries, development, energy, income, consumption, capital, environmental, investment, period, panel, economy, global, evidence, price, time, financial, significant, market	Saint Akadiri, Alola, Akadiri, and Alola (2019), *Energy Policy*; Asongu, Roux, and Biekpe (2018), *Technological Forecasting and Social Change*; Bloch, Rafiq, and Salim (2015), *Economic Modelling*

Note: Figure in colours for the digital version.

descriptions in columns one and two on the basis of their qualitative content, of the mostly cited papers. This mapping provides an overview of research directions of sustainability. Within each cluster, we present three research themes detailing the respective cluster. They are described by their characteristic signal words resulting from the topic modelling analysis. Furthermore, we list three articles representative of each theme within a cluster (research direction). According to the *Web of Science* database, these articles were most frequently cited by others (relative citations per year). In other words, the signal words and the top three articles in columns three and four of Table 8.1 are the results of our topic modelling analysis.

2.3 Overview of Corporate Sustainability Definitions and Content Patterns

In the following, we take a closer look at definitions of corporate sustainability. Meuer et al. (2020) identified 33 different definitions of 'corporate sustainability'. We examined these definition for recurring content patterns. Our results are shown in Table 8.2. Supported by these results, we recognise some recurrent patterns that might be characteristic of a business perspective on the sustainability concept:

a. The differentiation into three sustainability dimensions – 'People, Planet, Profit' ('3 Ps') – is found in (more than) three out of four definitions. However, the most frequent explicit reference in this sample (88%) is to the social dimension of sustainability.
b. Most definitions aim to integrate the three sustainability dimensions or the related value creation. Only two definitions describe corporate sustainability as the active reduction of the negative consequences of corporate action (mitigation).
c. However, it is also evident that some definitions (24%) place one 'P' in the foreground. In six cases, for example, the sustainability dimension 'profit' becomes dominant insofar as 'people' and 'planet" become a condition for 'profit" and are to be included, integrated, or taken into account accordingly (e.g., Salzmann, Ionescu-somers, and Steger (2005); Steger (2004) or Hahn et al. (2014)).
d. An explicit future orientation, mainly in the form of ensuring the ability to act and perform in the future, is found in some (24%) of the definitions analysed.

These results provide additional knowledge about corporate perspectives on sustainability. They shed light on existing knowledge *about* (or business perspectives on) sustainability and demonstrate differences depending on the respective definitions used. A question open for further investigation is if the definitions that do not refer to the environmental aspect can be considered truly sustainable as they do not take into account existing resource limitations. The same applies to the realisation of the future perspective (d), if the explicit temporal future orientation is missing, as is the case with the majority of these definitions. Moreover, if profit dominates the other dimensions (c), how can planet

Table 8.2. Definitions of Corporate Sustainability and Content Characteristics.

Source	Definition	Action	Mechanism/Target	'People' (Social Goals)	'Planet' (Environmental Goals)	'Profit' (Economic Goals)	'P' – Dominance/Priority	Future Focus	Other Focus
Elkington (1997)	'The attempt by firms to balance social, economic, and environmental goals'.	Balance goals	Compensation (integration)	x	x	x			
Atkinson (2000)	'Corporate sustainability means full-cost accounting with regard to all externalities caused by the firm based on the idea that corporations contribute or inhibit sustainable development'.	Account for externalities	Assume responsibility (costs)						All externalities
Bansal and Roth (2000)	'A set of corporate initiatives aimed at mitigating a firm's impact on the natural environment'.	Mitigate negative impact	Mitigation		x				
Dyllick and Hockerts (2002)	'Corporate sustainability can be defined as meeting the needs of a firm's direct and indirect stakeholders (such as shareholders, employees, clients, pressure groups, communities, etc.), without compromising its ability to meet the needs of future stakeholders as well'.	Meet needs; no compromising future abilities	Value added	x				x	
Funk (2003)	'A sustainable organization is one whose characteristics and actions are designed to lead a "desirable future state" for all stakeholders'.	Designed to deliver value	Value added	x				x	

(Continued)

Table 8.2. (*Continued*)

Source	Definition	Action	Mechanism/ Target	'People' (Social Goals)	'Planet' (Environmental Goals)	'Profit' (Economic Goals)	'P' - Dominance/ Priority	Future Focus	Other Focus
Hart and Milstein (2003)	'Contributes to sustainable development by delivering simultaneously economic, social, and environmental benefits. Sustainable development is the process of achieving human development in an inclusive, connected, equitable, prudent, and secure manner'.	Deliver benefits	Value added	x	x	x	People		
Marshall and Brown (2003)	'An "ideal" sustainable organization will not use natural resources faster than the rates of renewal, recycling, or regeneration of those resources'.	Not overuse resources	Sufficiency		x				
van Marrewijk and Marco (2003)	'In general, corporate sustainability and CSR refer to company activities – voluntary by definition – demonstrating the inclusion of social and environmental concerns in business operations and in interactions with stakeholders'.	Take actions; include	Integration	x	x	x	Profit		
Wilson (2003)	'A new and evolving corporate management paradigm that recognises that corporate growth and	Pursue goals	Integration	x	x	x			

	Definition				
	customer relationships, and the quality of products and services as well as adopting and pursuing ethical business practices, creating sustainable jobs, building value for all the stakeholders, and attending the needs of the underserved'.				
Neubaum and Zahra (2006)	'The ability of a firm to nurture and support growth over time by effectively meeting the expectations of diverse stakeholders'.	Nurture and support growth; meet expectations	Growth	x	x
Russell, Haigh, and Griffiths (2007)	'Working towards long-term economic performance, working towards positive outcomes for the natural environment, supporting people and social outcomes, adopting a holistic approach'.	Perform; support	Integration	x	x x
Hahn and Figge (2011)	'The pursuit of environmental, social, and economic goals in order to achieve long-term prosperity of the firm (organizational target level) or to contribute to the long-term prosperity of society and humankind (societal target level)'.	Pursue goals; contribute	Integration, long-term livelihood	x	x x
Porter and Kramer (2011)	'Policies and practices that enhance the competitiveness of a company while simultaneously advancing the economic and social conditions in the communities in which operates'.	Enhance competitiveness; advancing conditions	Competitiveness	x	x

(Continued)

Table 8.2. (*Continued*)

Source	Definition	Action	Mechanism/Target	'People' (Social Goals)	'Planet' (Environmental Goals)	'Profit' (Economic Goals)	'P' - Dominance/Priority	Future Focus	Other Focus
Lozano (2012)	'Corporate activities that proactively seek to contribute to sustainability equilibria, including the economic, environmental, and social dimensions of today, as well as their interrelations within and throughout the time dimension while addressing the company's system (including Operations and production, Management and strategy, Organizational systems, Procurement and marketing, and Assessment and communication); and its stakeholders'.	Proactively contribute to equilibria	Value added	x	x	x		x	
Valente (2012)	'A step toward a proactive orientation to sustainability. Firms need to find ways to interconnect social, economic, and ecological systems using "coordinated approaches social, ecological, and economic stakeholders operating as unified network or system"'.	Proactively integrate	Integration	x	x	x			
Milne and Gray (2012)	'Incorporating an entity's economic, environmental,		Assuming responsibility	x	x	x			

Source	Definition	Measure performance holistically	(performance reporting)			Profit	
	'and social performance indicators into its management and reporting processes'.						
Schaltegger, Beckmann, and Hansen (2013)	'The successful market-oriented realization and integration of ecological, social, and economic challenges to a company'.	Integrate challenges	Integration	x	x		
Bansal and DesJardine (2014)	'The ability of firms to respond to their short-term financial needs without compromising their (or others') ability to meet their future needs'.	Respond to needs, without compromising	Need satisfaction	x	x		x
Benn, Dunphy, and Griffiths (2014)	'Sustainable organizations engage in activities that (a) extend the socially useful life of organizations, (b) enhance the planet's ability to maintain and renew the viability of the biosphere and protect all living species, (c) enhance society's ability to maintain itself and to solve its major problems, and (d) maintain a decent level of welfare for present and future generations of humanity'.	Take actions; enhance; maintain	Value added	x	x		x
Eccles et al. (2014)	'Integrating social and environmental issues into a company's strategy and business model through the adoption of corporate policies'.	Integrate issues	Integration	x	x		

(Continued)

Table 8.2. (*Continued*)

Source	Definition	Action	Mechanism/ Target	'People' (Social Goals)	'Planet' (Environmental Goals)	'Profit' (Economic Goals)	'P' – Dominance/ Priority	Future Focus	Other Focus
Hahn, Preuss, Pinkse, and Figge (2014)	'A concept that "refers to a company's activities [. . .] demonstrating the inclusion of social and environmental concerns in business operations and in interactions with stakeholders'.	Take actions; include	Integration	x	x	x	Profit		
Sharma (2014)	'The achievement of a firm's short-term financial, social, and environmental performance without compromising its long-term financial, social, and environmental performance'.	Perform; without compromising	Value added	x	x	x		x	
Sterman (2015)	'Sustainability initiatives that are framed as (also) helping to heal the world'.	Help	Value added						'Heal the world"
Dočekalová and Kocmanová (2016)	'A key concept for companies to achieve long-term benefits by integrating activities associated with sustainability into their strategy'.	Achieve long-term benefits; integrate	Integration						Long-term
Dyllick and Muff (2015)	'A truly sustainable company understanding how it can create a significant, positive impact in critical and relevant areas for society and the planet'.	Create impact	Value added	x	x	x	Planet		

| Schaltegger et al. (2016) | 'Sustainability management refers to approaches dealing with social, environmental, and economic issues in an integrated manner to transform organizations in a way that they contribute to the sustainable development of the economy and society, within the limits of the ecosystem'. | Deal with and integrate issues; contribute; respect limits | Integration, value creation |

Source: Adapted From Meuer et al., 2020, p. 324ff.

and people be more than simply add-ons? In how far do such definitions contribute to sustainability-as-a-buzzword or 'greenwashing' tendencies? There-fore, in the next section, we aim to explore the types of knowledge and business models that foster action in order to walk the sustainability talk.

3. KNOWLEDGE *FOR* SUSTAINABILITY

The notion of 'knowledge for sustainability' refers to action orientation or competencies that support knowledge creation that enables organisations or individuals to act more sustainably. This includes the capabilities of 'diagnosing' (cf. Lewin, 1946) the sustainability of practices in specific local contexts in order to act accordingly. To provide an illustrative example: The issue of the sustain-ability of biomass heating could be evaluated differently in a context of a country of excess regrowth of wood or de-forestation (Bosch, van de Pol, & Philp, 2015). Consequently, knowledge for sustainability also enables contextual judgement.

3.1 Knowledge Types

Caniglia et al. (2021, p. 95ff) refer to 'three dimensions of actions for sustain-ability', i.e. 'intentional design', 'shared agency' and 'contextual realization', and related types of knowledge supporting these actions:

(1) 'Knowledge informing intentional design': 'Generative knowledge' enables finding alternative solutions based on a variety of perspectives. 'Prescriptive knowledge' on sustainability provides guidance and inspires actors to implement change. 'Strategic knowledge' allows for defining action priorities, anticipating consequences and reacting to changing circumstances. It enables bringing intention and context into a fit.

(2) 'Knowledge enhancing shared agency': 'Critical knowledge' is necessary to challenge existing distributions, institutions and basic assumptions. 'Empowering knowledge' supports knowledge for collective action. And, the expertise and knowledge generated by collaborative practices that bring together diverse perspectives, views and interests are also crucial for enhancing shared agency (i.e., 'co-produced knowledge').

(3) 'Knowledge enabling contextual realization': 'Emergent knowledge' results from 'open cycles of intervention, reflection and evaluation'. It is important to identify possible pathways and to understand changing circumstances and experiences. 'Tactical knowledge' is needed to build networks, leverage existing resources and understand interventions' short and long-term conse-quences. Additionally, 'situated knowledge' relates to the specific context, e.g., regional conditions, and enables situative action.

These types of knowledge are particularly crucial to translate 'actions for sustainability' into concrete changes on an individual and group level. They have wide-ranging effects, for example on the sustainability of business models, which will be discussed next.

3.2 (More) Sustainable Business Models

A business model explains how a company works, i.e., it reflects the core of its value-creating activities. It can help to understand and define the nature and logic of this entrepreneurial core as defined by Geissdoerfer, Vladimirova and Evans (2018, p. 402): 'Simplified representations of the value proposition, value creation, and delivery, and value capture elements and the interactions between these elements within an organizational unit'.

(More) sustainable business models are based on the '3 Ps' (People, Planet, Profit) conception and thus aim to create economic, social and ecological value in a long-term perspective. Anchoring sustainability at the company's core can represent an important competitive advantage (Bocken, Short, Rana, & Evans, 2014; Porter & Kramer, 2011). However, there is no business model for sustainability per se. Sustainability can only be incorporated in specific business models to a greater or lesser extent. This means that all business models depend on some kind of resources. The aim of integrating sustainability into a business model is, for instance, to waste less. However, a fully sustainable business model is hard to imagine as this would theoretically imply no use of resources. Even circular economy conceptions do not fully achieve net zero. The underlying and highly disputed question is if a complete de-coupling of resource use is possible (e.g. Lehmann, Delbard, & Lange, 2022).

The following section presents selected contributions on archetypal strategies and principles for designing and evaluating frameworks for determining the maturity of (more) sustainable business models.

3.3 Domains and Strategies for (More) Sustainable Business Models

Bocken et al. (2014) developed archetypal strategies for (more) sustainable business models in their widely cited paper. Categorised into three domains (i.e., technology, social and organisation), these provide action orientation for the development of concrete and context-specific measures. They are listed in Fig. 8.2. Furthermore, the authors give examples per strategy in their paper (Bocken et al., 2014, p. 48).

3.4 Sustainable Circular Economy Business Models

A particular category of (more) sustainable business models is sustainable circular business models (Geissdoerfer, Vladimirova, et al., 2018); Fig. 8.3 illustrates their particularities (Geissdoerfer, Morioka, de Carvalho, & Evans, 2018, p. 714). Although these do not drop the "people' and "profit' dimensions, the sustainable use of natural resources is at the forefront of circular business models (Pieroni, McAloone, & Pigosso, 2019, p. 209).

3.5 Principles for the Design of (More) Sustainable Business Models

In the strategies presented in Table 8.3, we recognise three pillars that can be considered foundational for the design of (more) sustainable business models – especially those of the circular economy. These can be found early and regularly in the German-speaking ('grey') (e.g., von Winterfeld, 2007) but also in the English literature (Huber, 2000) and are regarded as essential principles of sustainability (Bohnenberger, 2021, p. 172; Gunarathne & Lee, 2021). These pillars are (i) Sufficiency – '*less*': Resource consumption is to be reduced (in absolute terms) by eliminating or minimising the need for resources, (ii) Efficiency – '*better*': The use of resources is to be improved – i.e., the ratio of output to the input of materials and energy is to be increased – to achieve higher resource productivity, (iii) Consistency – '*different*': Environmentally harmful/damaging resources/technologies/processes are to be substituted by environmentally friendly resources/technologies/processes.

3.6 Evaluation and Maturity Assessment of (More) Sustainable Business Models

Implementing sustainability strategies leads to changes in the business model, if it the efforts go beyond 'greenwashing'. These changes can happen either incrementally or radically, whereas the former form is more common. To compare and classify business models and, above all, to evaluate (and plan) corporate sustainability development, several framework models can be found in the literature that allow the maturity of corporate sustainability to be determined. Three selected models are presented in more detail in the subsequent paragraphs.

Kleine and von Hauff (2009) present a management tool ('Integrative Sustainability Triangle') that is based on the so-called triple bottom line that we discussed earlier. It allows for specifying and systematising success indicators, action options, goals and stakeholders to plan and evaluate concrete measures. It can help to make the overall sustainability performance graphically visible as an evaluation tool. Appropriately measurable success indicators can be integrated into the triangle to measure the company's success 'three-dimensionally', i.e., in line with the requirements of a holistic sustainability concept. Furthermore, Kleine and von Hauff (2009, p. 523) offer a schematic representation of the management tool; they bring examples for representing specific contents in their integrative sustainability triangle.

Complementary to the integrative sustainability triangle, which can be used both at the level of individual measures and for aggregated performance measurement, van Marrewijk and Werre (2003) developed a stage model of corporate sustainability that can be used to evaluate the 'sustainability maturity level' of the entire company. Based on six stages, the development of a company can be described in terms of its sustainability orientation.

A very similar, albeit extended, unified model of stages of corporate sustainability is presented by Landrum (2018), which can also be used to evaluate the maturity of corporate sustainability. To this end, the author integrated 22 models of corporate sustainability, corporate social responsibility, environmental management and

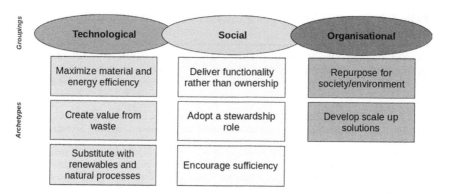

Fig. 8.2.   Archetypes of Sustainable Business Models. *Source*: Adapted from
Bocken et al., 2014, p. 48.

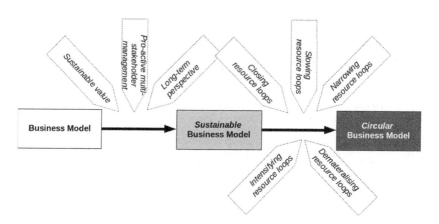

Fig. 8.3.   Comparison of Traditional, Sustainable and Circular Economy
Business Models. *Source*: Adapted from Geissdoerfer, Morioka, et al., 2018, p. 714.

sustainable development. The model of van Marrewijk and Werre (2003) is also
included to gain a holistic understanding of sustainability and to show different
interpretations of the concept. This results in a spectrum of degrees of sustainability
that can be systematised along the continuum between 'weak sustainability' and
'strong sustainability'. This can be the basis for determining the maturity of a
company's sustainability orientation, giving it a better understanding 'of what is
needed to achieve sustainability and reduce environmental degradation' (p. 288).
The five stages are described as follows (Landrum, 2018, p. 299ff):

(1) Level 1 – *'Compliance'* (very weak sustainability): Companies respond with
    sustainability measures that are externally enforced.
(2) Level 2 – *'Business-centred'* (weak sustainability): Companies proactively
    implement business-centred sustainability measures that are beneficial to the
    company's economic success (self-benefit, costs, profit, image/reputation,

Table 8.3. Strategies for Designing (More) Sustainable Circular Economy Business Models.

Lacy and Rutqvist (2015), OECD (2019, p. 25)	Ellen MacArthur Foundation (2015, p. 9)	Henry, Bauwens, Hekkert, and Kirchherr (2020, p. 5)	Pieroni, McAloone, and Pigosso (2020, p. 5)	Salvador, Barros, Freire, Halog, Piekarski, and De Francisco (2021, p. 5)
Circular procurement: Use of renewable energies, ecological or fully recyclable raw materials (as a substitute for raw materials with only one life cycle). *Material recovery*: Recovery of useful resources/energy from disposed products/ components. *Product life extension*: Extending the life cycle of products/ components through repair, upgrade and resale. *Sharing platforms*: Increased use of products through sharing/ownership. *Product as a service*: Provision of services instead of ownership (circular resource productivity).	*'Regenerate'*: Conversion to renewable energy and materials; recovery, maintenance and restoration of ecosystem condition; return of recovered biological resources to the biosphere. *'Share'*: Sharing assets (e.g., machines, space, tools); reuse/ second-hand; extend life through maintenance, design for longevity, expandability, etc. *'Optimise'*: Increase performance/ efficiency; eliminate waste in production/supply chains; use of Big Data, automation, remote management/ control. *'Loop'*: Reprocessing of products or components; recycling of materials; extraction of valuable raw materials from wastes. *'Virtualise'*: Direct dematerialisation (e.g., books → e-books, business	*'Regenerate'*: Maintaining and enhancing the performance (benefits) of ecological systems for society (e.g., urban agriculture or green roofs). *'Reduce'*: Increase efficiency (improved use) by avoiding or minimising hazardous materials (design, production). *'Reuse'*: Returning products to the economic cycle after their first use; extending the life of products and their components (repair, second-hand market, etc.) *'Recycle'*: Processing of used materials for new use with the same (upcycling) or lower (downcycling) quality. *'Recover'*: Energy recovery.	*Manufacturing side (upstream)*: *Circular production* and *distribution*: On-demand, eco-efficiency, collection/retrieval/ recycling of end-of-life materials. *Circular procurement*: Asset management, cooperation/ symbiosis. *Sales/customer side (downstream)*: *Dematerialisation* and increased *efficiency*: Services instead of products, promotion of sufficiency. *Collaborative consumption*: Sharing, pooling. *Product-service Systems*: Access models, performance/ outcome models. *Longevity*: 'Lifelong' products, serviceable products, hybrid models. *'Next Life'*: Direct reuse, second-hand market, product transformation, component/raw material recycling.	Strategic partnerships Cooperation/ Symbiosis Waste prevention Ecological use of materials Product service systems Dematerialisation Digital technologies Reuse Recycling Reprocessing Reprocessing Extension of the product life Take-back systems Repair and maintenance

Table 8.3. *(Continued)*

Lacy and Rutqvist (2015), OECD (2019, p. 25)	Ellen MacArthur Foundation (2015, p. 9)	Henry, Bauwens, Hekkert, and Kirchherr (2020, p. 5)	Pieroni, McAloone, and Pigosso (2020, p. 5)	Salvador, Barros, Freire, Halog, Piekarski, and De Francisco (2021, p. 5)
	travel → video conferencing); indirect dematerialisation (e.g., online shopping). *'Exchange'*: Replace old materials with modern and non-renewable materials; use new technologies; use new products/ services (e.g., multimodal transportation).			

recruitment, risk management). At this stage, companies address one or two 'Ps' and pursue a fundamental growth- and consumption-oriented strategy, which resembles a 'business-as-usual' approach with gradual changes. Sustainability is understood as 'doing less bad'.

(3) Level 3 – *'Systemic'* (medium sustainability): Companies work with others and integrate the entire sustainability spectrum ('3 Ps') to bring about systemic change. Sustainability is understood as 'doing more good', although the company fundamentally follows a growth and consumption-oriented strategy and continues to take an anthropocentric view of the world.

(4) Level 4 – *'Regenerative'* (strong sustainability): Sustainability is inherent in entrepreneurial activity and questions growth and resource consumption. Qualitative development is pursued without quantitative growth. Thus, the limits of growth and ecological performance are explicitly recognised. The company actively pursues the restoration and regeneration of natural resources. Nevertheless, the anthropocentric view of the world is maintained.

(5) Level 5 – *'Co-evolutionary'* (very strong sustainability): People, companies and societies see themselves in equal partnership with the natural world, giving as much as they take; the anthropocentric worldview is dropped. It is not about 'managing' the environment but about a mutually supportive and beneficial relationship and synergy in a 'we are part of the environment' way of thinking.

An alternative model for classifying different business models in terms of sustainability is by Dyllick and Muff (2015). It describes four maturity levels of corporate sustainability along with a simplified view of value creation (inputs/problem/'what', outputs/'what for' and processes/'how'). The four stages of their model are described as follows (Dyllick & Muff, 2015, p. 163ff):

(1) Stage 1 – *'Business-as-Usual'*: The focus is exclusively on economic considerations (e.g., cheap raw materials, efficient processes, strong market position) to maximise profit (shareholder value), which leads to the externalisation of costs. In line with the premise that 'the business of business is business' (c.f. Friedman, 1970), an 'inside-out' strategy is pursued, which places the pursuit of profit at the centre of the corporate target system.

(2) Stage 2 – *'Business Sustainability 1.0'* – *'broadening the business concern'*: It is recognised that there are social and environmental challenges outside the usual market mechanics that represent economic risks and economic opportunities for the company. These challenges are addressed by integrating them into the business model. Nevertheless, the fundamental logic of the business model remains untouched; profit is in the foreground.

(3) Stage 3 – *'Business Sustainability 2.0'* – *'expanding the value created'*: In this stage, sustainability is not only seen as a market and business opportunity but changes the target system of the company; value creation goes beyond the pursuit of profit (shareholder value), environmental aspects and stakeholders move into the focus of holistic value creation ('triple bottom line – 3 Ps').

(4) Stage 4 - *'Business Sustainability 3.0'* – *'changing the perspective'*: This stage is described as 'true sustainability'. Here, the perspective is shifted to 'outside-in' so that it is not just a matter of minimising the negative impacts of the usual business model ('inside-out'), but of transforming the core of corporate activity in such a way that a significantly positive impact is achieved for society and the environment.

The competencies for sustainability and diverse approaches and typologies to facilitate business model advancement towards sustainability can be considered knowledge *for* sustainability as they aim to get into action and walk the talk towards the goal of more sustainable actions. They aim to provide valuable nuances as a business model is hardly ever 0 or 100% sustainable. The assessment depends upon the perspective, contextual interpretation, on the individual dimensions focused on – or their integration – and temporal considerations. In terms of time, more sustainable equals more long-term thinking. Avoiding the buzzword-like use of sustainability implies that all these issues have to be taken into account in concrete cases as well as acknowledging and working on resolving tensions and trade-offs. Privileging any other than the environmental dimension is kind of cutting off one's nose to spite one's face as economy and society rely onto nature's resources to exist.

4. CONCLUSIONS

This work aimed to build foundations for knowledge *about* sustainability and knowledge *for* sustainability. To trace and present the current discourse on sustainability, a comprehensive analysis of English-language literature identified research directions, topics and representative contributions in each case to map knowledge *about* sustainability. In a further step, over 30 definitions of sustainability identified by Meuer et al. (2020) were analysed. The chapter demonstrated that the target triad of 'people', 'planet' and 'profit', i.e., the integration of social, ecological and economic goals, is central. So is the long-term time horizon. Moreover, the distinct approaches found in literature regarding sustainability offer an overview regarding research framings and directions that future works might aim to connect. As this work does not discuss the epistemological and ontological assumptions of the respective research directions, future work could build upon this chapter and critically examine the basic assumptions made in the distinct approaches basic assumptions.

In the second part (knowledge *for* sustainability), the three knowledge types for sustainability (Caniglia et al., 2021) were presented. They are key for context-specific interpretation and actions for more sustainability. This knowledge is reflected in actions towards (more) sustainable business models in companies, with circular economy business models as current forms of sustainable business models that focus mainly on the crucially important 'planet' target. Domains, strategies and derived principles for sustainable business models in the literature were identified and discussed. Furthermore, framework models presented in the literature for evaluating and determining the sustainability maturity level of a company were analysed. These approaches to walk the sustainability talk and make the path more transparent through the perspective of easy-to-grasp taxonomies aim to encourage action towards the goal of more sustainability. However, sustainability is not a target that can ever be reached fully but – depending on the perspective – involve tensions and trade-offs and therefore constant action and reflection processes. This holds especially true for temporal considerations.

This study is precious to new scholars researching sustainability that aim to understand definitions, dimensions and diversity of the field and practitioners trying to realise the concept in a meaningful way rather than using sustainability as a buzzword to gain attraction for their business. Notwithstanding the contributions, this research has some limitations. Namely, the restriction to the social sciences in the search, eliminating other areas, e.g., technology. Additionally, the search protocol could be improved to encompass synonyms and the use of Boolean markers. For future avenues, we envision the development of a tool for companies to measure and benchmark their maturity towards sustainability. Especially for SMEs, we diagnose a lack of a tailor-made tool to assess their maturity level of the corporate sustainability. Knowing about the concept is a prerequisite to diagnose respective starting points and start acting. We hope that this chapter provides the groundwork to make the meaning(s) of sustainability easier to grasp in order to walk the first step of action to implement sustainability principles in practice. Therefore, we conclude that (more) sustainable management is possible and we hope that our contribution can enable scholars and practitioners to gain knowledge *about* and *for* sustainability, to diagnose areas for improvement and to act more sustainably.

REFERENCES

Adams, R., Jeanrenaud, S., Bessant, J., Denyer, D., & Overy, P. (2015). Sustainability-oriented innovation: A systematic review. *International Journal of Management Reviews, 18*(2), 180–205. doi:10.1111/ijmr.12068

Aguinis, H., & Glavas, A. (2012). What we know and don't know about corporate social responsibility. *Journal of Management, 38*(4), 932–968. doi:10.1177/0149206311436079

Akadiri, S. S., Alola, A. A., Akadiri, A. C., & Alola, U. V. (2019). Renewable energy consumption in EU-28 countries: Policy toward pollution mitigation and economic sustainability. *Energy Policy, 132*, 803–810. doi:10.1016/j.enpol.2019.06.040

Aker, J. C. (2011). Dial "A" for agriculture: A review of information and communication technologies for agricultural extension in developing countries. *Agricultural Economics, 42*(6), 631–647. doi:10.1111/j.1574-0862.2011.00545.x

Arrow, K. J., Dasgupta, P., Goulder, L. H., Mumford, K. J., & Oleson, K. (2012). Sustainability and the measurement of wealth. *Environment and Development Economics, 17*(3), 317–353. doi:10.1017/s1355770x12000137

Asongu, S. A., Roux, S. L., & Biekpe, N. (2018). Enhancing ICT for environmental sustainability in sub-Saharan Africa. *Technological Forecasting and Social Change, 127*, 209–216. doi:10.1016/j.techfore.2017.09.022

Atkinson, G. (2000). Measuring corporate sustainability. *Journal of Environmental Planning and Management, 43*(2), 235–252. doi:10.1080/09640560010694

Avalos, B. (2011). Teacher professional development in Teaching and Teacher Education over ten years. *Teaching and Teacher Education, 27*(1), 10–20. doi:10.1016/j.tate.2010.08.007

Bansal, P., & DesJardine, M. R. (2014). Business sustainability: It is about time. *Strategic Organization, 12*(1), 70–78. doi:10.1177/1476127013520265

Bansal, P., & Roth, K. (2000). Why companies go green: A model of ecological responsiveness. *Academy of Management Journal, 43*(4), 717–736. doi:10.5465/1556363

Barneveld, K. van, Quinlan, M., Kriesler, P., Junor, A., Baum, F., Chowdhury, A., … Rainnie, A. (2020). The COVID-19 pandemic: Lessons on building more equal and sustainable societies. *Economic and Labour Relations Review, 31*(2), 133–157. doi:10.1177/1035304620927107

Baum, A., Checherita-Westphal, C., & Rother, P. (2013). Debt and growth: New evidence for the euro area. *Journal of International Money and Finance, 32*, 809–821. doi:10.1016/j.jimonfin.2012.07.004

Béné, C., Oosterveer, P., Lamotte, L., Brouwer, I. D., Haan, S. de, Prager, S. D., … Khoury, C. K. (2019). When food systems meet sustainability – Current narratives and implications for actions. *World Development, 113*, 116–130. doi:10.1016/j.worlddev.2018.08.011

Benjaafar, S., Kong, G., Li, X., & Courcoubetis, C. (2019). Peer-to-peer product sharing: Implications for ownership, usage, and social welfare in the sharing economy. *Management Science, 65*(2), 477–493. doi:10.1287/mnsc.2017.2970

Benn, S., Dunphy, D., & Griffiths, A. (2014). *Organizational change for corporate sustainability*. New York, NY: Routledge.

Bloch, H., Rafiq, S., & Salim, R. (2015). Economic growth with coal, oil and renewable energy consumption in China: Prospects for fuel substitution. *Economic Modelling, 44*, 104–115. doi:10.1016/j.econmod.2014.09.017

Bocken, N. M. P., Short, S. W., Rana, P., & Evans, S. (2014). A literature and practice review to develop sustainable business model archetypes. *Journal of Cleaner Production, 65*, 42–56.

Bohnenberger, K. (2021). Can 'sufficiency' reconcile social and environmental goals? A Q-methodological analysis of German housing policy. *Journal of Housing and the Built Environment, 36*(1), 171–189.

Bonsang, E., Adam, S., & Perelman, S. (2012). Does retirement affect cognitive functioning? *Journal of Health Economics, 31*(3), 490–501. doi:10.1016/j.jhealeco.2012.03.005

Bornhorst, T., Ritchie, J. R. B., & Sheehan, L. (2010). Determinants of tourism success for DMOs & destinations: An empirical examination of stakeholders' perspectives. *Tourism Management, 31*(5), 572–589. doi:10.1016/j.tourman.2009.06.008

Bosch, R., van de Pol, M., & Philp, J. (2015). Policy: Define biomass sustainability. *Nature, 523*(7562), Art. 7562. doi:10.1038/523526a

Bramwell, B. (2011). Governance, the state and sustainable tourism: A political economy approach. *Journal of Sustainable Tourism, 19*(4–5), 459–477. doi:10.1080/09669582.2011.576765

Brundiers, K., Wiek, A., & Redman, C. L. (2010). Real-world learning opportunities in sustainability: From classroom into the real world. *International Journal of Sustainability in Higher Education, 11*(4), 308–324. doi:10.1108/14676371011077540

Caniglia, G., Luederitz, C., von Wirth, T., Fazey, I., Martín-López, B., Hondrila, K., . . . Lang, D. J. (2021). A pluralistic and integrated approach to action-oriented knowledge for sustainability. *Nature Sustainability, 4*(2), 93–100.

Chaabane, A., Ramudhin, A., & Paquet, M. (2012). Design of sustainable supply chains under the emission trading scheme. *International Journal of Production Economics, 135*(1), 37–49. doi:10.1016/j.ijpe.2010.10.025

Cheng, B., Ioannou, I., & Serafeim, G. (2013). Corporate social responsibility and access to finance. *Strategic Management Journal, 35*(1), 1–23. doi:10.1002/smj.2131

Cheng, M. (2016). Sharing economy: A review and agenda for future research. *International Journal of Hospitality Management, 57*, 60–70. doi:10.1016/j.ijhm.2016.06.003

Crane, A., Palazzo, G., Spence, L. J., & Matten, D. (2014). Contesting the value of 'creating shared value. *California Management Review, 56*(2), 130–153.

Dembek, K., Singh, P., & Bhakoo, V. (2016). Literature review of shared value: A theoretical concept or a management buzzword?, *Journal of Business Ethics, 137*(2), 231–267.

Deutscher Bundestag. (1998). *Abschlussbericht Der Enquete-Kommission "Schutz Des Menschen Und Der Umwelt - Ziele Und Rahmenbedingungen Einer Nachhaltig Zukunftsverträglichen Entwicklung. The Concept of Sustainability. From Mission Statement to Implementation.* Retrieved from https://dserver.bundestag.de/btd/13/112/1311200.pdf

Dierendonck, D. van. (2010). Servant leadership: A review and synthesis. *Journal of Management, 37*(4), 1228–1261. doi:10.1177/0149206310380462

Dočekalová, M. P., & Kocmanová, A. (2016). Composite indicator for measuring corporate sustainability. *Ecological Indicators, 61*, 612–623. doi:10.1016/j.ecolind.2015.10.012

Doherty, B., Haugh, H., & Lyon, F. (2014). Social enterprises as hybrid organizations: A review and research agenda. *International Journal of Management Reviews, 16*(4), 417–436. doi:10.1111/ijmr.12028

Doren, J. V., Arns, M., Heinrich, H., Vollebregt, M. A., Strehl, U., & Loo, S. K. (2018). Sustained effects of neurofeedback in ADHD: A systematic review and meta-analysis. *European Child & Adolescent Psychiatry, 28*(3), 293–305. doi:10.1007/s00787-018-1121-4

Dyllick, T., & Hockerts, K. (2002). Beyond the business case for corporate sustainability. *Business Strategy and the Environment, 11*(2), 130–141. doi:10.1002/bse.323

Dyllick, T., & Muff, K. (2015). Clarifying the meaning of sustainable business. *Organization & Environment, 29*(2), 156–174. doi:10.1177/1086026615575176

Eccles, R. G., Ioannou, I., & Serafeim, G. (2014). The impact of corporate sustainability on organizational processes and performance. *Management Science, 60*(11), 2835–2857. doi:10.1287/mnsc.2014.1984

Egbue, O., & Long, S. (2012). Barriers to widespread adoption of electric vehicles: An analysis of consumer attitudes and perceptions. *Energy Policy, 48*, 717–729. doi:10.1016/j.enpol.2012.06.009

Elliot, S. (2011). Transdisciplinary perspectives on environmental sustainability: A resource base and framework for IT-enabled business transformation. *MIS Quarterly, 35*(1), 197–236. doi:10.2307/23043495

Elkington, J. (1997). *Cannibals with forks: The triple bottom line of 21st century business.* Oxford: Capstone Publishing Limited.

Ellen MacArthur Foundation. (2015). *Towards a circular economy: Business rationale for an acceler-ated transition*. Retrieved from https://ellenmacarthurfoundation.org/towards-a-circular-econ omy-business-rationale-for-an-accelerated-transition

European Commission. (2022). A European Green Deal: Striving to be the first climate-neutral continent). Retrieved from https://ec.europa.eu/info/strategy/priorities-2019-2024/european-green-deal_en. Accessed on May 27, 2022.

Faguet, J.-P. (2014). Decentralization and governance. *World Development, 53*, 2–13. doi:10.1016/j. worlddev.2013.01.002

Farley, J., & Costanza, R. (2010). Payments for ecosystem services: From local to global. *Ecological Economics, 69*(11), 2060–2068. doi:10.1016/j.ecolecon.2010.06.010

Friedman, M. (1970, September 13). The social responsibility of business is to increase its profits. *New York Times Magazine*.

Funk, K. (2003). Sustainability and performance. *MIT Sloan Management Review, 44*(2), 65.

Garnett, T. (2011). Where are the best opportunities for reducing greenhouse gas emissions in the food system (including the food chain)? *Food Policy, 36*, S23–S32. doi:10.1016/j.foodpol.2010.10.010

Gebler, M., Uiterkamp, A. J. M. S., & Visser, C. (2014). A global sustainability perspective on 3D printing technologies. *Energy Policy, 74*, 158–167. doi:10.1016/j.enpol.2014.08.033

Geels, F. W., Kern, F., Fuchs, G., Hinderer, N., Kungl, G., Mylan, J., ... Wassermann, S. (2016). The enactment of socio-technical transition pathways: A reformulated typology and a comparative multi-level analysis of the German and UK low-carbon electricity transitions (1990–2014). *Research Policy, 45*(4), 896–913. doi:10.1016/j.respol.2016.01.015

Geissdoerfer, M., Morioka, S. N., de Carvalho, M. M., & Evans, S. (2018). Business models and supply chains for the circular economy. *Journal of Cleaner Production, 190*, 712–721.

Geissdoerfer, M., Vladimirova, D., & Evans, S. (2018). Sustainable business model innovation: A review. *Journal of Cleaner Production, 198*, 401–416.

Ghosh, A. R., Kim, J. I., Mendoza, E. G., Ostry, J. D., & Qureshi, M. S. (2013). Fiscal fatigue, fiscal space and debt sustainability in advanced economies. *The Economic Journal, 123*(566), F4–F30. doi:10.1111/ecoj.12010

Gifford, R. (2011). The dragons of inaction: Psychological barriers that limit climate change mitigation and adaptation. *American Psychologist, 66*(4), 290–302. doi:10.1037/a0023566

Gonzales, A. (2015). The contemporary US digital divide: From initial access to technology mainte-nance. *Information, Communication & Society, 19*(2), 234–248. doi:10.1080/1369118x.2015. 1050438

Gonzalez, V. M., Coromina, L., & Galí, N. (2018). Overtourism: Residents' perceptions of tourism impact as an indicator of resident social carrying capacity—Case study of a Spanish heritage town. *Tourism Review, 73*(3), 277–296. doi:10.1108/tr-08-2017-0138

Gottschlich, D., & Friedrich, B. (2014). The legacy of sylvicultura oeconomica. A critical reflection on the notion of sustainability. A critical reflection on the legacy of sylvicultura oeconomica. A critical reflection on the notion of sustainability. *GAIA - Ecological Perspectives for Science and Society, 23*(1), 23–29.

Graham, S., Weingart, S., & Milligan, I. (2012). Getting started with topic modeling and MALLET. *Programming Historian, 1*. doi:10.46430/phen0017

Greco, S., Ishizaka, A., Tasiou, M., & Torrisi, G. (2018). On the methodological framework of composite indices: A review of the issues of weighting, aggregation, and robustness. *Social Indicators Research, 141*(1), 61–94. doi:10.1007/s11205-017-1832-9

Green, K. W., Zelbst, P. J., Meacham, J., & Bhadauria, V. S. (2012). Green supply chain management practices: Impact on performance. *Supply Chain Management: An International Journal, 17*(3), 290–305. doi:10.1108/13598541211227126

Grill, A. (2021). A German trade union and the transformation of work towards a more ecological, social and democratic future, In I. Bakhcheva, A. Dalla Costa, A. K. Grill, Y.-P. Hua, D. Lemos, S. S. A. Pasha, ... A. Zanchetta (Eds.), *Global issues – Local alternatives* (pp. 131–145). doi:10.17875/gup2021-1760

Grober, U. (2001). The idea of sustainability as a civilizational blueprint. *Politik Und Zeitgeschichte, 51*(24), 3–5.

Grunert, K. G., Hieke, S., & Wills, J. (2014). Sustainability labels on food products: Consumer motivation, understanding and use. *Food Policy, 44*, 177–189. doi:10.1016/j.foodpol.2013.12. 001

Gunarathne, N., & Lee, K. H. (2021). The link between corporate energy management and environmental strategy implementation: Efficiency, sufficiency and consistency strategy perspectives. *Journal of Cleaner Production, 293*, 126082.

Hahn, T., & Figge, F. (2011). Beyond the bounded instrumentality in current corporate sustainability research: Toward an inclusive notion of profitability. *Journal of Business Ethics, 104*(3), 325–345. doi:10.1007/s10551-011-0911-0

Hahn, T., Preuss, L., Pinkse, J., & Figge, F. (2014). Cognitive frames in corporate sustainability: Managerial sensemaking with paradoxical and business case frames. *Academy of Management Review, 39*(4), 463–487. doi:10.5465/amr.2012.0341

Hák, T., Janoušková, S., & Moldan, B. (2016). Sustainable development goals: A need for relevant indicators. *Ecological Indicators, 60*, 565–573.

Hall, C. M., Scott, D., & Gössling, S. (2020). Pandemics, transformations and tourism: Be careful what you wish for. *Tourism Geographies, 22*(3), 577–598. doi:10.1080/14616688.2020.1759131

Hamari, J., Sjöklint, M., & Ukkonen, A. (2015). The sharing economy: Why people participate in collaborative consumption. *Journal of the Association for Information Science and Technology, 67*(9), 2047–2059. doi:10.1002/asi.23552

Hart, S. L., & Milstein, M. B. (2003). Creating sustainable value. *Academy of Management Perspectives, 17*(2), 56–67. doi:10.5465/ame.2003.10025194

Harvey, M., & Pilgrim, S. (2011). The new competition for land: Food, energy, and climate change. *Food Policy, 36*, S40–S51. doi:10.1016/j.foodpol.2010.11.009

Helsper, E. J. (2012). A corresponding fields model for the links between social and digital exclusion. *Communication Theory, 22*(4), 403–426. doi:10.1111/j.1468-2885.2012.01416.x

Henry, M., Bauwens, T., Hekkert, M., & Kirchherr, J. (2020). A typology of circular start-ups: analysis of 128 circular business models. *Journal of Cleaner Production, 245*, 118528.

Herrington, G. (2021). Update to limits to growth: Comparing the World3 model with empirical data. *Journal of Industrial Ecology, 25*(3), 614–626.

Holden, E., Linnerud, K., & Banister, D. (2017). The imperatives of sustainable development. *Sustainable Development, 25*(3), 213–226.

Hong, Z., & Guo, X. (2019). Green product supply chain contracts considering environmental responsibilities. *Omega, 83*, 155–166. doi:10.1016/j.omega.2018.02.010

Huber, J. (2000). Towards industrial ecology: Sustainable development as a concept of ecological modernization. *Journal of Environmental Policy and Planning, 2*(4), 269–285.

Jiang, Y., & Wen, J. (2020). Effects of COVID-19 on hotel marketing and management: A perspective article. *International Journal of Contemporary Hospitality Management, 32*(8), 2563–2573. doi: 10.1108/ijchm-03-2020-0237

Kamble, S., Gunasekaran, A., & Dhone, N. C. (2019). Industry 4.0 and lean manufacturing practices for sustainable organisational performance in Indian manufacturing companies. *International Journal of Production Research, 58*(5), 1319–1337. doi:10.1080/00207543.2019.1630772

Karlin, B. E., Ruzek, J. I., Chard, K. M., Eftekhari, A., Monson, C. M., Hembree, E. A., ... Foa, E. B. (2010). Dissemination of evidence-based psychological treatments for posttraumatic stress disorder in the Veterans Health Administration. *Journal of Traumatic Stress, 23*(6), 663–673. doi:10.1002/jts.20588

Kivimaa, P., & Kern, F. (2016). Creative destruction or mere niche support? Innovation policy mixes for sustainability transitions. *Research Policy, 45*(1), 205–217. doi:10.1016/j.respol.2015.09.008

Kleine, A., & von Hauff, M. (2009). Sustainability-driven implementation of corporate social responsibility: Application of the integrative sustainability triangle. *Journal of Business Ethics, 85*(SUPPL. 3), 517–533.

Korhonen, J., Honkasalo, A., & Seppälä, J. (2018). Circular economy: The concept and its limitations. *Ecological Economics, 143*, 37–46. doi:10.1016/j.ecolecon.2017.06.041

Kragulj, F. (2023). *Knowledge management and sustainable value creation. Needs as a strategic focus for organizations.* Cham: Springer.

Lacy, P., & Rutqvist, J. (2015). *Waste to wealth. The circular economy advantage.* London: Palgrave Macmillan.

Landrum, N. E. (2018). Stages of corporate sustainability: Integrating the strong sustainability worldview. *Organization & Environment, 31*(4), 287–313.

Lee, T. H., & Jan, F.-H. (2019). Can community-based tourism contribute to sustainable development? Evidence from residents' perceptions of the sustainability. *Tourism Management, 70*, 368–380. doi:10.1016/j.tourman.2018.09.003

Lehmann, C., Delbard, O., & Lange, S. (2022). Green growth, a-growth or degrowth? Investigating the attitudes of environmental protection specialists at the German Environment Agency. *Journal of Cleaner Production, 336*, 130306. doi:10.1016/j.jclepro.2021.130306

Lewin, K. (1946). Action research and minority problems. *Journal of Social Issues, 2*(4), 34–46.

Long, R. D., Charles, A., & Stephenson, R. L. (2015). Key principles of marine ecosystem-based management. *Marine Policy, 57*, 53–60. doi:10.1016/j.marpol.2015.01.013

Lozano, R. (2012). Towards better embedding sustainability into companies' systems: An analysis of voluntary corporate initiatives. *Journal of Cleaner Production, 25*, 14–26. doi:10.1016/j.jclepro. 2011.11.060

Lubin, D. A., & Esty, D. C. (2010). The sustainability imperative. *Harvard Business Review, 88*(5), 42–50.

Magis, K. (2010). Community resilience: An indicator of social sustainability. *Society & Natural Resources, 23*(5), 401–416. doi:10.1080/08941920903305674

Markard, J., Raven, R., & Truffer, B. (2012). Sustainability transitions: An emerging field of research and its prospects. *Research Policy, 41*(6), 955–967. doi:10.1016/j.respol.2012.02.013

Marshall, R. S., & Brown, D. (2003). The strategy of sustainability: A systems perspective on environmental initiatives. *California Management Review, 46*, 101–126.

Martin, C. J. (2016). The sharing economy: A pathway to sustainability or a nightmarish form of neoliberal capitalism? *Ecological Economics, 121*, 149–159. doi:10.1016/j.ecolecon.2015.11.027

McCallum, A. K. (2002). *MALLET: A Machine Learning for Language Toolkit.* Retrieved from http://mallet.cs.umass.edu

McKinsey and Company. (2021). *Disruption & uncertainty. The state of grocery retail 2021 Europe.* Retrieved from https://www.mckinsey.com/~/media/mckinsey/industries/retail/our%20insights/the%20path%20forward%20for%20european%20grocery%20retailers/disruption-and-uncertainty-the-state-of-grocery-retail-2021-europe-final.pdf

Meadows, D., Meadows, D., Randers, J., & Behrens, W. W. (1972). *The Limits to Growth. A Report for the Club of Rome's Project on the Predicament of Mankind.* New York, NY: Universe Books.

Meadows, D., Randers, J., & Meadows, D. (2005). *Limits to growth. The 30-year update.* London: Earthscan.

Meuer, J., Koelbel, J., & Hoffmann, V. H. (2020). On the nature of corporate sustainability. *Organization & Environment, 33*(3), 319–341.

Milne, M. J., & Gray, R. (2012). W(h)ither ecology? The triple bottom line, the global reporting initiative, and corporate sustainability reporting. *Journal of Business Ethics, 118*(1), 13–29. doi: 10.1007/s10551-012-1543-8

Murray, A., Skene, K., & Haynes, K. (2015). The circular economy: An interdisciplinary exploration of the concept and application in a global context. *Journal of Business Ethics, 140*(3), 369–380. doi:10.1007/s10551-015-2693-2

Neubaum, D. O., & Zahra, S. A. (2006). Institutional ownership and corporate social performance: The moderating effects of investment horizon, activism, and coordination. *Journal of Management, 32*(1), 108–131. doi:10.1177/0149206305277797

Norgaard, R. B. (2010). Ecosystem services: From eye-opening metaphor to complexity blinder. *Ecological Economics, 69*(6), 1219–1227. doi:10.1016/j.ecolecon.2009.11.009

OECD. (2019). *Business models for the circular economy.* OECD. doi:10.1787/g2g9dd62-en

Ossewaarde, M., & Ossewaarde-Lowtoo, R. (2020). The EU's green deal: A third alternative to green growth and degrowth? *Sustainability, 12*(23), 9825.

Panter-Brick, C., Burgess, A., Eggerman, M., McAllister, F., Pruett, K., & Leckman, J. F. (2014). Practitioner Review: Engaging fathers – Recommendations for a game change in parenting interventions based on a systematic review of the global evidence. *Journal of Child Psychology and Psychiatry, 55*(11), 1187–1212. doi:10.1111/jcpp.12280

Paul, J., Modi, A., & Patel, J. (2016). Predicting green product consumption using theory of planned behavior and reasoned action. *Journal of Retailing and Consumer Services, 29*, 123–134. doi:10.1016/j.jretconser.2015.11.006

Peloza, J., & Shang, J. (2010). How can corporate social responsibility activities create value for stakeholders? A systematic review. *Journal of the Academy of Marketing Science, 39*(1), 117–135. doi:10.1007/s11747-010-0213-6

Pieroni, M. P. P., McAloone, T. C., & Pigosso, D. C. A. (2019). Business model innovation for circular economy and sustainability: A review of approaches. *Journal of Cleaner Production, 215*, 198–216.

Pieroni, M. P. P., McAloone, T. C., & Pigosso, D. C. A. (2020). From theory to practice: Systematising and testing business model archetypes for circular economy. *Resources, conservation and recycling* (Vol. 162). Elsevier. doi:10.1016/j.resconrec.2020.105029

Porter, M. E., & Kramer, M. R. (2006). Strategy and society: The link between competitive advantage and corporate social responsibility. *Harvard Business Review, 84*(12), 78–93.

Porter, M. E., & Kramer, M. R. (2011). The big idea: Creating shared value. *Harvard Business Review, 89*(1), 2.

Powlson, D. S., Gregory, P. J., Whalley, W. R., Quinton, J. N., Hopkins, D. W., Whitmore, A. P., … Goulding, K. W. T. (2011). Soil management in relation to sustainable agriculture and ecosystem services. *Food Policy, 36*, S72–S87. doi:10.1016/j.foodpol.2010.11.025

Ramkissoon, H., Smith, L. D. G., & Weiler, B. (2013). Testing the dimensionality of place attachment and its relationships with place satisfaction and pro-environmental behaviours: A structural equation modelling approach. *Tourism Management, 36*, 552–566. doi:10.1016/j.tourman.2012.09.003

Reidegeld, E. (2014). Sustainable forestry and timber savings art - Early forms of dealing with resource scarcity. *Leviathan, 42*(3), 433–462.

Rieckmann, M. (2012). Future-oriented higher education: Which key competencies should be fostered through university teaching and learning? *Futures, 44*(2), 127–135. doi:10.1016/j.futures.2011.09.005

Russell, S. V., Haigh, N., & Griffiths, A. (2007). Understanding corporate sustainability: Recognizing the impact of different governance systems. In S. Benn & D. Dunphy (Eds.), *Corporate governance and sustainability: Challenges for theory and practice* (pp. 36–56). New York, NY: Routledge.

Saberi, S., Kouhizadeh, M., Sarkis, J., & Shen, L. (2018). Blockchain technology and its relationships to sustainable supply chain management. *International Journal of Production Research, 57*(7), 2117–2135. doi:10.1080/00207543.2018.1533261

Sachs, J. D. (2012). From Millennium development goals to sustainable development goals. *The Lancet, 379*(9832), 2206–2211.

Safón, V., & Docampo, D. (2020). Analyzing the impact of reputational bias on global university rankings based on objective research performance data: The case of the Shanghai Ranking (ARWU). *Scientometrics, 125*, 2199–2227. doi:10.1007/s11192-020-03722-z

Salvador, R., Barros, M. V., Freire, F., Halog, A., Piekarski, C. M., & De Francisco, A. C. (2021). Circular economy strategies on business modeling: Identifying the greatest influences. *Journal of Cleaner Production* (299). doi:10.1016/j.jclepro.2021.126918

Salzmann, O., Ionescu-somers, A., & Steger, U. (2005). The business case for corporate sustainability. *European Management Journal, 23*(1), 27–36. doi:10.1016/j.emj.2004.12.007

Schaltegger, S., Beckmann, M., & Hansen, E. G. (2013). Transdisciplinarity in corporate sustainability: Mapping the field. *Business Strategy and the Environment, 22*(4), 219–229. doi:10.1002/bse.1772

Schaltegger, S., Hansen, E. G., & Lüdeke-Freund, F. (2016). Business models for sustainability: Origins, present research, and future avenues. *Organization & Environment, 29*(1), 3–10. doi:10.1177/1086026615599806

Schaltegger, S., & Wagner, M. (2011). Sustainable entrepreneurship and sustainability innovation: Categories and interactions. *Business Strategy and the Environment, 20*(4), 222–237. doi:10.1002/bse.682

Seraphin, H., Sheeran, P., & Pilato, M. (2018). Over-tourism and the fall of Venice as a destination. *Journal of Destination Marketing & Management, 9*, 374–376. doi:10.1016/j.jdmm.2018.01.011

Sharma, S. (2014). *Competing for a sustainable world: Building capacity for sustainable innovation.* New York, NY: Routledge.

Singh, G. G., Cisneros-Montemayor, A. M., Swartz, W., Cheung, W., Guy, J. A., Kenny, T.-A., ... Ota, Y. (2018). A rapid assessment of co-benefits and trade-offs among Sustainable Development Goals. *Marine Policy, 93*, 223–231. doi:10.1016/j.marpol.2017.05.030

Smith, A., & Raven, R. (2012). What is protective space? Reconsidering niches in transitions to sustainability. *Research Policy, 41*(6), 1025–1036. doi:10.1016/j.respol.2011.12.012

Smith, W. K., & Lewis, M. W. (2011). Toward a theory of paradox: A dynamic equilibrium model of organizing. *Academy of Management Review, 36*(2), 381–403. doi:10.5465/amr.2011.59330958

Steger, U. (2004). *The business of sustainability: Building industry cases for corporate sustainability.* Basingstoke: Palgrave Macmillan.

Sterman, J. (2015). Stumbling towards sustainability. In R. G. R. Henderson & M. Tushman (Eds.), *Leading sustainable change: An organizational perspective* (pp. 50–80). Oxford: Oxford University Press.

Sueyoshi, T., Yuan, Y., & Goto, M. (2017). A literature study for DEA applied to energy and environment. *Energy Economics, 62*, 104–124. doi:10.1016/j.eneco.2016.11.006

Tian, C., Peng, J., Zhang, W., Zhang, S., & Wang, J. (2019). Tourism environmental impact assessment based on improved AHP and picture fuzzy promethea II methods. *Technological and Economic Development of Economy, 26*(2), 355–378. doi:10.3846/tede.2019.11413

United Nations. (1987). *Report of the World Commission on Environment and Development: Our Common Future.* Retrieved from https://digitallibrary.un.org/record/139811

Valente, M. (2012). Theorizing firm adoption of sustaincentrism. *Organization Studies, 33*(4), 563–591. doi:10.1177/0170840612443455

van Eck, N. J., & Waltman, L. (2010). Software survey: VOSviewer, a computer program for bibliometric mapping. *Scientometrics, 84*(2), 523–538.

van Marrewijk, M., & Marco, W. (2003). Multiple levels of corporate sustainability. *Journal of Business Ethics, 44*(2–3), 107–119.

van Marrewijk, M., & Werre, M. (2003). Multiple levels of corporate sustainability. *Journal of Business Ethics, 44*, 107–119. doi:10.1023/A:1023383229086

Vargo, S. L., & Lusch, R. F. (2017). Service-dominant logic 2025. *International Journal of Research in Marketing, 34*(1), 46–67. doi:10.1016/j.ijresmar.2016.11.001

von Winterfeld, U. (2007). No sustainability without sufficiency. *Operations, 3*, 46–54.

Watermeyer, R., Crick, T., Knight, C., & Goodall, J. (2020). COVID-19 and digital disruption in UK universities: Afflictions and affordances of emergency online migration. *Higher Education, 81*(3), 623–641. doi:10.1007/s10734-020-00561-y

Wieland, J. (Ed.). (2017). *Creating shared value - Concepts, experience, criticism.* Cham: Springer.

Wilson, M. (2003). Corporate sustainability: What is it and where does it come from. *Ivey Business Journal, 67*(6), 1–5.

Zhang, C., & Anadon, L. D. (2014). A multi-regional input–output analysis of domestic virtual water trade and provincial water footprint in China. *Ecological Economics, 100*, 159–172. doi:10.1016/j.ecolecon.2014.02.006

CHAPTER 9

HOW THE UN SDGS HAVE AFFECTED SUSTAINABILITY REPORTING ACTIVITY OF SPANISH PUBLIC UNIVERSITIES?

Francisco Javier Andrades Peña,
Domingo Martinez Martinez and Manuel Larrán Jorge

ABSTRACT

Drawing on managerial innovation model proposed by Abrahamson (1991), this chapter tries to gain a better understanding of how the UN SDGs have impacted the practice of sustainability reporting of Spanish public universities. Data were collected from a variety of sources, such as: several email structured interviews with university managers, an examination of the Chancellor letters of sustainability reports of Spanish public universities, a detailed reading of some sustainability reports and a consultation of the website of each Spanish public university. The findings reveal that there has been an increasing number of Spanish public universities that have started to publish stand-alone sustainability reporting since the appearance of the UN SDGs. According to Abrahamson's framework, our findings reveal that governmental-policy forces have shaped the sustainability reporting landscape in the Spanish public university setting, and their behaviour is mostly explained by the forced-selection and fad/fashion perspectives.

Keywords: Sustainability reporting; Abrahamson's framework; managerial innovation; SDGs; Spanish public universities; efficient-choice; fad-fashion perspective

Innovation, Social Responsibility and Sustainability
Developments in Corporate Governance and Responsibility, Volume 22, 207–226
Copyright © 2024 Francisco Javier Andrades Peña, Domingo Martinez Martinez and Manuel Larrán Jorge
Published under exclusive licence by Emerald Publishing Limited
ISSN: 2043-0523/doi:10.1108/S2043-052320230000022009

1. INTRODUCTION

Since the late 1990s to the present, sustainability reporting has become a mainstream practice of the company's reporting strategy (Stubbs, Higgins, & Milne, 2013). Around 35% of the largest global companies produced a stand-alone sustainability report in 1999 (Higgins, Milne, & Van Gramberg, 2015). Meanwhile, 96% of these companies produced some kind of a sustainability report by 2020 (Jain, Islam, Keneley, & Kansal, 2022). This has meant that sustainability reporting has been recognised as a taken for granted practice among the largest and most publicly traded companies around the world (Farooq & de Villiers, 2019; Higgins, Stubbs, & Milne, 2018).

While this type of reporting has become something of a common feature on the corporate agenda, it has not been as popular in the public sector (Ball, Grubnic, & Birchall, 2014; Vinnari & Laine, 2013). It is quite surprising when public sector organisations (PSOs) have a role more explicitly related to the sustainable development agenda than private companies (Ball & Bebbington, 2008; Ball & Grubnic, 2007). Also, academic scholars have devoted less attention to how PSOs can advance towards sustainability (Farneti & Guthrie, 2009) in comparison to the vast body of empirical research that has examined the nature, extent and drivers of sustainability reporting in the for-profit oriented companies (Adams, 2002; Contrafatto, 2014).

The sustainability reporting landscape is constantly changing with organisations required to be responsive to ensure that this type of reporting satisfy multiple stakeholders (Cohen, 2022). The launch of the United Nations (UN) sustainable development goals (SDGs) in 2015 has been a well-recognised initiative to promote global awareness of sustainable development (Bebbington & Unerman, 2018). It has received considerable attention in the policy arena and different academics have highlighted the role that accounting should play in the path towards achieving the SDGs (Bebbington & Unerman, 2020). This calls for further research to explore how the UN SDGs have affected the practice of organisational sustainability reporting in the public sector. Until the current moment, these organisations have been slow to undertake sustainability reporting practices, with a limited number of PSOs producing stand-alone sustainability reports (Ball et al., 2014). In agreement with Marcuccio and Steccolini (2005), the appearance of the UN SDGs might resurge the interest in social and environmental reporting in PSOs. This raises the question of whether this initiative might drive the diffusion of sustainability reporting among PSOs. Consistent with Rogers (2003, p. 5), diffusion is 'the process in which an innovation is communicated through certain channels over time among members of a social system'. Prior empirical research has examined whether the diffusion of sustainability reporting is a managerial fad (Burritt & Schaltegger, 2010; Vinnari & Laine, 2013). However, little attention has been devoted to examine how the UN SDGs might affect the management oriented path to sustainability reporting.

To fill this research gap, and drawing on the managerial innovation model proposed by Abrahamson (1991), this chapter tries to gain a better understanding of how the UN SDGs have impacted the practice of sustainability reporting of

Spanish public universities. Data were collected from different sources, including email structured interviews with university managers, the examination of the Chancellor letters of sustainability reports of Spanish public universities and the analysis of the website of each Spanish public university.

The public university sector is selected for the following reasons: (1) They are typically large in size (Ball & Grubnic, 2007) and (2) their mission is to create and transfer knowledge to society (Adams, 2013; Godemann, Bebbington, Herzig, & Moon, 2014). Universities have an opportunity to contribute to SDG achievement by preparing sustainability reports aimed at measuring and reporting on their social, environmental and economic impacts (Bebbington & Unerman, 2020). In particular, the Spanish university setting is relevant because the central government along with the Conference of Rectors of Spanish Universities (CRUE in Spanish) have promoted the commitment of public universities towards SDGs achievement. This urges to investigate how Spanish public universities have addressed their sustainability concerns according to the governmental and policy actions developed by Spanish organisations aligned with the UN SDGs.

The chapter makes the following contributions to the accounting research. On a theoretical level, few empirical papers, to our knowledge, have used Abrahamson's model to examine the reasons associated with sustainability reporting activity (Marcuccio & Steccolini, 2005; Vinnari & Laine, 2013). It differs from the most commonly theoretical approaches adopted in previous research on sustainability accounting and reporting (Adams, 2002; Bebbington, Higgins, & Frame, 2009). Thus, it is from Abrahamson's model that we try to contribute to the sustainability accounting and reporting research. Previous research (Adams & Larrinaga, 2019) called for employing other approaches, beyond political economic theories, to enrich the conceptual understanding of the practice of sustainability reporting. On a practical level, this research tries to fill an absence in the literature of sustainability reporting: the SDG-motivated research (Bebbington & Unerman, 2020). Relying on Abrahamson's model, this study tries to understand the extent to which the UN SDGs has been an innovation in the field of sustainability reporting in the public university setting.

The remainder of the chapter is structured as follows. First, the institutional background is explained, followed by the theoretical framework. Next, we discuss the sample and methods. Then, we report the findings, followed by the discussion, conclusions and limitations, and finally suggestions for future research are proposed.

2. THE UN SDGS: A BOOST OF THE PRACTICE OF SUSTAINABILITY REPORTING

Before the appearance and approval of the UN SDGs, different governmental initiatives were launched to promote the commitment to sustainability reporting in the public and private sectors, such as the Global Reporting Initiative or the United Nations Global Compact (Contrafatto, 2014). In response to a broad range of social and environmental concerns, the UN approved a new global sustainable development agenda in September 2015, called as 'Transforming Our World: The 2030 Agenda for Sustainable Development' (Owens, 2017). This 2030 Agenda is comprised of 17 Sustainable Development Goals (SDGs) to 'stimulate action over the next 15 years in areas of critical importance for humanity and the planet' (UN, 2015, p. 3). The announcement of the UN SDGs has renewed the key role that accounting professionals and academics should play in developing organisational and operational SDGs-related practices (Bebbington & Unerman, 2020). In this way, Bebbington and Unerman (2018) manifested the link between the SDGs and the accounting discipline in the following quote 'elements of the accounting profession are among actors who have enthusiastically embraced the SDGs, seeing a pivotal role for accountants and accounting in supporting and their realization' (p. 2). Moreover, as they wrote, the 'SDGs provide a context for (re)invigorating accounting's contribution to sustainable development debates' (p. 1).

Among all the UN SDGs, the goal 12 is clearly linked to accounting, as it aims to ensure sustainable consumption and production patterns. Within this goal, the following targets, among others, show a clear connection with the accounting discipline:

- 12.2. By 2030, achieve the sustainable management and efficient use of natural resources;
- 12.4. By 2030, achieve the environmentally sound management of chemicals and all wastes throughout their life cycle, in accordance with agreed international frameworks, and significantly reduce their release to air, water and soil in order to minimise their adverse impacts on human health and the environment;
- 12.5. By 2030, substantially reduce waste generation through prevention, reduction, recycling and reuse;
- 12.6. Encourage companies, especially large and transnational companies, to adopt sustainable practices and to integrate sustainability information into their reporting cycle.

In addition to this, the goal number 16, in its target 16.6, also calls for increased sustainability reporting, through the development of effective, accountable and transparent institutions at all levels. (Niemann & Hoppe, 2018). As these authors noted, it appears to be that the UN SDGs represents a clear evidence that sustainability reporting is on the rise.

In parallel with this, some attempts have been produced to develop metrics and frameworks to measure the SDG performance in the university setting, such as The Times Higher Education (THE) Impact Rankings. They are global performance tables that assess universities against the UN SDGs across four main university activities: teaching-learning, research, management and community outreach.[1] The Sustainable Development Solutions Network (SDSN),[2] published the report 'Getting started with the SDGs in universities' in 2017 which is a guide to help universities their contributions to the SDGs implementation.[3]

The launch of the UN SDGs has also been accompanied by the approval of strategies by national governments to move the world forward on a sustainable path (Bisogno, Cuadrado-Ballesteros, Rossi, & Peña-Miguel, 2023). In the particular case of Spain, the central government approved a policy titled 'An Action Plan for the Implementation of the 2030 Agenda: Towards a Spanish Strategy for Sustainable Development'. It shows the long-term commitment of the Central Government in Spain to achieve a sustainable society in collaboration with the different regional governments. In addition to this, the Spanish Central Government approved its own national strategy 2030 to make possible the SDGs achievement and implementation. It requires that all public administrations should assume their commitment to establish a strategic policy aligned with the achievement of the SDGs.

Previous scholars have manifested that when a governmental policy is undertaken it is indicating that the dependent organisations must align their behaviour to this initiative (Marquis & Qian, 2014). In this way, the Conference of Rectors of Spanish Universities (CRUE in Spanish) has been preparing an annual report to reveal the pivotal role that universities should play in SDGs achievement since 2018. In March 2019, CRUE created its own SDG Committee to coordinate the set of actions related to the contribution of universities towards SDGs achievement. Since then, this Committee has annually published a report to describe the list of initiatives that have been carried out by CRUE in regards to the Spanish universities' progress towards SDGs implementation.

In the context of our study, this means that Spanish public universities, as they are largely funded by the government, could be coerced to conform to governmental pressures derived from the approval of the national strategy 2030 on SDG achievement to gain legitimacy (Carpenter & Feroz, 2001; Collin, Tagesson, Andersson, Cato, & Hansson, 2009).

3. LITERATURE REVIEW

Over the last decade, there have been a growing number of academic articles addressing the topic of sustainability reporting at the university level (Alonso-Almeida, Marimon, Casani, & Rodríguez-Pomeda, 2015; Moggi, 2019). While many of these papers have examined the internal and external drivers

---

[1] *Source*: https://www.timeshighereducation.com/impactrankings
[2] It is an initiative of SDSN Australia/Pacific in collaboration with the Australasian campuses towards sustainability, the global SDSN, and Australian and New Zealand universities.
[3] The SDSN Spain has elaborated a version of this Guide in Spanish language.

motivating universities to undertake sustainability reporting practices (Andrades, Martinez-Martinez, & Larran, 2021; Brusca, Labrador, & Larran, 2018), others explored the extent of sustainability disclosure provided by these organisations in their annual or sustainability reports (Fonseca, Macdonald, Dandy, & Valenti, 2011; Lozano, 2011).

The announcement of the UN SDGs has remarked the role that universities could play in the transition to a sustainable society by achieving these goals (Bebbington & Unerman, 2018; Yañez, Uruburu, Moreno, & Lumbreras, 2019). In particular, the goal 4 is oriented to ensure inclusive and equitable quality education and promote lifelong learning opportunities for all.[4] Connecting education with sustainability, the target 4.7 states that all learners should acquire the knowledge and skills needed to promote sustainable development by 2030. While there is substantial literature on SDG-related research in the university setting from an educational perspective (Albareda-Tiana, Vidal-Raméntol, & Fernández-Morilla, 2018; Leal Filho, Shiel et al., 2019; Leal Filho, Skanavis et al., 2019), the research on SDG reporting at the university level is in its early stages of development. To the best of our knowledge, there have been few attempts to explain how the UN SDGs has impacted the practice of sustainability reporting within the university sector. Therefore, there is a call for further research to explore how universities are engaged in the achievement of SDGs through their reporting practices. The actual managerial practices adopted by public universities cannot be examined as isolated from their environment (Marcuccio & Steccolini, 2005). In this way, the current institutional context in the Spanish public university setting has been taking shape through the appearance of the UN SDGs. It could explain the adoption of new organisational practices, like stand-alone sustainability reports, to conform to the expectations of different actors (e.g. the government and CRUE) in exchange for legitimacy.

Under such premises and, to fill a research gap in the field of sustainability reporting in universities, we use Abrahamson's (1991) managerial innovation framework to decipher how Spanish public universities are responding to the appearance of the UN SDGs. In agreement with Vinnari and Laine (2013), the voluntary nature of sustainability reporting in the public sector may be conceived as a managerial innovation rather than an external reporting standard. As Biondi and Bracci (2018) highlighted, the lack of mandatory reporting requirements for PSOs has supposed that the uptake of sustainability reporting has been varied and changing which raises the question of the existence of managerial fashions behind this practice. Therefore, the theory of managerial innovation offers insightful ideas about the reasons behind the adoption of sustainability reporting practices in Spanish public universities.

---

[4]https://sdgs.un.org/goals/goal4

4. THEORETICAL FRAMEWORK

Previous studies have sought to explain the diffusion of sustainability reporting from different theoretical standpoints (Thoradeniya, Ferreira, Lee, & Tan, 2021). Managerial innovation framework represents the most commonly used theoretical perspective to explain the diffusion of an innovation (Gunarathne & Senaratne, 2017). Relying on this perspective, it is proposed framework of innovation diffusion considering the presence of four main strategies efficient-choice, forced-selection, fad and fashion (Vinnari & Laine, 2013). In line with Thoradeniya et al. (2021), these strategies share some similarities with the notion of institutional isomorphism.

Extracted from Vinnari and Laine (2013, p. 1111) the efficient-choice strategy is 'premised upon the beliefs that organisations are able to freely choose an innovation, efficiency of the innovation in terms of whether it enables the attainment of those objectives'. This perspective explains that, when organisations have a performance gap between their goals and those that can be achieved, they tend to innovate to gain efficiency (Thoradeniya et al., 2021). Consistent with the typology of Abrahamson (1991), inside-influential forces could promote the diffusion of sustainability reporting in those organisations that have adopted an efficient choice. Previous studies have revealed the relevance of internal champions in initiating the path towards sustainability reporting (Adams & McNicholas, 2007; Vinnari & Laine, 2013). In such a way, Spanish public universities which have adopted the efficient choice are those that have persistently been producing a stand-alone sustainability report for a long time to improve their accountability for their social and environmental impacts (Tan & Egan, 2018). These organisations have routinised sustainability reporting activity in their managerial decision making process and it makes help to accelerate the progress towards SDGs achievement and implementation (Farooq & de Villiers, 2019; Yañez et al., 2019).

The forced-selection strategy assumes that 'certain outsider organisations, often political or other governmental bodies, are strong enough to impose their will on other organisations to the extent that those organisations adopt an innovation, regardless of whether it fits with their goals and interests' (Vinnari & Laine, 2013, p. 1111). Similar to the coercive force of institutional theory, this perspective is premised upon the powerful influence exerted by outside organisations in relation to the diffusion of an innovation (Gunarathne & Senaratne, 2017). As it has been mentioned earlier, the Spanish central government has developed some policies and initiatives to promote the contribution of Spanish universities towards SDGs achievement and implementation. According to the forced-selection perspective, Spanish public universities can undertake sustainability reporting practices to meet the demands of the government because they need their approbation to be legitimate (Andrades, Muriel, & Larrán, 2022). Following this logic, these organisations might have conformed to the governmental policy established by the Spanish central government because they can exercise their power to coerce universities to fulfil their demands (Farneti, Casonato, Montecalvo, & De Villiers, 2019).

The fashion perspective is premised upon the idea that uncertainty prevails in relation to organisational goals, environmental pressures or the technical efficiency of an innovation (Vinnari & Laine, 2013). Under such assumption, and in line with the mimetic force of institutional theory, organisations might imitate fashion-setting organisations in response to uncertainty as well as fashion-setters are capable of inspiring the trust in the managerial choice of organisations (Bebbington et al., 2009). These fashion-setters are outside organisations, such as consulting firms or business schools, which promote the fashion of an innovation (Gunarathne & Senaratne, 2017; Thoradeniya et al., 2021). Previous studies have highlighted the possible influence exerted by reporting standards developed by fashion-setting organisations, like the Global Reporting Initiative (GRI), to promote the diffusion of sustainability reporting practices (Bebbington et al., 2009; Montecalvo, Farneti, & De Villiers, 2018). For our study, the UN could be configured as a fashion-setting organisation by inspiring the trust of other organisations, like Spanish public universities, in relation to the publication of stand-alone sustainability reports.

The fad strategy is also premised upon the assumption of organisational uncertainty but, in this case, organisations tend to imitate successful practices adopted by their peers because they are sensible to what their peers are doing (Higgins & Larrinaga, 2014; Zhao & Patten, 2016). Based on the fad perspective, some Spanish public universities could feel pressured to conform to a managerial innovation and then they could undertake sustainability reports by imitating other universities that previously adopted this activity in order to be legitimate (Bebbington et al., 2009). In agreement with Jain et al. (2022) the growth in the diffusion of sustainability reporting could lead to a social contagion phase in which companies try to copy this practice to gain legitimacy and reduce uncertainty.

Drawing on the fad/fashion perspectives, Spanish public universities may have adopted sustainability reporting practices to symbolically manage public impressions by projecting an appearance consistent with societal expectations (Merkl-Davies & Brennan, 2007; Vinnari & Laine, 2013). Thus, the discourse of sustainability in their reports responds to the progressive façade that privileges social and environmental innovation (Cho, Laine, Roberts, & Rodrigue, 2015).

5. RESEARCH DESIGN

This paper is comprised of the 50 Spanish public universities that belongs the university system because they are highly visible due to these organisations are mostly funded by the government (Andrades et al., 2021). This might suppose that Spanish public universities could undertake sustainability reporting practices to conform to governmental and other societal pressures (Larran, Andrades, & Herrera, 2019).

To do this, our qualitative research combines different data sources, such as structured interviews with 20 university managers by email and the analysis of the Chancellor letters of 101 stand-alone sustainability reports published by the 50

Spanish public universities from 2015 to 2021. The initial year is 2015, just when the 2030 Agenda by UN and its 17 SDGs is launched. In third place, we consult the website of all Spanish public universities during the period of data analysis to provide a complementary overview of the findings and to improve the reliability of our results (Archel, Husillos, & Spence, 2011).

First, we carried out structured interviews via written email with 20 university managers from mid-January 2022 to the end of January 2023. Interviews are an effective research methodology because it facilitates the achievement of invaluable knowledge to the researcher according to the opinion of the interviewees (Farneti et al., 2019; Feldermann & Hiebl, 2020). Despite the fact that the semi-structured interview is the most common method employed in the qualitative research (Montecalvo et al., 2018), a structured interview is useful for our purposes because 'they are based on a rigid set of pre-established questions from which neither the interviewer nor the interviewee can deviate (Farneti et al., 2019, p. 566)',. In particular, we used structured interviews by email written for the following reasons (Hawkins, 2018): (1) cost reduction, because the transcription of data does not require any payment or to take a trip; (2) sample diversity as it facilitates the process of data gathering; (3) clarity and concise data because participants tend to provide shorter responses compared to oral ones and this might be useful to analyse data. As in previous research (Dahlin, 2021), we developed the following open-ended questions to encourage interviewees to express their opinion about three main themes.

(1) Reasons to adopt sustainability reporting practices;
(2) Reasons to maintain the sustainability reporting activity over time;
(3) Barriers associated with the adoption of sustainability reporting.

According to these questions, the responses provided by participants can provide us valuable information in relation to the factors that promote the diffusion of sustainability reporting among Spanish public universities. These questions were written in the Spanish language and revised by the three authors. Then, an external member of the research validated the content of these questions. The responses provided by interviewees were translated to English language by one researcher following the procedure defined by Feldermann and Hiebl (2020). This means that the translation from Spanish to English was not directly literal but maintaining the sense of meaning provided by participants in their responses.

The data was collected during a long period of time since semi-structured interviews by e-mail are not limited to time constrains (Hawkins, 2018). In a first phase, we sent two e-mails to the managers of the 50 Spanish public universities: an initial e-mail and a second message in which we remind to those managers who did not reply to the first contact. In total, we obtained 17 responses from 15 January to 9 February 2022. In a second phase carried out in January 2023, we contacted key personnel from some universities who had some kind of responsibility in the preparation of sustainability reports.

This allowed us receiving three additional responses. Hence, the list of interviewees who participated in the research was 20. Each manager is coded with a number according to when he/she responded to the interview.

Second, we performed a detailed examination of the Chancellor letter from 101 sustainability reports of 50 Spanish public universities from 2015 to 2021. The initial period for the analysis of Chancellor letters is 2015 because it is the moment in which the UN SDGs were launched. For longitudinal studies, the Chancellor letter is a main data source because it is the primary section of a corporate report (Amernic, Craig, & Tourish, 2010). These letters 'are an important focus of scrutiny because they can be perceived to mirror the corporate culture' (Mäkelä & Laine, 2011, p. 220). They tend to be the most read part of corporate annual reports as are usually positioned at the beginning of the report (Palmer, King, & Kelleher, 2004). The analysis of these letters is helpful for identifying top-management discourse and how their organisations have addressed sustainability challenges in their reports (Mäkelä & Laine, 2011). For our purposes, we selected excerpts from different sustainability reports to determine whether and how the UN SDGs have affected the diffusion of sustainability reporting activity of Spanish public universities.

This analysis involved an initial phase in which one researcher made a careful reading of these letters by taking some notes about key messages provided in these texts. Next, this researcher read the letters again in a more comprehensive way and he extracted some quotes from them to reveal whether and how the UN SDGs affected the practice of sustainability reporting in Spanish public universities. The participation in the data analysis process by only one researcher was conducted to avoid inter-coder variability (Kansal, Joshi, Babu, & Sharma, 2018). Moreover, we conducted an extensive reading of some sustainability reports to have a better understanding of whether universities have focused on providing qualitative or quantitative disclosures and to ascertain whether they prepared their reports according to an accepted standard. The whole analysis of letters and reports was performed from June 2022 to January 2023.

The previous data sources were complemented by the analysis of the website of the 50 Spanish public universities to have comprehensive picture of the influence of the UN SDGs on sustainability reporting activity.

6. ANALYSIS AND DISCUSSION

6.1 Longitudinal Analysis of the Sustainability Reporting Activity in the Spanish Public University Sector

Table 9.1 shows the evolution of the uptake of sustainability reporting in the Spanish public university setting from 2010 to 2021. This analysis tries to contextualise whether the UN SDGs has increased the number of universities adopting stand-alone sustainability reports. For such reason, a 10-year period analysis is performed to examine the extent to which universities have produced this type of reporting pre and post the UN SDGs. In such a way, it is necessary to

Table 9.1. Evolution of Sustainability Reporting Activity in the Spanish Public University Field.

Year	Number of Reporters	Proportion of Reporters
2010	12	24%
2011	13	26%
2012	13	26%
2013	9	18%
2014	9	18%
2015	12	24%
2016	11	22%
2017	13	26%
2018	14	28%
2019	18	36%
2020	18	36%
2021	16	32%
Total	158	31.60%

understand how the context from social, organisational and institutional levels might drive the diffusion of sustainability reporting practices (Contrafatto, 2014).

Before the approval of the UN SDGs, some initiatives helped to build an appropriate environment to start to adopt sustainability reporting practices, such as the launch of the consecutive reporting standards by GRI in their first, second and third versions. The foundation of the United Nations Global Compact in 2000 represents another movement to align the organisational behaviour to sustainability principles. In Spain, the central government approved the University Strategy in 2010 to promote the commitment to sustainability in Spanish universities. Also, the Law on Sustainable Economy was launched in 2011 in which the alignment with sustainability issues was promoted for the university sector. In spite of this, few Spanish public universities produced stand-alone sustainability reports over the period from 2010 to 2015. The trend in the number of reporters remained stable during the years from 2010 to 2012, while the number of reporters in 2013 and 2014 experienced some changes (Table 9.2). In particular, six universities did not produce a sustainability report for the 2013 year. Therefore, the previous initiatives had a limited impact on the number of reporting organisations since less than a third of Spanish public universities adopted stand-alone sustainability reports from 2010 to 2015.

The evolution of the number of reporters begins to change from 2015 to now, so the launch of the 2030 Agenda and its 17 UN SDGs could have something to do with this behaviour. In particular, it is relevant how the number of Spanish public universities adopting sustainability reports has increased since 2019.[5]

---

[5]Some managers manifested that their universities are working in the elaboration of their sustainability reports for the 2021 period.

Table 9.2. Detailed Analysis of the Trend in Sustainability Reporting Activity in the Spanish Public University Field.

Year	Number of Reporters	Reporters Who Maintained This Practice	New Reporters	Reporters Who Stop to Produce Reports
2010	12	–	–	
2011	13	11	2	1
2012	13	11	2	2
2013	9	7	2	6
2014	9	6	3	3
2015	12	7	5	2
2016	11	8	3	4
2017	13	8	3	5
2018	14	11	3	2
2019	18	11	7	3
2020	18	13	5	5
2021	16	10	6	8

During the last three years (2019, 2020 and 2021), the number of new reporters notably increased compared to the previous years, especially when compared to the period from 2010–2012. Although the UN SDGs were launched in 2015, governmental policies may take time to materialise and this could explain why the growth in the number of reporting organisations is materialised especially from 2019.

In overall, 31.4% of the entire population of Spanish public universities have elaborated sustainability reporting practices for the period 2010–2021, although the number of reporters has grown substantially in recent years. Our expectation is that the trend in the subsequent years will be for a greater number of universities adopting this type of reporting. Relying on Abrahamson's managerial innovation framework, these findings reveal that external pressures derived from governmental-policy initiatives have shaped the sustainability reporting landscape in the Spanish public university setting. According to this theoretical perspective, the behaviour of Spanish public universities is mostly explained by the combined influence of the forced-selection and fad/fashion perspectives. Following this logic, organisations outside the Spanish public university system have determined the diffusion of sustainability reporting practices of these universities.

6.2 Forces Driving the Adoption of Sustainability Reporting: A Combined Perspective of Forced-Selection and Fad/Fashion

Based on the forced-selection perspective, we find three main sources of external pressures from government policies. First, the adoption of sustainability reporting practices is explained by the compliance with pre-existing reporting requirements as Vinnari and Laine (2013) manifested. Some universities have manifested that their sustainability reports contribute to the UN SDGs following the recommendations established in the target 12.6. In line with Oliver (1991), the voluntary diffusion of the target 12.6, by recommending organisations to adopt sustainability reporting practices, represents an evidence of the voluntary diffusion of norms. Thus, Spanish public universities might have adhered to this norm by producing stand-alone sustainability reports. Second, some Chancellors have declared in their sustainability reports that they have adopted this type of reporting 'due to the need to advance in the achievement of the SDGs in line with the strategy adopted by our regional government in relation to the 2030 Agenda'. In the same way, a manager (University 7) manifested that the adoption of initiatives related to sustainability engagement is of an imperative nature for our university as it is shown in our agreement to the 2030 Agenda to achieve the SDGs. Another manager (University 11) stated that we are obliged to maintain the commitment to sustainability aligned with the 17 SDGs. Previous studies revealed that organisations tend to adopt managerial practices to conform to governmental pressures because these organisations are constrained by their external dependence on resources (Carpenter & Feroz, 2001; Collin et al., 2009). Thus, Spanish public universities might have adhered to the UN SDGs because they have to meet to demands of the Central State (Andrades, Martinez-Martinez, Herrera, & Larrán, 2023). Consistent with previous studies, these universities might have used the sustainability report to align their behaviour with SDGs achievement because they are externally pressured from the government to enhance their legitimacy (Gunarathne & Senaratne, 2017; Thoradeniya et al., 2021). Third, other universities have manifested that CRUE plays a pivotal role in the promotion of the commitment of Spanish public universities towards SDGs achievement. The preamble of the first sustainability report of a university highlights the influence exerted by the CRUE in relation to the achievement of the UN SDGs in the university setting. This has been materialised in the approval of a Committee responsible for coordinating the contributions of the different Spanish public universities to the 17 SDGs. As a result, this university published its first stand-alone sustainability report in 2019, among other things, to align efforts around the 17 SDGs. In agreement with previous literature, some universities have adopted sustainability reporting practices to meet the demands of a particular stakeholder, the CRUE (Esteban-Arrea & Garcia-Torea, 2022). This organisation is exerting pressure on Spanish public universities so that they carry out practices aligned with the achievement of the SDGs (Gunarathne & Senaratne, 2017).

Based on the fad and fashion perspectives, the evidence obtained through data sources reveals that the launch of the UN SDGs has represented a sustainability hype for Spanish public universities. After its launch, many universities have created sustainability-related management units to undertake stand-alone reports aligned with SDGs achievement. An examination of the Chancellor's letter from different sustainability reports clearly reveals the same message: the need for universities to be aligned with the achievement of the UN SDGs and the compliance with 2030 Agenda. One Chancellor declared that 'since 2015, we have assumed the challenge of implementing the 2030 Agenda for Sustainable Development in our university and it is an opportunity to introduce positive changes in our governance model'. Another Chancellor declared in its sustainability report for 2018–2019 that the achievement of SDGs is a pivotal element of our university as it was announced as part of our strategy at the end of 2017. Another university, in its 2017 sustainability report, contemplates that their commitment with the 2030 Agenda and the achievement of UN SDGs. Another Chancellor declared that our government action is to be aligned with the SDGs and the 2030 Agenda. The opinion manifested by some university managers corroborate these findings. One interviewee (University 18) stated that one motivation to approve our first sustainability report was 'to identify and demonstrate our contribution to the fulfilment of the 2030 Agenda and SDGs implementation'. Another manager (University 12) stated that 'we have the responsibility and commitment to introduce sustainability themes in our main activities: management, teaching and research and this is recognized in our 2019-2022 Strategic Plan... Our recent sustainability reports have been aligned with the UN SDGs'. Manager coded as University 3 declared that 'our university cannot ignore the commitment with the 2030 Agenda and its 17 UN SDGs'.

Consistent with Abrahamson's (1991) managerial innovation framework, the diffusion of sustainability reporting practices in these universities mostly corresponds to the perspectives of fad and fashion, indicating that it was driven by the wish to imitate a fashion-setting organisation, the UN. Consistent with Vinnari and Laine (2013), this has supposed that some Spanish public universities adopted an innovator role and later adopters imitated the sustainability reporting practice of these innovator universities. Consistent with Jain et al. (2022), the growth in the number of reporters has been isomorphic because later adopters copied fashionable practice to improve their legitimacy and reduce uncertainty. Thus, fad and fashion appear to have worked in parallel.

However, some scholars have criticised that the pressure from fad/fashion perspectives may arise from the need of organisations to conform to institutional norms to be legitimate (Thoradeniya et al., 2021). Once the fashion wears off, organisations are not driven to persistently maintain the adoption of sustainability reporting practices (Vinnari & Laine, 2013). In these cases, organisations adopt symbolic sustainability reporting as a legitimation strategy and to manage stakeholder perceptions with little substantial impact on organisations (Gunarathne & Senaratne, 2017; Rodrigue, Magnan, & Cho, 2013). In line with these arguments, the reading of some sustainability reports published by Spanish public universities reveals that they are mostly narrative and qualitative. These reports do not usually provide quantitative evidence of the social and environmental impacts of university's activity. Most of these reports have been elaborated without following an accepted standard for measuring and reporting on sustainability. As Cho et al. (2015) manifested, this evidences that sustainability reporting can be described as an organised hypocrite and an organisational façade. According to Abrahamson and Baumard (2008, p. 437), organisational façade means 'a symbolic front erected by organizational participants designed to reassure their organizational stakeholders of the legitimacy of the organization and its management'. Thus, the notion of organisational façade might be considered as another theoretical lens to support that sustainability reporting is aimed at creating organisational legitimacy with respect to stakeholders (Cho et al., 2015). Some university managers (University 5 and University 6) reinforced these assumptions by highlighting that the diffusion of sustainability reporting is mostly explained by legitimising reasons rather than to provide transparent information to stakeholders.

6.3 Sustainability Reporting as an Efficient Choice

Some Spanish public universities (a total of seven) have been producing a stand-alone sustainability report for a long period of time even long before the launch of the UN SDGs. For these organisations, sustainability reporting has become a taken for granted practice because this activity has been embedded in their management decisions (Tarquinio & Xhindole, 2022). In this way, one manager (University 9) manifested that 'our university, for many years, assumed their responsibility with society, and it required to acquire a commitment to sustainability that should translate into an improvement in efficiency and performance...'. He/she also stated that 'the persistent adoption of sustainability reporting has created a culture in the university community of being socially responsible and it has allowed the integration of sustainability into our mission, vision, and strategic goals'. Consistent with the opinion of this university manager, sustainability reporting has allowed the concept of sustainability has permeated the organisational discourse of this organisation and it has helped to improve the accountability for their social and environmental externalities (Farooq & de Villiers, 2019). Another university has persistently published a sustainability report with the idea of developing a culture that promotes social and environmental values as the Chancellor stated in its first sustainability report. Manager from University 20 declared that our university uses the sustainability report as an accountability tool to meet the demands of our stakeholders. Another public university from the north of Spain has published 14 sustainability reports since 2008 to the current date. Its current strategic plan (2019–2023) contemplates sustainability as a transversal element of this organisation. This resulted in the approval of its Management Plan for University Social Responsibility to support the implementation of sustainability at all levels of the university.

Consistent with the efficient choice perspective, these Spanish public universities, through the leadership exerted by an internal champion, perceived that they had a gap in the measurement of their social and environmental impacts. As Larrinaga and Perez (2008) noted, ethical motivations of people employed in the public university sector should be more consistent with the sustainable development agenda. Therefore, these public universities would produce stand-alone sustainability reports because this practice is coherent with their organisational goals. As it has been noted previously, public universities have a social purpose the continued existence of sustainability reporting might be signalling that they are morally and implicitly engaged with society (Adams, Muir, & Hoque, 2014; Fusco & Ricci, 2019).

7. CONCLUSIONS

This research is drawn on Abrahamson's (1991) managerial innovation framework to analyse how the launch of the UN SDGs has impacted the diffusion of sustainability reporting practices in the Spanish public university setting. Data was collected through different sources, such as a set of structured interviews with key university managers and an examination of Chancellor's letter from sustainability reports.

This paper finds that there has been an increasing number of Spanish public universities that have started to publish stand-alone sustainability reporting since the appearance of the UN SDGs. The behaviour of these universities is mostly explained by the combined influence of the forced-selection and fad/fashion perspectives. According to the theoretical perspective selected, our findings reveal that governmental-policy forces have shaped the sustainability reporting landscape in the Spanish public university setting. On the one hand, governments and international organisations, through the development of policies, declarations and initiatives, have driven the commitment of Spanish public universities towards SDG achievement by producing sustainability reports. These universities might be coerced to meet the demands of governments and international organisations as they represent powerful stakeholders compared to others, like students (Larran et al., 2019). On the other hand, the proliferation of reporters within the Spanish public university setting may be associated with the appearance of a fad, in which the adoption of sustainability reporting would be a greenwashing attempt with a little impact in the accountability for their social and environmental impacts (Cho et al., 2015). This is contrary to the behaviour of other Spanish public universities that have routinised the sustainability discourse in their management decisions through the persistent production of sustainability reports over time (Yañez et al., 2019).

However, there is still a long way to go for the whole implementation of sustainability reporting practices in the Spanish public university field. Although the launch of the UN SDGs has meant that a greater number of Spanish public universities have begun to prepare sustainability reports, many universities in Spain have not yet developed this type of reporting. Some university managers (University 1 and University 5) remarked the lack of enforcing mechanisms as a possible explanation of why Spanish public universities have not published stand-alone sustainability reports. The Spanish sustainability reporting regulation does not establish any requirement for public universities to adopt this type of reporting (Andrades et al., 2021). Also, university managers manifested, among other reasons, the following barriers to explain why Spanish public universities are resistant to produce sustainability reports: the lack of internal leadership exerted by senior management teams (Universities 2, 11 and 12), the lack of financial, human and technical resources (Universities 7 and 8) and the lack of understanding of the sustainability which is materialised in a lack of sustainability training (Universities 3 and 8). Although it has not been evidenced through interviews, previous studies have manifested the lack of involvement of stakeholders, such as students, in the production of sustainability reports (Larran et al., 2019). Students' demands are often different from the social and environmental impacts of universities (Godemann et al., 2014). They are more interested in receiving information about the quality of teaching rather than to sustainability (Adams, 2013).

From a theoretical standpoint, this paper provides valuable insights on the forces that promote the diffusion of sustainability reporting by relying on Abrahamson's (1991) managerial innovation framework. It is an alternative theory in comparison with the most commonly used in previous sustainability reporting research (Esteban-Arrea & Garcia-Torea, 2022). According to this perspective, we have found that the UN SDGs have supposed an initial diffusion of sustainability reporting in some Spanish public universities, which could be associated as a managerial innovation.

At a practical level, we recommend to equip university managers and other faculty members with the necessary sustainability skills to adopt sustainability reporting practices. The lack of professionalisation within senior management teams of universities has been highlighted by some managers as a potential limitation to produce stand-alone sustainability reports. Also, the evidence from interviews reveals that it is recommendable that policy makers extend the mandatory sustainability reporting requirements for public universities.

This study has also its limitations. First, this paper is focused on the Spanish public university setting and the interpretation of findings have to be limited to this context. In the future, it could be interesting to extend this research to other European countries to determine whether the organisational, social and cultural context influence the diffusion of sustainability reporting activity.

REFERENCES

Abrahamson, E. (1991). Managerial fads and fashions: The diffusion and rejection of innovations. *Academy of Management Review, 16*(3), 586–612.
Abrahamson, E., & Baumard, P. (2008). What lies behind organizational façades and how organizational façades lie: An untold story of organizational decision making. In G. Gerard, P. Hodgkinson, & W. H. Starbuck (Eds.), *The Oxford handbook of organizational decision making* (pp. 437–452). Oxford: Oxford University Press.
Adams, C. A. (2002). Internal organisational factors influencing corporate social and ethical reporting: Beyond current theorising. *Accounting, Auditing & Accountability Journal, 15*(2), 223–250.
Adams, C. A. (2013). Sustainability reporting and performance management in universities: Challenges and benefits. *Sustainability Accounting, Management and Policy Journal, 4*(3), 384–392.
Adams, C. A., & Larrinaga, C. (2019). Progress: Engaging with organisations in pursuit of improved sustainability accounting and performance. *Accounting, Auditing & Accountability Journal, 32*(8), 2367–2394.
Adams, C. A., & McNicholas, P. (2007). Making a difference: Sustainability reporting, accountability and organisational change. *Accounting, Auditing & Accountability Journal, 20*(3), 382–402.
Adams, C., Muir, S., & Hoque, Z. (2014). Measurement of sustainability performance in the public sector. *Sustainability Accounting, Management and Policy Journal, 5*(1), 46–67.

Albareda-Tiana, S., Vidal-Raméntol, S., & Fernández-Morilla, M. (2018). Implementing the sustainable development goals at University level. *International Journal of Sustainability in Higher Education*, *19*(3), 473–497.

Alonso-Almeida, M. M., Marimon, F., Casani, F., & Rodríguez-Pomeda, J. (2015). Diffusion of sustainability reporting in universities: Current situation and future perspectives. *Journal of Cleaner Production*, *106*, 144–154.

Amernic, J., Craig, R., & Tourish, D. (2010). *Measuring and assessing tone at the top using annual report CEO letters*. Edinburgh: Institute of Chartered Accountants in Scotland.

Andrades, J., Martinez-Martinez, D., Herrera, J., & Larrán, M. (2023). Is water management really transparent? A comparative analysis of ESG reporting of Andalusian publicly-owned enterprises. *Public Money & Management*. doi:10.1080/09540962.2023.2171844.

Andrades, J., Martinez-Martinez, D., & Larran, M. (2021). Corporate governance disclosures by Spanish universities: How different variables can affect the level of such disclosures? *Meditari Accountancy Research*, *29*(1), 86–109.

Andrades, J., Muriel, M. J., & Larrán, M. (2022). How far can mandatory requirements drive increased levels of disclosure? *Public Money & Management*. doi:10.1080/09540962.2022.2045124.

Archel, P., Husillos, J., & Spence, C. (2011). The institutionalisation of unaccountability: Loading the dice of Corporate Social Responsibility discourse. *Accounting, Organizations and Society*, *36*(6), 327–343.

Ball, A., & Bebbington, J. (2008). Accounting and reporting for sustainable development in public service organizations. *Public Money & Management*, *28*(6), 323–326.

Ball, A., & Grubnic, S. (2007). Sustainability accounting and accountability in the public sector. In J. Unerman, J. Bebbington, & B. O'Dwyer (Eds.), *Sustainability accounting and accountability*. London: Routledge.

Ball, A., Grubnic, S., & Birchall, J. (2014). Sustainability accounting and accountability in the public sector. In J. Unerman, J. Bebbington, & B. O'Dwyer (Eds.), *Sustainability accounting and accountability* (pp. 176–196). London: Routledge.

Bebbington, J., Higgins, C., & Frame, B. (2009). Initiating sustainable development reporting: Evidence from New Zealand. *Accounting, Auditing & Accountability Journal*, *22*(4), 588–625.

Bebbington, J., & Unerman, J. (2018). Achieving the United Nations sustainable development goals. *Accounting, Auditing & Accountability Journal*, *31*(1), 2–24.

Bebbington, J., & Unerman, J. (2020). Advancing research into accounting and the UN sustainable development goals. *Accounting, Auditing & Accountability Journal*, *33*(7), 1657–1670.

Biondi, L., & Bracci, E. (2018). Sustainability, popular and integrated reporting in the public sector: A fad and fashion perspective. *Sustainability*, *10*(9), 3112.

Bisogno, M., Cuadrado-Ballesteros, B., Rossi, F. M., & Peña-Miguel, N. (2023). Sustainable development goals in public administrations: Enabling conditions in local governments. *International Review of Administrative Sciences*. doi:10.1177/00208523221146458.

Brusca, I., Labrador, M., & Larran, M. (2018). The challenge of sustainability and integrated reporting at universities: A case study. *Journal of Cleaner Production*, *188*, 347–354.

Burritt, R. L., & Schaltegger, S. (2010). Sustainability accounting and reporting: Fad or trend? *Accounting, Auditing & Accountability Journal*, *23*(7), 829–846.

Carpenter, V. L., & Feroz, E. H. (2001). Institutional theory and accounting rule choice: An analysis of four US state governments' decisions to adopt generally accepted accounting principles. *Accounting, Organizations and Society*, *26*(7–8), 565–596.

Cho, C. H., Laine, M., Roberts, R. W., & Rodrigue, M. (2015). Organized hypocrite, organizational façades, and sustainability reporting. *Accounting, Organizations and Society*, *40*, 78–94.

Cohen, S. (2022). Debate: Climate change, environmental challenges, sustainable development goals and the relevance of accounting. *Public Money & Management*, *42*(2), 55–56.

Collin, S. O., Tagesson, T., Andersson, A., Cato, J., & Hansson, K. (2009). Explaining the choice of accounting standards in municipal corporations. *Critical Perspectives on Accounting*, *20*(2), 141–174.

Contrafatto, M. (2014). The institutionalization of social and environmental reporting: An Italian narrative. *Accounting, Organizations and Society*, *39*(6), 414–432.

Dahlin, E. (2021). Email interviews: A guide to research design and implementation. *International Journal of Qualitative Methods, 20*, 1–10.

Esteban-Arrea, R., & Garcia-Torea, N. (2022). Strategic responses to sustainability reporting regulation and multiple stakeholder demands: An analysis of the Spanish EU non-financial reporting directive transposition. *Sustainability Accounting, Management and Policy Journal, 13*(3), 600–625.

Farneti, F., Casonato, F., Montecalvo, M., & De Villiers, C. (2019). The influence of integrated reporting and stakeholder information needs on the disclosure of social information in a state-owned enterprise. *Meditari Accountancy Research, 27*(4), 556–579.

Farneti, F., & Guthrie, J. (2009). Sustainability reporting by Australian public sector organisations: Why they report. *Accounting Forum, 33*(2), 89–98.

Farooq, M. B., & de Villiers, C. (2019). Understanding how managers institutionalise sustainability reporting: Evidence from Australia and New Zealand. *Accounting, Auditing & Accountability Journal, 32*(5), 1240–1269.

Feldermann, S. K., & Hiebl, M. R. (2020). Using quotations from non-English interviews in accounting research. *Qualitative Research in Accounting and Management, 17*(2), 229–262.

Fonseca, A., Macdonald, A., Dandy, E., & Valenti, P. (2011). The state of sustainability reporting at Canadian universities. *International Journal of Sustainability in Higher Education, 12*(1), 22–40.

Fusco, F., & Ricci, P. (2019). What is the stock of the situation? A bibliometric analysis on social and environmental accounting research in public sector. *International Journal of Public Sector Management, 32*(1), 21–41.

Godemann, J., Bebbington, J., Herzig, C., & Moon, J. (2014). Higher education and sustainable development: Exploring possibilities for organisational change. *Accounting, Auditing & Accountability Journal, 27*(2), 218–233.

Gunarathne, N., & Senaratne, S. (2017). Diffusion of integrated reporting in an emerging South Asian (SAARC) nation. *Managerial Auditing Journal, 32*(4/5), 524–548.

Hawkins, J. E. (2018). The practical utility and suitability of email interviews in qualitative research. *Qualitative Report, 23*(2), 493–501.

Higgins, C., & Larrinaga, C. (2014). Sustainability reporting: Insights from institutional theory. In J. Bebbington, J. Unerman, & B. O'Dwyer (Eds.), *Sustainability accounting and accountability* (2nd ed., pp. 273–285). London: Routledge.

Higgins, C., Milne, M. J., & Van Gramberg, B. (2015). The uptake of sustainability reporting in Australia. *Journal of Business Ethics, 129*, 445–468.

Higgins, C., Stubbs, W., & Milne, M. (2018). Is sustainability reporting becoming institutionalised? The role of an issues-based field. *Journal of Business Ethics, 147*(2), 309–326.

Jain, A., Islam, M. A., Keneley, M., & Kansal, M. (2022). Social contagion and the institutionalisation of GRI-based sustainability reporting practices. *Meditari Accountancy Research, 30*(5), 1291–1308.

Kansal, M., Joshi, M., Babu, S., & Sharma, S. (2018). Reporting of corporate social responsibility in central public sector enterprises: A study of post mandatory regime in India. *Journal of Business Ethics, 151*(3), 813–831.

Larran, M., Andrades, F. J., & Herrera, J. (2019). An analysis of university sustainability reports from the GRI database: An examination of influential variables. *Journal of Environmental Planning and Management, 62*(6), 1019–1044.

Larrinaga, C., & Perez, V. (2008). Sustainability accounting and accountability in public water companies. *Public Money & Management, 28*(6), 337–343.

Leal Filho, W., Shiel, C., Paço, A., Mifsud, M., Ávila, L. V., Brandli, L. L., …, Caeiro, S. (2019). Sustainable Development Goals and sustainability teaching at universities: Falling behind or getting ahead of the pack? *Journal of Cleaner Production, 232*, 285–294.

Leal Filho, W., Skanavis, C., Kounani, A., Brandli, L. L., Shiel, C., do Paco, A., …, Shula, K. (2019). The role of planning in implementing sustainable development in a higher education context. *Journal of Cleaner Production, 235*, 678–687.

Lozano, R. (2011). The state of sustainability reporting in universities. *International Journal of Sustainability in Higher Education, 12*(1), 67–78.

Mäkelä, H., & Laine, M. (2011). A CEO with many messages: Comparing the ideological representations provided by different corporate reports. *Accounting Forum, 35*(4), 217–231.

Marcuccio, M., & Steccolini, I. (2005). Social and environmental reporting in local authorities: A new Italian fashion? *Public Management Review, 7*(2), 155–176.

Marquis, C., & Qian, C. (2014). Corporate social responsibility reporting in China: Symbol or substance? *Organization Science, 25*(1), 127–148.

Merkl-Davies, D. M., & Brennan, N. (2007). Discretionary disclosure strategies in corporate narratives: Incremental information or impression management? *Journal of Accounting Literature, 26*, 116–196.

Moggi, S. (2019). Social and environmental reports at universities: A Habermasian view on their evolution. *Accounting Forum, 43*(3), 283–326.

Montecalvo, M., Farneti, F., & De Villiers, C. (2018). The potential of integrated reporting to enhance sustainability reporting in the public sector. *Public Money & Management, 38*(5), 365–374.

Niemann, L., & Hoppe, T. (2018). Sustainability reporting by local governments: A magic tool? Lessons on use and usefulness from European pioneers. *Public Management Review, 20*(1), 201–223.

Oliver, C. (1991). Strategic response to institutional processes. *Academy of Management Review, 16*(1), 145–179.

Owens, T. L. (2017). Higher education in the sustainable development goals framework. *European Journal of Education, 52*(4), 414–420.

Palmer, I., King, A. W., & Kelleher, D. (2004). Listening to Jack: GE's change conversations with shareholders. *Journal of Organizational Change Management, 17*(6), 593–614.

Rodrigue, M., Magnan, M., & Cho, C. H. (2013). Is environmental governance substantive or symbolic? An empirical examination. *Journal of Business Ethics, 114*(1), 107–129.

Rogers, E. M. (2003). *Diffusion of innovations* (5th ed.). New York, NY: Free Press.

Stubbs, W., Higgins, C., & Milne, M. (2013). Why do companies not produce sustainability reports? *Business Strategy and the Environment, 22*(7), 456–470.

Tan, L. K., & Egan, M. (2018). The public accountability value of a triple bottom line approach to performance reporting in the water sector. *Australian Accounting Review, 28*(2), 235–250.

Tarquinio, L., & Xhindole, C. (2022). The institutionalisation of sustainability reporting in management practice: Evidence through action research. *Sustainability Accounting, Management and Policy Journal, 13*(2), 362–386.

Thoradeniya, P., Ferreira, A., Lee, J., & Tan, R. (2021). The diffusion of sustainability key performance indicators in a developing country context. *Accounting, Auditing & Accountability Journal, 34*(5), 1246–1274.

United Nations (UN). (2015). *Transforming our world: The 2030 Agenda for Sustainable Development.* New York, NY: United Nations. Retrieved from https://sustainabledevelopment.un.org/content/documents/21252030%20Agenda%20for%20Sustainable%20Development%20web.pdf. Accessed March 7, 2016.

Vinnari, E., & Laine, M. (2013). Just a passing fad?: The diffusion and decline of environmental reporting in the Finnish water sector. *Accounting, Auditing & Accountability Journal, 26*(7), 1107–1134.

Yañez, S., Uruburu, A., Moreno, A., & Lumbreras, J. (2019). The sustainability report as an essential tool for the holistic and strategic vision of higher education institutions. *Journal of Cleaner Production, 207*, 57–66.

Zhao, N., & Patten, D. M. (2016). An exploratory analysis of managerial perceptions of social and environmental reporting in China. *Sustainability Accounting, Management and Policy Journal, 7*(1), 80–98.